The European Tour Yearbook 2002

OFFICIAL EUROPEAN TOUR PUBLICATION

Wentworth Club, West Course: Hole 2, Par 3

ecutive Editor
tchell Platts

duction Editor
nessa O'Brien

torial Consultants
ris Plumridge
rdon Simpson

ture Editors
vid Cannon
phen Munday
drew Redington

Director
Leney
Communications Plc

duced By
don Print & Design Plc

e European Tour Yearbook 2002
published by The PGA European
r, Wentworth Drive, Virgina Water,
rey GU25 4LX.

tributed through Aurum Press Ltd.
Bedford Avenue
don WC1B 3AT

our reproduction through Essex
our.

nting and binding by Mohn Media.
PGA European Tour.

N 1-85410-818-2

Introduction from The European Tour

The record-breaking achievement of Retief Goosen in becoming the first player to win the US Open Championship and the Volvo Order of Merit in the same year fully deserves to take pride of place among the numerous outstanding achievements by European Tour Members during 2001.

Sandy Lyle (1985), Severiano Ballesteros (1988) and Nick Faldo (1992) are the only other Members during the first 30 years of The European Tour to win a Major Championship and the Volvo Order of Merit in the same year although in their case it was the Open Championship.

We offer our congratulations to Retief because in winning the US Open Championship he not only led from start to finish to follow his South African compatriots Gary Player and Ernie Els onto the US Open roll of honour, but also demonstrated his strength of character in beating the American Mark Brooks in the play-off at Southern Hills Country Club in Tulsa. His win took the total number of Major Championship victories by European Tour Members to 26 since Severiano won the Open Championship in 1979.

Retief also won The Scottish Open at Loch Lomond, one of a record 48 tournaments allocated in 24 countries to The 2001 European Tour International Schedule, and with his success in the Telefonica Open de Madrid he became the first non-European winner of the Volvo Order of Merit since Greg Norman in 1982 and the first South African since Dale Hayes in 1975.

There were no fewer than 12 first time winners, and players from no fewer than 17 countries enjoyed tournament victories. Henrik Stenson (Benson and Hedges International Open) was one of the new winners as he graduated from his success in finishing Number One on the 2000 European Challenge Tour, and we now congratulate the 16 leading players led by Mark Foster from the 2001 European Challenge Tour for securing their cards to compete on The 2002 European Tour International Schedule. Another slice of history was made in 2001 with the leading 115 in the Volvo Order of Merit all winning in excess of £100,000.

With our minds always on the future, we were also delighted by the success of Great Britain and Ireland, under the inspirational leadership of Peter McEvoy, at the Walker Cup. Luke Donald, Nick Dougherty and Steven O'Hara are three Members of that team whom The European Tour has already welcomed to the professional ranks and Paul Casey, a member of the 1999 team, launched his career in superb style by winning the Gleneagles Scottish PGA Championship in only his 11th European Tour event. We congratulate Paul in becoming the 2001 Sir Henry Cotton Rookie of the Year.

Sam Torrance was the Rookie of the Year in 1972 - the year when The European Tour officially started - and with the postponement of The 2001 Ryder Cup Matches to 2002, a decision taken following the enormity of the tragedy in the United States on September 11, he will, as Captain, assemble The European Team alongside that of The United States, captained by Curtis Strange, at The De Vere Belfry in September, 2002.

Sam would be the first to point out that The 34th Ryder Cup Matches will now take place less then one year away from him becoming eligible for the European Seniors Tour which enjoyed a year of outstanding performances highlighted by that of Ian Stanley in winning the Senior British Open, presented by MasterCard, and The 2001 European Seniors Tour Order of Merit.

The steady growth pattern of all three Tours continues and in this the 14th Edition of The European Tour Yearbook the game's leading writers and photographers have captured all the many wonderful and poignant moments from 2001. We hope you enjoy the content in addition to witnessing first hand Tour competition at all our superb locations in 2002.

Kenneth D Schofield CBE
Executive Director, The European Tour

Contents

Something in the Air

When Retief Goosen finally closed the deal on him becoming Europe's top golfer of 2001 by leading the Volvo Order of Merit he did so in typical fashion. This is to say he accepted the ultimate accolade quietly, modestly and in a voice so naturally low and soft you had to lean forward and listen intently to pick up on his words.

This is the way it always has been with this particular South African whose instinct is to set aside any large trumpets and to rely instead on his play and his statistics to underline the quality of his golf. This graceful, high note of humility in an often overly-hyped world is as reassuring as is his ability to first encounter and then to overcome adversity.

It is a strength first learned as a teenager in South Africa when he discovered early that timing is everything and that being in the wrong place at the wrong time may wreck a life. Certainly the lightning strike that zapped him as he practised his game while still an amateur in South Africa taught Goosen a major life-enforcing lesson: in condensed form this amounts to 'just when you feel you have got it made in life, someone or something tends to push you over.'

Make no mistake, this electrical charge all but burned out young Goosen's body, leaving him for several weeks to reflect painfully in hospital on what had happened. What he reflected on, of course, was the ancient riddle posed to those who have been alarmingly close to a premature departure. What Goosen tried to work out 17 years ago was whether he was now lucky to be alive or if he had been desperately unfortunate to have been struck in the first place.

TaylorMade
TaylorMade
USGA
IZOD CLUB

Retief with his wife Tracy

There is no simple answer to this elemental question but what is without doubt is that he left that hospital a quieter, more reflective and certainly a more deeply introspective young man. Even for a kid, this experience had been alarming enough to encourage the realisation that any human being, no matter how content, may be erased by a fickle, fateful moment.

It is a knowledge he has carried with him since and that has made him both stronger than most and yet more vulnerable than many, the usual, and necessary, embryonic champion's arrogance hugely diluted by that bolt from a leaden African sky. Nowhere was this fallibility, this lack of total conviction more vividly illustrated than during the US Open Championship in Tulsa, Oklahoma. Equally it was here that his strength was laid out for public admiration.

His unfortunate putting ordeal - three strokes from ten feet, for goodness sake - on the 72nd green, when this glittering Championship was within his grasp, would have crushed a lesser man. Yet while television commentators and journalists instantly queried his ability to return the following morning to the minefield that was Southern Hills still upright, never mind in the correct

Mel Pyatt (left), President & CEO, Volvo Event Management, and Ken Schofield (right), Executive Director of The European Tour, presented Retief Goosen with the 2001 Volvo Order of Merit Trophy at the Volvo Masters Andalucia in November.

mental mode to take on Mark Brooks in the only remaining 18 hole play-off in high-level professional golf, Goosen knew otherwise.

The fact is we all underestimated Goosen. While we fretted, he did two things. First, he spoke with his 'mind coach' Jos Vanstiphout, a diminutive middle-aged Belgian who once played in a rock band called The Mayfair Set. Vanstiphout spoke with his client for half an hour. "I expected to find a wreck but he was fine. He told me he knew he was playing well and that he knew he had just missed an opportunity. Just as he was leaving he said 'You know Jos, the one thing I now know is that I can beat everyone.' That was the moment I knew he was going to win." The second thing Goosen did was to go to bed early. And instantly fall asleep. Extraordinary.

It remains true, however, that until this year no-one underestimated Retief Goosen more than he did himself. Despite previous success, despite his laid-back nature and his slow-burn grin, Goosen remained a golfer who knew he was very good but who constantly doubted his ability to claw his way forward and to turn good into great.

All this changed in Oklahoma. Retief admits brutally that missing the original short putt could have "wrecked my career." Instead, as he now realises, it has made him. Four weeks after America he

triumphed in Scotland on another devilishly demanding course, by capturing The Scottish Open at Loch Lomond. Once again he was all focus and control, a player in charge of himself and his emotions and whose swing thus was freed to fulfil its natural potential. He still moved slow but, clearly, he had learned fast as success in The Scottish Open at Loch Lomond underlined.

The following week he was 13th in the Open Championship and by the time he secured his Volvo Order of Merit Number One title with another win in the Telefonica Open de Madrid in Spain in October he had been some sort of contender every time he teed it up. This, in the wickedly contrary world of professional golf, is phenomenal.

Along the way he at last has moved away from the large shadow cast by his amiable compatriot and good friend Ernie Els. All his life Goosen has moved slowly behind Els. As an amateur he was acknowledged as supremely gifted but not quite as gifted as the big man. It has been the same as a professional. Even Gary Player, usually so generous and perceptive in his analysis of others, failed to notice properly the steely determination within a golfer who, to be fair to Player, seemed to most of us too ready to accept close-run failure when the really big moments beckoned ever to make the demanding journey to Major Champion.

There is, of course, no such annoyingly smirking monkey on either of those broad shoulders now for the man who divides his domestic life betwixt the clamour of Johannesburg and the village calm of Sunninghill just down the road from The European Tour's elegant headquarters at Wentworth. "It's hard for it to sink in properly that I am the best player in Europe in 2001," he whispered in Madrid, that trumpet still nowhere to be seen. "What I do know is that it's been a dream year winning a Major, the Volvo Order of Merit, The Scottish Open at Loch Lomond and now the Telefonica Open de Madrid here in the Spanish capital. I've put in a lot of work with Jos and this is the year it's all begun to pay off."

So Retief Goosen becomes the first non-European to take the Volvo Order Of Merit since Greg Norman swaggered his way ahead of everyone else 19 years ago. He does so in the year that he becomes the third South African, after Els and Player, to win the US Open Championship. In modern times, of course, no European has managed to beard the Americans in their national Championship. Clearly there must be something in the South African water, although, in Goosen's case, it is more likely that there was something in the air all those years ago.

Bill Elliott

1999 PAYNE STEWART
2000 TIGER WOODS
2001 RETIEF GOOSEN

Breathtaking Structure

Andrew Oldcorn

The time has long since past when comparisons with other golfing arenas were essential in order to assess the importance of European golf on the global stage. Such sidelong glances are simply no longer necessary because of the breathtaking structure that now stands in place to encourage the best golfers from all over the world on an annual pilgrimage that knows no national boundaries.

Indeed, if sport is a unifying influence, in that excellence and performance are the only criteria by which an individual should be judged, then The European Tour International Schedule remains a shining example of that philosophy because its campaigners of so many different nationalities demonstrate intense rivalry on the field of play yet also bond effectively with each other when required to work as a team.

Part of this is due, of course, to the shared experience of globe-trotting and the need to adapt to whatever conditions of climate, culture, food and golf that await them wherever The European Tour stops each week on its round-the-world odyssey. Part is also due to the nature of the game and its demands which prompt a collective awareness of what the other man is going through whether good or bad. The net result is an all-embracing atmosphere of family in which, despite occasional distractions, goodwill prevails.

Moreover, the degree of skill The European Tour International Schedule now requires for success can be measured not only in terms of improved scoring but in the number of resounding achievements its Members have demonstrated in forays to other parts in 2001, none more so than those of South Africa's Retief Goosen. His dramatic play-off victory for the US Open Championship at Southern Hills Country Club in Tulsa in June underlined the global aspect of the sport in that it formed the basis of his triumphant campaign to become the first non-European for 19 years to top the Volvo Order of Merit.

It was additional proof that the old theory about being obliged to play constantly in the United States in order to win there was quite superfluous as Germany's Bernhard Langer, Spain's José Maria Olazábal and Welshman Ian Woosnam, among others, had shown at various times by popping over from Europe to win their respective Masters Tournament titles.

Other excursions brought ample rewards, too, as Sweden's Pierre Fulke reached the final of the World Golf Championships-Accenture Match Play in Australia in January and earned sufficient prize money to sustain him at the top of the Volvo Order of Merit table for five months until dislodged by New Zealander Michael Campbell, who was then displaced by Angel Cabrera from Argentina.

Cabrera's reign was short-lived when Goosen soared to the top of the list with his US Open Championship win and remained the elusive target for his closest challengers, Ireland's Padraig Harrington, Northern Ireland's Darren Clarke and South Africa's Ernie Els, for the rest of the season. Indeed it is a measure of the rich rewards now on offer for supreme skills that Goosen had earned 2,007,723 euro (£1,204,833) in prize money even before the Open Championship in July, and eventually took his total official winnings to 2,862,806 euro (£1,760,476).

He was, in fact, one of five multiple winners during the 2001 season because in addition to the US Open Championship he captured The Scottish Open at Loch Lomond title a week before the Open Championship at Royal Lytham & St Annes - where the American David Duval scored his first Major victory - and later took the

Retief Goosen

Telefonica Open de Madrid in a play-off to put himself beyond reach in the race for Volvo Order of Merit honours.

Scotland's Colin Montgomerie showed customary resilience after his run of seven successive Volvo Order of Merit titles came to an end in 2000, and bounced back to win the Murphy's Irish Open and the Volvo Scandinavian Masters. Indeed, he had shown earlier in the year signs that he was in determined mood when he won the Ericsson Masters in Melbourne, Australia, in February.

Langer's enduring talent brought him two victories - The TNT Open and the Linde German Masters - while last year's Masters Champion, Vijay Singh, of Fiji, made his mark with victories in the Carlsberg Malaysian Open and the Caltex Singapore Masters in consecutive weeks.

Of course, in strict terms the ultimate multiple winner was American Tiger Woods, the world's leading golfer, because he captured the Johnnie Walker Classic and the Deutsche Bank-SAP Open TPC of Europe in addition to the 2001 Masters Tournament. This made Woods the first golfer in history to hold all four Major titles at the same time with the US Open Championship, Open Championship and US PGA Championship from the 2000 season. Later he captured the WGC-NEC Invitational and it is a reflection of the wider awareness of his responsibilities that he, too, plans a competitive programme on an international scale.

Padraig Harrington might very well have been included in the list of multiple winners for he finished runner-up no fewer than seven times during the year. Therefore it was a tribute to his strength of character that he should produce a performance that smacked of courage and class in the season-ending Volvo Masters Andalucia where his triumph in a tense finish at Montecastillo Hotel and Golf Resort in Jerez, Spain, was applauded by all and, most importantly, by his peers. The win moved Harrington into the top ten in the Official World Ranking and, as the season closed in Europe and the United States, there were no fewer than five European Tour Members in the top ten, nine in the top 20 and 16 in the top 40.

The overall health of The European Tour International Schedule is extremely robust with a contingent of no fewer than 12 first time winners in 2001, and some old favourites proving they still possess the desire and ability to produce golf of the highest quality. Indeed, Irishman Des Smyth's Madeira Island Open victory at the age of 48 years and 34 days, making him the oldest ever winner on The European Tour International Schedule and beating the record previously held by Neil Coles by 20 days, has stirred the hopes and ambitions of much younger though similarly experienced campaigners who now realise they, too, may have many years left before the action has to stop.

In fact, longevity of service was a keynote of the 2001 season because the veteran Englishman Roger Chapman reached an impressive milestone by playing in his 500th event. So, too, did England's Malcolm Mackenzie while the remarkable Irishman Eamonn Darcy, at the age of 49, played in his 600th tournament. More evidence, if required, of the broad church that exists within the professional game and allows each individual to achieve personal goals to the limit.

For some, however, it was just the start, particularly those who experienced the thrill of winning on The European Tour for the first time. Paul Casey, the English newcomer, made a speedy impact by achieving a victory in only his 11th event when he took the Gleneagles Scottish PGA Championship, on the way to becoming the

Left to Right: Roger Chapman, Edward Asprey and Des Smyth

Lee Westwood and Colin Montgomerie

Bernhard Langer

Sir Henry Cotton Rookie of the Year, while Tobias Dier from Nürnberg in Germany held his nerve to win the North West of Ireland Open by a stroke.

Darren Fichardt from South Africa became the Sao Paulo Brazil Open champion and Adam Scott, from Australia, earned the Alfred Dunhill Championship title in South Africa. But, perhaps, the most dramatic line-up of newcomers emerged from Argentina with Jorge Berendt winning the Cannes Open in France, Ricardo Gonzalez taking the Omega European Masters in Switzerland and Angel Cabrera the Open de Argentina on home soil.

There were wins for Americans Steve Stricker (WGC - Accenture Match Play) and David Toms (US PGA Championship). At 19 years old, Australia's Aaron Baddeley also triumphed for the first time on The European Tour International Schedule, beating Spain's Sergio Garcia in a play-off for the Greg Norman Holden International in Sydney, Australia. Sweden's Henrik Stenson captured his first title at the Benson and Hedges International Open, and in so doing graduated in superb style from winning the 2000 European Challenge Tour Rankings. Then, as the sun began to set on another season, three times French Amateur champion Gregory Havret became the second Frenchman to win on The 2001 European Tour International Schedule by claiming his maiden title in his rookie season. He closed with a 69 to win the Atlanet Italian Open at Is Molas Golf Club, Sardinia. The tournament also marked another significant milestone for The European Tour as, for the first time, the leading 115 in the Volvo Order of Merit all won in excess of £100,000.

The early part of the year had a case-hardened appearance to it with Mark McNulty from Zimbabwe, playing in his 25th consecutive season, holding on to the Mercedes-Benz South African Open and foiling a spirited attempt by England's Justin Rose to win his first title. Campbell was back in form to win the Heineken Classic when The European Tour moved "Down Under" to The Vines Resort in Perth.

When the assembled cast teed up for the Dubai Desert Classic at The Emirates in early March it was generally assumed that Woods would be the dominant figure and so it transpired until the final hole when the Danish professional Thomas Björn put the American star under pressure as they were tied for the lead and proved to be the more resolute in what had essentially turned into a match play encounter between them.

Zimbabwe's Tony Johnstone maintained the triumphant march of the "oldies" with a win in the Qatar Masters, but by April the young lions began to find their stride with England's Ian Poulter taking the Moroccan Open, Sweden's Robert Karlsson the Via Digital Open de España and Welshman Phillip Price the Algarve Open de Portugal in successive weeks.

Olazábal regained the winning touch in the Novotel Perrier Open de France. Yet, perhaps, the most heartening win of the season was that

Padraig Harrington and Darren Clarke

Paul Casey

of Andrew Oldcorn. He started the Volvo PGA Championship at Wentworth Club as a 150-1 outsider yet upstaged the stars to take the title which proved to be rightful reward for his tenacity and determination after earlier setbacks.

By the time French professional Thomas Levet won the Victor Chandler British Masters, Australian Peter O'Malley had taken The Compass Group English Open and Scotland's Andrew Coltart The Great North Open, players from 15 different countries had won on The European Tour. By the end of the season in which The European Tour visited 23 different countries and had attracted competitors of 25 nationalities there were winners from Argentina, Australia, Denmark, England, Fiji, France, Germany, Ireland, New Zealand, Northern Ireland, Scotland, South Africa, Spain, Sweden, United States, Wales and Zimbabwe.

One of the most triumphant performances came from Clarke, winner of the Dimension Data Pro-Am in South Africa and the Chunichi Crowns in Japan earlier in the year, who, in front of thousands of jubilant fans, became the first Irishman to win on home soil for 19 years as he took the Smurfit European Open at The K Club outside Dublin. Paul McGinley was another Irishman to win but in his case it was on Welsh soil as he captured The Celtic Manor Resort Wales Open.

Ricardo Gonzalez

By this time, too, The European Tour had a customary feel and balance to it as the new brigade mingled comfortably with the experienced old guard and the arrival of American John Daly, winner of the 1991 US PGA Championship and the 1995 Open Championship, in the BMW International Open served to underline that eternal truth that form varies but class endures. Daly became a winner for the first time in six years with a score of 27 under par 261 at Golfclub München Nord-Eichenried which, had it not been for preferred lies on Saturday, would have tied the lowest under par total in the history of The European Tour. Moreover, the American professional came very close to a double success but was narrowly foiled by Langer in the Linde German Masters.

Indeed, during a year in which stamina and perseverance (plus a large helping of self-belief) characterised so many victories, some of the best were yet to come as Woosnam staged a command performance to win the Cisco World Match Play Championship by earning the title in three separate decades (and two different centuries for that matter). His victims included the US Open Champion Goosen, as well as Montgomerie and 2000 Volvo Order of Merit winner Lee Westwood, of England, whose form was frustratingly elusive all season, and Harrington in the final.

On reflection, Woosnam's remarkable performance was compensation in part for the dreadful mix-up at the Open Championship when he was penalised for having one club too many in his bag following the start of the final round - a setback which some genuinely believe cost this inspirational player perhaps his best chance so far of victory in the Open. His Wentworth Club win was followed by a similar comeback exploit at St Andrews by Scotland's Paul Lawrie as the 1999 Open Champion scored a dramatic last green victory on the Old Course to take the Dunhill Links Championship.

During the interim Garcia spread his talent successfully to both sides of the Atlantic by following two wins on the US PGA Tour by capturing the Trophée Lancôme in Paris. His success on American soil underlined a wider impact as Sweden's Jesper Parnevik again became a US winner, and the remarkable Argentinian José Coceres, who required three attempts to qualify for The European Tour, then toiled for 11 years, suddenly broke through at the age of 38 to win two US events.

A tribute to longevity, of course. But more than this, living proof that a vibrant European Tour, which offers opportunity, incentive and challenge to players as they emerge and develop, creates a climate for champions and can be judged by the quality and number of its heroes. It is, after all, the sole raison d'etre for The European Tour International Schedule. And one that it fulfils completely.

Michael McDonnell

Home from Home

ALPINE GOLF & SPORTS CLUB, BANGKOK, THAILAND

Tiger Woods was in a slump, or so some observers suggested, when he arrived at the Alpine Golf & Sports Club in Bangkok for the first event on The 2001 European Tour International Schedule. For the first time in 18 months, Woods had gone three tournaments without a win. The almond-eyed one, however, was flashing that famous toothy smile again as for the tenth time in a glittering, record-breaking year he strolled to victory.

With typical metronomic ease, Woods followed an opening 68 with three successive 65s for a 25 under par total of 263 to finish three shots ahead of the Australian Geoff Ogilvy and seven shots in front of New Zealand's Michael Campbell, the defending champion.

Tiger Woods

"It's always special to win in Thailand because it's my mother's home country and part of my culture and heritage," said Woods. "It was great to get such a warm reception and see family and friends out there watching."

Woods, of course, is always in demand as befits a man considered to be the most important sportsman since Muhammed Ali. In Thailand it was more so the case. Off the fairways, he still had time to accept an honorary degree and adopt an elephant. More importantly, he staged a clinic especially enjoyed by the 18 children who joined him on the range. He revealed to them: "This isn't even my best year! That was when I was 11. I had the cutest girlfriend in school. They let us out to play three times a day. Oh, and I won 33 straight junior tournaments."

Winning, of course, is now what matters, not the money, although that was not always the case. "I know how it feels to be on the outside," he said. "I used to play in junior tournaments without a practice round because we couldn't afford hotels."

The practice range has become home from home for Woods. In Thailand, he moved through the now familiar routine - "I need only three practice swings on the range to determine what sort of day it's going to be" - before setting off in search of the title. He managed six birdies in the first round but there were also a number of

Michael Campbell

The Course

A spectacular opening hole, incorporating the waterfall, leads to an excellent course, with a serious set of par threes including the sixth, possibly the most difficult hole on the outward nine, which closes with a dramatic par four finishing hole which requires great accuracy off the tee.

Jesper Parnevik

uncharacteristic errors so that by the end of the day he was in a share of fourth place as the Australian Wayne Smith led the way on 65. Nevertheless, Woods was reasonably happy since he had the worst of the conditions during the afternoon with a tricky breeze drying out the already firm greens.

By the end of the second day, Woods had moved into the lead with an 11 under par halfway total of 133 - one ahead of the Australian Rodney Pampling. Paul Lawrie, three shots behind after a 69, said: "You know Tiger is going to play well so you have to play even better. But there is no intimidation factor. You can't change what he is doing, so you have to play your own game. He is the best player in the game by a long way, and I have great respect for what he is doing."

Woods notched eight birdies against one bogey, coming home in 31, but he was outscored by Sergio Garcia, who followed an opening 74 with a 64. Woods said: "The greens were a lot more receptive than on the first day and there was no wind either."

The third round produced a flawless exhibition from Woods. His 65 moved him to 198 and three ahead of Campbell, who set a new record for the course with a 63, and Pampling. Lawrie did move alongside Woods in the lead, but back to back bogeys early on his inward nine proved costly.

Rodney Pampling

On the previous evening, Woods was behind the bar serving the sponsor's product. There was more of a commotion on the course in the third round when a snake appeared at the 14th and caused brief panic in the gallery of more than 10,000 following the American.

Campbell's confidence was high after his superb 63 and with four early birdies in the final round he launched a challenge on Woods. But he failed to get up and down from a tricky lie in the rough at the ninth where Woods made a six foot birdie putt to move four in front. Ogilvy, with four birdies in five holes from the tenth, took up the challenge but Woods chipped close for a birdie at the 14th then collected two more at the 16th and 17th to come home strongly.

Ogilvy said: "I have never started the weekend being two behind, shot 67 and 64 and lost by three. It's ridiculous and that's as good as I could play. All credit to Tiger. He is the best; he is the king."

Mitchell Platts

Shot of the Week

Peter Baker secured the first ace on The 2001 European Tour International Schedule when with his ninth shot of the tournament he holed in one at the 198 yards third with a five iron. The ball took two bounces and disappeared into the cup.

ALPINE GOLF & SPORTS CLUB, BANGKOK, THAILAND 16-19 NOVEMBER, 2000, PAR 72, 6989 YARDS, 6391 METRES

Pos.	Name		Rd1	Rd2	Rd3	Rd4	Total	Par	Prize Money Euro	£
1	Tiger WOODS	USA	68	65	65	65	263	-25	221134.47	133330.00
2	Geoff OGILVY	Aus	68	67	67	64	266	-22	147411.92	88880.00
3	Michael CAMPBELL	NZ	71	67	63	69	270	-18	83060.18	50080.00
4	Rodney PAMPLING	Aus	68	66	67	71	272	-16	61300.01	36960.00
	Paul LAWRIE	Scot	67	69	67	69	272	-16	61300.01	36960.00
6	Jesper PARNEVIK	Swe	72	65	69	70	276	-12	43122.30	26000.00
	Wayne SMITH	Aus	65	70	68	73	276	-12	43122.30	26000.00
8	Anthony PAINTER	Aus	71	68	73	65	277	-11	33171.00	20000.00
9	Lian-Wei ZHANG	PRC	72	67	69	71	279	-9	26890.63	16213.34
	Nick O'HERN	Aus	69	72	72	66	279	-9	26890.63	16213.34
	David PODLICH	Aus	69	70	69	71	279	-9	26890.63	16213.34
12	Richard GREEN	Aus	71	70	71	68	280	-8	22091.89	13320.00
	Peter O'MALLEY	Aus	72	70	68	70	280	-8	22091.89	13320.00
14	Paul GOW	Aus	66	70	73	72	281	-7	19106.50	11520.00
	Kenny DRUCE	Aus	70	68	68	75	281	-7	19106.50	11520.00
	Soren HANSEN	Den	70	69	73	69	281	-7	19106.50	11520.00
	Rolf MUNTZ	Hol	69	75	70	67	281	-7	19106.50	11520.00
18	Craig JONES	Aus	72	73	70	67	282	-6	17116.24	10320.00
19	Chawalit PLAPHOL	Thai	74	68	70	71	283	-5	15050.16	9074.29
	Sergio GARCIA	Sp	74	64	75	70	283	-5	15050.16	9074.29
	Brett OGLE	Aus	71	73	69	70	283	-5	15050.16	9074.29
	Prayad MARKSAENG	Thai	71	70	72	70	283	-5	15050.16	9074.29
	Lucas PARSONS	Aus	72	70	69	72	283	-5	15050.16	9074.29
	Stephen A LINDSKOG	Swe	71	74	70	68	283	-5	15050.16	9074.29
	Daisuke MARUYAMA	Jpn	69	72	69	73	283	-5	15050.16	9074.29
26	Tom GILLIS	USA	72	68	72	72	284	-4	12804.01	7720.00
	Carlos RODILES	Sp	71	70	73	70	284	-4	12804.01	7720.00
	Christian CÉVAER	Fr	72	69	70	73	284	-4	12804.01	7720.00
	Wei-Tze YEH	Twn	71	71	70	72	284	-4	12804.01	7720.00
30	Costantino ROCCA	It	70	75	71	69	285	-3	11012.77	6640.00
	Shane TAIT	Aus	72	67	72	74	285	-3	11012.77	6640.00
	Steen TINNING	Den	71	72	73	69	285	-3	11012.77	6640.00
	Peter BAKER	Eng	71	74	71	69	285	-3	11012.77	6640.00
	Thongchai JAIDEE	Thai	71	71	74	69	285	-3	11012.77	6640.00
35	Wayne RILEY	Aus	71	70	72	73	286	-2	9287.88	5600.00
	Mike HARWOOD	Aus	73	72	70	71	286	-2	9287.88	5600.00
	Anders HANSEN	Den	72	70	71	73	286	-2	9287.88	5600.00
	Des TERBLANCHE	SA	75	70	71	70	286	-2	9287.88	5600.00
	Peter LONARD	Aus	70	69	78	69	286	-2	9287.88	5600.00
	Scott HEND	Aus	68	72	72	74	286	-2	9287.88	5600.00
41	Ian POULTER	Eng	73	72	71	71	287	-1	7828.36	4720.00
	No-Seok PARK	R.Kor	71	71	71	74	287	-1	7828.36	4720.00
	Jarrod MOSELEY	Aus	69	74	72	72	287	-1	7828.36	4720.00
	Alex CEJKA	Ger	70	74	71	72	287	-1	7828.36	4720.00
	Chie-Hsiang LIN	Taipei	70	71	72	74	287	-1	7828.36	4720.00
46	Andre STOLZ	Aus	73	68	73	74	288	0	6368.83	3840.00
	Wook-Soon KANG	S.K.	74	71	71	72	288	0	6368.83	3840.00
	Thomas LEVET	Fr	71	70	74	73	288	0	6368.83	3840.00
	Satoshi OIDE	Jpn	72	71	67	78	288	0	6368.83	3840.00
	Ter-Chang WANG	Twn	71	74	69	74	288	0	6368.83	3840.00
	Rodrigo CUELLO	Phil	70	75	71	72	288	0	6368.83	3840.00
52	Nick FALDO	Eng	71	73	74	71	289	1	4776.62	2880.00
	Michael LONG	NZ	70	71	75	73	289	1	4776.62	2880.00
	Trevor IMMELMAN	SA	76	68	70	75	289	1	4776.62	2880.00
	Jonathan LOMAS	Eng	74	69	73	73	289	1	4776.62	2880.00
	Christopher D GRAY	Aus	74	69	71	75	289	1	4776.62	2880.00
	Erol SIMSEK	Ger	70	72	75	72	289	1	4776.62	2880.00
58	Greg TURNER	NZ	71	70	75	74	290	2	3914.18	2360.00
	Gerry NORQUIST	USA	71	71	77	71	290	2	3914.18	2360.00
60	Rodger DAVIS	Aus	70	73	75	73	291	3	3317.10	2000.00
	Peter SENIOR	Aus	72	71	73	75	291	3	3317.10	2000.00
	Jeev Milkha SINGH	Ind	68	74	71	78	291	3	3317.10	2000.00
	Chia-Yuh HONG	Twn	73	71	75	72	291	3	3317.10	2000.00
	Neil KERRY	Aus	74	71	74	72	291	3	3317.10	2000.00
	Andrew MCLARDY	SA	70	73	73	75	291	3	3317.10	2000.00
	Scott GARDINER	Aus	69	75	74	73	291	3	3317.10	2000.00
67	Wayne GRADY	Aus	73	70	75	74	292	4	2477.82	1493.97
	Soren KJELDSEN	Den	72	69	75	76	292	4	2477.82	1493.97
	John SENDEN	Aus	73	70	74	75	292	4	2477.82	1493.97
	Matthew ECOB	Aus	71	71	76	74	292	4	2477.82	1493.97
	Ulrik GUSTAFSSON	Swe	73	72	68	79	292	4	2477.82	1493.97
72	Olle NORDBERG	Swe	73	72	71	77	293	5	1987.00	1198.03
73	Mardan MAMAT	Sing	70	73	73	78	294	6	1976.50	1191.70
	Tim ELLIOTT	Aus	72	72	74	76	294	6	1976.50	1191.70
	Scott LAYCOCK	Aus	70	71	79	74	294	6	1976.50	1191.70
	Henrik NYSTROM	Swe	70	74	73	77	294	6	1976.50	1191.70
	Nico VAN RENSBURG	SA	70	73	80	71	294	6	1976.50	1191.70
	Tobias DIER	Ger	69	75	71	79	294	6	1976.50	1191.70
79	Shane ROBINSON	Aus	74	71	76	74	295	7	1966.00	1185.37
80	Yang-Jin SHIN	R.Kor	70	71	76	79	296	8	1963.00	1183.56
81	Stephen COLLINS	Aus	72	72	84	72	300	12	1960.00	1181.76

A Chance to Dream

THE METROPOLITAN GOLF CLUB, MELBOURNE, AUSTRALIA

It is doubtful whether any player epitomises the pendulous nature of professional golf better than Pierre Fulke. One year earlier, the 29 year old Swede had been at a low ebb with his career threatened by a back problem.

And, although Fulke lost to American Steve Stricker in the final of the World Golf Championships-Accenture Match Play at The Metropolitan Golf Club in Melbourne, his performance throughout the week saw him draw admiring glances from many quarters.

It also saw him gather an abundance of Official World Golf Ranking Points, too, raising the former European Challenge Tour player to 32nd on the list, his highest ever position and a far cry from the 203rd place he occupied just one week before the 1999 Ryder Cup in Boston.

Such was the magnitude of his performance - he earned 532,592 euro (£334,336) "Down Under", Fulke's place in the European Team bound for The De Vere Belfry in September was already assured, ensuring he became at least the fifth Swede to play in the biennial contest, following in the footsteps of Joakim Haeggman, Per-Ulrik Johansson, Jesper Parnevik and Jarmo Sandelin.

Pierre Fulke

"I was disappointed to lose to Steve in the final, of course, but before I went to sleep I was pretty pleased," said Fulke. "It had been a great week. It was only the beginning of January, I had earned half a million and I knew I could now prepare properly for The Ryder Cup."

Fulke's Antipodean exploits continued a glorious five-month spell following his victories in 2000 in the Scottish PGA Championship at The Gleneagles Hotel and the Volvo Masters at Montecastillo.

Before that, his first Tour title had come in France in September 1999 when he captured the Trophée Lancôme, but in between them, he had the real worry of a potentially serious injury with which to contend.

"After winning the Lancôme I was out for about seven months with a wrist problem which actually turned out to be referred pain from my neck and back," said Fulke. "Initially the pain came straight away and I pulled out of the Belgacom Open (the week after his Trophée Lancôme win) and I treated it like an injury to the wrist.

"I saw the best hand surgeon in Sweden. We never did surgery but he opened it up, went in, and had a look around but found nothing

Andrew Coltart

Padraig Harrington

wrong structurally with it. He cleaned up the tendons a bit and I seemed to recover.

"I then went down to Dubai in mid-March (2000) to practise and it came back within a week. Obviously it was something else and that was when I went to a chiropractor in Stockholm called Michael Jansch. It was my idea. He was into a bit of eastern medicine and yoga so I thought it would be a good idea to give him a call and after four or five treatments with him, the problem was solved.

"The problem was that the vertebrae in my neck and back were in the wrong place and therefore were sending out the wrong signals to the rest of my body. He just put them back in place and everything was fine."

Fulke admitted that during his darkest hours, it had occurred to him that he might never play golf at the highest level again. He said: "It came into my mind, very briefly, in Dubai. I had only hit about 300 balls in six days and the problem recurred. You do think about it."

But with his health on an even keel, Fulke began to play the golf he knew he was capable of and began to climb the Official World Golf Ranking. His victory in the Trophée Lancôme moved him from 203rd to 99th, his Scottish PGA Championship success saw him rise to 68th and after the Volvo Masters he stood 48th.

So while the Australian spectators, who lined the fairways at The Metropolitan Golf Club, might not have been too aware of the

The Course

The layout is regarded as a classic and a tribute to American architect Dick Wilson. Adorned by glorious native trees, Peter Thomson once said of The Metropolitan Golf Club: "It is no exaggeration that this course is comparable with anything in the world."

Swede before the event began, they most certainly did so as he reached the final with victories over Americans Fred Funk and Glen Day, New Zealand's Michael Campbell, a third American, Brad Faxon, and tournament favourite Ernie Els of South Africa.

Meanwhile Stricker came through impressively with wins against Ireland's Padraig Harrington, American compatriots Scott Verplank and Justin Leonard, Australia's Nick O'Hern and Japan's Toru Taniguchi.

In the 36 hole final Stricker lunched two-up, but at the 16th (34th) in the afternoon it appeared that Fulke would square the match. Stricker had hit from a fairway bunker into a greenside bunker, but he came out to five feet from where he holed for the all-important half which kept him one up with two to play.

It was just the boost Stricker required and when Fulke's 12 foot putt at the 17th to keep the match alive stayed above ground, the American was the champion.

So Stricker collected the $1 million first prize, the biggest cheque of his career, with what was his first victory since 1996. He said: "It had been a long time, with a lot of lows, but what a way to start the year - any year!"

Scott Crockett

Nick O'Hern

THE METROPOLITAN GOLF CLUB, MELBOURNE, AUSTRALIA, 3-7 JANUARY 2001, PAR 72, 7066 YARDS, 6461 METRES

First Round	Second Round	Third Round	Quarter Finals	Semi Finals
1 Ernie Els / 64 Greg Kraft	**Els 4 & 2**	**Els 1 hole**	**Els at the 1st extra hole**	**Els 1 hole**
32 Hidemichi Tanaka / **33 Bernhard Langer**	Tanaka 1 hole			
16 Duffy Waldorf / **49 Jean Van de Velde**	**Van de Velde 1 hole**	Van de Velde 4 & 3		
17 Retief Goosen / 48 Steve Lowery	**Goosen 2 & 1**			
8 John Huston / 57 Craig Stadler	Stadler 4 & 2	Stadler 7 & 6	Stadler at the 1st extra hole	
25 Dennis Paulson / 40 Craig Parry	Parry 1 hole			
9 David Toms / 56 Hirofumi Miyase	Toms 1 hole	**Coltart 4 & 2**		
24 Phillip Price / **41 Andrew Coltart**	**Coltart 3 & 2**			
4 Tom Lehman / 61 Greg Chalmers	Lehman 2 & 1	Lehman 3 & 2	Faxon 1 hole	**Fulke at the 1st extra hole**
29 Naomichi Joe Ozaki / 36 Jeff Sluman	Sluman 3 & 2			
13 Chris Perry / 52 Jonathan Kaye	Perry 2 holes	Faxon 1 hole		
20 José Coceres / 45 Brad Faxon	Faxon 3 & 2			
5 Michael Campbell / **60 Mathias Grönberg**	**Campbell 4 & 3**	**Campbell 6 & 4**	**Fulke 1 hole**	
28 Toshi Izawa / 37 Steve Pate	Izawa 1 hole			
12 Kirk Triplett / 53 Glen Day	Day 3 & 1	**Fulke at the 2nd extra hole**		
21 Pierre Fulke / 44 Fred Funk	**Fulke 5 & 4**			

Final: **Fulke 2 & 1** (semi final) — Stricker 2 & 1 (semi final)

WINNER
STEVE STRICKER
2 & 1

THE CONSOLATION MATCH
TORU TANIGUCHI beat ERNIE ELS
4 & 3

Semi Finals	Quarter Finals	Third Round	Second Round	First Round
Stricker 2 & 1	Stricker at the 2nd extra hole	**O'Hern 5 & 4**	**O'Hern 5 & 3**	**O'Hern 1 hole**	Hal Sutton 2 / **Nick O'Hern 63**
			Herron 3 & 1	Franklin Langham 31 / Tim Herron 34
		Hart 5 & 4	Allenby 2 & 1	Robert Allenby 15 / Nobuhito Sato 50
			Hart 6 & 5	Dudley Hart 18 / Skip Kendall 47
		Stricker 6 & 5	Leonard at the 2nd extra hole	Leonard 6 & 5	Justin Leonard 7 / **Patrick Sjöland 58**
			Orr 2 & 1	**Gary Orr 26** / **Paul McGinley 39**
		Stricker 3 & 2	Stricker 2 & 1	**Padraig Harrington 10** / Steve Stricker 55
			Verplank 1 hole	Scott Verplank 23 / Brent Geiberger 42
	Taniguchi 2 & 1	Taniguchi 2 & 1	Taniguchi 1 hole	Singh 4 & 2	Vijay Singh 3 / Kevin Sutherland 52
			Taniguchi 3 & 2	Toru Taniguchi 30 / Bob Estes 35
		Appleby 4 & 3	Appleby 2 holes	Stuart Appleby 14 / Kenny Perry 51
			Johansson 5 & 4	Steve Flesch 19 / **Per-Ulrik Johansson 46**
		Maruyama 4 & 3	**McNulty 5 & 4**	**McNulty 1 hole**	Stewart Cink 6 / **Mark McNulty 59**
			Lawrie 5 & 4	**Paul Lawrie 27** / Chris DiMarco 36
		Maruyama at the 4th extra hole	**May 2 & 1**	**Bob May 11** / Tom Scherrer 54
			Maruyama 2 & 1	Shigeki Maruyama 22 / Scott Dunlop 43

PRIZE MONEY
Champion €1,065,188
Runner-Up €532,592
Third Place €426,075
Fourth Place €319,556
Quarter Finalists €159,778
Third Round €79,889
Second Round €53,259
First Round €26,629

In Good Hands

HOUGHTON GOLF CLUB, JOHANNESBURG, SOUTH AFRICA

Houghton, just a few miles from the fashionable Sandton district of Johannesburg, is just one of several fine clubs which have played a vital part in South African golf history over the years. They still talk there of the great golfing battles of the past played out in beautiful surroundings on a course which has the well manicured look of a botanical garden thanks, it must be said, to the untiring dedication of club member Barbey Jacobson. He supervised, and indeed paid for, many of the hundreds of trees and bushes that help give the Club its unique character. Houghton is very special. The members respect the game and appreciate great golf at the Alfred Dunhill Championship.

Adam Scott and Justin Rose

The pre-tournament disappointment felt at the non-appearance of local favourite and diligent Sunshine Tour supporter Ernie Els, on duty in America, was forgotten by the end of a week that saw two 20 year olds, England's Justin Rose and Australian Adam Scott both sure to play an important part in international golf over the next two decades, battling it out for the title with Nick Faldo, the 43 year old six times Major winner, and gutsy 30 year old Scot Dean Robertson.

In the end Scott, son of a Queensland professional and coached by him until he met Tiger Woods's guru Butch Harmon while studying at the University of Nevada, Las Vegas, came back after losing a four stroke advantage on the final day to edge out Rose for the title with a deft pitch and a three foot putt at the last.

After his difficult baptism in the professional ranks where he missed his first 21 halfway cuts following his tied fourth finish as an amateur in the 1998 Open Championship, Rose's Houghton performance was a welcome relief. Few could have handled the early disappointments as gracefully and intelligently. So coping with the disappointment of losing at Houghton when in contention for the first time, was relatively easy.

Shot of the Week

Adam Scott's four iron at the par five 16th in the third round - a classic, fairway bunker shot which by finding the green kept him in contention on the way to victory.

Dean Robertson

Yet this was Scott's week. He secured his first victory in only his ninth start as a professional on The European Tour. He had played with distinction as an amateur in some early Tour events in 2000, including third place in the Benson and Hedges International Open at The De Vere Belfry, so his quick success was hardly unexpected. In his latter days as an amateur he had been rated World Number Two and had upstaged the professionals by firing a course record 63 in the Greg Norman Holden International when fans first noticed how similar his style was to that of Woods - coach Harmon's most high profile pupil.

Nick Faldo

The swings of the two players are almost identical and it was clear again at Houghton that Scott has the temperament to succeed on the multi-national European Tour and also on the world stage. In Johannesburg, however, Scott re-iterated his well-proven route. Many of today's international stars, including Greg Norman, Nick Price, Vijay Singh and the "Big Easy" Els to name just four, have learned to play a variety of shots on all kinds of grasses and in all weathers in Europe before moving on to become winners of Major Championships.

Last summer Scott had taken the opportunity to mention to Tiger, when they were practising together at Las Vegas, that he was considering turning professional rather earlier than planned. His decision to do so was influenced by the World Number One's confidence boosting reply: "Go on, go out there, play hard and let them have it."

He did just that at Houghton, helped by a word of advice he received from Harmon on the phone on Saturday night. Scott had led before going into the final round and failed to win so this time Harmon advised him to forget about winning. "Just go out and play golf," said Butch and he did until the last hour and a half when in danger of losing his competitive instincts took over. Three birdies in the last five holes enabled him to handle the spirited challenge of Rose.

What was so commendable throughout a week mercifully free from any serious weather disruptions, was the spirit in which the two young men conducted themselves throughout - an indication that the future well being of the game is in good hands. In the end Scott summed up his feelings as succinctly as you might expect of someone who has studied communications. "I've experienced the taste of winning now and want it even more," he said.

On the evidence of another highly memorable Alfred Dunhill Championship Adam Scott should have little trouble in filling up the shelves of his trophy cabinet.

Renton Laidlaw

Anthony Wall

The Course

Houghton, a long, scenic, parkland course, was in immaculate condition leading up to the tournament, despite unseasonal heavy rain. The fact that it stood up to the test under severe problems was a tribute to the work of the staff who had the greens in perfect shape.

HOUGHTON GOLF CLUB, JOHANNESBURG, SOUTH AFRICA 18-21 JANUARY, 2001, PAR 72, 7284 YARDS, 6660 METRES

Pos.	Name		Rd1	Rd2	Rd3	Rd4	Total	Par	Prize Money Euro	Prize Money £
1	Adam SCOTT	Aus	67	66	65	69	267	-21	123071.73	79000.00
2	Justin ROSE	Eng	66	67	66	69	268	-20	89577.53	57500.00
3	Nick FALDO	Eng	68	65	68	68	269	-19	46151.90	29625.00
	Dean ROBERTSON	Scot	62	70	67	70	269	-19	46151.90	29625.00
5	Anthony WALL	Eng	69	64	70	67	270	-18	32247.91	20700.00
6	Malcolm MACKENZIE	Eng	68	68	67	68	271	-17	27574.30	17700.00
7	Brian DAVIS	Eng	69	70	69	64	272	-16	21070.19	13525.00
	Retief GOOSEN	SA	73	68	67	64	272	-16	21070.19	13525.00
9	Sven STRÜVER	Ger	71	70	69	63	273	-15	16825.00	10800.00
10	Ricardo GONZALEZ	Arg	69	64	70	71	274	-14	14072.76	9033.33
	Greg OWEN	Eng	66	70	69	69	274	-14	14072.76	9033.33
	Michael KIRK	SA	68	66	69	71	274	-14	14072.76	9033.33
13	Jeev Milkha SINGH	Ind	70	66	69	70	275	-13	11580.17	7433.34
	Steve WEBSTER	Eng	66	70	72	67	275	-13	11580.17	7433.34
	Bradley DREDGE	Wal	67	68	68	72	275	-13	11580.17	7433.34
16	Brenden PAPPAS	SA	68	67	73	68	276	-12	9908.05	6360.00
	Carl SUNESON	Sp	70	67	72	67	276	-12	9908.05	6360.00
	Jonathan LOMAS	Eng	72	67	69	68	276	-12	9908.05	6360.00
	Paul MCGINLEY	Ire	67	71	68	70	276	-12	9908.05	6360.00
	Mathias GRÖNBERG	Swe	66	70	71	69	276	-12	9908.05	6360.00
21	Nic HENNING	SA	68	69	69	71	277	-11	8763.02	5625.00
	Sean LUDGATER	SA	69	67	71	70	277	-11	8763.02	5625.00
23	Mark MCNULTY	Zim	67	70	72	69	278	-10	7384.31	4740.00
	Anders HANSEN	Den	71	68	71	68	278	-10	7384.31	4740.00
	Peter BAKER	Eng	73	66	67	72	278	-10	7384.31	4740.00
	David FAUGHT	SA	72	67	71	68	278	-10	7384.31	4740.00
	Bobby LINCOLN	SA	69	68	70	71	278	-10	7384.31	4740.00
	Des TERBLANCHE	SA	68	65	72	73	278	-10	7384.31	4740.00
	Andrew RAITT	Eng	71	68	70	69	278	-10	7384.31	4740.00
	Markus BRIER	Aut	69	69	70	70	278	-10	7384.31	4740.00
	David HIGGINS	Ire	69	70	71	68	278	-10	7384.31	4740.00
	Ashley ROESTOFF	SA	66	70	72	70	278	-10	7384.31	4740.00
33	Marco BERNARDINI	It	73	68	72	66	279	-9	6309.37	4050.00
34	Bradford VAUGHAN	SA	70	71	70	69	280	-8	5686.23	3650.00
	Trevor IMMELMAN	SA	75	66	71	68	280	-8	5686.23	3650.00
	Paul BROADHURST	Eng	66	70	71	73	280	-8	5686.23	3650.00
	Justin HOBDAY	SA	70	67	73	70	280	-8	5686.23	3650.00
	Stephen DODD	Wal	69	70	70	71	280	-8	5686.23	3650.00
	Ian GARBUTT	Eng	68	71	73	68	280	-8	5686.23	3650.00
	Alastair FORSYTH	Scot	68	66	77	69	280	-8	5686.23	3650.00
41	David HOWELL	Eng	71	69	69	72	281	-7	4517.82	2900.00
	Raphaël JACQUELIN	Fr	71	68	70	72	281	-7	4517.82	2900.00
	Peter HANSON	Swe	73	65	69	74	281	-7	4517.82	2900.00
	Gregory HAVRET	Fr	71	68	74	68	281	-7	4517.82	2900.00
	Van PHILLIPS	Eng	69	72	73	67	281	-7	4517.82	2900.00
	Craig KAMPS	SA	67	74	71	69	281	-7	4517.82	2900.00
	Simon DYSON	Eng	69	66	77	69	281	-7	4517.82	2900.00
	Bradley DAVISON	SA	71	70	72	68	281	-7	4517.82	2900.00
49	Chris WILLIAMS	Eng	72	67	73	70	282	-6	3583.10	2300.00
	Jamie SPENCE	Eng	69	69	73	71	282	-6	3583.10	2300.00
	Adilson DA SILVA	Bra	69	69	71	73	282	-6	3583.10	2300.00
	Mikael LUNDBERG	Swe	71	70	72	69	282	-6	3583.10	2300.00
53	Tony JOHNSTONE	Zim	69	68	71	75	283	-5	2609.43	1675.00
	Deane PAPPAS	SA	69	70	67	77	283	-5	2609.43	1675.00
	Marco GORTANA	SA	68	72	71	72	283	-5	2609.43	1675.00
	Mark HILTON	Eng	72	68	72	71	283	-5	2609.43	1675.00
	Ian POULTER	Eng	67	72	72	72	283	-5	2609.43	1675.00
	Paul EALES	Eng	65	74	73	71	283	-5	2609.43	1675.00
	Jean HUGO	SA	71	67	76	69	283	-5	2609.43	1675.00
	Olivier EDMOND	Fr	70	68	72	73	283	-5	2609.43	1675.00
	Neil CHEETHAM	Eng	70	67	76	70	283	-5	2609.43	1675.00
	Brett LIDDLE	SA	70	70	72	71	283	-5	2609.43	1675.00
63	Ian PALMER	SA	69	72	71	72	284	-4	1756.89	1127.75
	Darren FICHARDT	SA	72	65	75	72	284	-4	1756.89	1127.75
	Hennie WALTERS	SA	69	71	71	73	284	-4	1756.89	1127.75
	Steen TINNING	Den	71	68	74	71	284	-4	1756.89	1127.75
	Richard S JOHNSON	Swe	68	72	68	76	284	-4	1756.89	1127.75
	Johan RYSTRÖM	Swe	71	69	70	74	284	-4	1756.89	1127.75
	James KINGSTON	SA	74	66	74	70	284	-4	1756.89	1127.75
	Robert COLES	Eng	75	66	76	67	284	-4	1756.89	1127.75
	Doug McGUIGAN	Scot	70	66	74	74	284	-4	1756.89	1127.75
72	Donald GAMMON	SA	72	69	72	72	285	-3	1165.00	747.82
73	Warren BENNETT	Eng	69	68	72	78	287	-1	1157.50	743.00
	Michele REALE	It	73	68	73	73	287	-1	1157.50	743.00
	Ryan DREYER	SA	71	66	75	75	287	-1	1157.50	743.00
	Trevor MOORE	SA	69	71	75	72	287	-1	1157.50	743.00
77	Desvonde BOTES	SA	72	69	75	72	288	0	1148.50	737.22
	Erol SIMSEK	Ger	67	71	74	76	288	0	1148.50	737.22
79	Ulrich VAN DEN BERG	SA	69	70	77	73	289	1	1144.00	734.34
80	Nicolas COLSAERTS	Bel	70	69	73	78	290	2	1141.00	732.41
81	Simon MCCARTHY	Eng	69	71	74	77	291	3	1138.00	730.48

Pro-Golf 2002

Pro-Golf, the European Tour Media Guide respected throughout the golfing world as an essential work of reference, has been chronicling the achievements of The European Tour for 31 years and the 2002 edition is packed full of records and revealing statistics.

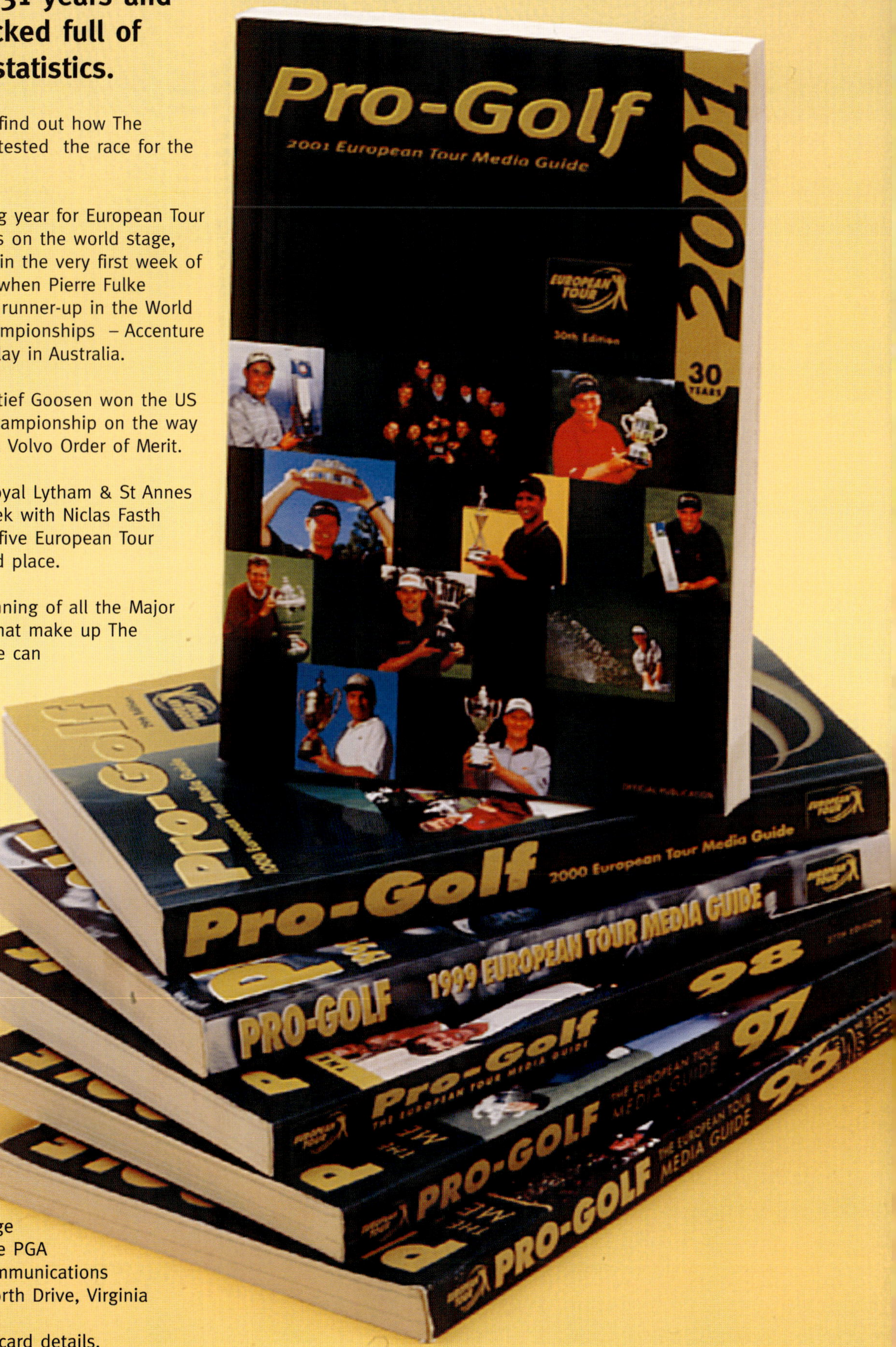

In an arena full of great champions find out how The European Tour's leading players contested the race for the Volvo Order of Merit title.

The 2001 season was an outstanding year for European Tour Members on the world stage, starting in the very first week of January when Pierre Fulke finished runner-up in the World Golf Championships – Accenture Match Play in Australia.

Then Retief Goosen won the US Open Championship on the way to finishing Number One in the 2001 Volvo Order of Merit.

The 130th Open Championship at Royal Lytham & St Annes proved to be another exemplary week with Niclas Fasth finishing second and no fewer than five European Tour Members finishing in a share of third place.

The facts and figures behind the winning of all the Major Championships plus all the events that make up The European Tour International Schedule can be found in Pro-Golf 2002.

The tremendous progress of The European Tour over the past three decades, notable achievements, detailed biographies of all the international stars who make The European Tour unique, records and statistics are all meticulously chronicled in almost 600 pages in the illustrated 2002 Pro-Golf. Quite simply, it is a must for the library of every golf enthusiast.

Ordering a copy of Pro-Golf 2002 is simple: send a cheque for £15 UK and Europe (which includes postage and packaging) and £20 Overseas (which includes postage and packaging), made payable to the PGA European Tour to Emily Doughty, Communications Division, The European Tour, Wentworth Drive, Virginia Water, Surrey GU25 4LX or call +44 1344 840442 with credit card details.

Lethal Mixture

EAST LONDON GOLF CLUB, EAST LONDON, SOUTH AFRICA

Mark McNulty was only six years old when the Mercedes-Benz South African Open was last played at East London. Gary Player, 13 times winner of the Championship, took the title 37 years ago and had he been present for the Championship this year he would have seen few changes to a course that by modern-day standards could be described accurately enough as old fashioned.

Professionals these days have become accustomed to playing American-style target golf but at East London the secret to scoring well requires imagination, patience, a strong mind-set, a comprehensive repertoire of shots and an ability to read grainy greens. McNulty proved over the four rounds - the last played in a testing swirling wind that got up in the afternoon – that, at times, there is nothing to beat experience. There are other, younger, players who hit the ball further than McNulty - although a new driver has helped him add ten yards off the tee - and there are fitter, more athletic younger players around, but it was McNulty's 20 years experience that enabled the respected international campaigner to score his second Mercedes-Benz South African Open triumph.

Sven Strüver

Winning these days is never easy and McNulty left it late. He could not claim his victory until after he had holed a 25 foot putt on the last green to get the better of talented 20 year old Justin Rose, runner-up for the second week running on the 'Sunshine Tour Swing' of The European Tour International Schedule. For McNulty, who had not won on The European Tour since taking the 1996 TNT Dutch Open, it was an emotional moment.

For a long-time campaigner McNulty's success at East London was his 49th international victory. Only five players have done better than him in European Tour, Sunshine Tour events and National Championships. Seve Ballesteros, whose 88 international successes only underlines the contribution he made to European and world golf, may be, sadly, just a shadow of himself, but the record is there to celebrate the fact that he remains the most prolific winner on Tour ahead of Arnold Palmer and Gary Player, on the list because

Shot of the Week

Mark McNulty's 25 foot putt at the last on the final day to beat Justin Rose - he showed steely nerves to make the all-important stroke of the tournament.

Thomas Björn

Simon Dyson

they are both Honorary Life Members, Bernhard Langer and Greg Norman. McNulty comes in at sixth spot despite having suffered a series of injuries over the years that have severely disrupted his schedules. His all round game is a lethal mixture of competence, consistency and class. Consider, for example, this statistic on the McNulty CV. In a 12 year spell between 1985 and 1996 he played 172 European Tour events and missed the cut just 17 times.

The South African-based Zimbabwean is the complete professional and when the wind blew for the later starters on the final day at East London there was ample proof of that. While others were bamboozled by the breeze which blew strongly off the Indian Ocean most days, he mastered it superbly and was equal to the challenge thrown down in particular by Rose. South Africans Hennie Otto and Roger Wessels, Sweden's Challenge Tour graduate Mickael Lundberg and Danish Ryder Cup star Thomas Björn were also involved in the title hunt but for Rose and McNulty, playing together on the last day, the battle assumed an engrossingly exciting match-play characteristic of enthusiasm against experience. In the end as they battled head to head, a missed putt of eight feet on the 11th and a bogey at the 12th, proved expensive mistakes for Rose.

The English golfer's overall performance, however, underlined how much he has improved as a player. He never stopped believing in

Roger Wessels

himself despite all his gut-wrenching early knock backs. Following his runners-up spot to Adam Scott at Houghton the week before, Rose had achieved one of his early goals. After having had to cope three times with the traumatic tensions of the Qualifying School, the 212,401 euro (£135,443) he had earned in two weeks was more than enough to ensure his card for 2002. Rose then identified victory as his next target to match that of Scott, who had to pull out of the East London tournament with a recurrence of knee trouble.

Amazingly Rose might never have been in East London but for the generosity of local professional Shane Howe, who had been offered a guest spot in the event. Keen to give Rose, whose official ranking was too low for automatic entry, a spot in the field, officials took an unusual step. They asked Howe if he would withdraw to let the young Englishman in and he graciously agreed.

Yet nothing Rose did on the week can deflect from the proud performance of 47 year old McNulty who, by grinding out this latest triumph, became the oldest player from Southern Africa to take a European Tour title. He has holed many crucial putts in his illustrious career but that 25 foot winner at East London was certainly one of his most impressive - indeed a perfect match for those luxury saloons that roll off sponsor Mercedes Benz's assembly line a few miles down the coast.

Renton Laidlaw

Hennie Otto

The Course

East London, a traditional championship venue dating back to 1906, returned to the tournament rota for the Mercedes-Benz South African Open for the first time since 1967, and the players were treated to a picturesque, elegantly manicured lay out with a definite links feel right on the Indian Ocean coastline.

Justin Rose

EAST LONDON GOLF CLUB, EAST LONDON, SOUTH AFRICA, 25-28 JANUARY, 2001, PAR 72, 6847 YARDS, 6287 METRES

Pos.	Name		Rd1	Rd2	Rd3	Rd4	Total	Par	Prize Money Euro	Prize Money £
1	Mark McNULTY	Zim	69	71	69	71	280	-8	169283.00	107948.02
2	Justin ROSE	Eng	72	69	68	72	281	-7	122823.62	78321.90
3	Thomas BJÖRN	Den	72	67	71	72	282	-6	63120.66	40250.65
	Roger WESSELS	SA	67	69	72	74	282	-6	63120.66	40250.65
5	Hennie OTTO	SA	65	70	71	77	283	-5	40692.01	25948.39
	Mikael LUNDBERG	Swe	71	67	73	72	283	-5	40692.01	25948.39
7	Malcolm MACKENZIE	Eng	76	68	77	63	284	-4	28409.64	18116.20
	Bradford VAUGHAN	SA	71	74	70	69	284	-4	28409.64	18116.20
9	Desvonde BOTES	SA	70	71	74	70	285	-3	18110.77	11548.84
	Arjun ATWAL	Ind	72	70	72	71	285	-3	18110.77	11548.84
	Justin HOBDAY	SA	70	70	70	75	285	-3	18110.77	11548.84
	Johan RYSTRÖM	Swe	71	71	75	68	285	-3	18110.77	11548.84
	Stephen GALLACHER	Scot	70	71	71	73	285	-3	18110.77	11548.84
	Tobias DIER	Ger	71	66	76	72	285	-3	18110.77	11548.84
	Simon DYSON	Eng	69	72	69	75	285	-3	18110.77	11548.84
16	David HOWELL	Eng	71	67	73	75	286	-2	13478.56	8594.98
	Brian DAVIS	Eng	73	70	74	69	286	-2	13478.56	8594.98
	Peter BAKER	Eng	72	73	75	66	286	-2	13478.56	8594.98
	Ignacio GARRIDO	Sp	66	73	73	74	286	-2	13478.56	8594.98
	Martin MARITZ	SA	69	71	74	72	286	-2	13478.56	8594.98
21	Michael ARCHER	Eng	71	73	71	72	287	-1	11427.94	7287.34
	Paul MCGINLEY	Ire	71	72	70	74	287	-1	11427.94	7287.34
	Bradley DREDGE	Wal	67	70	74	76	287	-1	11427.94	7287.34
	Retief GOOSEN	SA	71	68	73	75	287	-1	11427.94	7287.34
	Erol SIMSEK	Ger	72	70	75	70	287	-1	11427.94	7287.34
26	Jeev Milkha SINGH	Ind	71	71	70	76	288	0	9425.38	6010.36
	Bruce VAUGHAN	USA	70	71	74	73	288	0	9425.38	6010.36
	Trevor IMMELMAN	SA	72	73	69	74	288	0	9425.38	6010.36
	James KINGSTON	SA	68	74	73	73	288	0	9425.38	6010.36
	David LYNN	Eng	72	72	75	69	288	0	9425.38	6010.36
	Greg OWEN	Eng	67	69	74	78	288	0	9425.38	6010.36
	David PARK	Wal	74	68	76	70	288	0	9425.38	6010.36
	Markus BRIER	Aut	70	73	68	77	288	0	9425.38	6010.36
34	Grant MULLER	SA	69	73	72	75	289	1	8010.24	5107.95
	Shaun P WEBSTER	Eng	72	71	75	71	289	1	8010.24	5107.95
	Rolf MUNTZ	Hol	75	69	73	72	289	1	8010.24	5107.95
	Trevor DODDS	Nam	70	73	75	71	289	1	8010.24	5107.95
38	Paul EALES	Eng	71	72	74	73	290	2	6835.40	4358.78
	Wayne BRADLEY	SA	71	74	73	72	290	2	6835.40	4358.78
	Daren LEE	Eng	75	70	76	69	290	2	6835.40	4358.78
	Alastair FORSYTH	Scot	74	70	69	77	290	2	6835.40	4358.78
	Bradley DAVISON	SA	71	73	74	72	290	2	6835.40	4358.78
	Doug McGUIGAN	Scot	74	69	70	77	290	2	6835.40	4358.78
	Carl PETTERSSON	Swe	72	73	75	70	290	2	6835.40	4358.78
45	Sven STRÜVER	Ger	70	73	77	71	291	3	5446.96	3473.41
	Nasho KAMUNGEREMU	Zim	69	71	72	79	291	3	5446.96	3473.41
	Derek CRAWFORD	Scot	70	73	76	72	291	3	5446.96	3473.41
	André CRUSE	SA	70	74	73	74	291	3	5446.96	3473.41
	David HIGGINS	Ire	70	73	77	71	291	3	5446.96	3473.41
	Ashley ROESTOFF	SA	72	73	75	71	291	3	5446.96	3473.41
51	Wayne RILEY	Aus	69	71	79	73	292	4	4485.73	2860.45
	Brenden PAPPAS	SA	68	72	73	79	292	4	4485.73	2860.45
	Peter HANSON	Swe	72	72	78	70	292	4	4485.73	2860.45
54	Dean VAN STADEN	SA	75	70	73	75	293	5	3738.11	2383.71
	Ian POULTER	Eng	72	70	79	72	293	5	3738.11	2383.71
	Paolo QUIRICI	Swi	67	73	75	78	293	5	3738.11	2383.71
	Michele REALE	It	71	74	75	73	293	5	3738.11	2383.71
	Jaco VAN DER MERWE (AM)	SA	72	72	76	73	293	5		
59	Deane PAPPAS	SA	72	70	79	73	294	6	3097.29	1975.07
	Jean-Francois REMESY	Fr	70	74	78	72	294	6	3097.29	1975.07
	Gary EMERSON	Eng	75	70	74	75	294	6	3097.29	1975.07
	Mathias GRÖNBERG	Swe	76	69	73	76	294	6	3097.29	1975.07
	Matthew WILCOX	Eng	70	71	81	72	294	6	3097.29	1975.07
	Jaco VAN ZYL (AM)	SA	75	67	72	80	294	6		
65	Raphaël JACQUELIN	Fr	71	71	76	77	295	7	2616.68	1668.60
	Wallie COETSEE	SA	72	73	71	79	295	7	2616.68	1668.60
	Bobby LINCOLN	SA	70	69	76	80	295	7	2616.68	1668.60
	Ted HENDRIKS	SA	72	73	75	75	295	7	2616.68	1668.60
69	Richard KAPLAN	SA	72	72	80	72	296	8	2296.27	1464.28
	Lindani NDWANDWE	SA	73	71	74	78	296	8	2296.27	1464.28
71	Ian KENNEDY	SA	72	72	79	74	297	9	2136.06	1362.12
72	Chris DAVISON	SA	71	74	79	76	300	12	2029.25	1294.01

Father's Day

THE VINES RESORT, PERTH, AUSTRALIA

Michael Campbell has never made any secret of the importance he attaches to being a father. Indeed, after the birth of his first child, Thomas, the New Zealander publicly attributed the responsibility of parenthood for his improved 1999 season.

Therefore, it should not have been a surprise that the arrival of his second son, Jordan, in December 2000, heralded another bountiful spell, one which manifested itself in a successful defence of the Heineken Classic at The Vines Resort in Perth.

Going into the final round only two strokes off the lead might be enough to give some golfers, if not a sleepless night, then certainly a restless morning. But not Campbell. His initial concern was spending quality time with his family, sitting round the breakfast table like any normal father on a Sunday morning.

An hour-long practice session on the putting green the previous evening had reassured Campbell normal service would be restored in that department, after three days where his stubborn putter had given him little assistance. Such was his personal contentment and professional confidence it enabled the New Zealander to focus on the task ahead, rather than look back.

It meant he was able to play for four hours in the blistering heat without once losing his mental stability. It meant he comfortably overtook third round leader Nick O'Hern with a closing 64. It meant he was the champion again.

"When you get into that zone, nothing disturbs you,"said Campbell who eventually finished five shots clear of fellow New Zealander David Smail with O'Hern in third. "You are so focused. I am in my own little bubble and no other influence in the world can distract me from my goal. Sometimes you don't even hear the wind or the crowds roaring or anything else apart from your own thoughts."

Greg Turner

Nick O'Hern

The Course

The Vines, which is regularly included in the list of Australia's top courses, provides an interesting and at times demanding challenge especially when the wind is blowing. Designed by Perth-based Graham Marsh and Ross Watson in the attractive Swan Valley, noted for producing some of the country's finest wines, the course is set in pleasant rolling countryside.

The professional search for perfection can be interrupted by a technical flaw, but more often than not it can be attributed to a simple distraction. Suddenly the fairways narrow, the greens appear to be halved in size by bunkers and a sense of claustrophobia takes over. Campbell claimed even if a 747 had roared overhead into the Perth sky, he would not have heard it.

It has always been in Campbell's nature to shoot for the pins at all times. Even so, his closing 64 was an impressive performance from the moment he followed an opening bogey with three successive birdies to serve notice on O'Hern that there was to be a titanic challenge on the superbly prepared course.

In fact, O'Hern contributed to his own downfall as he relinquished his advantage by taking eight at the sixth. Dean Robertson had held the lead following a first round of 65, one ahead of Greg Norman and O'Hern, but at the halfway stage O'Hern (69) shared the lead with Steen Tinning, who followed a 69 with a 66. "If I win the tournament, fantastic," said O'Hern. "If not there are plenty more to play. It's not something I'm going to lose sleep over."

O'Hern had good reason to remain in a similar mood as, playing in front of a gallery that included family and friends, he played the last 11 holes in five under for another 69 for 204 - two ahead of Campbell and three in front of Peter Lonard, Robertson and Tinning.

Steen Tinning

Dean Robertson

Greg Norman and Adam Scott

The left-hander however, went from pacesetter to pursuer as, at the sixth hole, he plunged from 14 under to ten under, from two ahead of Campbell to two behind. O'Hern had struck his tee shot in the right fairway bunker on the 437 yards hole and, in his own words, "probably made the wrong decision with his next shot. I should have gone out sideways, rather than going for too much. From there I just got a couple of bad lies. Eight shots is pretty easy to rack up on this course."

O'Hern was to be applauded for the manner in which he fought back, even if after a 72 he was passed for second place by Smail, who shot a second successive 66. But for all that, this was a tournament that belonged to Campbell.

He made ten birdies and two bogeys for the low round of the tournament and his 64 was just one short of the course record. Moreover, it was Campbell's sixth win in 33 tournaments. "I putted unbelievably in the last round," said Campbell. "I knew I had played so well from tee to green on the first three days that I only had to start making some putts to be right in it. Now I want to become one of the top five golfers in the world."

In years to come Thomas and Jordan might appreciate that fact but for the moment they are more concerned with daddy's qualities as a father. To them of course, in that realm, he is already Number One.

Mitchell Platts

Shot of the Week

Michael Campbell knew he was home and dry, but his 260 yards three wood at the last was still a memorable blow. It set up his final birdie of the championship, his tenth of a remarkable afternoon, and one which made victory all the sweeter.

THE VINES RESORT, PERTH, AUSTRALIA, 1-4 FEBRUARY, 2001, PAR 72, 7101 YARDS, 6492 METRES

Pos.	Name		Rd1	Rd2	Rd3	Rd4	Total	Par	Prize Money Euro	£
1	Michael CAMPBELL	NZ	69	70	67	64	270	-18	195498.92	123449.87
2	David SMAIL	NZ	71	72	66	66	275	-13	110782.73	69954.93
3	Nick O'HERN	Aus	66	69	69	72	276	-12	73312.09	46293.70
4	Paul DEVENPORT	NZ	71	68	69	69	277	-11	42358.10	26747.47
	Steen TINNING	Den	69	66	72	70	277	-11	42358.10	26747.47
	Jarrod MOSELEY	Aus	70	70	70	67	277	-11	42358.10	26747.47
	Dean ROBERTSON	Scot	65	74	68	70	277	-11	42358.10	26747.47
8	Robert KARLSSON	Swe	72	66	72	70	280	-8	29324.83	18517.48
	Ian GARBUTT	Eng	78	66	68	68	280	-8	29324.83	18517.48
	Thomas BJÖRN	Den	67	71	73	69	280	-8	29324.83	18517.48
11	Greg TURNER	NZ	70	71	69	72	282	-6	20201.56	12756.49
	Kenny DRUCE	Aus	72	72	66	72	282	-6	20201.56	12756.49
	Peter LONARD	Aus	70	71	66	75	282	-6	20201.56	12756.49
	Fredrik JACOBSON	Swe	71	72	70	69	282	-6	20201.56	12756.49
	Henrik NYSTROM	Swe	75	69	70	68	282	-6	20201.56	12756.49
16	Greg NORMAN	Aus	66	73	70	74	283	-5	14264.18	9007.27
	Craig PARRY	Aus	70	70	69	74	283	-5	14264.18	9007.27
	Brett RUMFORD	Aus	72	70	71	70	283	-5	14264.18	9007.27
19	Soren HANSEN	Den	76	69	71	68	284	-4	11580.60	7312.69
	Phillip PRICE	Wal	75	70	69	70	284	-4	11580.60	7312.69
	David CARTER	Eng	73	70	71	70	284	-4	11580.60	7312.69
	Nathan GREEN	Aus	72	70	72	70	284	-4	11580.60	7312.69
23	David HOWELL	Eng	72	73	66	74	285	-3	8773.31	5540.00
	Justin ROSE	Eng	70	75	68	72	285	-3	8773.31	5540.00
	Paul BROADHURST	Eng	74	69	70	72	285	-3	8773.31	5540.00
	Anthony GILLIGAN	Aus	71	73	69	72	285	-3	8773.31	5540.00
	Pierre FULKE	Swe	67	76	69	73	285	-3	8773.31	5540.00
	Markus BRIER	Aut	71	73	68	73	285	-3	8773.31	5540.00
	Christopher HANELL	Swe	74	70	72	69	285	-3	8773.31	5540.00
	Brendan JONES	Aus	72	70	69	74	285	-3	8773.31	5540.00
	Scott GARDINER	Aus	71	72	71	71	285	-3	8773.31	5540.00
32	John WADE	Aus	73	70	70	73	286	-2	6625.25	4183.58
	Scott LAYCOCK	Aus	67	74	74	71	286	-2	6625.25	4183.58
34	Sven STRÜVER	Ger	72	71	73	71	287	-1	5864.97	3703.50
	Wayne SMITH	Aus	69	73	72	73	287	-1	5864.97	3703.50
	Gary EVANS	Eng	72	73	71	71	287	-1	5864.97	3703.50
	Lucas PARSONS	Aus	72	73	70	72	287	-1	5864.97	3703.50
	Andrew TSCHUDIN	Aus	73	68	71	75	287	-1	5864.97	3703.50
39	Richard GREEN	Aus	69	76	74	69	288	0	4778.86	3017.66
	Andre STOLZ	Aus	73	71	70	74	288	0	4778.86	3017.66
	Shane TAIT	Aus	67	72	77	72	288	0	4778.86	3017.66
	Michael LONG	NZ	71	72	73	72	288	0	4778.86	3017.66
	John BICKERTON	Eng	74	66	73	75	288	0	4778.86	3017.66
44	Anthony PAINTER	Aus	70	72	73	74	289	1	3801.37	2400.42
	Ignacio GARRIDO	Sp	68	75	76	70	289	1	3801.37	2400.42
	Bradley KING	Aus	69	74	70	76	289	1	3801.37	2400.42
	Gerry NORQUIST	USA	71	74	68	76	289	1	3801.37	2400.42
48	Peter SENIOR	Aus	69	72	73	76	290	2	2796.72	1766.02
	Matthew ECOB	Aus	73	72	75	70	290	2	2796.72	1766.02
	Richard S JOHNSON	Swe	77	68	71	74	290	2	2796.72	1766.02
	Joakim HAEGGMAN	Swe	73	71	75	71	290	2	2796.72	1766.02
	Martyn ROBERTS	Wal	73	72	70	75	290	2	2796.72	1766.02
	Stephen SCAHILL	NZ	74	70	75	71	290	2	2796.72	1766.02
54	Jeff WAGNER	Aus	77	68	71	75	291	3	2356.85	1488.26
	Marcus CAIN	Aus	71	73	72	75	291	3	2356.85	1488.26
	Matthew LANE	NZ	72	73	73	73	291	3	2356.85	1488.26
	David LYNN	Eng	72	73	73	73	291	3	2356.85	1488.26
58	Rodney PAMPLING	Aus	76	69	76	71	292	4	2302.53	1453.96
59	Maarten LAFEBER	Hol	70	73	75	75	293	5	2280.82	1440.25
60	Roger CHAPMAN	Eng	73	67	74	80	294	6	2237.38	1412.82
	John SENDEN	Aus	76	68	77	73	294	6	2237.38	1412.82
	Rolf MUNTZ	Hol	72	72	72	78	294	6	2237.38	1412.82
63	Stuart BOUVIER	Aus	73	71	78	73	295	7	2193.93	1385.38
64	Roger WINCHESTER	Eng	72	73	74	77	296	8	2161.36	1364.81
	Niclas FASTH	Swe	73	72	79	72	296	8	2161.36	1364.81
66	Henrik STENSON	Swe	69	74	76	78	297	9	2128.76	1344.23
67	Justin COOPER	Aus	74	70	70	84	298	10	2074.46	1309.94
	Charles HOWELL III	USA	70	73	77	78	298	10	2074.46	1309.94
	Robert FLOYD	USA	75	69	75	79	298	10	2074.46	1309.94
	James MCLEAN	Aus	74	67	86	71	298	10	2074.46	1309.94

Olympic Gold

THE LAKES GOLF CLUB, SYDNEY, AUSTRALIA

There are few more vibrant cities in the world than Sydney and, following hard on the heels of arguably the most successful of Olympic Games, it was fitting that the Greg Norman Holden International should unfold into a classic festival of golf.

Aaron Baddeley moved centre-stage by capturing the title but the supporting cast captivated the audience with moments of such great theatre that no critic could fail to be impressed by the majestic performances of the players.

Aaron Baddeley

Baddeley's victory, his second as a professional following a successful defence of the Australian Open which he had won as an amateur in 1999, earned him a two-year exemption on The European Tour which co-sanctions the Greg Norman Holden International with the Australasian PGA Tour. It was also seen by many observers as a defining moment in the sport. Both Sergio Garcia and Baddeley, with their stars in the ascendancy, showed commendable composure and courage in a truly sporting confrontation as they moved into a play-off. The Australian newspapers informed their readers that the tournament would be remembered as fundamental to golf in their country producing, as it did, a showdown between two of the youngest, brightest golfers in the world.

This was golf at its best. There was joy and tears, highs and lows, as a compelling story unfolded from the start with Greg Norman, the host, taking up the challenge set by the "Young Guns". The Australians could point to the likes of Scott Gardiner, James McLean, Brett Rumford, Adam Scott and Baddeley, all born within a couple of years of each other, as being as promising a group as Seve Ballesteros, Nick Faldo, Bernhard Langer, Sandy Lyle and Ian Woosnam, while Ian Poulter, Carlos Rodiles, Justin Rose and Garcia further advertised the new force coming together in Europe.

Sergio Garcia

Ian Poulter

Garcia's opening 64 gave him a one shot lead ahead of Pierre Fulke with Steve Alker, Daren Lee and Phillip Price being joined on 66 by Norman. Garcia's 64 was one shot short of the record at The Lakes set by Scott as an amateur a year earlier. Garcia had played in the morning when the flags barely moved, but in the afternoon the wind came up to set an altogether sterner test. Baddeley's 67 late in the day was a round that emphasised his steely reserve and smacked of class.

Baddeley had good reason to feel that he would profit by playing early the next day, and a round of 68 was a sound effort. Garcia, however, stayed out in front with a 69 for a 13 under par total of 133 - one ahead of Norman (68) with Baddeley and Price (69) on 135. So now Garcia and The Shark would play together in the third round. There were those who wanted to see Baddeley and Garcia together, and they would be granted their wish on the final day, but as Norman asked with mock hurt: "What's wrong with Garcia-Norman?"

The age factor, of course, had been the talking point all week. McLean, 22, who suffers from Vaso-vagal Syndrome, a condition that can cause fainting spells, was now in the hunt after a 67 for 136 and 20 year old Scott was only two further back after a 67. So with 21 year old Garcia leading, and 19 year old Baddeley sharing third place, Norman was asked if he felt like an old lion going into battle with the young cubs.

Shot of the Week

Peter Lonard will not forget the four iron he flushed at the 195 yards 18th in round three - the ball landed, rolled across the green, disappeared into the hole and won him a Holden VX Commodore SS car.

Norman said: "Well, they're all skin and bones so there's not much to eat there! I'm in there in the hunt. The kids today are so experienced. Their approach to golf is far better than I can remember when I was 19-20-21. I wish I were 21 now."

By a strange coincidence Norman celebrated his 46th birthday on the Saturday. His caddie, Tony Navaro, bought him an atlas to keep on the bridge of his new boat. Peter Lonard did not require a map of any description at the 18th in the third round where he holed in one with a four iron which took him to 13 under par for a share of fifth place with Jarrod Moseley, behind Baddeley and Garcia on 16 under, Poulter on 15 and Norman at 14 under.

Garcia would have led by two but he was penalised two shots for not taking the correct relief for a temporary immovable obstruction on the first hole. Garcia was less than pleased, but Poulter had good reason to smile after a best of the day 65.

The 25 year old from Leighton Buzzard had a group of supporters following him. They wore T-shirts with "Tiger Who?" on the front and "Poulter's Barmy Army" on the back. "They're mates of mine," said Poulter, the 2000 Sir Henry Cotton Rookie of the Year. "They're out here on holiday, and I hope I gave them a bit of a show today."

Phillip Price

The Course

There are still those who say the old Lakes course laid out in 1928 was better than the new one forced on the Club in 1968 when the Sydney City authorities decreed that some of the original holes must go to make way for a super highway to the nearby Kingsford-Smith International Airport. Even so, the replacement course, designed by Bob Hagge, has been toughened up in more recent years by Jack Newton and his architectural team, and sets a superb test with many challenging holes.

Greg Norman

Poulter did much more than that on the final day. Baddeley was out in 34 to the 35s of Garcia, Norman and Poulter. Garcia birdied the 11th, 13th and 14th to reach 20 under but by then Poulter, with birdies at the tenth, 12th and 14th had joined Baddeley at 19 under. The Shark was still snapping at their heels after birdies at the 13th and 15th took him to 17 under.

Baddeley's 25 foot birdie at the 15th moved him to 20 under and, sensationally, Poulter holed a bunker shot of 30 yards for an eagle at the 17th to share the lead with Baddeley and Garcia. Baddeley and Garcia both edged clear again with birdies at the 17th and, like Poulter, shot 68s but with 21 under par totals of 271 they finished one clear of their English rival with Norman, also round in 68 with birdies at the 17th and 18th, one shot further adrift.

Baddeley and Garcia are destined to have many duels in the future, but on this occasion the Australian claimed gold as he holed a 16 foot putt at the first extra hole for a winning birdie. Moreover, he earned a place in history as one of the few golfers to have made their first appearance in a European Tour event a winning one.

Mitchell Platts

Nick Faldo

Greg Norman and Ian Poulter

THE LAKES GOLF CLUB, SYDNEY, AUSTRALIA, 8-11 FEBRUARY, 2001, PAR 73, 6904 YARDS, 6315 METRES

Pos.	Name		Rd1	Rd2	Rd3	Rd4	Total	Par	Prize Money Euro	Prize Money £
1	Aaron BADDELEY	Aus	67	68	68	68	271	-21	223593.91	142401.99
2	Sergio GARCIA	Sp	64	69	70	68	271	-21	126703.21	80694.46
3	Ian POULTER	Eng	70	69	65	68	272	-20	83847.72	53400.75
4	Greg NORMAN	Aus	66	68	71	68	273	-19	59625.04	37973.86
5	Nick O'HERN	Aus	70	69	72	65	276	-16	49687.54	31644.89
6	Jarrod MOSELEY	Aus	72	68	66	71	277	-15	42234.41	26898.16
	Peter LONARD	Aus	74	66	66	71	277	-15	42234.41	26898.16
8	Carlos RODILES	Sp	70	72	69	67	278	-14	30557.84	19461.61
	Craig PARRY	Aus	69	68	71	70	278	-14	30557.84	19461.61
	Robert KARLSSON	Swe	74	69	68	67	278	-14	30557.84	19461.61
	Phillip PRICE	Wal	66	69	74	69	278	-14	30557.84	19461.61
	Scott GARDINER	Aus	71	72	66	69	278	-14	30557.84	19461.61
13	Steve ALKER	NZ	66	72	71	70	279	-13	20309.78	12934.85
	David SMAIL	NZ	71	68	71	69	279	-13	20309.78	12934.85
	Rodney PAMPLING	Aus	70	71	69	69	279	-13	20309.78	12934.85
	Pierre FULKE	Swe	65	71	73	70	279	-13	20309.78	12934.85
17	Marc FARRY	Fr	68	70	73	69	280	-12	14611.24	9305.57
	Peter BAKER	Eng	71	68	70	71	280	-12	14611.24	9305.57
	David PARK	Wal	71	72	72	65	280	-12	14611.24	9305.57
	David CARTER	Eng	68	74	72	66	280	-12	14611.24	9305.57
21	Stephen LEANEY	Aus	71	71	68	71	281	-11	12223.13	7784.64
	Kenny DRUCE	Aus	72	69	71	69	281	-11	12223.13	7784.64
	Justin ROSE	Eng	75	69	66	71	281	-11	12223.13	7784.64
	Fredrik JACOBSON	Swe	68	74	72	67	281	-11	12223.13	7784.64
	Daren LEE	Eng	66	71	76	68	281	-11	12223.13	7784.64
26	Anders HANSEN	Den	75	69	72	66	282	-10	9341.26	5949.24
	David BRANSDON	Aus	70	73	66	73	282	-10	9341.26	5949.24
	Joakim HAEGGMAN	Swe	70	70	73	69	282	-10	9341.26	5949.24
	Raymond RUSSELL	Scot	71	71	71	69	282	-10	9341.26	5949.24
	Adam SCOTT	Aus	70	67	74	71	282	-10	9341.26	5949.24
31	Roger CHAPMAN	Eng	70	70	70	73	283	-9	7096.00	4519.28
	John SENDEN	Aus	69	72	72	70	283	-9	7096.00	4519.28
	Søren HANSEN	Den	67	72	72	72	283	-9	7096.00	4519.28
	Matthew LANE	NZ	72	70	71	70	283	-9	7096.00	4519.28
	Peter O'MALLEY	Aus	68	74	71	70	283	-9	7096.00	4519.28
	Niclas FASTH	Swe	70	70	70	73	283	-9	7096.00	4519.28
	Dean ROBERTSON	Scot	75	68	69	71	283	-9	7096.00	4519.28
	John BICKERTON	Eng	72	72	69	70	283	-9	7096.00	4519.28
39	Marcus NORGREN	Swe	70	72	75	68	285	-7	5217.19	3322.71
	Søren KJELDSEN	Den	72	68	73	72	285	-7	5217.19	3322.71
	Ian GARBUTT	Eng	71	72	74	68	285	-7	5217.19	3322.71
	David LYNN	Eng	70	71	70	74	285	-7	5217.19	3322.71
	Charles HOWELL III	USA	75	68	69	73	285	-7	5217.19	3322.71
	Nathan GREEN	Aus	67	69	77	72	285	-7	5217.19	3322.71
	James MCLEAN	Aus	69	67	75	74	285	-7	5217.19	3322.71
46	Brett RUMFORD	Aus	72	67	74	73	286	-6	4223.43	2689.81
47	Tim ELLIOTT	Aus	71	73	73	70	287	-5	3395.32	2162.40
	Shane TAIT	Aus	70	68	74	75	287	-5	3395.32	2162.40
	Elliot BOULT	NZ	74	70	70	73	287	-5	3395.32	2162.40
	Paolo QUIRICI	Swi	70	73	71	73	287	-5	3395.32	2162.40
	Bob FRIEND	USA	72	71	75	69	287	-5	3395.32	2162.40
	Andrew RAITT	Eng	72	72	69	74	287	-5	3395.32	2162.40
53	Wayne RILEY	Aus	74	70	72	72	288	-4	2715.42	1729.39
	Anthony WALL	Eng	70	71	77	70	288	-4	2715.42	1729.39
	Marcus CAIN	Aus	72	69	73	74	288	-4	2715.42	1729.39
	Greg OWEN	Eng	69	72	74	73	288	-4	2715.42	1729.39
	Terry PRICE	Aus	71	72	74	71	288	-4	2715.42	1729.39
58	Richard S JOHNSON	Swe	75	69	72	73	289	-3	2633.44	1677.18
59	Scott LAYCOCK	Aus	74	70	69	77	290	-2	2583.76	1645.54
	Gary EVANS	Eng	72	72	70	76	290	-2	2583.76	1645.54
	Lucas PARSONS	Aus	74	65	76	75	290	-2	2583.76	1645.54
62	Stephen COLLINS	Aus	68	73	75	75	291	-1	2521.65	1605.98
	Roger WESSELS	SA	73	69	73	76	291	-1	2521.65	1605.98
64	Rodger DAVIS	Aus	71	72	73	76	292	0	2459.54	1566.43
	Henrik STENSON	Swe	76	68	72	76	292	0	2459.54	1566.43
	Philip TATAURANGI	NZ	75	69	72	76	292	0	2459.54	1566.43
67	Andre STOLZ	Aus	74	70	75	74	293	1	2397.43	1526.87
	Anthony PAINTER	Aus	75	68	75	75	293	1	2397.43	1526.87
69	Maarten LAFEBER	Hol	70	72	75	77	294	2	2360.15	1503.13
70	Adrian PERCEY	Aus	70	74	71	80	295	3	2335.31	1487.31
71	John WADE	Aus	71	72	78	76	297	5	2298.05	1463.58
	Martyn ROBERTS	Aus	78	66	77	76	297	5	2298.05	1463.58

Charming the Cobra

SAUJANA GOLF AND COUNTRY CLUB, KUALA LUMPUR, MALAYSIA

Vijay Singh's career has turned full circle since the day he arrived to play in the Malaysia PGA Championship as an unknown 21 year old professional golfer with precious few dollars in his pocket but an untapped reservoir of ambition seeking an escape valve from within his 6 feet 2 inches frame.

Singh felt the early stirrings of a love affair with Malaysia that week. The hard work ethic he learned from his father, Mohan, and developed as a precocious 13 year old on Viti Levu, Fiji's largest island, manifested itself in the form of a first professional victory.

From Fiji, Singh had embarked on an equatorial safari through Borneo, sometimes playing for exorbitant sums which his wallet could not withstand, to a successful adventure on The European Tour and then to the US PGA Tour where he went on to win the 1998 US PGA Championship and the 2000 Masters Tournament.

His affection for Malaysia deepened when he married his Malaysian wife, Ardina. So there was an element of homecoming when Singh's jet touched down in Kuala Lumpur for the 2001 Carlsberg Malaysian Open. By the time his plane departed the teeming Malaysian capital seven days later, the love he felt was unconditional.

This time he was one of the star attractions, having achieved a celebrity status which would have been beyond his wildest dreams 17 years earlier. This time he was Vijay Singh, reigning Masters champion and one of the world's greatest golfers.

Victory at Saujana Golf and Country Club would be the first of back to back wins for Singh on The European Tour in February 2001, courtesy of a three-hole play-off against Ireland's Padraig Harrington, after the pair had completed regulation play deadlocked on 14 under par.

The 2000 Masters champion looked to have handed the title to Harrington, last year's runner-up, when he drove out of bounds on the 17th on his way to a double bogey six. But the Fijian birdied the final hole in regulation to force extra holes with the pair tied on 274.

Vijay can!

Twice they visited the 18th, before Singh finally ended the duel with a birdie three on the 17th hole, his gamble of driving the green on the 360 yards dogleg paying off. For the first time that week Harrington also pulled out the driver on the 17th but came up just short in the rough. He bravely chipped to six feet but his putt to continue the contest just fell away from the hole and Singh was crowned champion for the second time following his victory in 1992.

"I thought I had given it away with the double bogey on the 17th," said Singh. "But then I made birdie. I'm glad the way things turned out. Padraig played very well all round and came back strongly at the end. The crowd was behind me, which was nice. I had a lot of friends out there who I had met through the years."

Singh had earlier seemed in total control when he broke out of a four way tie for the lead with birdies on the 12th, 13th and 16th to open a two shot lead. But when he drove out of bounds and Harrington picked up birdies on the 15th an 16th, the Irishman was two clear with two to play.

More drama followed on the 17th as Harrington was too aggressive with his pitch, flew the green and was unable to save his par. Ahead of him Singh played a great approach to the last, pitching within a foot of the hole and leaving himself with a six foot putt which he duly converted to set up the dramatic finale.

Harrington still had a chance to win but could not convert his 15 foot birdie putt. Twice more the pair returned to the 18th, matching each other with par fives the first time when Singh's 12 footer lipped out and then both making birdie fours the second time around, before heading back to the 17th where Singh calmly two putted for victory.

"I had a good feeling coming here to Malaysia," said Singh, with masterly understatement. "Every win is good for the confidence."

The play-off combatants were among 65 players who had to return to the course at 8am on Sunday to complete their rain-interrupted third round after the skies had opened and cut short play on Thursday and Friday. Once the skies - and the muddled picture on

The Course

Saujana's Palm course is regarded as one of the most challenging golf courses in all Malaysia. The 6,945 yards championship layout was designed by Ronald Fream and the course is more affectionately known as "The Cobra" as it snakes its way through an old palm oil plantation.
The 'Cobra' nickname is not taken lightly as deadly cobra snakes and mischievous monkeys frequent the layout where water comes into play on at least six holes.

Shot of the Week

Vijay Singh delivered the telling shot of the Carlsberg Malaysian Open, finding the front of the green at the third extra hole, the 360 yards par 17th , with a full-blooded driver to seal victory over Padraig Harrington. The Fijian's stroke of brilliance was all the more impressive in the heat of a play-off as he had driven out-of-bounds on the same hole nearly 90 minutes earlier, carding a double-bogey.

the course - had cleared, Holland's Maarten Lafeber was left in the lead after the first round with a five under par 67.

Harrington then shot a 66 to share the halfway lead with Michael Campbell of New Zealand while a third round 68 propelled him into a two stroke lead from Singh, who also shot 68. However the real drama centred on that long Sunday, with Singh emerging triumphant over Harrington with American Ahmad Dan Bateman and Charlie Wi, of the Republic of Korea, tied for third place two strokes adrift of the play-off protagonists.

Bernie McGuire

José Manuel Lara

Padraig Harrington

SAUJANA GOLF AND COUNTRY CLUB, KUALA LUMPUR, MALAYSIA 15-18 FEBRUARY, 2001, PAR 72, 6945 YARDS, 6350 METRES

Pos.	Name		Rd1	Rd2	Rd3	Rd4	Total	Par	Prize Money Euro	Prize Money £
1	Vijay SINGH	Fiji	68	70	68	68	274	-14	163655.69	104665.29
2	Padraig HARRINGTON	Ire	70	66	68	70	274	-14	109107.39	69779.16
3	Charlie WI	RepKor	70	70	67	69	276	-12	55285.32	35357.49
	Ahmad Dan BATEMAN	USA	72	69	68	67	276	-12	55285.32	35357.49
5	Soren HANSEN	Den	69	70	70	69	278	-10	41635.84	26628.02
6	Ter-Chang WANG	Taiwan	69	71	68	71	279	-9	34369.21	21980.68
7	Maarten LAFEBER	Hol	67	72	69	72	280	-8	22742.59	14544.92
	Desvonde BOTES	SA	72	67	71	70	280	-8	22742.59	14544.92
	Michael CAMPBELL	NZ	69	67	71	73	280	-8	22742.59	14544.92
	Thongchai JAIDEE	Thai	75	67	68	70	280	-8	22742.59	14544.92
	Carl PETTERSSON	Swe	72	69	67	72	280	-8	22742.59	14544.92
12	Mardan MAMAT	Sing	70	70	70	71	281	-7	16349.92	10456.52
	Olle KARLSSON	Swe	73	65	72	71	281	-7	16349.92	10456.52
14	Soren KJELDSEN	Den	70	69	72	71	282	-6	14140.47	9043.48
	Thammanoon SRIROJ	Thai	71	67	72	72	282	-6	14140.47	9043.48
	Jean HUGO	SA	75	69	73	65	282	-6	14140.47	9043.48
	John DALY	USA	72	72	69	69	282	-6	14140.47	9043.48
18	Jose Manuel LARA	Sp	75	68	71	69	283	-5	11489.14	7347.83
	Justin HOBDAY	SA	69	69	71	74	283	-5	11489.14	7347.83
	Ignacio GARRIDO	Sp	72	69	73	69	283	-5	11489.14	7347.83
	Robert COLES	Eng	68	73	71	71	283	-5	11489.14	7347.83
	Patrik SJÖLAND	Swe	75	65	68	75	283	-5	11489.14	7347.83
	Henrik NYSTROM	Swe	71	71	70	71	283	-5	11489.14	7347.83
	Yong-Eun YANG	RepKor	72	70	67	74	283	-5	11489.14	7347.83
25	Clay DEVERS	USA	75	67	67	75	284	-4	9623.38	6154.59
	Wook-Soon KANG	S.K.	72	65	75	72	284	-4	9623.38	6154.59
	Alex CEJKA	Ger	75	69	69	71	284	-4	9623.38	6154.59
	Robert HUXTABLE	USA	71	71	67	75	284	-4	9623.38	6154.59
	Gerald ROSALES	Phil	72	69	74	69	284	-4	9623.38	6154.59
30	Jean-Francois REMESY	Fr	72	74	71	68	285	-3	8297.71	5306.76
	Garry HOUSTON	Wal	76	70	72	67	285	-3	8297.71	5306.76
	Des TERBLANCHE	SA	69	75	73	68	285	-3	8297.71	5306.76
	John BICKERTON	Eng	74	70	72	69	285	-3	8297.71	5306.76
34	Kyi Hla HAN	Myan	72	71	71	72	286	-2	6873.84	4396.13
	Wayne RILEY	Aus	73	71	70	72	286	-2	6873.84	4396.13
	Anders HANSEN	Den	70	71	74	71	286	-2	6873.84	4396.13
	Felix CASAS	Phil	72	69	73	72	286	-2	6873.84	4396.13
	Tjaart VAN DER WALT	SA	75	71	72	68	286	-2	6873.84	4396.13
	Gustavo ROJAS	Arg	75	70	74	67	286	-2	6873.84	4396.13
	Stephen SCAHILL	NZ	75	71	71	69	286	-2	6873.84	4396.13
	Tobias DIER	Ger	71	74	71	70	286	-2	6873.84	4396.13
42	Costantino ROCCA	It	69	76	69	73	287	-1	5597.27	3579.71
	Elliot BOULT	NZ	72	66	71	78	287	-1	5597.27	3579.71
	Arjun ATWAL	Ind	71	69	75	72	287	-1	5597.27	3579.71
	Anthony KANG	RepKor	71	73	72	71	287	-1	5597.27	3579.71
	Fredrik ANDERSSON	Swe	74	70	72	71	287	-1	5597.27	3579.71
47	Thomas LEVET	Fr	72	72	74	70	288	0	4713.49	3014.49
	Erol SIMSEK	Ger	74	71	72	71	288	0	4713.49	3014.49
	Mikael LUNDBERG	Swe	72	70	75	71	288	0	4713.49	3014.49
	Ted PURDY	USA	72	69	72	75	288	0	4713.49	3014.49
51	Lian-Wei ZHANG	PRC	71	75	71	72	289	1	3547.39	2268.72
	Marc FARRY	Fr	74	72	72	71	289	1	3547.39	2268.72
	Jim RUTLEDGE	Can	74	72	70	73	289	1	3547.39	2268.72
	Simon YATES	Scot	72	72	70	75	289	1	3547.39	2268.72
	Joakim HAEGGMAN	Swe	75	69	71	74	289	1	3547.39	2268.72
	Andrew RAITT	Eng	73	70	72	74	289	1	3547.39	2268.72
	Danny ZARATE	Phil	71	71	74	73	289	1	3547.39	2268.72
	Robert FLOYD	USA	72	73	70	74	289	1	3547.39	2268.72
59	Chawalit PLAPHOL	Thai	74	71	72	73	290	2	2847.73	1821.25
60	Gary EVANS	Eng	70	72	75	74	291	3	2749.54	1758.46
61	Chia-Yuh HONG	Taiwan	74	71	74	73	292	4	2454.94	1570.05
	Rodrigo CUELLO	Phil	74	72	71	75	292	4	2454.94	1570.05
	Graeme STORM	Eng	71	73	72	76	292	4	2454.94	1570.05
	Amandeep JOHL	Ind	75	71	73	73	292	4	2454.94	1570.05
	Holden KIM	RepKor	73	73	74	72	292	4	2454.94	1570.05
66	R NACHIMUTHU	Mal	74	71	75	73	293	5	2111.25	1350.24
	Mark PILKINGTON	Wal	78	68	71	76	293	5	2111.25	1350.24
68	S MURTHY	Mal	72	71	79	72	294	6	1963.95	1256.04
69	Yu-Shu HSIEH	C.Tai	76	67	78	74	295	7	1865.76	1193.24
70	Peter MITCHELL	Eng	71	74	78	73	296	8	1797.77	1149.76
71	Frankie MINOZA	Phil	77	68	77	75	297	9	1473.00	942.05
72	Zaw MOE	Myan	69	72	78	79	298	10	1470.00	940.13
73	Stephen DODD	Wal	70	73	80	79	302	14	1467.00	938.21

On the Double

SINGAPORE ISLAND COUNTRY CLUB, SINGAPORE

At six foot two inches tall, Vijay Singh is well used to literally towering over his fellow competitors but metaphorically, too, the Fijian's golf is often to be found on a higher level than the rest.

It was somehow appropriate, therefore, that the first sight to greet visitors to Singapore was a giant poster of the man himself. Singh, after all, was the reigning Masters champion and had won the week before in the Carlsberg Malaysian Open. His initial promotional prominence was understandable and, by the end of the week, his overall playing prominence was undeniable.

Mikael Lundberg

Alongside the prints of Singh were similar-size posters of Colin Montgomerie who, like the Fijian, arrived in The Lion City harbouring a winning feeling, having captured the Ericsson Masters in Australia the previous week in his first tournament outing of the year.

The duo had last played together at the Singapore Island Golf Club eight years earlier in the Johnnie Walker Classic where Montgomerie finished second to Nick Faldo and Singh took ninth. As it turned out, both men were to take centre stage once again on the Bukit Course as the tussle for the 154,616 euro (£97,662) first prize unfolded.

They were not, however the only protagonists in the drama. The field for the co-sanctioned event between The European Tour and the Asian PGA's Davidoff Tour also featured talents such as Ireland's Padraig Harrington, who had lost in a play-off to Singh in Malaysia, and England's Warren Bennett.

Eighteen months previously, Bennett looked to have the world at his feet. The 29 year old from Kent had just won five times on the European Challenge Tour on his way to topping the Rankings and, having graduated to The European Tour, won the Scottish PGA Championship at Gleneagles in the summer of 1999.

Anthony Wall

Maarten Lafeber

The Course

The Bukit Course at Singapore Island Country Club may not be one of the longest on The European Tour at only 6,751 yards but still posed plenty of problems during the week. The first thing players had to get used to was the cow grass particularly when chipping. Many European players had not encountered the broad leaf grass before and the Asian players were noticeably more at home around the greens.

But in a cruel twist of fate, Bennett was struck down by pneumonia within weeks of his winning breakthrough. Weakened by the illness, he then suffered a recurrence of a neck injury, restricting him to just six starts on the 2000 season. At his lowest point he even considered giving up the game and for six months didn't pick up a club as he fought to regain his fitness, both mentally and physically

But having been inspired by the birth of his first child, Tom, a month earlier, and with his health finally on an even keel, Bennett, playing on The 2001 European Tour on a medical exemption, at last showed what he was capable of with an excellent first round 63.

The eight under par effort was matched by Harrington who looked on course to repeat the feat of winning a tournament the week after losing in a play-off - the previous occurrence being in April 2000 when the Dubliner claimed the Brazil Sao Paulo 500 Years Open, seven days after surrendering in extra holes to Roger Chapman in the Brazil Rio de Janeiro 500 Years Open.

Incredibly, the low scoring of the first day was surpassed on the second as records were smashed. It is not often Montgomerie has opened with rounds of 66 and 67 and found himself some nine shots off the pace. Even Singh, with rounds of 64 and 63, could not keep up with Frankie Minoza, the leader at the halfway stage.

The Filipino notched seven birdies on the inward half of his second round to come home in 28 strokes and set a new course record of 61, ten under par. His 36 hole total of 125, 17 under par, also set a new European Tour record. But, as is often said, a golf tournament is a marathon not a sprint, and Minoza was to be overhauled as the pace quickened over the weekend.

If ever a lightning delay arrived at the right time it was during the third afternoon. Montgomerie needed something special to move into contention but had only picked up three birdies when the klaxon sounded to halt proceedings. Nothing was happening, but when play resumed the Scot flew from the traps with three birdies in four holes to move within three shots of the lead, now held by Singh. The only hole Montgomerie failed to birdie was the 16th when his eight iron approach was, if anything, too accurate, hitting the pin and ricocheting off the green.

Playing partner Bennett also birdied three of the last four holes to remain in the hunt along with Swedish rookie Mikael Lundberg, who birdied the 17th and 18th to move to 16 under par and two shots off the lead.

All the pieces were in place for a thrilling final day with Singh leading from Bennett, Lundberg and Minoza, with Harrington and Montgomerie within striking distance, but from the outset Singh was in command. Two birdies in the first four holes moved the Fijian clear as the chasing pack faltered. Despite bogeys at the seventh and eighth, a real challenge to Singh failed to materialise on the final lap and when he birdied the ninth, 13th and 15th, the title was his.

While Singh marched to his second consecutive victory, eyes were focused on the battle for second. Harrington had moved into the frame with a run of birdies but his charge halted when his ball moved as he addressed it on the 16th. The resulting one stroke penalty moved him back into a share of fifth place with Dane Anders Hansen, who moved up the final rankings with a six under par 65.

Bennett and Montgomerie had fought together over the final two rounds with Montgomerie edging a stroke clear playing the par five final hole. But in one final twist of the tale, Bennett chipped in for eagle from the back of the green to snatch second place and earn the biggest cheque of his career - 103,077 euro (£65,108).

Montgomerie, who like Singh had not carded over 68 all week, had to settle for a share of third place with Holland's Maarten Lafeber. The Dutchman continued his good run of form, following his joint seventh place finish in Malaysia the week before, with an excellent closing 65.

Roddy Williams

Shot of the Week

Warren Bennett's chip in from the back of the 18th green for an eagle. From a difficult lie, Bennett calmly chipped in to snatch second place from Colin Montgomerie and the biggest cheque of his career. It also confirmed his return to fitness after 18 months of anguish.

Vijay Singh and W[illegible]n Bennett

SINGAPORE ISLAND COUNTRY CLUB, SINGAPORE 22-25 FEBRUARY, 2001, PAR 71, 6751 YARDS, 6173 METRES

Pos.	Name		Rd1	Rd2	Rd3	Rd4	Total	Par	Prize Money Euro	£
1	Vijay SINGH	Fiji	64	63	68	68	263	-21	154616.94	97662.88
2	Warren BENNETT	Eng	63	69	65	68	265	-19	103077.96	65108.59
3	Maarten LAFEBER	Hol	64	67	70	65	266	-18	52232.06	32992.07
	Colin MONTGOMERIE	Scot	66	67	65	68	266	-18	52232.06	32992.07
5	Padraig HARRINGTON	Ire	63	67	71	66	267	-17	35903.75	22678.39
	Anders HANSEN	Den	69	64	69	65	267	-17	35903.75	22678.39
7	Frankie MINOZA	Phil	64	61	71	72	268	-16	25513.00	16115.14
	Mikael LUNDBERG	Swe	69	64	64	71	268	-16	25513.00	16115.14
9	Prayad MARKSAENG	Thai	67	63	69	70	269	-15	20781.49	13126.51
10	Clay DEVERS	USA	70	65	70	65	270	-14	18554.91	11720.10
11	Andrew PITTS	USA	71	67	67	66	271	-13	15988.14	10098.81
	Chia-Yuh HONG	Taiwan	66	71	65	69	271	-13	15988.14	10098.81
	Keng-Chi LIN	Taiwan	67	69	64	71	271	-13	15988.14	10098.81
14	Tom GILLIS	USA	69	66	70	67	272	-12	13637.86	8614.27
	Stephen DODD	Wal	69	66	66	71	272	-12	13637.86	8614.27
	Yong-Eun YANG	RepKor	67	66	72	67	272	-12	13637.86	8614.27
17	Costantino ROCCA	It	67	69	68	69	273	-11	11225.72	7090.66
	Chawalit PLAPHOL	Thai	67	66	70	70	273	-11	11225.72	7090.66
	Anthony WALL	Eng	64	71	65	73	273	-11	11225.72	7090.66
	Gary ORR	Scot	68	68	67	70	273	-11	11225.72	7090.66
	Robert COLES	Eng	68	69	69	67	273	-11	11225.72	7090.66
	Henrik NYSTROM	Swe	67	66	70	70	273	-11	11225.72	7090.66
	Gerald ROSALES	Phil	68	69	70	66	273	-11	11225.72	7090.66
24	Jeev Milkha SINGH	Ind	68	68	67	71	274	-10	9370.23	5918.65
	Carlos RODILES	Sp	72	67	66	69	274	-10	9370.23	5918.65
	Zaw MOE	Myan	68	67	68	71	274	-10	9370.23	5918.65
	Ignacio GARRIDO	Sp	70	68	69	67	274	-10	9370.23	5918.65
	Andrew COLTART	Scot	68	71	65	70	274	-10	9370.23	5918.65
29	José Manuel LARA	Sp	67	72	70	66	275	-9	7483.81	4727.10
	Steen TINNING	Den	67	68	70	70	275	-9	7483.81	4727.10
	Henrik BJORNSTAD	Nor	68	70	68	69	275	-9	7483.81	4727.10
	Anthony KANG	RepKor	66	69	71	69	275	-9	7483.81	4727.10
	Gustavo ROJAS	Arg	70	67	69	69	275	-9	7483.81	4727.10
	Stephen SCAHILL	NZ	68	70	70	67	275	-9	7483.81	4727.10
	Ted PURDY	USA	67	70	70	68	275	-9	7483.81	4727.10
	Wei-Tze YEH	Taiwan	68	70	66	71	275	-9	7483.81	4727.10
	Thongchai JAIDEE	Thai	73	66	66	70	275	-9	7483.81	4727.10
38	Mark MOULAND	Wal	66	66	71	73	276	-8	6030.34	3809.03
	Justin HOBDAY	SA	67	71	70	68	276	-8	6030.34	3809.03
	Eric MEEKS	USA	68	70	67	71	276	-8	6030.34	3809.03
	Gerry NORQUIST	USA	69	68	71	68	276	-8	6030.34	3809.03
	Gary RUSNAK	USA	67	71	67	71	276	-8	6030.34	3809.03
43	Richard GREEN	Aus	65	71	70	71	277	-7	5288.15	3340.23
	Olivier EDMOND	Fr	67	64	76	70	277	-7	5288.15	3340.23
	Massimo SCARPA	It	66	72	70	69	277	-7	5288.15	3340.23
46	David HOWELL	Eng	69	69	73	67	278	-6	4545.95	2871.42
	Arjun ATWAL	Ind	69	69	68	72	278	-6	4545.95	2871.42
	Charlie WI	RepKor	69	67	73	69	278	-6	4545.95	2871.42
	Alex CEJKA	Ger	68	69	71	70	278	-6	4545.95	2871.42
	Ahmad Dan BATEMAN	USA	70	69	75	64	278	-6	4545.95	2871.42
51	Wook-Soon KANG	S.K.	72	67	71	69	279	-5	3210.00	2027.58
	Paul EALES	Eng	68	69	72	70	279	-5	3210.00	2027.58
	Madasaamy MURUGIAH	Sing	68	70	71	70	279	-5	3210.00	2027.58
	Boonchu RUANGKIT	Thai	71	67	67	74	279	-5	3210.00	2027.58
	Jorge BERENDT	Arg	69	68	71	71	279	-5	3210.00	2027.58
	Des TERBLANCHE	SA	66	72	72	69	279	-5	3210.00	2027.58
	Mark PILKINGTON	Wal	67	70	70	72	279	-5	3210.00	2027.58
	Raymond RUSSELL	Scot	69	69	72	69	279	-5	3210.00	2027.58
	Graeme STORM	Eng	71	67	70	71	279	-5	3210.00	2027.58
	Unho PARK	Aus	70	68	73	68	279	-5	3210.00	2027.58
61	Olle NORDBERG	Swe	70	69	69	72	280	-4	2272.98	1435.71
	Peter MITCHELL	Eng	71	68	71	70	280	-4	2272.98	1435.71
	Rafael PONCE	Equa	69	70	72	69	280	-4	2272.98	1435.71
	Paul STREETER	Eng	71	66	72	71	280	-4	2272.98	1435.71
	Ter-Chang WANG	Taiwan	70	69	72	69	280	-4	2272.98	1435.71
	Pablo DEL OLMO	Mex	69	64	72	75	280	-4	2272.98	1435.71
67	Amandeep JOHL	Ind	72	67	72	70	281	-3	1901.88	1201.31
	Ted OH	RepKor	69	68	74	70	281	-3	1901.88	1201.31
69	James KINGSTON	SA	72	67	72	71	282	-2	1732.71	1094.46
	Daisuke MARUYAMA	Jpn	69	70	72	71	282	-2	1732.71	1094.46
71	Elliot BOULT	NZ	69	69	74	71	283	-1	1392.00	879.25
72	Aaron MEEKS	USA	67	71	71	75	284	0	1386.00	875.46
	Yong-Jin SHIN	RepKor	69	70	73	72	284	0	1386.00	875.46
	Chih-Bing LAM	Sing	69	70	74	71	284	0	1386.00	875.46
75	Haruyuki TSUJIMURA	Jpn	70	69	71	76	286	2	1380.00	871.67
76	Raul BALLESTEROS	Sp	71	68	72	76	287	3	1377.00	869.77

DUBAI DESERT CLASSIC

Coming of Age

EMIRATES GOLF CLUB, DUBAI

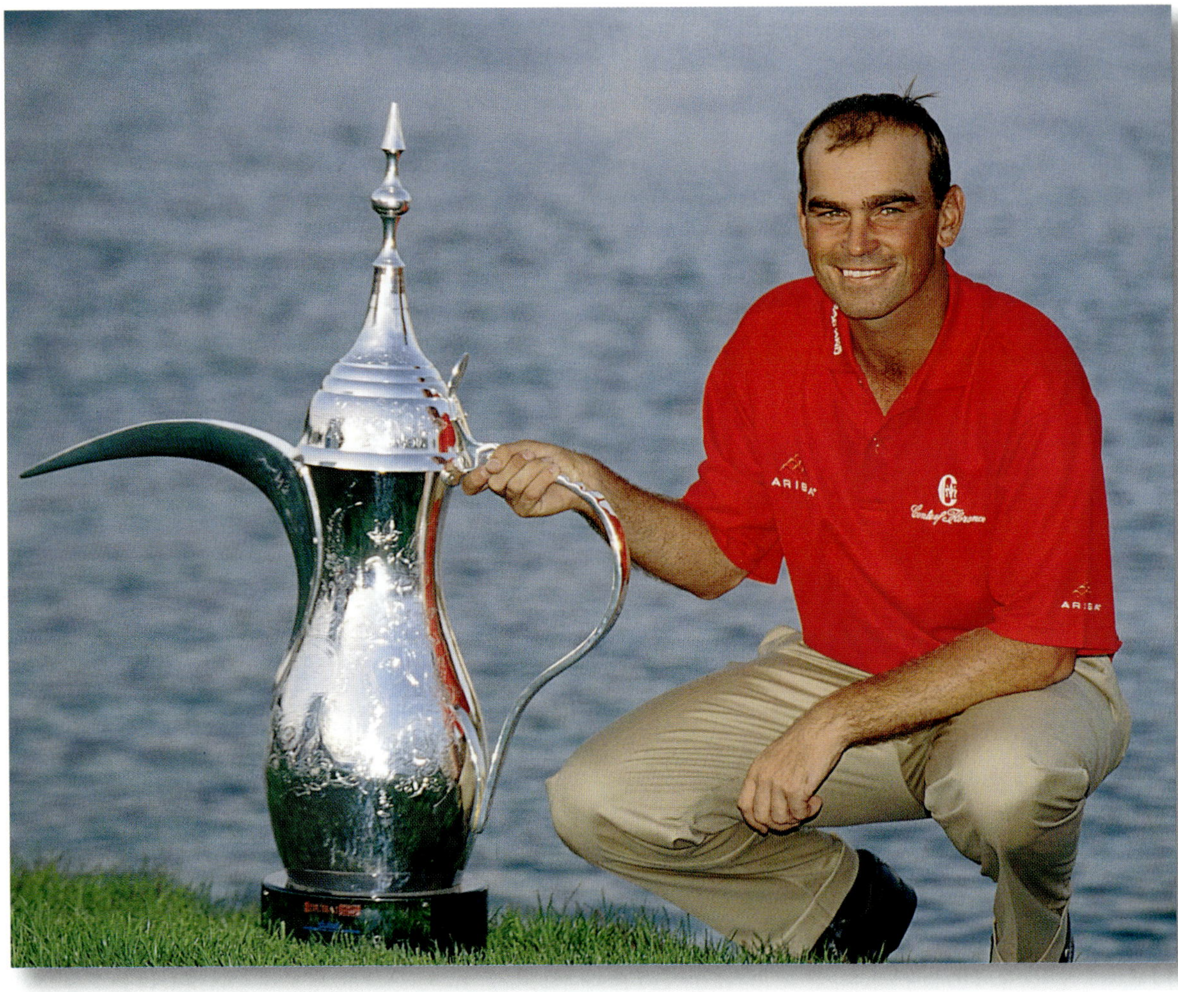

The duel in the desert may go down in the history books for a far more significant reason than just for proving Tiger Woods to be human.

Thomas Björn's truly magnificent triumph after four days stalking the king of the golfing jungle marked a coming of age for the great Dane. It came less than a year after he had suffered the entire opposite in the company of the World Number One.

Björn's memory still carried the scars of that ill-fated meeting in the third round of the US Open at Pebble Beach. It was his first bout of Saturday contention in a Major and, alongside Woods, he could not handle the situation. His mind was anywhere but on the job and as his concentration wavered, the shots mounted - all 82 of them.

Lesser men would have considered throwing themselves off the Pebble Beach rocks into the Pacific, but when the mists cleared from Björn's mind, realisation set in. If he was ever going to meet his objective of being one of the world's best golfers, he would have to learn to live and play with them and they came no better than Woods.

Padraig Harrington and Tiger Woods

Björn dedicated himself to that end. "You have to get used to the 250 yards three irons and the drives which go 340 yards into the wind," he said. "Your own game can get dragged down watching somebody that impressive."

Long before the final round on the banks of The Gulf, Björn had shown he had learned his lesson and there was no great gulf in class. There would be no intimidation factor this time.

The duo were paired with one another for the first two rounds and Björn could have been forgiven for wondering what on earth he had been let in for again. Woods shot 64-64, but Björn refused to bend and was only two shots back when the pairings were made for the third round.

Björn would have preferred a break from the Woods circus - all bodyguards and bustle - but his own prowess had denied it him. They set off in tandem again and this time the European outscored the American 67 to 68. They would be together again for a fourth straight day.

While Padraig Harrington and Ian Woosnam offered early signs of intent, Björn prepared himself mentally on the range. Just minutes

Jeev Milkha Singh

Shot of the Week

It was not the most spectacular shot of a truly memorable tournament, but it was the most decisive. Thomas Björn's 300 yards drive on the 72nd could not have been placed in a better position, but it was not where it finished, but when it came which was decisive. Björn had to put his nearest rival Tiger Woods under pressure and he did - taking the tiger line and inviting the World Number One to better it. He failed and the Dane triumphed.

Tiger Woods

before tee-off Björn received a gentle reminder of what he faced. Coach Pete Cowen's words hit him in the middle of his psyche. "This is what all those long hours on the range are for," said the blunt Yorkshireman.

"It might not be a Major or the biggest tournament in the world, but it's still big and it is you against the best golfer in the world."

Björn knew this was his time, his chance to follow Darren Clarke and Lee Westwood and beat arguably the greatest golfer there has ever been. His time to announce himself. He let nobody down.

The duel was relentless, but Woods headed into the back nine with a two shot lead and one hand on the giant, silver coffee pot. Björn bided his time and then pounced. He knew he had to birdie 17... and did. He knew he had to launch the perfect drive down 18... and did. How would Woods, whose lead had evaporated, respond? For once, the intimidator became the intimidated.

Woods made a wrong club selection, took driver instead of three wood and ended in territory known only to David Attenborough. When Tiger's third shot landed in water, Björn knew not only that he was the champion, but that he would never again be haunted by what had happened in the US Open.

Björn had spent four days in the company of the great one and would live to tell the tale over and over again. Only three of 26 players had ever bettered Woods on the occasions he had gone into the last round leading. Now there were four.

There were plenty more happy to help him celebrate and he rewarded their ovation for him in the bar afterwards by buying all the 400 or so revellers a drink. They had come to watch Woods, but they left saluting another true champion.

Never again would Björn feel intimidated or uncomfortable in the company of Woods. "I now know I can look him in the eye and beat him," he said. It was a wonderful feeling.

Martin Hardy

Paul McGinley

The Course

All but three of the 82 weekend qualifiers finished under par which would suggest an easy track. The Emirates course is far from that, but it is superbly manicured and it does meander beautifully through the dunes.

If Tiger Woods could find no fault in it then who is to argue and if the players found a better-prepared one all season they were blessed.

Eamonn Darcy

EMIRATES GOLF CLUB, DUBAI 1-4 MARCH, 2001, PAR 72, 7127 YARDS, 6518 METRES

Pos.	Name		Rd1	Rd2	Rd3	Rd4	Total	Par	Prize Money Euro	£
1	Thomas BJÖRN	Den	64	66	67	69	266	-22	265152.73	166660.00
2	Tiger WOODS	USA	64	64	68	72	268	-20	138184.57	86855.00
	Padraig HARRINGTON	Ire	66	69	64	69	268	-20	138184.57	86855.00
4	Ian WOOSNAM	Wal	69	68	64	69	270	-18	73503.27	46200.00
	Mathias GRÖNBERG	Swe	68	68	66	68	270	-18	73503.27	46200.00
6	Jeev Milkha SINGH	Ind	67	66	67	71	271	-17	51706.85	32500.00
	Brian DAVIS	Eng	69	65	67	70	271	-17	51706.85	32500.00
8	Trevor IMMELMAN	SA	66	73	68	65	272	-16	39774.50	25000.00
9	Elliot BOULT	NZ	69	69	70	65	273	-15	32243.86	20266.67
	Paul MCGINLEY	Ire	70	64	67	72	273	-15	32243.86	20266.67
	Angel CABRERA	Arg	66	70	65	72	273	-15	32243.86	20266.67
12	Eamonn DARCY	Ire	68	67	70	69	274	-14	24628.37	15480.00
	Jean-Francois REMESY	Fr	68	68	68	70	274	-14	24628.37	15480.00
	Anders HANSEN	Den	70	66	67	71	274	-14	24628.37	15480.00
	Richard GREEN	Aus	67	73	67	67	274	-14	24628.37	15480.00
	Greg OWEN	Eng	70	68	67	69	274	-14	24628.37	15480.00
17	Andrew OLDCORN	Scot	71	66	68	70	275	-13	20205.45	12700.00
	David LYNN	Eng	70	71	66	68	275	-13	20205.45	12700.00
	Lee WESTWOOD	Eng	66	70	69	70	275	-13	20205.45	12700.00
	Retief GOOSEN	SA	70	68	67	70	275	-13	20205.45	12700.00
21	Gary EMERSON	Eng	70	67	65	74	276	-12	17023.49	10700.00
	Colin MONTGOMERIE	Scot	69	70	65	72	276	-12	17023.49	10700.00
	Russell CLAYDON	Eng	67	70	71	68	276	-12	17023.49	10700.00
	Phillip PRICE	Wal	66	72	69	69	276	-12	17023.49	10700.00
	Ricardo GONZALEZ	Arg	71	67	69	69	276	-12	17023.49	10700.00
	Paul LAWRIE	Scot	70	67	71	68	276	-12	17023.49	10700.00
	John BICKERTON	Eng	68	67	70	71	276	-12	17023.49	10700.00
28	Jamie SPENCE	Eng	72	66	68	71	277	-11	14159.72	8900.00
	Søren HANSEN	Den	69	69	68	71	277	-11	14159.72	8900.00
	Rolf MUNTZ	Hol	71	69	66	71	277	-11	14159.72	8900.00
	Dean ROBERTSON	Scot	69	68	69	71	277	-11	14159.72	8900.00
	Thongchai JAIDEE	Thai	73	67	68	69	277	-11	14159.72	8900.00
33	Anders FORSBRAND	Swe	71	67	72	68	278	-10	11152.77	7010.00
	Tony JOHNSTONE	Zim	71	69	63	75	278	-10	11152.77	7010.00
	Warren BENNETT	Eng	70	69	69	70	278	-10	11152.77	7010.00
	Sven STRÜVER	Ger	71	68	68	71	278	-10	11152.77	7010.00
	John SENDEN	Aus	68	71	67	72	278	-10	11152.77	7010.00
	Tjaart VAN DER WALT	SA	68	72	70	68	278	-10	11152.77	7010.00
	Nicolas COLSAERTS	Bel	70	70	65	73	278	-10	11152.77	7010.00
	Jarrod MOSELEY	Aus	69	70	70	69	278	-10	11152.77	7010.00
	Andrew COLTART	Scot	70	69	70	69	278	-10	11152.77	7010.00
	Wei-Tze YEH	Taiwan	70	70	67	71	278	-10	11152.77	7010.00
43	Des SMYTH	Ire	69	69	68	73	279	-9	8909.49	5600.00
	David HOWELL	Eng	69	69	72	69	279	-9	8909.49	5600.00
	Carl SUNESON	Sp	69	72	65	73	279	-9	8909.49	5600.00
	Tobias DIER	Ger	68	72	67	72	279	-9	8909.49	5600.00
47	Ignacio GARRIDO	Sp	68	73	67	72	280	-8	7636.71	4800.00
	Roger WESSELS	SA	70	70	70	70	280	-8	7636.71	4800.00
	Bradley DREDGE	Wal	70	65	73	72	280	-8	7636.71	4800.00
	Robert COLES	Eng	68	70	68	74	280	-8	7636.71	4800.00
51	Lian-Wei ZHANG	PRC	70	69	70	72	281	-7	6363.92	4000.00
	Carlos RODILES	Sp	67	70	72	72	281	-7	6363.92	4000.00
	Raymond RUSSELL	Scot	68	69	72	72	281	-7	6363.92	4000.00
	Marco BERNARDINI	It	70	70	70	71	281	-7	6363.92	4000.00
55	Steve WEBSTER	Eng	71	70	68	73	282	-6	5250.23	3300.00
	Wook-Soon KANG	S.K.	72	69	71	70	282	-6	5250.23	3300.00
	Fredrik JACOBSON	Swe	70	71	66	75	282	-6	5250.23	3300.00
58	Mark ROE	Eng	71	69	71	72	283	-5	4216.10	2650.00
	Ross BAIN	Scot	71	69	71	72	283	-5	4216.10	2650.00
	Jose Manuel LARA	Sp	66	72	68	77	283	-5	4216.10	2650.00
	Jean HUGO	SA	70	67	71	75	283	-5	4216.10	2650.00
	Michele REALE	It	72	69	70	72	283	-5	4216.10	2650.00
	Gary EVANS	Eng	70	66	72	75	283	-5	4216.10	2650.00
	Darren CLARKE	N.Ire	71	69	70	73	283	-5	4216.10	2650.00
	Peter LONARD	Aus	68	71	72	72	283	-5	4216.10	2650.00
66	Thomas LEVET	Fr	73	68	72	71	284	-4	3420.61	2150.00
	Diego BORREGO	Sp	72	69	73	70	284	-4	3420.61	2150.00
68	Mark MCNULTY	Zim	66	74	71	74	285	-3	3038.77	1910.00
	Johan RYSTRÖM	Swe	69	70	72	74	285	-3	3038.77	1910.00
	Christopher HANELL	Swe	71	70	69	75	285	-3	3038.77	1910.00
71	Costantino ROCCA	It	70	71	70	75	286	-2	2378.50	1494.99
	Raphaël JACQUELIN	Fr	67	72	71	76	286	-2	2378.50	1494.99
	Per HAUGSRUD	Nor	70	71	77	68	286	-2	2378.50	1494.99
	Peter MITCHELL	Eng	68	72	73	73	286	-2	2378.50	1494.99
	Thomas GÖGELE	Ger	69	70	73	74	286	-2	2378.50	1494.99
	Lucas PARSONS	Aus	70	70	73	73	286	-2	2378.50	1494.99
77	Maarten LAFEBER	Hol	70	69	74	74	287	-1	2365.00	1486.51
	Justin ROSE	Eng	71	70	71	75	287	-1	2365.00	1486.51
	Daren LEE	Eng	71	70	70	76	287	-1	2365.00	1486.51
80	Joakim HAEGGMAN	Swe	71	67	77	73	288	0	2357.50	1481.79
	Jarmo SANDELIN	Swe	69	72	72	75	288	0	2357.50	1481.79
82	Ian POULTER	Eng	71	69	72	77	289	1	2353.00	1478.96

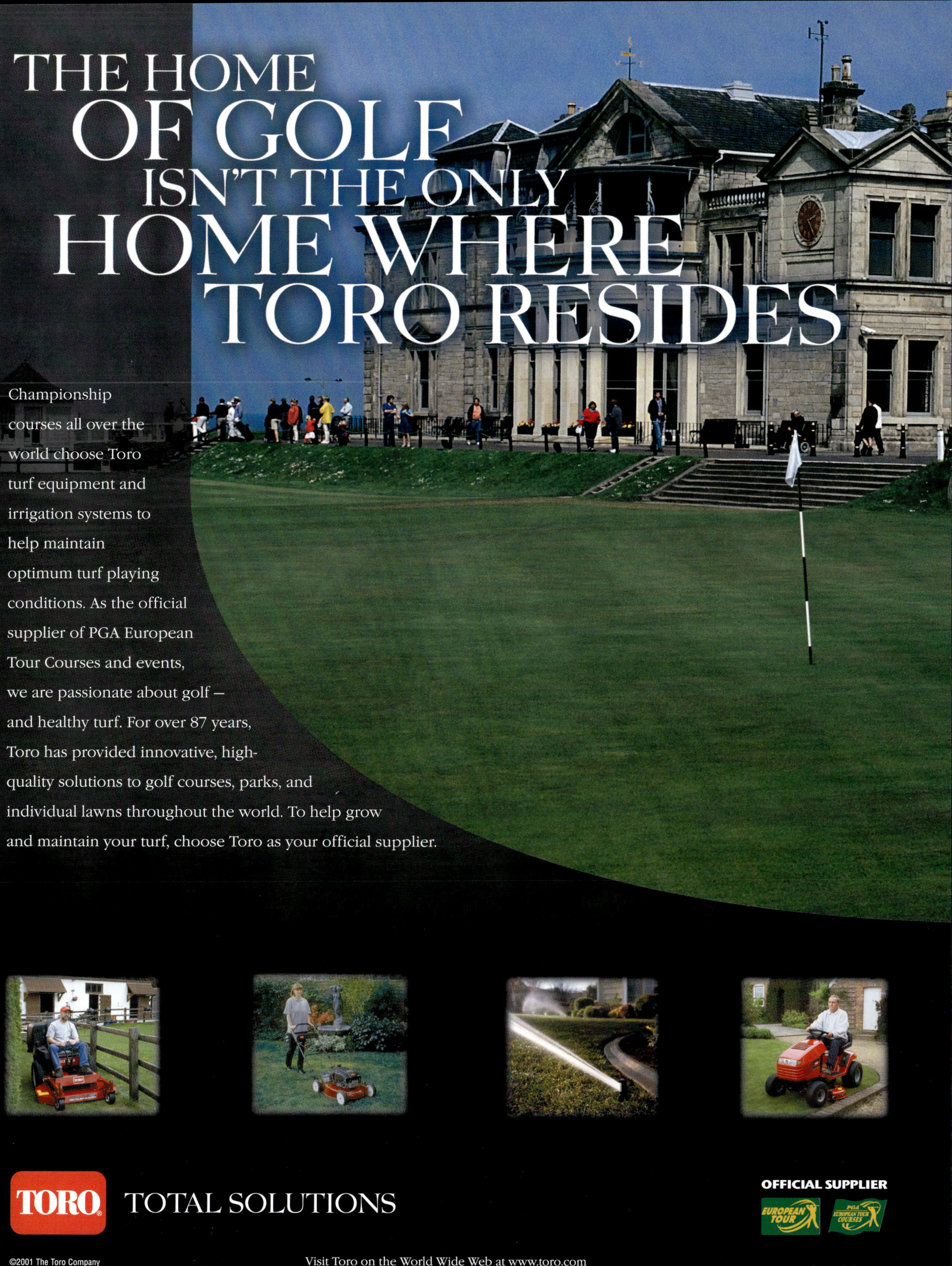
THE HOME
OF GOLF
ISN'T THE ONLY
HOME WHERE
TORO RESIDES
Championship courses all over the world choose Toro turf equipment and irrigation systems to help maintain optimum turf playing conditions. As the official supplier of PGA European Tour Courses and events, we are passionate about golf – and healthy turf. For over 87 years, Toro has provided innovative, high-quality solutions to golf courses, parks, and individual lawns throughout the world. To help grow and maintain your turf, choose Toro as your official supplier.
TORO
TOTAL SOLUTIONS
OFFICIAL SUPPLIER
EUROPEAN TOUR
PGA EUROPEAN TOUR COURSES
©2001 The Toro Company
Visit Toro on the World Wide Web at www.toro.com

The Enigma

DOHA GOLF CLUB, QATAR

Tony Johnstone is an enigma, a bona fide bundle of contradictions. The aimiable Zimbabwean is a fitness fanatic who smokes his way round the golf course. He is a small man whose lengthy arms should belong to a strapping six-footer. And he is blessed with sublime bunker play while being cursed by putting problems.

It should not come as a surprise then, that the 44 year old revelled in the ecstasy of a tournament victory a mere two months after wallowing in the agony of a form slump so severe, it made the former Volvo PGA champion give serious consideration to quitting golf altogether.

Dean Robertson

Elliot Boult

As always, the root of the problem for Johnstone was his putting. He had been striking the ball well and manoeuvring it cleverly around the course, but once on the green, it was a different story. Chance after chance slipped past the hole turning potential 66s into 72s and turning Johnstone's thoughts to another career.

"I was in South Africa and I said to my wife that I wasn't going to play another golf tournament until I found a way to putt," he said. "It was probably a good thing because it galvanised me into action and made me try a couple of radical alterations."

Catalyst for change was a meeting with his long-term friend and advisor Dr Ken West, a Doctor of Optometry with an acute eye for problem solving. Three years earlier West had advised Johnstone to cut back on caffeine as it was dehydrating his eyes, causing stigmatism. The Zimbabwean did as instructed and a fortnight later won the Alfred Dunhill South African PGA Championship at Houghton.

This time, during a day trip to Johnstone's Sunningdale home, the University of Virginia-based academic spotted a problem with his alignment caused primarily by his elongated arms. Having arrived at a solution, based around holding the putter as if it were a sand wedge, Johnstone set off for a fortnight in The Gulf.

Armed with a new blade and a fresh desire for hard work under the tutelage of coach Simon Holmes, Johnstone's new-found confidence manifested itself in the guise of a superb third round 63 in the Dubai Desert Classic at the Emirates Golf Club.

The encouraging signs were there and continued in the first round of the Qatar Masters where a steady four under par 68 left Johnstone in a share of 20th place, five shots adrift of joint leaders Robert Karlsson and Mark Pilkington.

The Swede and the Welshman had both tossed back their respective duvets long before light dawned on Doha, but the pain of such an act was quickly soothed by the benign early morning conditions, the absence of the traditional Shamal wind a major factor in their joint course record 63s.

While Karlsson was to feature in the higher echelons of the leaderboard for the entire tournament, Pilkington's moment in the spotlight was brief, his second round 79 making sure of that, the former Welsh amateur champion eventually finishing tied for 46th.

A second round 70 saw Karlsson open up a two shot lead over his nearest challengers, New Zealander Elliot Boult and Frenchman Olivier Edmond, Johnstone's own 70 moving him into the top ten as the tougher, windier conditions took hold.

Karlsson, whose three victories on The European Tour had come in the odd-numbered years 1995, 1997 and 1999, remained poised to

Olivier Edmond

Shot of the Week

Several of Tony Johnstone's shots in the tense closing stages could qualify - the Zimbabwean's drive to the back of the green at the 16th which set up the crucial birdie three or, of course, the birdie putt on the 18th. But perhaps the most vital stroke came on the short 17th. In the right hand bunker from the tee, Johnstone called on his mastery of sand play to splash out to six inches and save par, giving him the impetus to go on and win.

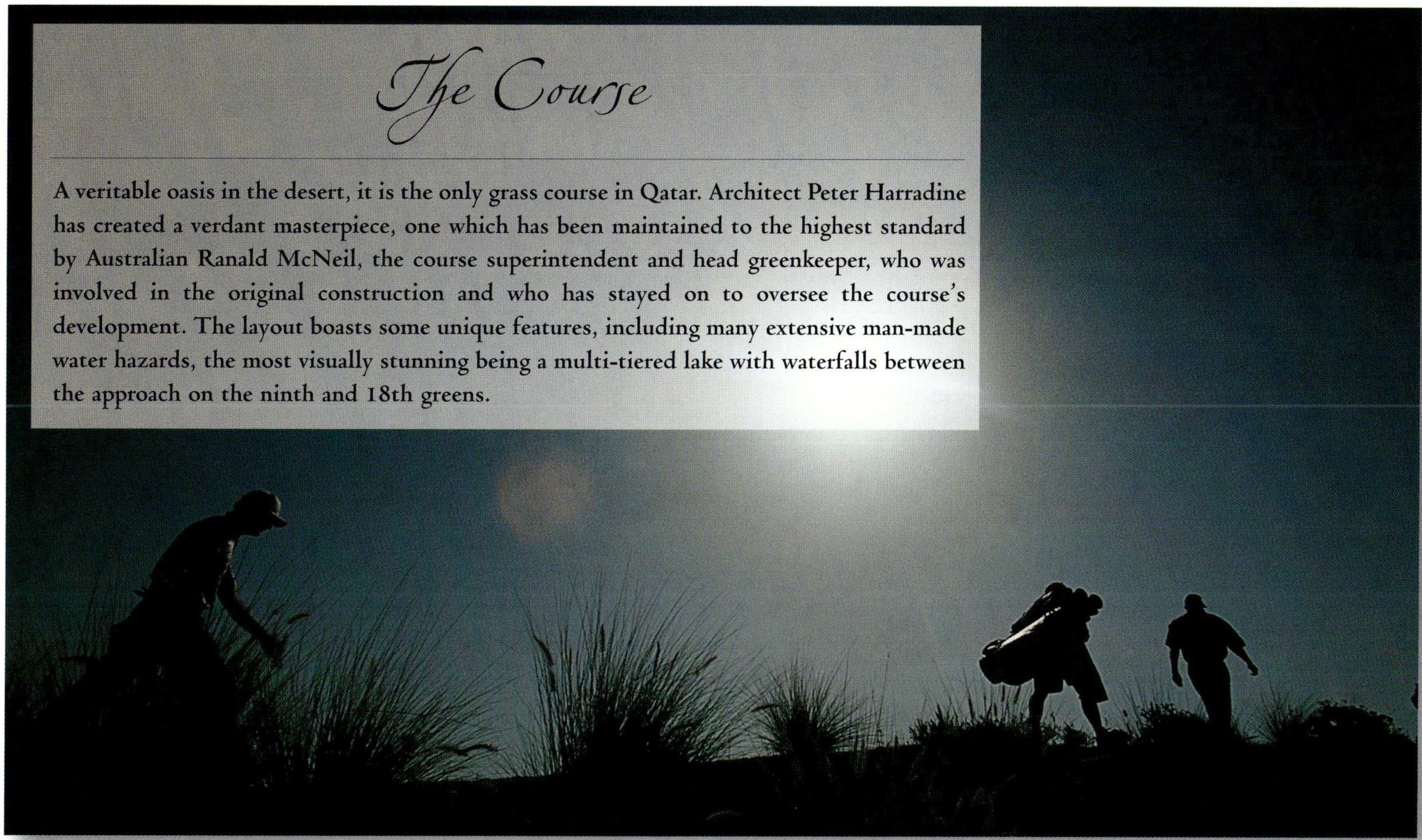

The Course

A veritable oasis in the desert, it is the only grass course in Qatar. Architect Peter Harradine has created a verdant masterpiece, one which has been maintained to the highest standard by Australian Ranald McNeil, the course superintendent and head greenkeeper, who was involved in the original construction and who has stayed on to oversee the course's development. The layout boasts some unique features, including many extensive man-made water hazards, the most visually stunning being a multi-tiered lake with waterfalls between the approach on the ninth and 18th greens.

continue the sequence with a third round 70 which saw him share the lead on 203 with Argentina's Angel Cabrera going into the final afternoon.

Paisley's Dean Robertson stood one shot adrift of the leading duo after his 68 but the most positive move was that by Johnstone, whose flawless 66, which featured three birdies in a row to finish, saw him join the Scot on 204. It was a telling thrust.

The final round saw the most demanding conditions of the week with the Shamal at its swirling peak. While most players groaned, Johnstone's face creased into a wry smile as he threw back his bedroom curtains and saw the palm trees bent double.

"It definitely helped me," he admitted. "I went to University in Durban which is a very windy town so I had a lot of experience in those conditions. It also negates the long game to a degree. In the wind it's difficult to get the ball close and so everybody was going to miss greens. Then it's down to the short game and that week my short game was as good as it's ever been."

Johnstone proved the point conclusively on the opening hole, pitching in from the back of the green for an audacious eagle three. It propelled him into the lead and into a position he was not to relinquish.

John Senden

Lucas Parsons

With Cabrera and Robertson failing to make ground and Boult having secured third place with a closing 71, the destiny of the championship rested in the hands of Johnstone and Karlsson.

The Zimbabwean grabbed the initiative at the 306 yards 16th where he drove the green before pitching and putting for a vital birdie three and a one shot lead. A crucial sand save at the 17th maintained his advantage before Johnstone found himself standing over a 12 foot birdie putt at the last.

The curling left to right putt, the most difficult for right-handers to read, would have been an impossibility for Johnstone eight weeks previously but such had been his progress, he stroked the ball with authority and dropped to his knees in delight as the ball found the centre of the cup.

He knew then Karlsson had to make an eagle to tie and although his pitch and run attempt was brave, it ran past the hole - the fact the Swede missed the return birdie effort a concern only for the statisticians.

Johnstone had won, and won well. The player bedevilled by putting woes had triumphed thanks to holing one of the toughest putts on the final green. It was the final contradiction.

Scott Crockett

Thomas Björn

DOHA GOLF CLUB, QATAR, 8-11 MARCH, 2001, PAR 72, 7110 YARDS, 6500 METRES

Pos.	Name		Rd1	Rd2	Rd3	Rd4	Total	Par	Prize Money Euro	Prize Money £
1	Tony JOHNSTONE	Zim	68	70	66	70	274	-14	133832.77	84889.65
2	Robert KARLSSON	Swe	63	70	70	73	276	-12	89218.28	56590.83
3	Elliot BOULT	NZ	68	67	72	71	278	-10	50267.59	31884.55
4	Olivier EDMOND	Fr	65	70	71	73	279	-9	37098.45	23531.41
	Dean ROBERTSON	Scot	67	69	68	75	279	-9	37098.45	23531.41
6	John SENDEN	Aus	69	73	68	71	281	-7	26097.39	16553.48
	Angel CABRERA	Arg	66	70	67	78	281	-7	26097.39	16553.48
8	Anders HANSEN	Den	71	69	71	71	282	-6	16541.73	10492.36
	Steve WEBSTER	Eng	71	70	73	68	282	-6	16541.73	10492.36
	Ricardo GONZALEZ	Arg	67	71	70	74	282	-6	16541.73	10492.36
	Greg OWEN	Eng	69	71	69	73	282	-6	16541.73	10492.36
	David HIGGINS	Ire	70	72	72	68	282	-6	16541.73	10492.36
13	Ian WOOSNAM	Wal	71	70	71	71	283	-5	11356.67	7203.49
	Maarten LAFEBER	Hol	69	73	68	73	283	-5	11356.67	7203.49
	Paul MCGINLEY	Ire	71	67	71	74	283	-5	11356.67	7203.49
	Rolf MUNTZ	Hol	70	69	74	70	283	-5	11356.67	7203.49
	Fredrik JACOBSON	Swe	70	71	69	73	283	-5	11356.67	7203.49
	David CARTER	Eng	69	71	74	69	283	-5	11356.67	7203.49
	Martin MARITZ	SA	70	69	70	74	283	-5	11356.67	7203.49
20	Roger CHAPMAN	Eng	72	71	72	69	284	-4	9341.53	5925.30
	Jarrod MOSELEY	Aus	67	74	75	68	284	-4	9341.53	5925.30
	David LYNN	Eng	67	71	70	76	284	-4	9341.53	5925.30
23	Thomas BJÖRN	Den	69	71	70	75	285	-3	8471.61	5373.51
	Daren LEE	Eng	67	72	75	71	285	-3	8471.61	5373.51
	Lucas PARSONS	Aus	73	70	68	74	285	-3	8471.61	5373.51
	Marco BERNARDINI	It	66	73	71	75	285	-3	8471.61	5373.51
27	Eamonn DARCY	Ire	69	68	72	77	286	-2	6914.69	4385.96
	Des SMYTH	Ire	71	71	68	76	286	-2	6914.69	4385.96
	Soren KJELDSEN	Den	70	71	71	74	286	-2	6914.69	4385.96
	Carl SUNESON	Sp	69	71	73	73	286	-2	6914.69	4385.96
	Mathias GRÖNBERG	Swe	68	72	70	76	286	-2	6914.69	4385.96
	Paul LAWRIE	Scot	68	70	69	79	286	-2	6914.69	4385.96
	Peter LONARD	Aus	69	74	72	71	286	-2	6914.69	4385.96
	Van PHILLIPS	Eng	67	72	75	72	286	-2	6914.69	4385.96
	Carl PETTERSSON	Swe	70	69	75	72	286	-2	6914.69	4385.96
36	David HOWELL	Eng	68	71	73	75	287	-1	5540.68	3514.43
	Lian-Wei ZHANG	PRC	70	70	70	77	287	-1	5540.68	3514.43
	Brian DAVIS	Eng	71	67	72	77	287	-1	5540.68	3514.43
	Thomas GÖGELE	Ger	71	71	70	75	287	-1	5540.68	3514.43
	Roger WESSELS	SA	66	73	74	74	287	-1	5540.68	3514.43
41	Craig HAINLINE	USA	70	73	69	76	288	0	4737.68	3005.09
	Trevor IMMELMAN	SA	70	68	73	77	288	0	4737.68	3005.09
	Neil CHEETHAM	Eng	69	71	73	75	288	0	4737.68	3005.09
	Stephen DODD	Wal	68	73	75	72	288	0	4737.68	3005.09
	Ignacio GARRIDO	Sp	72	68	70	78	288	0	4737.68	3005.09
46	Mark ROE	Eng	72	70	70	77	289	1	3452.89	2190.16
	Jean-Francois REMESY	Fr	71	70	67	81	289	1	3452.89	2190.16
	Fredrik HENGE	Swe	72	71	71	75	289	1	3452.89	2190.16
	Richard S JOHNSON	Swe	69	70	73	77	289	1	3452.89	2190.16
	Johan RYSTRÖM	Swe	68	71	73	77	289	1	3452.89	2190.16
	Jorge BERENDT	Arg	71	71	72	75	289	1	3452.89	2190.16
	Massimo SCARPA	It	66	73	73	77	289	1	3452.89	2190.16
	Bradley DREDGE	Wal	72	71	69	77	289	1	3452.89	2190.16
	Mark PILKINGTON	Wal	63	79	72	75	289	1	3452.89	2190.16
	Andrew COLTART	Scot	71	69	75	74	289	1	3452.89	2190.16
	Matthew BLACKEY	Eng	70	72	75	72	289	1	3452.89	2190.16
57	Russell CLAYDON	Eng	69	74	72	75	290	2	2449.14	1553.48
	Henrik NYSTROM	Swe	67	71	75	77	290	2	2449.14	1553.48
59	Tom GILLIS	USA	67	76	75	73	291	3	2047.64	1298.81
	Gregory HAVRET	Fr	71	69	73	78	291	3	2047.64	1298.81
	Soren HANSEN	Den	67	73	75	76	291	3	2047.64	1298.81
	Jeremy ROBINSON	Eng	71	69	73	78	291	3	2047.64	1298.81
	Michele REALE	It	70	73	73	75	291	3	2047.64	1298.81
	Jonathan LOMAS	Eng	71	72	74	74	291	3	2047.64	1298.81
	Markus BRIER	Aut	66	70	73	82	291	3	2047.64	1298.81
	Patrik SJÖLAND	Swe	69	74	71	77	291	3	2047.64	1298.81
67	Sven STRÜVER	Ger	70	73	76	73	292	4	1571.19	996.60
	Kenneth FERRIE	Eng	68	74	75	75	292	4	1571.19	996.60
	Henrik STENSON	Swe	70	70	70	82	292	4	1571.19	996.60
	Tobias DIER	Ger	71	70	72	79	292	4	1571.19	996.60
71	Marc FARRY	Fr	71	70	72	80	293	5	1204.00	763.69
72	Massimo FLORIOLI	It	71	70	74	79	294	6	1201.00	761.79
73	Santiago LUNA	Sp	73	70	77	75	295	7	1196.50	758.94
	Barry LANE	Eng	68	75	77	75	295	7	1196.50	758.94
75	Raphaël JACQUELIN	Fr	69	71	75	81	296	8	1192.00	756.08
76	Hennie OTTO	SA	71	72	71	DISQ	214	-2		

Master Chef

SANTO DA SERRA, MADEIRA

Oh, what sights that old gunslinger's narrowed eyes had witnessed. Laugh-lines created by ten thousand and one days in the sun crinkled deeper and deeper yet. He had been everywhere, seen everything and done most of that which is granted to all but the greatest. And yet this was fresh, new, unexpected.

The thoughts that tumbled through the mind of this particular veteran can only have been imagined as he stepped forward on the beautiful little Portuguese island in the Atlantic Ocean and responded to the invocation of the man in the green blazer.

Des Smyth

"And the winner, with a score of 270, 18 under par, is ..... Des Smyth," intoned Mikael Eriksson, the Tournament Director of the Madeira Island Open on that sunny evening in March. And as the man of the moment stepped forward to receive his cheque and the acclamation of the gallery, he must have wondered if this was real.

As he went into the tournament, Smyth had a crystal-clear perception of why he was there in the first place. At 48, his salad days on The European Tour were long gone, but he kept on plugging away because, first and foremost, he was a competitor down to his bones and, second, he was keeping himself in competitive trim and marking time until his 50th birthday, when he could become young again by joining the ranks of senior professional golf as a rookie.

And now what had happened? He'd only gone and won the thing, beating in the process countless young Turks who were at the stage in their careers through which he had walked 30 years ago, and more.

That Smyth is one of the Tour's nice guys is beyond dispute. You could wait a day, a month, a year, a lifetime before you would find anybody with a bad word to say about 'Dessie'. But if you'd asked if he had it in him to be a winner again, the answer might have been different. Listen, 48 year olds just don't win on The European Tour any more, right?

Massimo Scarpa

The Course

Santo da Serra was, by general consent, in the best condition it had ever been in the nine-years history of the tournament. Tough on the feet and the lungs and even more leg-wearying for caddies, the venue was complemented by a beautifully refurbished clubhouse. A delight up the mountain.

Shot of the Week

If Des Smyth's seven iron out of trees on the seventh hole on the final day — it led to a surprising birdie — was the stroke that saved him from losing the title, his second shot on the 571 yards 11th was the one that won it. The piercing, raking four iron left him with a four foot putt for an eagle three.

Wrong. In doing so, he became the oldest winner in the 30 years history of The European Tour. At 48 years and 34 days, he was 20 days older than Neil Coles, now the Chairman of the Tour's Board of Directors, had been when he won the Sanyo Open at Sant Cugat in 1982. Furthermore, now he was also that rarest of birds, a winner in four different decades.

After his opening round of 66, with which he had shared the lead with Malcolm Mackenzie, a mere stripling at 39, Smyth said that, his desire to remain competitive until he reached the magic half-century aside, his prime objective was to keep his player's rights for 2001. The exemption he won 2,300 feet above sea level at Santo da Serra – the rest of the season plus two years – meant he would not have to worry about the latter until after he had qualified for the former.

He had seven birdies on that first day, including four in the first half-dozen holes, and only one bogey, while Mackenzie's most notable blow was his lob wedge on the 14th. Having risked all with a driver off the tee and got away with it, he threw his ball 15 feet beyond the pin then watched in delight as it sucked back into the hole for an unlikely eagle two.

Smyth marked time a little in the second round, leaving the way clear for Niclas Fasth, the defending champion, to rampage through the

Massimo Florioli

field with a 63 that was flawless in style and execution. Nine birdies told the story as he finished on 12 under par.

This was a day that was brimming with delicious eccentricities. There was the welcome, if rare, sight of Severiano Ballesteros signing for a 68, a score he has not beaten since the Italian Open in 1999, James Hepworth's 11 and Hank Kuehne's ten on the par four 11th and, finally, the tale of the amazing retreating golf ball.

The perpetrator was Ulrik Gustafsson, the young Swede, whose 300 yards tee shot on the 18th hit a cart path to the left of the fairway, then rolled and bounced all the way back down the hill until it drew to a halt 50 yards behind the tee it had just left. Gustafsson traipsed back, chipped out sideways, then hit two six irons, the last of which gave him a two foot putt for the best bogey of his life. The ball, meanwhile, must have been exhausted — it had travelled 1,085 yards on what should have been only a 385 yards journey.

John Bickerton had his second 67 of the tournament to lie in second place two strokes behind Fasth, and Smyth was one of seven players on eight under.

Bickerton was still there or thereabouts on day three, a 69 leaving him sharing second place with David Lynn, two strokes behind Massimo Florioli, whose aim to become the third Italian winner in recent times behind Costantino Rocca and Massimo Scarpa was helped no end by a 65. Smyth, meanwhile, continued his waiting game, sharing fourth place on 12 under par with Stephen Dodd, Craig Hainline, and Fasth.

The events of that Saturday in the sun provided a richly sauced casserole on its menu of possibilities for the final round. As the leaders started, nobody could have expected that, in the end, it would be the most piquant creation of the lot that would be the main course of the day.

As other, younger men left the high table, their appetites for victory blunted, it was the master chef who kept on serving up dishes fit for a king. Smyth was irresistible, his 66 taking him to his first victory for eight years, two strokes ahead of Bickerton with the pack two further back.

It was then that he provided the most memorable quote of the week. "You chase that elusive dream for so long that when it finally happens, you can't quite believe it," he said. It was not long before he did.

Mel Webb

Gary Emerson

SANTO DA SERRA, MADEIRA, 15-18 MARCH, 2001, PAR 72, 6661 YARDS, 6090 METRES

Pos.	Name		Rd1	Rd2	Rd3	Rd4	Total	Par	Prize Money Euro	£
1	Des SMYTH	Ire	66	70	68	66	270	-18	91660.00	58181.31
2	John BICKERTON	Eng	67	67	69	69	272	-16	61110.00	38789.66
3	Massimo FLORIOLI	It	68	68	65	73	274	-14	26125.00	16582.88
	Stephen DODD	Wal	71	67	66	70	274	-14	26125.00	16582.88
	Massimo SCARPA	It	69	68	70	67	274	-14	26125.00	16582.88
	Niclas FASTH	Swe	69	63	72	70	274	-14	26125.00	16582.88
7	Pehr MAGNEBRANT	Swe	70	70	69	66	275	-13	15125.00	9600.61
	David LYNN	Eng	68	71	64	72	275	-13	15125.00	9600.61
9	Jose Manuel LARA	Sp	68	68	71	69	276	-12	11660.00	7401.20
	Craig HAINLINE	USA	69	70	65	72	276	-12	11660.00	7401.20
11	Gary EMERSON	Eng	69	67	72	70	278	-10	9212.50	5847.65
	Peter MITCHELL	Eng	72	70	70	66	278	-10	9212.50	5847.65
	Gary CLARK	Eng	71	68	71	68	278	-10	9212.50	5847.65
	Jarmo SANDELIN	Swe	69	69	73	67	278	-10	9212.50	5847.65
15	Andrew OLDCORN	Scot	67	69	69	74	279	-9	7296.67	4631.57
	Peter FOWLER	Aus	69	68	71	71	279	-9	7296.67	4631.57
	Steve WEBSTER	Eng	74	68	68	69	279	-9	7296.67	4631.57
	Simon KHAN	Eng	68	73	69	69	279	-9	7296.67	4631.57
	Francis VALERA	Sp	73	65	70	71	279	-9	7296.67	4631.57
	Graeme STORM	Eng	71	71	68	69	279	-9	7296.67	4631.57
21	Santiago LUNA	Sp	70	72	67	71	280	-8	5967.50	3787.88
	Eric CARLBERG	Swe	69	72	70	69	280	-8	5967.50	3787.88
	Fredrik HENGE	Swe	70	68	69	73	280	-8	5967.50	3787.88
	Stuart LITTLE	Eng	72	66	70	72	280	-8	5967.50	3787.88
	Jeremy ROBINSON	Eng	68	72	69	71	280	-8	5967.50	3787.88
	Ian GARBUTT	Eng	71	67	72	70	280	-8	5967.50	3787.88
27	Philip GOLDING	Eng	67	72	69	73	281	-7	5307.50	3368.94
	Gary ORR	Scot	71	72	70	68	281	-7	5307.50	3368.94
29	Malcolm MACKENZIE	Eng	66	73	70	73	282	-6	4895.00	3107.11
	Simon HURD	Eng	73	69	67	73	282	-6	4895.00	3107.11
	Alastair FORSYTH	Scot	69	75	69	69	282	-6	4895.00	3107.11
32	Mårten OLANDER	Swe	75	68	70	70	283	-5	4033.33	2560.16
	Henrik STENSON	Swe	70	66	73	74	283	-5	4033.33	2560.16
	Thomas GÖGELE	Ger	72	72	71	68	283	-5	4033.33	2560.16
	Andrew BEAL	Eng	73	70	70	70	283	-5	4033.33	2560.16
	Russell CLAYDON	Eng	70	72	72	69	283	-5	4033.33	2560.16
	Birgir HAFTHORSSON	Ice	69	71	74	69	283	-5	4033.33	2560.16
	Markus BRIER	Aut	68	68	71	76	283	-5	4033.33	2560.16
	David CARTER	Eng	68	74	70	71	283	-5	4033.33	2560.16
	Nic HENNING	SA	73	71	69	70	283	-5	4033.33	2560.16
41	Mark MOULAND	Wal	70	69	70	75	284	-4	3190.00	2024.86
	Philip WALTON	Ire	67	75	70	72	284	-4	3190.00	2024.86
	Marc PENDARIES	Fr	70	71	68	75	284	-4	3190.00	2024.86
	Greg OWEN	Eng	69	74	71	70	284	-4	3190.00	2024.86
	Johan SKOLD	Swe	67	71	75	71	284	-4	3190.00	2024.86
	Lee S JAMES	Eng	72	68	71	73	284	-4	3190.00	2024.86
47	Seve BALLESTEROS	Sp	71	68	70	76	285	-3	2475.00	1571.01
	Shaun P WEBSTER	Eng	72	71	71	71	285	-3	2475.00	1571.01
	Hennie OTTO	SA	68	71	74	72	285	-3	2475.00	1571.01
	John HAWKSWORTH	Eng	71	73	71	70	285	-3	2475.00	1571.01
	Simon D. HURLEY	Eng	70	73	69	73	285	-3	2475.00	1571.01
	Matthew BLACKEY	Eng	68	75	71	71	285	-3	2475.00	1571.01
	Hank KUEHNE	USA	67	76	71	71	285	-3	2475.00	1571.01
54	Richard BLAND	Eng	70	73	73	70	286	-2	1826.00	1159.06
	Robin BYRD	USA	71	70	73	72	286	-2	1826.00	1159.06
	Dennis EDLUND	Swe	74	70	67	75	286	-2	1826.00	1159.06
	Raimo SJÖBERG	Swe	68	73	73	72	286	-2	1826.00	1159.06
	Stephen SCAHILL	NZ	68	74	73	71	286	-2	1826.00	1159.06
59	Wayne RILEY	Aus	71	72	73	71	287	-1	1540.00	977.52
	Soren KJELDSEN	Den	70	70	71	76	287	-1	1540.00	977.52
	José ROMERO	Sp	74	67	72	74	287	-1	1540.00	977.52
62	Jean-François LUCQUIN	Fr	71	71	73	73	288	0	1347.50	855.33
	Jorge BERENDT	Arg	68	72	75	73	288	0	1347.50	855.33
	Stuart CAGE	Eng	69	70	73	76	288	0	1347.50	855.33
	Benoit TEILLERIA	Fr	72	67	76	73	288	0	1347.50	855.33
66	David HOWELL	Eng	70	73	72	74	289	1	1104.00	700.77
	Gregory HAVRET	Fr	69	75	72	73	289	1	1104.00	700.77
	Fredrik ANDERSSON	Swe	72	72	72	73	289	1	1104.00	700.77
	Iain PYMAN	Eng	75	69	74	71	289	1	1104.00	700.77
	Marcus KNIGHT	Eng	70	72	73	74	289	1	1104.00	700.77
71	Sam WALKER	Eng	74	70	75	71	290	2	825.00	523.67
72	Steven RICHARDSON	Eng	72	71	75	73	291	3	819.00	519.86
	António SOBRINHO	Port	72	71	75	73	291	3	819.00	519.86
	Dean ROBERTSON	Scot	69	72	79	71	291	3	819.00	519.86
75	Mats LANNER	Swe	73	71	75	73	292	4	811.50	515.10
	Kenneth FERRIE	Eng	72	72	71	77	292	4	811.50	515.10
77	Robert Jan DERKSEN	Hol	73	71	77	72	293	5	805.50	511.29
	Ulrik GUSTAFSSON	Swe	70	72	75	76	293	5	805.50	511.29
79	Paul SHERMAN	Eng	72	71	81	75	299	11	801.00	508.44
80	Paddy GRIBBEN	Ire	70	71	73	DISQ	214	-2		

SAO PAULO BRAZIL OPEN

Right on Cue

SAO PAULO GOLF CLUB, SAO PAULO, BRAZIL

They say lightning never strikes in the same place twice, but nobody ever said anything about three times.

With a regularity you could set your watch by, thunder and lightning arrived from seemingly clear blue skies every afternoon at Sao Paulo Golf Club to send the players scurrying for the sanctuary of the clubhouse. The first round stretched into Friday, the second round into Saturday and eventually the third and final round into Sunday as a forecast for more of the same meant the tournament had to be reduced to 54 holes.

It all meant a tortuous wait for the leading contenders, and none more so than eventual winner Darren Fichardt, who had not struck a blow in anger since completing a brilliant, and ultimately decisive, second round 61 on Friday lunchtime. Imagine that, sitting on a seven shot lead at one stage, seeing it whittled down to four by José Coceres and then three by Brett Rumford, not knowing if you had 36 holes in which to protect that lead or just 18 standing between you and victory.

And not just any victory, but a first European Tour win and one that would, without hyperbole, change your golfing career. For the South African was not even certain to get into the 144-man field having missed his card at the Qualifying School in November and yet was suddenly within touching distance of the 125,000 euro (£78,242) first prize and an even more valuable two year Tour exemption.

Just a few things then to occupy Fichardt's mind as he sat around the clubhouse on Saturday afternoon waiting for the second round to be completed and then preparing for the start of the third. With still 60 minutes to go before zero hour, however, a thunderstorm of biblical proportions arrived right on cue and Fichardt's march to glory was put back until 8am on Sunday.

Another night to sleep on it, and consider again and again all the ramifications, did not appear to have done the 25 year old from Pretoria any favours when the final round eventually began as a

Brett Rumford

The Course

An oasis of lush greenery that appears almost magically out of nowhere in the world's third most populous city, Sao Paulo Golf Club exhibits its heritage in a setting typical of many English parkland courses, a legacy of the group of British engineers who moved the course - designed by Stanley Thompson - to its present location in 1915.

Richard S Johnson

José Coceres

bogey on the second coupled with a birdie on the fourth from Rumford meant a three shot lead was suddenly down to one. Fichardt had a secret weapon, however, in wife Natasha, performing the dual role of caddie and mental coach, using her studies in sports psychology to great effect.

"I was a bit nervous because I've never had a lead and had to wait two nights to go and play," Fichardt admitted. "I was a bit shaky but once I made the first birdie on the fifth I felt more relaxed. Natasha was my mental strength all week and she was great."

That mental fortitude had also been vital off the course earlier in the year when Fichardt's sister, Debbie, was tragically killed in a road accident shortly before the Mercedes-Benz South African Open in East London. Darren and Natasha cancelled their tickets three times before the family persuaded them that Debbie, who had two young children, would have wanted him to play. To no-one's surprise he missed the cut and lost any motivation to play.

"After my sister passed away it was hard and I didn't feel like playing the summer Tour," Fichardt added. "But my family encouraged me and I'm sure Debbie would be proud today."

Proud indeed and with good reason as Fichardt refused to buckle after that early mistake and a later charge from Coceres, who enjoyed a run of birdie-birdie-eagle from the sixth hole. Fichardt's response was equally impressive, a birdie from six feet on the fifth steadying the nerves and three more in a row, including a near hole in one on seven, seeing him to the turn in 32 and back in charge.

Coceres did reduce the gap to three with a birdie on the 12th but the Argentinian dropped back again with a bogey two holes later and Fichardt made absolutely certain by holing from 30 feet for birdie on the 16th. That just left the battle for second place which came down to the final green and four putts, two holed and two missed that would decide the outcome.

Firstly Sweden's Richard S Johnson holed from 20 feet for birdie to complete a superb 65 and move to 13 under, followed in the next group by South African Nic Henning, who missed from 15 feet for par to drop back to 12 under. Then it was the turn of Rumford to complete a hat-trick of closing birdies to match Johnson's total before Coceres missed a putt that would have given him outright second in his first tournament of the year.

Johnson therefore matched his best ever finish on Tour while Rumford demonstrated his potential by recovering from a double bogey seven in the final round and seems destined to match the feats of compatriots Aaron Baddeley and Adam Scott, both winners already by this time on The 2001 European Tour International Schedule.

Nic Henning

"It's definitely a breakthrough for me," said Fichardt, who won the South African Tour Players' Championship one month earlier by four shots despite a two shot penalty in the final round. "The win in South Africa was big because people like Ernie Els and Mark McNulty were playing and it was a stepping stone, but this is a major breakthrough. It means I can pick and choose tournaments and no longer need to rely on invites. It makes an enormous difference."

So the victory that had eluded him in his native South Africa just over a year ago - when his attempt for eagle from 80 yards on the 72nd hole at Randpark to force a play-off with Mathias Grönberg somehow stayed above ground as it spun back to the flag - was safely secured, and with something to spare.

And not even another thunderstorm that arrived, bang on schedule as usual, shortly after the presentation ceremony, could dampen Fichardt's spirits or those of the Tour's South African contingent, who made sure plenty of the local firewater "Caiparinha" was downed in celebration!

Phil Casey

SAO PAULO GOLF CLUB, SAO PAULO, BRAZIL 22-25 MARCH, 2001, PAR 71, 6646 YARDS, 6077 METRES

Pos.	Name		Rd1	Rd2	Rd3	Rd4	Total	Par	Prize Money Euro	£
1	Darren FICHARDT	SA	67	61	67		195	-18	125000.00	78242.36
2	Richard S JOHNSON	Swe	68	67	65		200	-13	55926.67	35006.68
	José COCERES	Arg	68	64	68		200	-13	55926.67	35006.68
	Brett RUMFORD	Aus	66	65	69		200	-13	55926.67	35006.68
5	Raphaël JACQUELIN	Fr	66	70	65		201	-12	29025.00	18167.88
	Nic HENNING	SA	70	64	67		201	-12	29025.00	18167.88
7	Anthony WALL	Eng	71	67	64		202	-11	22500.00	14083.63
8	Simon D. HURLEY	Eng	69	69	65		203	-10	16087.50	10069.79
	Neil CHEETHAM	Eng	69	67	67		203	-10	16087.50	10069.79
	Matthew BLACKEY	Eng	67	68	68		203	-10	16087.50	10069.79
	Christopher HANELL	Swe	68	65	70		203	-10	16087.50	10069.79
12	Robin BYRD	USA	68	69	67		204	-9	12900.00	8074.61
13	Gustavo ROJAS	Arg	67	68	70		205	-8	11775.00	7370.43
	Daren LEE	Eng	68	68	69		205	-8	11775.00	7370.43
15	Philip WALTON	Ire	69	66	71		206	-7	10140.00	6347.02
	Kenneth FERRIE	Eng	70	67	69		206	-7	10140.00	6347.02
	Thomas GÖGELE	Ger	70	67	69		206	-7	10140.00	6347.02
	Massimo FLORIOLI	It	69	68	69		206	-7	10140.00	6347.02
	Tomas Jesus MUÑOZ	Sp	71	66	69		206	-7	10140.00	6347.02
20	Peter FOWLER	Aus	70	70	67		207	-6	8260.71	5170.70
	Warren BENNETT	Eng	70	68	69		207	-6	8260.71	5170.70
	Carlos RODILES	Sp	69	71	67		207	-6	8260.71	5170.70
	Eduardo PESENTI	Bra	71	69	67		207	-6	8260.71	5170.70
	Diego BORREGO	Sp	68	67	72		207	-6	8260.71	5170.70
	Benoit TEILLERIA	Fr	70	68	69		207	-6	8260.71	5170.70
	Alexandre ROCHA	Bra	74	69	64		207	-6	8260.71	5170.70
27	Thomas LEVET	Fr	67	71	70		208	-5	7012.50	4389.40
	Per NYMAN	Swe	65	73	70		208	-5	7012.50	4389.40
	Jorge BERENDT	Arg	75	66	67		208	-5	7012.50	4389.40
	Angel ROMERO	Col	70	69	69		208	-5	7012.50	4389.40
31	Mark ROE	Eng	67	70	72		209	-4	5675.00	3552.20
	Jesus AMAYA	Col	69	70	70		209	-4	5675.00	3552.20
	Andrew BEAL	Eng	68	73	68		209	-4	5675.00	3552.20
	Olle KARLSSON	Swe	70	71	68		209	-4	5675.00	3552.20
	Christophe POTTIER	Fr	72	71	66		209	-4	5675.00	3552.20
	Johan SKOLD	Swe	70	65	74		209	-4	5675.00	3552.20
	Erol SIMSEK	Ger	67	71	71		209	-4	5675.00	3552.20
	Hank KUEHNE	USA	67	69	73		209	-4	5675.00	3552.20
	Carl PETTERSSON	Swe	74	69	66		209	-4	5675.00	3552.20
40	Bradford VAUGHAN	SA	72	67	71		210	-3	4425.00	2769.78
	Christophe RAVETTO	Fr	69	69	72		210	-3	4425.00	2769.78
	Henrik STENSON	Swe	75	67	68		210	-3	4425.00	2769.78
	Joakim HAEGGMAN	Swe	70	70	70		210	-3	4425.00	2769.78
	Francisco CEA	Sp	70	69	71		210	-3	4425.00	2769.78
	Jose ADERBAL	Bra	67	71	72		210	-3	4425.00	2769.78
	Adam ARMAGOST	USA	69	71	70		210	-3	4425.00	2769.78
47	Mårten OLANDER	Swe	68	70	73		211	-2	3375.00	2112.54
	Stephen SCAHILL	NZ	73	68	70		211	-2	3375.00	2112.54
	Paul STREETER	Eng	71	68	72		211	-2	3375.00	2112.54
	Andrew RAITT	Eng	73	67	71		211	-2	3375.00	2112.54
	Gary CLARK	Eng	69	71	71		211	-2	3375.00	2112.54
	Mauricio MOLINA	Arg	70	69	72		211	-2	3375.00	2112.54
	Shannon SYKORA	USA	73	69	69		211	-2	3375.00	2112.54
54	Gregory HAVRET	Fr	73	66	73		212	-1	2550.00	1596.14
	Ricardo GONZALEZ	Arg	70	67	75		212	-1	2550.00	1596.14
	Han LEE	USA	71	68	73		212	-1	2550.00	1596.14
	Rafael BARCELLOS	Bra	75	65	72		212	-1	2550.00	1596.14
58	Santiago LUNA	Sp	67	72	74		213	0	1912.50	1197.11
	Marc PENDARIES	Fr	69	73	71		213	0	1912.50	1197.11
	Felix LUBENAU	Ger	73	69	71		213	0	1912.50	1197.11
	Scott DRUMMOND	Scot	70	73	70		213	0	1912.50	1197.11
	Henrik BJORNSTAD	Nor	71	68	74		213	0	1912.50	1197.11
	Paul EALES	Eng	72	71	70		213	0	1912.50	1197.11
	Marcello SANTI	It	73	70	70		213	0	1912.50	1197.11
	Charles CHALLEN	Eng	69	74	70		213	0	1912.50	1197.11
	Rafael GONZALEZ	Bra	71	72	70		213	0	1912.50	1197.11
	Sebastian FERNANDEZ	Arg	72	71	70		213	0	1912.50	1197.11
68	Van PHILLIPS	Eng	75	68	71		214	1	1308.40	818.98
	Simon KHAN	Eng	73	70	71		214	1	1308.40	818.98
	Michael JONZON	Swe	68	69	77		214	1	1308.40	818.98
	Marco BERNARDINI	It	68	70	76		214	1	1308.40	818.98
	Gustavo ACOSTA	Arg	70	73	71		214	1	1308.40	818.98
73	Jeremy ROBINSON	Eng	72	71	72		215	2	1116.00	698.55
	Paul DWYER	Eng	70	69	76		215	2	1116.00	698.55
	Erik ANDERSSON	Swe	69	73	73		215	2	1116.00	698.55
76	Hennie OTTO	SA	72	69	75		216	3	1110.00	694.79
77	Jose Priscilo DINIZ	Bra	73	70	74		217	4	1107.00	692.91
78	Peter HANSON	Swe	72	71	75		218	5	1102.50	690.10
	Sergio BRASIL	Bra	72	70	76		218	5	1102.50	690.10

Follow the European Tours LIVE at the touch of a button!
EUROPEAN SENIORS TOUR
EUROPEAN TOUR
EUROPEAN CHALLENGE TOUR
europeantour.com
Official Website of the PGA European Tour
europeantour.com your instant access to *live scoring*, the *latest news* and *everything* you want to know about the European, Seniors and Challenge Tours
europeantour.com
OFFICIAL WEBSITE OF THE PGA EUROPEAN TOUR

Dedicated Dream

THE JOCKEY CLUB, BUENOS AIRES, ARGENTINA

It is often said the hardest victory of them all is the first one and they don't get much tougher than your national Open in front of an expectant home crowd.

With The European Tour visiting Argentina for the first time for a co-sanctioned tournament, Angel Cabrera arrived at the immaculate Jockey Club in Buenos Aires for the 96th Open de Argentina hoping to right two wrongs. Never before had he won his national title, and neither had he mounted the winners' rostrum on The European Tour.

Admittedly, he had been close on a number of occasions, finishing second on The European Tour four times, third twice and scooping a top ten positions on 17 other occasions. However, that maiden victory somehow managed to elude him.

Shot of the Week

It was only a 15 foot putt but it proved critical in the outcome of the tournament. With only three holes to play Angel Cabrera was on the brink of winning his maiden title but Carl Pettersson had followed his birdie on the 15th with another on the 16th. The gap was briefly down to a single stroke until Cabrera rolled in his own birdie putt on the 16th to restore his two shot lead and secure victory.

Argentine players have had a huge influence on The European Tour over the years. The defending champion at The Jockey Club, Vicente Fernandez, will long be remembered for his victory jig on the 18th green at The De Vere Belfry after holing a monster putt to win the English Open in 1992. In 2000, Eduardo Romero captured the European Masters for the second time, winning his seventh European Tour title, but for Romero the start of a new millennium brought another dream to reality - confirmation that the Open de Argentine would feature on The European Tour International Schedule.

Romero also dreamed of winning the title in 2001, but if it was not to be him then he hoped the tournament would provide the breakthrough that Cabrera deserved. Romero has been more than just a friend and mentor to his fellow Argentinian. Romero saw in Cabrera, who started out as a caddie in Cordoba, an abundance of talent and used his own money to sponsor his young protégé on The European Tour. With Romero's help and advice Cabrera made good progress, climbing to tenth and 14th in the Volvo Order of Merit in 1999 and 2000 respectively.

Late in 2000, Buenos Aires Golf Club had hosted the World Golf Championships - EMC^2 World Cup. Cabrera partnered Romero and they finished a close second to David Duval and Tiger Woods. With memories of that superb performance still fresh in their minds, spectators were expecting great things from their own players in the Open de Argentina.

Costantino Rocca and caddie Brian McFeat

Carl Pettersson

Mark Mouland

Graeme Storm and caddie Mark Steers

From the outset it was clear the golfing gods were smiling down on Cabrera. His tee shot at the seventh disappeared up a pine tree. Just as he was about to give up the search, and return to the tee, the ball toppled from the branches back into play. From there he saved his par and never looked back.

Cabrera opened with a three under par 67 but trailed first round leader Angel Franco of Paraguay by three. Cabrera stepped up a gear with a five under par 65 in the second round to open a two stroke lead at the halfway stage ahead of another Argentine player Ricardo Gonzalez, Swedes Olle Karlsson and Carl Pettersson and former Amateur Champion Graeme Storm of England. Pettersson, the 23 year old European Amateur Champion embarking on his rookie season as a professional, shot a third round 67 to join Cabrera (69) in the lead with four players two shots off the pace snapping at their heels.

Conditions could not have been better on the final day and Cabrera arrived on the first tee with the cheers from the home fans reverberating in his ears. "I think the toughest moment was on the first tee of that final round," he said afterwards. "Everyone was watching and expecting Cabrera to win his first tournament in Argentina. That was when I felt the pressure."

There was no doubt who the favourite was but Pettersson struck first with a birdie at the opening hole. Two holes later the lead was reversed. Pettersson overclubbed, and could do no better than a bogey four, while Cabrera birdied. It was a lead he was never to relinquish.

Pettersson trailed by three with four holes to play but he still applied pressure on the leader with a birdie on the 15th and then another on the 16th, holing from 25 feet. Even so Cabrera kept his nose in front with his own birdie on the 16th from 15 feet to set up his victory on home soil.

"This is one of the most important moments of my life," he said afterwards. "I have longed for this victory for a long time - to win this tournament in my own country. I could never do it before and now I am very happy. I knew that it was going to happen sooner or later. We all have opportunities - this was my opportunity."

As he waited on the 18th green for the presentation he sat among the great golfers in Argentine golf history. Fernandez was there as was possibly the greatest of them all - Robert de Vicenzo, the 1967 Open Champion. And, of course, there was Romero.

"Eduardo has helped me a lot with my career and supported me unconditionally," said Cabrera. " He is a person loved and welcomed everywhere he goes and without his help I wouldn't be playing on The European Tour. I dedicate this win to him from my heart."

At the end it was hard to know who had the biggest smile, Cabrera or Romero, but it was entirely fitting that upon his graduation, the pupil should give thanks to his tutor.

Roddy Williams

Vicente Fernandez

The Course

A true test of golf designed by world renowned architect Dr Alister MacKenzie, the course resembles an arboretum as the narrow fairways wind their way around some magnificent trees and shrubs. In true MacKenzie style the greens pose the greatest test with plenty of undulations over what was undoubtedly one of the finest courses to host a European Tour event.

THE JOCKEY CLUB, BUENOS AIRES, ARGENTINA, 29 MARCH - 1 APRIL, 2001, PAR 71, 6730 YARDS, 6303 METRES

Pos.	Name		Rd1	Rd2	Rd3	Rd4	Total	Par	Prize Money Euro	£
1	Angel CABRERA	Arg	67	65	69	67	268	-12	130697.23	81626.08
2	Carl PETTERSSON	Swe	65	69	67	69	270	-10	87127.75	54415.05
3	Graeme STORM	Eng	68	66	69	69	272	-8	49092.68	30660.50
4	Mark MOULAND	Wal	69	68	69	68	274	-6	30859.38	19273.02
	Costantino ROCCA	It	71	67	65	71	274	-6	30859.38	19273.02
	Henrik BJORNSTAD	Nor	70	70	66	68	274	-6	30859.38	19273.02
	Matthew BLACKEY	Eng	66	70	71	67	274	-6	30859.38	19273.02
8	Vicente FERNANDEZ	Arg	69	72	65	69	275	-5	16155.10	10089.56
	Hennie OTTO	SA	70	67	68	70	275	-5	16155.10	10089.56
	Olle KARLSSON	Swe	65	69	72	69	275	-5	16155.10	10089.56
	Daren LEE	Eng	72	66	67	70	275	-5	16155.10	10089.56
	Nic HENNING	SA	70	69	71	65	275	-5	16155.10	10089.56
13	Anthony WALL	Eng	68	70	68	70	276	-4	11559.52	7219.42
	Ricardo GONZALEZ	Arg	70	64	69	73	276	-4	11559.52	7219.42
	Ruben ALVAREZ	Arg	71	72	66	67	276	-4	11559.52	7219.42
	Angel FRANCO	Par	64	72	71	69	276	-4	11559.52	7219.42
	Christopher HANELL	Swe	70	69	69	68	276	-4	11559.52	7219.42
18	Eduardo ROMERO	Arg	70	66	69	72	277	-3	9442.11	5897.01
	Jose Manuel LARA	Sp	65	71	71	70	277	-3	9442.11	5897.01
	Thomas LEVET	Fr	69	70	70	68	277	-3	9442.11	5897.01
	Paul EALES	Eng	69	69	70	69	277	-3	9442.11	5897.01
	Tomas Jesus MUÑOZ	Sp	69	66	67	75	277	-3	9442.11	5897.01
	Matias ANSELMO (AM)	Arg	73	64	70	70	277	-3		
24	Simon D. HURLEY	Eng	73	64	70	71	278	-2	8508.88	5314.16
	Massimo FLORIOLI	It	71	68	70	69	278	-2	8508.88	5314.16
26	Darren FICHARDT	SA	68	72	70	69	279	-1	7214.90	4506.02
	Miguel FERNANDEZ	Arg	73	69	71	66	279	-1	7214.90	4506.02
	Diego BORREGO	Sp	69	72	71	67	279	-1	7214.90	4506.02
	Francisco CEA	Sp	69	70	70	70	279	-1	7214.90	4506.02
	Johan SKOLD	Swe	73	68	66	72	279	-1	7214.90	4506.02
	Mauricio MOLINA	Arg	70	69	66	74	279	-1	7214.90	4506.02
	Mikael LUNDBERG	Swe	66	72	72	69	279	-1	7214.90	4506.02
	Martin LONARDI	Arg	72	70	73	64	279	-1	7214.90	4506.02
	Julio ZAPATA	Arg	69	69	68	73	279	-1	7214.90	4506.02
35	Craig HAINLINE	USA	71	70	70	69	280	0	5803.29	3624.41
	Jorge BERENDT	Arg	70	65	69	76	280	0	5803.29	3624.41
	Erol SIMSEK	Ger	65	71	71	73	280	0	5803.29	3624.41
	Dave BISHOP	USA	67	71	69	73	280	0	5803.29	3624.41
39	Mark ROE	Eng	73	65	75	68	281	1	4862.22	3036.67
	John WADE	Aus	73	67	70	71	281	1	4862.22	3036.67
	Richard S JOHNSON	Swe	65	71	73	72	281	1	4862.22	3036.67
	Nicolas COLSAERTS	Bel	75	67	71	68	281	1	4862.22	3036.67
	Horacio CARBONETTI	Arg	71	67	70	73	281	1	4862.22	3036.67
	Gustavo ROJAS	Arg	72	70	69	70	281	1	4862.22	3036.67
	Van PHILLIPS	Eng	71	71	69	70	281	1	4862.22	3036.67
	Stephen SCAHILL	NZ	69	67	73	72	281	1	4862.22	3036.67
47	Raphaël JACQUELIN	Fr	72	71	65	74	282	2	3607.45	2253.01
	Jesus AMAYA	Col	71	70	70	71	282	2	3607.45	2253.01
	Marcello SANTI	It	72	69	72	69	282	2	3607.45	2253.01
	Jonathan LOMAS	Eng	70	72	72	68	282	2	3607.45	2253.01
	Andrew RAITT	Eng	70	68	70	74	282	2	3607.45	2253.01
	Simon HURD	Eng	72	69	70	71	282	2	3607.45	2253.01
	Ariel LICERA	Arg	67	71	76	68	282	2	3607.45	2253.01
	Alexandre ROCHA	Bra	74	68	69	71	282	2	3607.45	2253.01
55	Dennis EDLUND	Swe	71	70	72	70	283	3	2603.64	1626.09
	Gary CLARK	Eng	69	69	70	75	283	3	2603.64	1626.09
	Michael JONZON	Swe	72	67	71	73	283	3	2603.64	1626.09
	Hank KUEHNE	USA	72	71	69	71	283	3	2603.64	1626.09
	Ramon FRANCO	Par	68	74	69	72	283	3	2603.64	1626.09
60	Kenneth FERRIE	Eng	70	72	71	71	284	4	2078.21	1297.93
	Carlos RODILES	Sp	73	67	75	69	284	4	2078.21	1297.93
	Gregory HAVRET	Fr	72	70	72	70	284	4	2078.21	1297.93
	Simon KHAN	Eng	70	71	71	72	284	4	2078.21	1297.93
	Ariel CAÑETE	Arg	73	65	72	74	284	4	2078.21	1297.93
	Roberto COCERES	Arg	70	71	71	72	284	4	2078.21	1297.93
66	Olivier EDMOND	Fr	70	73	69	73	285	5	1764.51	1102.01
	Eduardo ARGIRO	Arg	69	70	75	71	285	5	1764.51	1102.01
68	Thomas GÖGELE	Ger	75	68	67	76	286	6	1607.67	1004.06
	Donald DONAHUE	USA	74	69	76	67	286	6	1607.67	1004.06
70	Cesar MONASTERIO	Arg	74	66	75	72	287	7	1370.42	855.89
	Esteban ISASI	Par	72	69	71	75	287	7	1370.42	855.89
	Damian HALE	T&T	72	71	72	72	287	7	1370.42	855.89
73	Tim HEGNA	USA	73	70	73	72	288	8	1173.00	732.59
74	Steven RICHARDSON	Eng	72	71	72	74	289	9	1170.00	730.72
75	Christian CEVAER	Fr	69	72	76	73	290	10	1165.50	727.91
	Fredrik ANDERSSON	Swe	69	74	77	70	290	10	1165.50	727.91
77	Adan SOWA	Arg	72	71	75	73	291	11	1159.50	724.16
	Andrew BEAL	Eng	72	71	76	72	291	11	1159.50	724.16
	Fernando CHIESA (AM)	Arg	70	73	72	76	291	11		
80	Simon DYSON	Eng	72	71	75	74	292	12	1155.00	721.35
81	Philip WALTON	Ire	72	70	79	73	294	14	1152.00	719.47

Perfect Six

AUGUSTA NATIONAL, AUGUSTA, GEORGIA, USA

One day he was duelling modern golfing lions like David Duval and Phil Mickelson for a unique place in the game's history. The next he was taking on past sporting gods such as Muhammad Ali and Joe DiMaggio for a unique place in the annals of all sport.

One unforgettable Sunday afternoon in Augusta and Tiger Woods slipped into a green jacket that symbolised his unquestioned position as the premier sportsman of his generation.

One memorable Monday all over the world and every columnist worth his or her salt rushed into print to begin a more hotly contested debate. Well, was it? Did winning the Masters to complete a clean sweep of all four Major Championships constitute the most breathtaking sporting feat the globe has yet seen?

Golfers are magnanimous by nature so let's just say that those of us in Woods's corner believe we have a heck of a case. Heavens, we have masses of evidence. Let's start with witness number one, the previously incomparable Jack Nicklaus.

Few people argue that until Woods came along Nicklaus was the greatest golfer who ever lived. But how many consecutive Majors did Nicklaus ever manage to win? That's right, not four, not even three, but two.

Witness number two is Colin Montgomerie. Anybody dispute that Montgomerie is up there with the great European golfers of all time? Thought not. But Montgomerie is still waiting to win any Major Championship, let alone Majors consecutively.

The example of Montgomerie, therefore, tells us how hard it is to win just one of these things, and Nicklaus the difficulty of winning consecutively.

David Duval

Phil Mickelson

Then again, golfers know all this don't they? That is why up to three years ago it was thought of as next to impossible for all four to end up in the same household.

Each year at the Masters the same question was posed to the winner of the green jacket. Do you think you can win the Grand Slam? Every April the champion would allow himself a wry chuckle, attempt a joke along the lines of 'Well, no-one else can this year,' and accept it was hardly within the bounds of comprehension, let alone their ability.

Now all right, Woods's feat might not be a Grand Slam in the very purest sense of the term but arguing over that is, as Nicklaus pointed out, completely irrelevant.

"I don't care what you call it but what I call it is by far the most remarkable golfing feat we have ever seen," the great man said.

Shot of the Week

The approach to the 11th is so fraught with danger that Ben Hogan used to say that if you ever saw him on that green in two it meant he had pulled his second shot.
Tiger Woods came to the 11th on Sunday tied for the lead. A wonderful drive left him 145 yards from the pin. In years gone by he might have hit a high wedge and hoped it travelled the right distance. This time he struck a beautifully controlled knockdown eight iron. It finished inches from the hole for a certain birdie. Woods was ahead again, and would remain so to the end.

Bernhard Langer

What made Woods's Slam so pleasurable to so many was the manner of it, and the places he won. First, the 100th US Open Championship at America's most evocative course, Pebble Beach, the victory margin the small matter of 15 strokes.

Next he became the youngest player to complete the career Grand Slam, winning the Open Championship at St Andrews of all places, by eight shots. Then the US PGA Championship after a thrilling last day shootout with Bob May.

So to Augusta National. Yes, the same Augusta National that Bobby Jones built; the Bobby Jones who won the Grand Slam as it was constituted in 1930 (the Amateur and Open Championships of Great Britain and America). Do you think this boy has good timing?

It proved one amazing week. It even lived up to the incredible hype. From Monday at 8am the patrons came, queuing to buy their souvenirs, as if they instinctively knew that this was going to be the tournament of tournaments.

From the moment Woods began 70-66 to mirror exactly his scores when he won by 12 in 1997 there was the feeling that this result was somehow pre-ordained.

Such a thought perhaps does less than justice to Woods's incredible desire and the hundreds of hours of practice he puts in to be perfect in each department of the game.

But when you see his name rise up the leaderboard tournaments take on a fateful air; you can almost sense the feeling of helplessness in the opposition, the feeling that as Woods moves freely through the gears there is nothing they can do.

A 68 in the third round and now Woods was one stroke ahead. Thomas Björn and Lee Westwood are two of a select group of players who know what it feels like to reel Woods in when he is leading with a round to play. So, too, does Mickelson, who just happened to be his partner on the last day.

In Major Championships, however, Woods made it a perfect six for six, demonstrating again his unerring ability to deliver when it matters most. The following morning the television networks summed up the mood of the nation when they christened it Tiger Woods Day. It was the only appropriate honour for a man who had transcended his chosen game with a feat that, at the very least, puts him up there with the other sporting immortals on Mt Olympus.

Derek Lawrenson

Ernie Els

The Course

Augusta National has evolved considerably over the years and will do so again for 2002 when several of the par fours are lengthened. Two things that have remained the same are its reputation as one of the great tests of golf, and its status as the most picturesque inland course in the world.

Chris DiMarco

AUGUSTA NATIONAL, AUGUSTA, GEORGIA, USA, 5-8 APRIL, 2001, PAR 72, 6985 YARDS, 6387 METRES

Pos.	Name		Rd1	Rd2	Rd3	Rd4	Total	Par	Prize Money Euro	£
1	Tiger WOODS	USA	70	66	68	68	272	-16	1146236.00	710359.44
2	David DUVAL	USA	71	66	70	67	274	-14	687741.60	426215.67
3	Phil MICKELSON	USA	67	69	69	70	275	-13	433022.50	268358.02
4	Toshimitsu IZAWA	Jpn	71	66	74	67	278	-10	280191.00	173643.41
	Mark CALCAVECCHIA	USA	72	66	68	72	278	-10	280191.00	173643.41
6	Bernhard LANGER	Ger	73	69	68	69	279	-9	206163.30	127766.05
	Jim FURYK	USA	69	71	70	69	279	-9	206163.30	127766.05
	Ernie ELS	SA	71	68	68	72	279	-9	206163.30	127766.05
	Kirk TRIPLETT	USA	68	70	70	71	279	-9	206163.30	127766.05
10	Brad FAXON	USA	73	68	68	71	280	-8	146463.50	90768.16
	Steve STRICKER	USA	66	71	72	71	280	-8	146463.50	90768.16
	Miguel Angel JIMÉNEZ	Sp	68	72	71	69	280	-8	146463.50	90768.16
	Angel CABRERA	Arg	66	71	70	73	280	-8	146463.50	90768.16
	Chris DIMARCO	USA	65	69	72	74	280	-8	146463.50	90768.16
15	José Maria OLAZÁBAL	Sp	70	68	71	72	281	-7	108255.60	67089.49
	Paul AZINGER	USA	70	71	71	69	281	-7	108255.60	67089.49
	Rocco MEDIATE	USA	72	70	66	73	281	-7	108255.60	67089.49
18	Vijay SINGH	Fiji	69	71	73	69	282	-6	92335.67	57223.39
	Tom LEHMAN	USA	75	68	71	68	282	-6	92335.67	57223.39
20	Mark O'MEARA	USA	69	74	72	68	283	-5	74186.94	45976.04
	Jesper PARNEVIK	Swe	71	71	72	69	283	-5	74186.94	45976.04
	John HUSTON	USA	67	75	72	69	283	-5	74186.94	45976.04
	Jeff MAGGERT	USA	72	70	70	71	283	-5	74186.94	45976.04
24	Darren CLARKE	N.Ire	72	67	72	73	284	-4	61132.58	37885.83
25	Tom SCHERRER	USA	71	71	70	73	285	-3	56038.20	34728.68
26	Fred COUPLES	USA	74	71	73	68	286	-2	50943.82	31571.53
27	Padraig HARRINGTON	Ire	75	69	72	71	287	-1	46167.84	28611.70
	Justin LEONARD	USA	73	71	72	71	287	-1	46167.84	28611.70
	Mike WEIR	Can	74	69	72	72	287	-1	46167.84	28611.70
	Steve JONES	USA	74	70	72	71	287	-1	46167.84	28611.70
31	Stuart APPLEBY	Aus	72	70	70	76	288	0	37762.11	23402.40
	Mark BROOKS	USA	70	71	77	70	288	0	37762.11	23402.40
	Duffy WALDORF	USA	72	70	71	75	288	0	37762.11	23402.40
	Lee JANZEN	USA	67	70	72	79	288	0	37762.11	23402.40
	David TOMS	USA	72	72	71	73	288	0	37762.11	23402.40
36	Hal SUTTON	USA	74	69	71	75	289	1	32795.08	20324.17
37	Loren ROBERTS	USA	71	74	73	72	290	2	29929.49	18548.27
	Chris PERRY	USA	68	74	74	74	290	2	29929.49	18548.27
	Scott HOCH	USA	74	70	72	74	290	2	29929.49	18548.27
40	Steve LOWERY	USA	72	72	78	70	292	4	26108.71	16180.41
	Shingo KATAYAMA	Jpn	75	70	73	74	292	4	26108.71	16180.41
	Franklin LANGHAM	USA	72	73	75	72	292	4	26108.71	16180.41
43	Dudley HART	USA	74	70	78	71	293	5	22287.92	13812.54
	Bob MAY	USA	71	74	73	75	293	5	22287.92	13812.54
	Jonathan KAYE	USA	74	71	74	74	293	5	22287.92	13812.54
46	Carlos Daniel FRANCO	Par	71	71	77	75	294	6	19740.73	12233.97
47	Robert ALLENBY	Aus	71	74	75	75	295	7	18467.13	11444.68
48	Sergio GARCIA	Sp	70	76			146	2	5685.69	3523.61
	Davis LOVE III	USA	71	75			146	2	5685.69	3523.61
	José COCERES	Arg	77	69			146	2	5685.69	3523.61
	Thomas BJÖRN	Den	70	76			146	2	5685.69	3523.61
	Dennis PAULSON	USA	73	73			146	2	5685.69	3523.61
	Notah BEGAY III	USA	73	73			146	2	5685.69	3523.61
	James DRISCOLL (AM)	USA	68	78			146	2		
55	Sandy LYLE	Scot	74	73			147	3	5685.69	3523.61
	Shigeki MARUYAMA	Jpn	77	70			147	3	5685.69	3523.61
	Scott VERPLANK	USA	69	78			147	3	5685.69	3523.61
	Joe DURANT	USA	73	74			147	3	5685.69	3523.61
59	Jack NICKLAUS	USA	73	75			148	4	5685.69	3523.61
	Eduardo ROMERO	Arg	75	73			148	4	5685.69	3523.61
	Tom WATSON	USA	78	70			148	4	5685.69	3523.61
	Ian WOOSNAM	Wal	71	77			148	4	5685.69	3523.61
	Greg CHALMERS	Aus	76	72			148	4	5685.69	3523.61
	Nick PRICE	Zim	73	75			148	4	5685.69	3523.61
	Larry MIZE	USA	74	74			148	4	5685.69	3523.61
	Rory SABBATINI	SA	73	75			148	4	5685.69	3523.61
67	Gary PLAYER	SA	73	76			149	5	5685.69	3523.61
	Fuzzy ZOELLER	USA	77	72			149	5	5685.69	3523.61
	Stewart CINK	USA	75	74			149	5	5685.69	3523.61
	Colin MONTGOMERIE	Scot	73	76			149	5	5685.69	3523.61
	Paul LAWRIE	Scot	73	76			149	5	5685.69	3523.61
	Retief GOOSEN	SA	75	74			149	5	5685.69	3523.61
73	Steve FLESCH	USA	74	76			150	6	5685.69	3523.61
	Grant WAITE	NZ	79	71			150	6	5685.69	3523.61
	Aaron BADDELEY	Aus	75	75			150	6	5685.69	3523.61
76	Nick FALDO	Eng	75	76			151	7	5685.69	3523.61
	Raymond FLOYD	USA	76	75			151	7	5685.69	3523.61
	Mikko ILONEN (AM)	Fin	72	79			151	7		
79	Seve BALLESTEROS	Sp	76	76			152	8	5685.69	3523.61
	Craig STADLER	USA	79	73			152	8	5685.69	3523.61
	Charles COODY	USA	80	72			152	8	5685.69	3523.61
	Pierre FULKE	Swe	73	79			152	8	5685.69	3523.61
83	Greg NORMAN	Aus	71	82			153	9	5685.69	3523.61
	Michael CAMPBELL	NZ	78	75			153	9	5685.69	3523.61
	D J TRAHAN (AM)	USA	78	75			153	9		
86	Jeff QUINNEY (AM)	USA	80	76			156	12		
	Greg PUGA (AM)	USA	76	80			156	12		
88	Arnold PALMER	USA	82	76			158	14	5685.69	3523.61
89	Ben CRENSHAW	USA	81	78			159	15	5685.69	3523.61
90	Tommy AARON	USA	81	82			163	19	5685.69	3523.61
91	Billy CASPER	USA	87	80			167	23	5685.69	3523.61
92	Gay BREWER	USA	84	RETD			190	12	5685.69	3523.61
93	Doug FORD	USA	W/D				190	0	5685.69	3523.61

Poulter Heist

ROYAL GOLF DAR ES SALAM, RABAT, MOROCCO

It was rather apt that Ridley Scott was shooting his latest film just down the road from Royal Golf Dar Es Salam during the 11th Moroccan Open.

The greatly respected course had already witnessed many gladiatorial golfing battles and The European Tour's fourth visit to Rabat provided another epic.

This time it was Ian Poulter pitting himself against all-comers. After an absorbing contest, the Bedfordshire professional followed up his victory in the 2000 Italian Open in Sardinia, with a two stroke success in Rabat.

David Lynn

Gary Evans

Nick Faldo may have done it at an earlier age, but 25 year old Poulter had already achieved exactly the same feat. He had won in his first year and claimed the Sir Henry Cotton Rookie of the Year Award. Then he had followed up with victory in his second year. Poulter was following the route of his golfing hero and, with a climb to sixth at the time on Europe's Ryder Cup table, he could dream of success similar to that Faldo has enjoyed.

Poulter began his victory quest quietly, hardly surprising as he was suffering tonsillitis which needed antibiotics. His opening 71 left him four strokes behind the first-day leader Paul McGinley. But never was the old adage 'beware the sickly golfer' more in evidence than in the second round.

At first it looked as though the never-say-die Paolo Quirici was going to mount another bid for a maiden European Tour title when the Swiss player put Royal Golf Dar Es Salam to the sword with eight birdies in 12 holes. It was only fleeting success. Quirici left the arena that day bloodied by two double bogeys after his glorious run, wounded badly enough to be no threat from there on.

Instead of a trident, Poulter used another sharp blade - his putter - to take command, netting his birdies and protecting his rear and front with just 22 putts in the second round, 14 of them singles. Poulter fashioned a two shot lead over an American seeking to win back the card he had lost the year before, Craig Hainline. Although the new leader had also discovered another trusty weapon in a new driver picked up in America during his Tour break, it was the putter which won the day for him in the end.

Shot of the Week

Ian Poulter's magnificent drive which covered nearly 320 yards at the tenth in the final round, needed only an eight iron approach to the par five, which he hit with aplomb to just three feet. The eagle enabled Poulter to stave off all-comers. "I busted the drive and the eight iron was all over the flag," said the winner.

The second round, too, provided a breakthrough for a new young warrier not even in the professional ranks, Nick Dougherty, schooled by Britain's greatest master of the arena, Nick Faldo. The exciting 18 year old from Lancashire celebrated making his first cut among the professionals.

As a scorching third round unfolded, several of the cast from Oscar-winning Scott's film 'Black Hawk Down' came to Royal Golf Dar Es Salam to watch the golfing gladiators. One of them was Ewan McGregor, star of Star Wars and Trainspotting. Saturday, then, was star spotting. As he is from Crieff, McGregor decided to watch his fellow Scot Stephen Gallacher, nephew of Bernard. His attention inspired Gallacher, who went on to post his best result of the year up to that point.

While the day belonged to Poulter as his solid 69 established a four-stroke lead over Gary Evans, Robert Karlsson and Thomas Levet, the round belonged to a man who had duelled in Europe for a decade successfully but without a title, Australian Peter Lonard. Sickness and personal problems had dogged the burly Australian but he looked over all his troubles as he cut and thrust his way to a course record equalling 66. A hole-in-one helped him equal Howard Clark's 14 year record, and took him within five shots of Poulter. Evans was another to equal the record but Poulter looked imperious, only off guard late on as he found the cork trees on the 16th for his only bogey.

Robert Karlsson

Thomas Levet

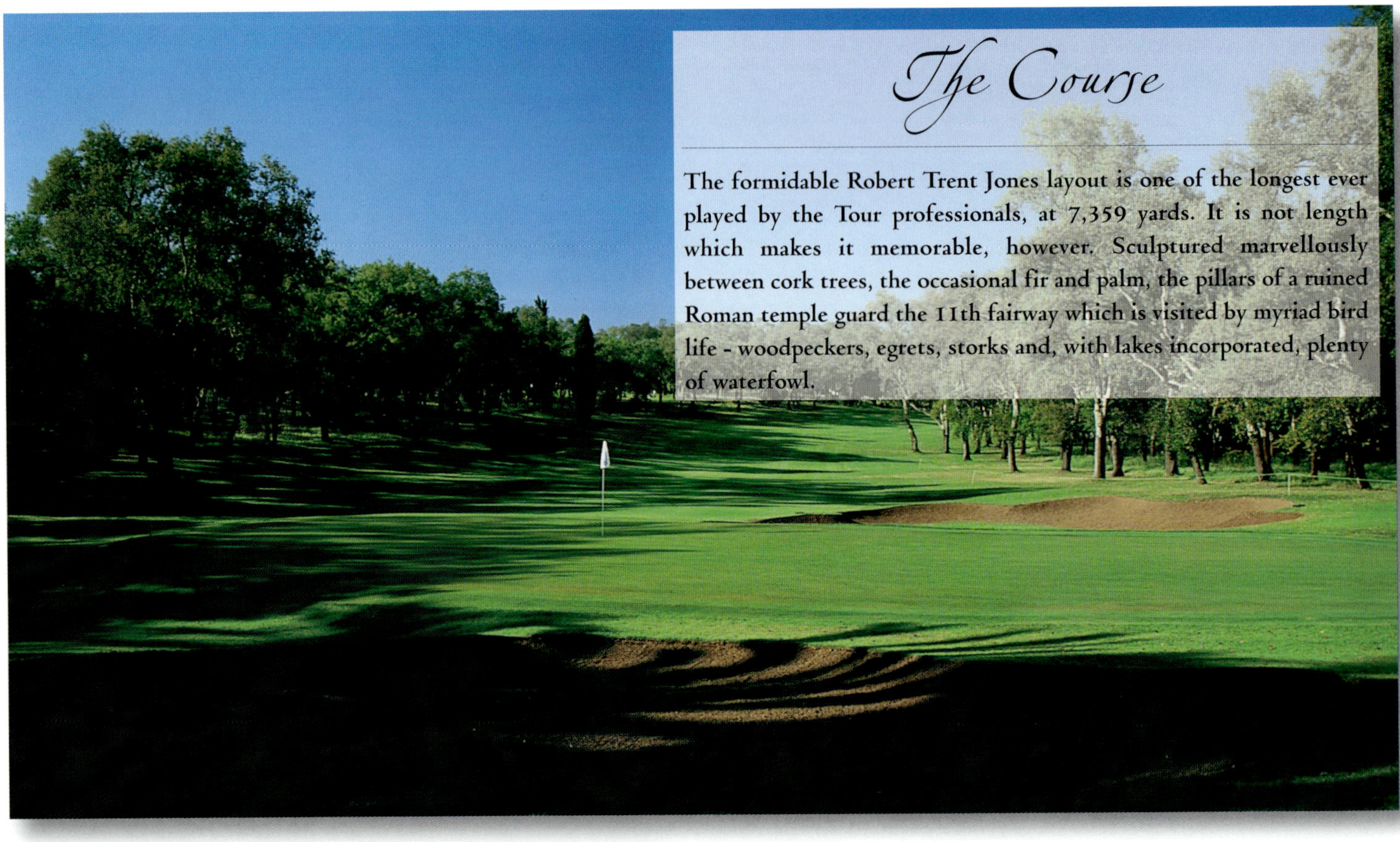

The Course

The formidable Robert Trent Jones layout is one of the longest ever played by the Tour professionals, at 7,359 yards. It is not length which makes it memorable, however. Sculptured marvellously between cork trees, the occasional fir and palm, the pillars of a ruined Roman temple guard the 11th fairway which is visited by myriad bird life - woodpeckers, egrets, storks and, with lakes incorporated, plenty of waterfowl.

Gary Clark

The final round witnessed Poulter with his back to the wall as his chief weapon of the week seemed blunted from its earlier endeavours. While his trusty putter found the target at the second from 25 feet to increase his lead, from there it betrayed him time and again. It needed a supreme eagle on the tenth to settle his escalating nerves. From there the golfing gladiator could again rely on his putter as a series of vital saves kept him always two strokes better than anyone else.

Opponents came and went but Poulter vanquished them all until there was but one, an English contemporary David Lynn. Lynn's attack came with a thrilling run of birdies, but not sufficient enough to deny the Gladiator slaying "David" on this occasion.

Norman Dabell

Peter Lonard and caddie Ken Herring

ROYAL GOLF DAR ES SALAM, RABAT, MOROCCO, 12-15 APRIL, 2001, PAR 73, 7359 YARDS, 6729 METRES

Pos.	Name		Rd1	Rd2	Rd3	Rd4	Total	Par	Prize Money Euro	£
1	Ian POULTER	Eng	71	67	69	70	277	-15	106506.68	66660.00
2	David LYNN	Eng	72	72	68	67	279	-13	71004.45	44440.00
3	Peter LONARD	Aus	71	75	66	68	280	-12	40007.91	25040.00
4	Thomas LEVET	Fr	73	68	70	71	282	-10	29526.61	18480.00
	Stephen GALLACHER	Scot	72	72	70	68	282	-10	29526.61	18480.00
6	Gary EVANS	Eng	70	75	66	72	283	-9	20770.88	13000.00
	Greg OWEN	Eng	73	70	70	70	283	-9	20770.88	13000.00
8	Peter HANSON	Swe	73	71	68	72	284	-8	13708.78	8580.00
	Paul MCGINLEY	Ire	67	75	70	72	284	-8	13708.78	8580.00
	Federico BISAZZA	It	72	71	69	72	284	-8	13708.78	8580.00
	Hank KUEHNE	USA	71	71	71	71	284	-8	13708.78	8580.00
12	Robert KARLSSON	Swe	70	71	70	74	285	-7	10992.59	6880.00
13	Gary EMERSON	Eng	73	72	68	73	286	-6	10033.93	6280.00
	Paolo QUIRICI	Swi	73	69	71	73	286	-6	10033.93	6280.00
15	Kenneth FERRIE	Eng	72	73	75	67	287	-5	8819.64	5520.00
	Craig HAINLINE	USA	68	72	73	74	287	-5	8819.64	5520.00
	Olivier EDMOND	Fr	71	72	70	74	287	-5	8819.64	5520.00
	Sam WALKER	Eng	69	76	67	75	287	-5	8819.64	5520.00
19	Andrew SHERBORNE	Eng	72	72	70	74	288	-4	7451.95	4664.00
	Peter FOWLER	Aus	74	72	68	74	288	-4	7451.95	4664.00
	Andrew MARSHALL	Eng	72	74	71	71	288	-4	7451.95	4664.00
	Jean HUGO	SA	71	74	70	73	288	-4	7451.95	4664.00
	Christophe POTTIER	Fr	73	69	71	75	288	-4	7451.95	4664.00
24	Wayne RILEY	Aus	71	74	73	71	289	-3	6263.22	3920.00
	Søren KJELDSEN	Den	71	72	71	75	289	-3	6263.22	3920.00
	Jean-François LUCQUIN	Fr	73	73	70	73	289	-3	6263.22	3920.00
	Carl SUNESON	Sp	74	71	72	72	289	-3	6263.22	3920.00
	Bradley DREDGE	Wal	70	76	70	73	289	-3	6263.22	3920.00
	Andrew COLTART	Scot	75	72	71	71	289	-3	6263.22	3920.00
	Simon DYSON	Eng	72	73	72	72	289	-3	6263.22	3920.00
31	Roger CHAPMAN	Eng	72	74	68	76	290	-2	4633.50	2900.00
	Raphaël JACQUELIN	Fr	71	75	70	74	290	-2	4633.50	2900.00
	Bradford VAUGHAN	SA	76	71	73	70	290	-2	4633.50	2900.00
	Hennie OTTO	SA	74	70	72	74	290	-2	4633.50	2900.00
	Trevor IMMELMAN	SA	74	74	71	71	290	-2	4633.50	2900.00
	Henrik BJORNSTAD	Nor	71	74	69	76	290	-2	4633.50	2900.00
	Simon D. HURLEY	Eng	77	69	71	73	290	-2	4633.50	2900.00
	Gregory HAVRET	Fr	73	70	72	75	290	-2	4633.50	2900.00
	Raimo SJÖBERG	Swe	74	70	72	74	290	-2	4633.50	2900.00
	Michael JONZON	Swe	68	75	72	75	290	-2	4633.50	2900.00
	Erol SIMSEK	Ger	71	75	72	72	290	-2	4633.50	2900.00
	Tobias DIER	Ger	71	75	73	71	290	-2	4633.50	2900.00
43	Anders FORSBRAND	Swe	73	71	73	74	291	-1	3515.07	2200.00
	Graham RANKIN	Scot	73	75	70	73	291	-1	3515.07	2200.00
	Massimo FLORIOLI	It	74	69	72	76	291	-1	3515.07	2200.00
	Gustavo ROJAS	Arg	75	70	72	74	291	-1	3515.07	2200.00
	Francis VALERA	Sp	73	74	70	74	291	-1	3515.07	2200.00
48	Marc FARRY	Fr	71	74	70	77	292	0	2812.06	1760.00
	Elliot BOULT	NZ	75	72	73	72	292	0	2812.06	1760.00
	Justin ROSE	Eng	75	71	69	77	292	0	2812.06	1760.00
	Massimo SCARPA	It	72	73	72	75	292	0	2812.06	1760.00
	Nic HENNING	SA	76	70	72	74	292	0	2812.06	1760.00
	James MCLEAN	Aus	74	68	74	76	292	0	2812.06	1760.00
54	Mark ROE	Eng	76	72	74	71	293	1	2036.00	1274.28
	Jean-Francois REMESY	Fr	72	74	73	74	293	1	2036.00	1274.28
	José ROMERO	Sp	73	72	75	73	293	1	2036.00	1274.28
	Didier DE VOOGHT	Bel	72	71	74	76	293	1	2036.00	1274.28
	Paul STREETER	Eng	72	76	71	74	293	1	2036.00	1274.28
	Gary CLARK	Eng	76	72	71	74	293	1	2036.00	1274.28
	David PARK	Wal	69	73	74	77	293	1	2036.00	1274.28
	Abdelkader EL HALI (AM)	Mor	74	74	70	75	293	1		
62	Malcolm MACKENZIE	Eng	72	70	73	79	294	2	1693.63	1060.00
	Raymond RUSSELL	Scot	71	75	76	72	294	2	1693.63	1060.00
	Nick DOUGHERTY (AM)	Eng	76	69	73	76	294	2		
65	Johan RYSTRÖM	Swe	73	73	74	75	295	3	1469.94	920.00
	Andrew BEAL	Eng	76	71	73	75	295	3	1469.94	920.00
	Stephen DODD	Wal	75	73	70	77	295	3	1469.94	920.00
	Adam MEDNICK	Swe	73	75	73	74	295	3	1469.94	920.00
	John BICKERTON	Eng	74	70	75	76	295	3	1469.94	920.00
70	Philip WALTON	Ire	71	71	75	79	296	4	1158.46	725.05
	Peter MITCHELL	Eng	75	72	74	75	296	4	1158.46	725.05
	Markus BRIER	Aut	74	74	75	73	296	4	1158.46	725.05
	Matthew BLACKEY	Eng	73	72	76	75	296	4	1158.46	725.05
74	Nils ROERBAEK	Den	73	75	75	74	297	5	954.50	597.40
	Dennis EDLUND	Swe	76	71	71	79	297	5	954.50	597.40
76	John WADE	Aus	75	71	74	78	298	6	947.00	592.70
	Russell CLAYDON	Eng	78	70	74	76	298	6	947.00	592.70
	Alastair FORSYTH	Scot	73	72	79	74	298	6	947.00	592.70
79	Andrew RAITT	Eng	72	74	77	76	299	7	939.50	588.01
	Benoit TEILLERIA	Fr	74	73	70	82	299	7	939.50	588.01
81	Neil CHEETHAM	Eng	68	76	74	82	300	8	933.50	584.26
	Juan A VIZCAYA	Sp	76	72	79	73	300	8	933.50	584.26
83	Roger WINCHESTER	Eng	75	73	75	78	301	9	929.00	581.44
84	Pascal EDMOND	Fr	72	76	73	81	302	10	926.00	579.56
85	Ross DRUMMOND	Scot	72	76	75	81	304	12	923.00	577.68

VIA DIGITAL OPEN DE ESPAÑA

Road to Damascus

EL SALER, VALENCIA, SPAIN

His greatest fear was that he would allow himself to get in front of himself. He had done it before, and it had cost him dear. This time it absolutely had to be different, and he made sure it was by not allowing anybody to get in front of him. The journey through the Via Digital Open de España was Robert Karlsson's road to Damascus, and the conversion he underwent was profound indeed.

Jean-Francois Remesy

During the week that brought the tall and elegant Swede the fourth victory of his European Tour career, he admitted that he was a moody character who, in the past, had been prone to get over-excited when in good positions and excessively depressed when things were not going so well. In 2000 he had had more bad times than good and had paid for it by finishing 114th in the Volvo Order of Merit.

It was a salutary lesson. This could not be allowed to continue. A stern re-appraisal was called for, but it had proved easier to hope for than to achieve. During the four days on the outskirts of Valencia, Spain's second city, he confessed again to a preference for attacking from behind rather than defending from in front, similar sentiments to those he had expressed during a valiant display in the Qatar Masters a few short weeks before.

His rationale was that if he were leading, there was only one way to go, and that was backwards. Among the dunes of the magnificent El Saler course, he discovered there was another choice, and that was to stay in front. Which is exactly what he did, with a total of 277, 11 under par, two strokes ahead of Jean-Francois Remesy, with Søren Hansen and Miguel Angel Jiménez third a further shot behind.

For the third tournament in succession, Karlsson played in the last group on the course on the final day. The man who hated leading was easing nicely into the job and he discovered that, on the whole, it was not so bad after all. A year before, if given the choice of being

Darren Clarke

Shot of the Week

Robert Karlsson was level with Darren Clarke going into the final round, but made an immediate impact on the first hole they played. A perfectly struck seven iron left him only 12 feet from the hole, and he made the putt for birdie. So is it the pitch or the putt that takes the accolade? Take your pick. Neither would have been possible without the other.

on top of a leaderboard at the start of the final day of a golf tournament or endeavouring to knit scrambled eggs, he would have called for the hen-fruit every time. No more - the eggs could go and boil in their own water.

Karlsson is tall. Very tall. At 6 feet 5 inches in his stockinged feet, he is the loftiest player on The European Tour. When his hand scratches the top of his head, it's in danger of going down with altitude sickness. In winter-time in his native Malmo, the upper reaches of his frame would run the risk of being covered in snow.

For that reason, among others, he now lives in Monaco, the tiny state where there are no taxes worth mentioning, a climate in which sustained rainfall is no more than an empty rumour and an ambience that reduces the rich and famous to the ranks of the ordinary citizen.

Walk down the streets of Monte Carlo, the town within a state, and you'll be lucky not to trip over a world-class Formula One driver, a big-name tennis player or an A-group golfer. Now, if he bent down ever so slightly, Karlsson could look them all in the eye as an equal.

He won this tournament in some considerable style. A 68 put him in a tie for eighth place after a first round that was dominated by Andrew Oldcorn, the Scot who had once been English, with a 64, but who would go on to finish tied for 32nd. Darren Clarke, who was to feature so dramatically later in the tournament, was three strokes adrift.

Søren Hansen and caddie Tim King

On the second day another 68 pushed Karlsson up into a share of third place, a stroke behind the emerging Clarke, who had an identical score, and Andrew Raitt, a surprise packet who eventually shared 16th place.

Like all links courses, El Saler is at its most testing when the wind pays a visit, and a gusty Saturday sorted *los hombres* from *los ninos*. Clarke, in his element in the conditions, had a 72. More crucially, Karlsson outscored him by a stroke, which meant that, in the company of Hansen, the young Dane, they would be playing together on the final day having finished on nine under par.

The scene was set for a classic confrontation between the willowy and stylish Swede and the sturdy, steadfast Ulsterman. Elegance won, hands down.

Karlsson made the first impact with a birdie on the opening hole and continued serenely, a man under total control of his mind and his game. One by one there were small bursts of activity from down the field, most notably from Remesy, who had seven birdies in his 66, the best round of the day.

But Karlsson had a plan of attack that involved nothing more ambitious than making sure of his pars and taking the birdie chances on the important holes. It worked perfectly.

Clarke was going along nicely without threatening Karlsson's hegemony until calamity struck on the par five 15th. He hit his drive into trees on the left then planted his second stroke into bushes on the right. He finally emerged from the thicket with the last of three increasingly desperate flails, came up short in six, went through the green with his seventh blow, chipped back and two-putted for a catastrophic ten.

The entire episode had taken no more than a few minutes, but they must have seemed like hours for Clarke. When he started the hole he had been tied for third place. When he finished it, he was down among the dead men in joint 32nd.

And that is where he stayed as Karlsson took the applause after a closing 70 that gave him a precious victory. No more would he worry about leading. No more would he have to concern himself with only being able to go backwards. He had found, to his benefit, that there was a lot to be said for staying exactly where he was.

Mel Webb

The Course

El Saler is acknowledged as one of the finest courses in all of Europe, and it did nothing to damage its status on this week. Darren Clarke entered the tournament purely because it was being played where it was, and there were scores of his peers who felt the same way about the peerless Valencian layout. Truly, a prince among golf courses.

Ian Woosnam

EL SALER, VALENCIA, SPAIN, 19-22 APRIL, 2001, PAR 72, 6952 YARDS, 6357 METRES

Pos.	Name		Rd1	Rd2	Rd3	Rd4	Total	Par	Prize Money Euro	£
1	Robert KARLSSON	Swe	68	68	71	70	277	-11	200000.00	123839.78
2	Jean-Francois REMESY	Fr	66	72	75	66	279	-9	133330.00	82557.79
3	Miguel Angel JIMÉNEZ	Sp	71	69	70	70	280	-8	67560.00	41833.08
	Søren HANSEN	Den	68	71	70	71	280	-8	67560.00	41833.08
5	Peter MITCHELL	Eng	71	72	71	67	281	-7	42960.00	26600.78
	Joakim HAEGGMAN	Swe	70	71	71	69	281	-7	42960.00	26600.78
	Gustavo ROJAS	Arg	72	69	74	66	281	-7	42960.00	26600.78
8	Raphaël JACQUELIN	Fr	74	71	72	65	282	-6	30000.00	18575.97
9	Malcolm MACKENZIE	Eng	72	67	74	70	283	-5	21274.29	13173.02
	Justin ROSE	Eng	70	73	72	68	283	-5	21274.29	13173.02
	Gary EMERSON	Eng	71	69	71	72	283	-5	21274.29	13173.02
	Domingo HOSPITAL	Sp	70	74	70	69	283	-5	21274.29	13173.02
	Jean HUGO	SA	70	72	69	72	283	-5	21274.29	13173.02
	Stephen SCAHILL	NZ	70	68	74	71	283	-5	21274.29	13173.02
	Jarmo SANDELIN	Swe	70	66	76	71	283	-5	21274.29	13173.02
16	Warren BENNETT	Eng	69	70	75	70	284	-4	15051.43	9319.83
	Sergio GARCIA	Sp	69	73	71	71	284	-4	15051.43	9319.83
	Steve WEBSTER	Eng	69	70	73	72	284	-4	15051.43	9319.83
	Jonathan LOMAS	Eng	70	69	74	71	284	-4	15051.43	9319.83
	Peter LONARD	Aus	71	72	72	69	284	-4	15051.43	9319.83
	Andrew RAITT	Eng	67	68	79	70	284	-4	15051.43	9319.83
	Carl PETTERSSON	Swe	67	69	74	74	284	-4	15051.43	9319.83
23	Gordon BRAND JNR.	Scot	71	72	73	69	285	-3	11760.00	7281.78
	Miguel Angel MARTIN	Sp	70	71	70	74	285	-3	11760.00	7281.78
	Søren KJELDSEN	Den	71	69	71	74	285	-3	11760.00	7281.78
	Gregory HAVRET	Fr	75	70	71	69	285	-3	11760.00	7281.78
	Thomas GÖGELE	Ger	68	72	76	69	285	-3	11760.00	7281.78
	Olle KARLSSON	Swe	72	71	74	68	285	-3	11760.00	7281.78
	Greg OWEN	Eng	70	73	73	69	285	-3	11760.00	7281.78
	Andrew COLTART	Scot	69	68	79	69	285	-3	11760.00	7281.78
	Dean ROBERTSON	Scot	71	70	71	73	285	-3	11760.00	7281.78
32	Andrew OLDCORN	Scot	64	73	78	71	286	-2	8676.00	5372.17
	Jose Manuel LARA	Sp	70	73	70	73	286	-2	8676.00	5372.17
	David GILFORD	Eng	71	71	73	71	286	-2	8676.00	5372.17
	Desvonde BOTES	SA	69	71	77	69	286	-2	8676.00	5372.17
	Nicolas COLSAERTS	Bel	76	69	74	67	286	-2	8676.00	5372.17
	Jarrod MOSELEY	Aus	70	74	72	70	286	-2	8676.00	5372.17
	Ian GARBUTT	Eng	68	74	73	71	286	-2	8676.00	5372.17
	Nicolas VANHOOTEGEM	Bel	75	70	72	69	286	-2	8676.00	5372.17
	Darren CLARKE	N.Ire	67	68	72	79	286	-2	8676.00	5372.17
	Raymond RUSSELL	Scot	72	69	76	69	286	-2	8676.00	5372.17
42	Des SMYTH	Ire	70	72	75	70	287	-1	6600.00	4086.71
	Jesus Maria ARRUTI	Sp	73	68	74	72	287	-1	6600.00	4086.71
	Neil CHEETHAM	Eng	73	71	74	69	287	-1	6600.00	4086.71
	Peter O'MALLEY	Aus	73	69	75	70	287	-1	6600.00	4086.71
	Fredrik JACOBSON	Swe	72	72	73	70	287	-1	6600.00	4086.71
	Stephen GALLACHER	Scot	72	72	69	74	287	-1	6600.00	4086.71
	Christopher HANELL	Swe	71	73	69	74	287	-1	6600.00	4086.71
49	Anders FORSBRAND	Swe	76	69	73	70	288	0	4680.00	2897.85
	Sven STRÜVER	Ger	72	72	74	70	288	0	4680.00	2897.85
	Michele REALE	It	73	71	76	68	288	0	4680.00	2897.85
	Gary EVANS	Eng	71	74	74	69	288	0	4680.00	2897.85
	Phillip PRICE	Wal	70	74	71	73	288	0	4680.00	2897.85
	Christian CEVAER	Fr	76	69	74	69	288	0	4680.00	2897.85
	Van PHILLIPS	Eng	74	70	72	72	288	0	4680.00	2897.85
	David LYNN	Eng	69	75	73	71	288	0	4680.00	2897.85
	Graeme STORM	Eng	70	71	75	72	288	0	4680.00	2897.85
58	David HOWELL	Eng	72	72	75	70	289	1	3300.00	2043.36
	Anders HANSEN	Den	75	69	72	73	289	1	3300.00	2043.36
	Diego BORREGO	Sp	69	72	74	74	289	1	3300.00	2043.36
	Ignacio GARRIDO	Sp	71	73	75	70	289	1	3300.00	2043.36
	Markus BRIER	Aut	75	70	73	71	289	1	3300.00	2043.36
	Simon DYSON	Eng	72	71	75	71	289	1	3300.00	2043.36
64	Andrew SHERBORNE	Eng	73	68	73	76	290	2	2524.29	1563.04
	Graham RANKIN	Scot	67	72	74	77	290	2	2524.29	1563.04
	Raul BALLESTEROS	Sp	70	73	72	75	290	2	2524.29	1563.04
	John BICKERTON	Eng	71	67	77	75	290	2	2524.29	1563.04
	Erol SIMSEK	Ger	74	69	79	68	290	2	2524.29	1563.04
	Mikael LUNDBERG	Swe	69	76	73	72	290	2	2524.29	1563.04
	Alastair FORSYTH	Scot	72	72	78	68	290	2	2524.29	1563.04
71	Santiago LUNA	Sp	73	71	76	71	291	3	1795.50	1111.77
	John SENDEN	Aus	74	71	75	71	291	3	1795.50	1111.77
	Patrik SJÖLAND	Swe	74	71	75	71	291	3	1795.50	1111.77
	Daren LEE	Eng	71	71	78	71	291	3	1795.50	1111.77
75	Carlos RODILES	Sp	67	77	76	72	292	4	1785.00	1105.27
	Fernando ROCA	Sp	71	73	71	77	292	4	1785.00	1105.27
	Fredrik ANDERSSON	Swe	70	74	75	73	292	4	1785.00	1105.27
78	Mark MOULAND	Wal	74	71	76	72	293	5	1779.00	1101.55
79	Johan RYSTRÖM	Swe	72	72	78	72	294	6	1774.50	1098.77
	Francis VALERA	Sp	69	72	77	76	294	6	1774.50	1098.77
81	Juan QUIROS	Sp	72	73	78	72	295	7	1770.00	1095.98
82	Tom WHITEHOUSE (AM)	Eng	71	74	79	74	298	10		
83	Brian DAVIS	Eng	72	73	81	76	302	14	1767.00	1094.12

Inner Strength

QUINTA DO LAGO, ALGARVE, PORTUGAL

Phillip Price had to wait more than a year for revenge, but when it came at Quinta do Lago it was absolute.

Fourteen months after being denied by a stunning Gary Orr eagle three at Penina's last hole, the 34 year old Welshman with the grey flecked hair and soft Rhonnda accent became the Algarve Open de Portugal champion for the second time with an irresistible 15 under par aggregate of 273.

In 1994 at Penha Longa he led virtually from start to finish. This time, through a capricious breeze and four days of unbroken sunshine, he made up the ground on the final day as spectacularly as a Welsh wing forward on the rugby field.

When Price began his fourth round at Quinta he had 14 players ahead of him. It seemed the 166,660 euro (£104,330) winner's cheque was destined to find its way into the hands of one of five players sharing the lead at 11 under par, England's Simon Dyson and David Gilford, Ireland's Padraig Harrington, New Zealand's Stephen Scahill and Germany's Sven Strüver.

A multiple play-off looked the most likely outcome. But, almost as quickly as it takes fellow Pontypriddian, Neil Jenkins, to kick a penalty goal, Price, was in the midst of the battle. Though built entirely differently, the Welshman's all-black outfit reminded some of us of a charging Gary Player in his heyday.

With five birdies in the first six holes, he tore through a faltering field and by the finish of an eight under par 64, which contained ten birdies in all, he was home with two shots to spare. This time it was right for Price. His seven year wait for his second victory on The European Tour was over.

Yet his immediate reaction was not of elation, but of relief. "I've finished second so many times that I was thinking over the last three holes, 'I do not want to blow this'," he said. "I've found it difficult to win, so to get the job done was very, very pleasing."

While hinting to a previous lack of belief, Price paved the way to this triumph six months earlier when he finished joint runner-up with Justin Leonard to Tiger Woods in the World Golf Championships-NEC Invitational in Akron, Ohio. To perform so

Sven Strüver

Padraig Harrington

The Course

Quinta do Lago is suprisingly hilly, and with so many trees, it requires accuracy and careful positioning from the tee, not an easy task since, being near the Atlantic coast, Quinta is rarely without a wind. The signature hole is the short 15th, which is played over a yawning lake to a well guarded green.

Ignacio Garrido

brilliantly in that company and on foreign soil proved to others, and, most importantly, to himself, that he had the inner strength as well as the game to compete at the highest level.

As it turned out, this 44th Algarve Open de Portugal, first won in 1953 by Eric Brown, was a tale of two golfers who have struggled to rid themselves of the tag of perennial runner-up.

Price felt it after losing to Orr's closing eagle at Penina in 2000 and again to José Maria Olazábal's eagle at the 17th a few weeks later in the Benson and Hedges International Open at The De Vere Belfry. Although by April in Portugal, Harrington had won three times in Europe, he also had to bear the frustration of having finished second 11 times.

A 12th "bridesmaid's" position did not look likely for the Irishman when he began with a 64 and held the lead, or a share of it, through the second and third rounds with scores of 70 and 71. However, the putter which served him so wonderfully well initially failed to function so tellingly on the final day.

He missed three times from inside 12 feet over the last four holes and was consigned to a share of second place with Strüver on 275, 13 under par.

Harrington could cite mitigating circumstances. While the Quinta do Lago fairways were as good as you would have found anywhere in the world, the grainy greens at times presented unexpected difficulties, especially late in the afternoon following a day's golfing traffic.

The wonder is that with 60,000 holiday rounds being played per annum, they were as good as they were. In any case, Price did not have a problem with them during his final flourish.

The drama of the final day brought smiles back to the faces of the organisers, devastated on the Friday evening by the favourite and former champion Colin Montgomerie's failure to make the "cut", rounds of 73 and 72 leaving him one shot beyond the 144 limit.

"I shouldn't be missing cuts", said Montgomerie before heading for Faro Airport and an extra week off to work on his game.

In the shake-up a younger Scot, Alastair Forsyth, once again showed his potential by climbing into equal fourth place alongside Ignacio Garrido and Scahill with a closing 69, which contained three birdies and an eagle from the 12th.

Jock MacVicar

Stephen Scahill

Alastair Forsyth

Shot of the Week

A tough choice between Phillip Price's chip-in for a birdie three at the 16th in the final round and Alastair Forsyth's five wood to eight feet for an eagle three at the 17th in the same round.
Price's holed chip showed the mettle of the man, having taken three putts on the previous green. However, in terms of a quality strike, Forsyth's towering five wood in the testing breeze at a time when more than half a dozen players were competing for the major prizes just edged it.

David Gilford

QUINTA DO LAGO, ALGARVE, PORTUGAL, 26-29 APRIL, 2001, PAR 72, 7099 YARDS, 6491 METRES

Pos.	Name		Rd1	Rd2	Rd3	Rd4	Total	Par	Prize Money Euro	Prize Money £
1	Phillip PRICE	Wal	72	67	70	64	273	-15	166660.00	104330.08
2	Padraig HARRINGTON	Ire	64	70	71	70	275	-13	86855.00	54371.71
	Sven STRÜVER	Ger	70	70	65	70	275	-13	86855.00	54371.71
4	Ignacio GARRIDO	Sp	69	68	70	70	277	-11	42466.67	26584.37
	Stephen SCAHILL	NZ	70	69	66	72	277	-11	42466.67	26584.37
	Alastair FORSYTH	Scot	68	68	72	69	277	-11	42466.67	26584.37
7	Alex CEJKA	Ger	70	73	70	65	278	-10	27500.00	17215.15
	Brett RUMFORD	Aus	74	68	67	69	278	-10	27500.00	17215.15
9	David HOWELL	Eng	67	70	69	73	279	-9	18233.33	11414.17
	Warren BENNETT	Eng	70	70	70	69	279	-9	18233.33	11414.17
	David GILFORD	Eng	66	70	69	74	279	-9	18233.33	11414.17
	Russell CLAYDON	Eng	70	72	71	66	279	-9	18233.33	11414.17
	Niclas FASTH	Swe	66	72	68	73	279	-9	18233.33	11414.17
	Simon DYSON	Eng	69	69	67	74	279	-9	18233.33	11414.17
15	Brian DAVIS	Eng	71	71	73	65	280	-8	13800.00	8638.88
	Elliot BOULT	NZ	67	73	69	71	280	-8	13800.00	8638.88
	Roger WESSELS	SA	73	68	66	73	280	-8	13800.00	8638.88
	Mikael LUNDBERG	Swe	70	72	69	69	280	-8	13800.00	8638.88
19	Santiago LUNA	Sp	71	70	72	68	281	-7	11342.86	7100.69
	Anders HANSEN	Den	68	71	69	73	281	-7	11342.86	7100.69
	Maarten LAFEBER	Hol	72	71	71	67	281	-7	11342.86	7100.69
	Richard GREEN	Aus	71	72	69	69	281	-7	11342.86	7100.69
	Trevor IMMELMAN	SA	68	73	67	73	281	-7	11342.86	7100.69
	David PARK	Wal	70	71	69	71	281	-7	11342.86	7100.69
	Patrik SJÖLAND	Swe	67	72	70	72	281	-7	11342.86	7100.69
	Nick DOUGHERTY (AM)	Eng	71	72	71	67	281	-7		
27	Roger CHAPMAN	Eng	68	70	72	72	282	-6	8760.00	5483.81
	Greg TURNER	NZ	69	74	69	70	282	-6	8760.00	5483.81
	Hennie OTTO	SA	71	73	70	68	282	-6	8760.00	5483.81
	Henrik STENSON	Swe	70	73	68	71	282	-6	8760.00	5483.81
	Nicolas COLSAERTS	Bel	71	70	70	71	282	-6	8760.00	5483.81
	Jeremy ROBINSON	Eng	71	68	72	71	282	-6	8760.00	5483.81
	Paolo QUIRICI	Swi	73	71	71	67	282	-6	8760.00	5483.81
	Joakim HAEGGMAN	Swe	68	72	68	74	282	-6	8760.00	5483.81
	Markus BRIER	Aut	70	72	69	71	282	-6	8760.00	5483.81
	Andrew COLTART	Scot	75	68	68	71	282	-6	8760.00	5483.81
37	Malcolm MACKENZIE	Eng	70	72	68	73	283	-5	6700.00	4194.24
	Søren KJELDSEN	Den	73	70	69	71	283	-5	6700.00	4194.24
	Desvonde BOTES	SA	73	69	71	70	283	-5	6700.00	4194.24
	Gregory HAVRET	Fr	71	72	75	65	283	-5	6700.00	4194.24
	Robin BYRD	USA	72	71	67	73	283	-5	6700.00	4194.24
	Paul MCGINLEY	Ire	71	69	70	73	283	-5	6700.00	4194.24
	Ricardo GONZALEZ	Arg	68	71	68	76	283	-5	6700.00	4194.24
44	Anders FORSBRAND	Swe	70	69	71	74	284	-4	5100.00	3192.63
	Ian WOOSNAM	Wal	74	70	69	71	284	-4	5100.00	3192.63
	Peter FOWLER	Aus	71	69	71	73	284	-4	5100.00	3192.63
	Steve WEBSTER	Eng	69	74	70	71	284	-4	5100.00	3192.63
	Francisco CEA	Sp	71	73	66	74	284	-4	5100.00	3192.63
	Jarmo SANDELIN	Swe	72	71	69	72	284	-4	5100.00	3192.63
	Henrik NYSTROM	Swe	72	71	71	70	284	-4	5100.00	3192.63
	John BICKERTON	Eng	69	73	70	72	284	-4	5100.00	3192.63
	David HIGGINS	Ire	66	77	72	69	284	-4	5100.00	3192.63
53	Mark MOULAND	Wal	70	70	73	72	285	-3	3514.29	2199.96
	Justin ROSE	Eng	70	71	74	70	285	-3	3514.29	2199.96
	Massimo SCARPA	It	76	66	74	69	285	-3	3514.29	2199.96
	Gustavo ROJAS	Arg	72	69	70	74	285	-3	3514.29	2199.96
	Bradley DREDGE	Wal	72	71	71	71	285	-3	3514.29	2199.96
	Raymond RUSSELL	Scot	72	71	69	73	285	-3	3514.29	2199.96
	Matthew BLACKEY	Eng	68	75	71	71	285	-3	3514.29	2199.96
60	Mark DAVIS	Eng	70	74	72	70	286	-2	2600.00	1627.61
	Justin HOBDAY	SA	70	70	76	70	286	-2	2600.00	1627.61
	Paul EALES	Eng	74	70	69	73	286	-2	2600.00	1627.61
	Johan RYSTRÖM	Swe	71	73	74	68	286	-2	2600.00	1627.61
	Mathias GRÖNBERG	Swe	72	71	74	69	286	-2	2600.00	1627.61
	Tomas Jesus MUÑOZ	Sp	68	75	70	73	286	-2	2600.00	1627.61
	David LYNN	Eng	66	75	76	69	286	-2	2600.00	1627.61
67	Manuel PIÑERO	Sp	75	68	72	72	287	-1	2006.00	1255.77
	Domingo HOSPITAL	Sp	70	73	72	72	287	-1	2006.00	1255.77
	Jorge BERENDT	Arg	68	75	68	76	287	-1	2006.00	1255.77
	Paul STREETER	Eng	72	72	68	75	287	-1	2006.00	1255.77
	Hank KUEHNE	USA	71	69	73	74	287	-1	2006.00	1255.77
72	Andrew OLDCORN	Scot	70	74	72	72	288	0	1497.00	937.13
	Ian POULTER	Eng	67	76	75	70	288	0	1497.00	937.13
	Roger WINCHESTER	Eng	69	74	71	74	288	0	1497.00	937.13
75	Kenneth FERRIE	Eng	68	74	70	77	289	1	1491.00	933.37
	Nuno CAMPINO (AM)	Port	72	71	74	72	289	1		
	David PRICE (AM)	Eng	70	73	72	74	289	1		
78	Shaun P WEBSTER	Eng	70	74	71	75	290	2	1485.00	929.62
	Christian CéVAËR	Fr	71	70	76	73	290	2	1485.00	929.62
	Andrew RAITT	Eng	70	74	73	73	290	2	1485.00	929.62
81	Craig HAINLINE	USA	72	69	73	77	291	3	1479.00	925.86
82	José RIVERO	Sp	70	74	76	73	293	5	1476.00	923.98

PROQUIP
BBC SPORT
Don't put your name
to anything less
ENGLISH GOLF UNION
Our total commitment to research, development and quality ensures each garment is designed to provide consistent protection - whatever the conditions.
Official Supplier since 1983
ENGLISH GOLF UNION
OFFICIAL SUPPLIER
Winning Weatherwear™
Part of Caledonian Golf Group
North Berwick, Scotland.
When you put your name on an item of sportswear, the choice you make speaks volumes about your company or club. So choose golf weatherwear that's acknowledged as the best you can buy. For more information, please call sales on 01620 892 219.

Staying Focused

LYON GOLF CLUB, VILLETTE D'ANTHON, FRANCE

José Maria Olazábal's victory in the Novotel Perrier Open de France at the Lyon Golf Club was a masterclass in mind over matter, a triumph of character and determination and a steely will-to-win over technical frailty and elements which taxed physical and mental strength to near breaking point.

Two Masters Tournament victories at Augusta National and 18 previous European Tour triumphs clearly indicated that the 35 year old Spaniard should have started favourite on paper, but, in reality, favourite he certainly was not.

He had finished 15th in the 2001 Masters Tournament but eight US Tour starts had yielded only three top 25 placings. On his only previous European Tour outing, in the Via Digital Open de España, he had failed embarrassingly to qualify for the final two rounds and warned: "My driving is still weak."

When torrential overnight rain flooded the Sangliers course forcing Tournament Director Mike Stewart, who had already ruled preferred lies would be permitted, to delay the start by four hours, the omens were not good.

Shot of the Week

Ireland's Paddy Gribben, on only his third Tour outing of the year, needed something special to happen after slipping back to four under par following three opening 68s and it came at the par four 16th, where he pitched straight into the hole from 152 yards with an eight iron for an eagle two en route to a closing 70, and a career best joint tenth prize of 21,505 euro (£13,362).

By the time play got under way, with the 571 yards fifth "shrunk" on Stewart's orders to a 177 yards par three and thus overall par from 72 to 70, the players, many of whom had left their beds before 6am for breakfast time tee-offs, were eager to get to the first tee.

Olazábal admitted: "It was a long delay and changed the whole day." The Spaniard's sensible solution was to find a quiet corner and snatch 40 winks. "I slept for 45 minutes and awoke refreshed," he declared.

An opening 66 left him tied seventh, three behind Australian Jarrod Moseley, with Daren Lee, an Englishman who prefers to walk and chart courses instead of playing practice rounds, shooting 64. Moseley in fact, completed his first round the next day, and the second round had to be suspended the following afternoon, another two and a half hours being lost to more heavy rain.

Greens and tees stood up magnificently to the deluge but a resumption was impossible before 3pm on Saturday - seven hours behind schedule.

Marc Farry

The Course

Constructed in 1991 and officially opened the following year the Sangliers course was designed by French architect Hugues Lambert and is carved through woodland at Villette d'Anthon 30 minutes drive from France's second city of Lyon. Six holes are adjacent to the River Rhone and water comes into play on eight.

Gregory Havret

With more that 13 hours lost to the elements it meant that the first two rounds were only finally completed on Saturday, by which time, Frenchman Marc Farry, with rounds of 68 and 65, led by one from young compatriot Gregory Havret and Denmark's Anders Hansen, with Olazábal tied fourth one further back.

Farry's one Tour victory had come in the 1996 BMW International Open in Munich when it was reduced to two rounds by flooding. Mike Stewart was the Tournament Director that week, too, but in Lyon a marginally more promising weather forecast encouraged him, in line with Tour policy, to stick with a cut to 70 and ties and target a full 72 holes. It meant another dawn two-tee start and a snatched sandwich for players and caddies between the third and fourth rounds.

A cut at level par - French Number One Jean Van de Velde missed by a stroke - left a logjam of 80 players covered by just seven shots.

Anything could happen - and did. Costantino Rocca, a sleeping giant for too long trailing in 62nd place in the Ryder Cup table, shot 64 to swoop from joint 22nd place, four strokes behind Farry, into the joint lead with Olazábal, who, after a modest 69, added a 66.

At nine under par the two had edged one clear of England's Neil Cheetham and Paul Eales and Spaniard Domingo Hospital. Norway's Henrik Bjornstad equalled Moseley's best-of-the-week 63 to join a group on seven under par which included New Zealand's Greg Turner.

The 44 year old Rocca, seeking a repeat of his 1993 Open de Lyon victory at the same venue, hinted that the stamina sapping conditions might be taking their toll when he bogeyed the first two holes of the final round, finding himself three behind when Olazábal birdied the third. But ten holes and three birdies later he was co-leader again.

Rocca duly set the ten below par target with his 69. Turner, having been sidelined with back and neck injuries, courageously matched it by following a double bogey six at the 16th with a swashbuckling 235 yards five wood to 12 feet for an eagle three at the 18th and a third successive 67.

The ever neat and tidy Eales moved to ten under with a three from 20 feet at the 11th and a four at the long 15th, but Olazábal, having made a crucial two with a five iron to five feet at the 14th to move 11 under par, remained cool, calm and collected. He threaded an exquisite long iron tee shot down the final fairway, laying up short of the water, then pitched to six feet for a final birdie four, a 67 and a two stroke victory with a 12 under par total of 268 ahead of Eales, Rocca and Turner.

He admitted: "It had been a year since my last victory in the Benson and Hedges International Open and it feels great. I didn't feel comfortable on the golf course. It was a good fight within myself just to stay calm and focused and get the most out of every shot.

"I was a little tired with the course being so wet. You need the extra energy and I never felt any lack of it over the last few holes. I am very happy with the way I scored but I need to work hard to improve the quality of the shots I hit, especially off the tee."

Gordon Richardson

Paul Eales

LYON GOLF CLUB, VILLETTE D'ANTHON, FRANCE, 3-6 MAY, 2001, PAR 70, 7175 YARDS, 6561 METRES

Pos.	Name		Rd1	Rd2	Rd3	Rd4	Total	Par	Prize Money Euro	£
1	José Maria OLAZÁBAL	Sp	66	69	66	67	268	-12	216660.00	134624.11
2	Costantino ROCCA	It	68	69	64	69	270	-10	96940.00	60234.75
	Greg TURNER	NZ	69	67	67	67	270	-10	96940.00	60234.75
	Paul EALES	Eng	66	69	67	68	270	-10	96940.00	60234.75
5	Gregory HAVRET	Fr	67	67	69	68	271	-9	55120.00	34249.43
6	Marc FARRY	Fr	68	65	71	68	272	-8	45500.00	28271.93
7	Anders HANSEN	Den	66	68	70	69	273	-7	33540.00	20840.45
	Paul MCGINLEY	Ire	72	67	69	65	273	-7	33540.00	20840.45
	Ian GARBUTT	Eng	68	71	70	64	273	-7	33540.00	20840.45
10	Alex CEJKA	Ger	67	70	70	67	274	-6	21505.71	13362.81
	Neil CHEETHAM	Eng	67	69	66	72	274	-6	21505.71	13362.81
	Jorge BERENDT	Arg	66	71	69	68	274	-6	21505.71	13362.81
	Paul LAWRIE	Scot	71	67	67	69	274	-6	21505.71	13362.81
	John BICKERTON	Eng	70	67	66	71	274	-6	21505.71	13362.81
	Paddy GRIBBEN	Ire	68	68	68	70	274	-6	21505.71	13362.81
	James MCLEAN	Aus	65	71	69	69	274	-6	21505.71	13362.81
17	Soren KJELDSEN	Den	70	68	71	66	275	-5	15067.00	9362.05
	Stephen LEANEY	Aus	72	67	66	70	275	-5	15067.00	9362.05
	Anthony WALL	Eng	69	68	67	71	275	-5	15067.00	9362.05
	Desvonde BOTES	SA	67	68	71	69	275	-5	15067.00	9362.05
	Domingo HOSPITAL	Sp	69	67	66	73	275	-5	15067.00	9362.05
	Roger WINCHESTER	Eng	66	69	72	68	275	-5	15067.00	9362.05
	Joakim HAEGGMAN	Swe	68	70	67	70	275	-5	15067.00	9362.05
	Peter O'MALLEY	Aus	72	67	70	66	275	-5	15067.00	9362.05
	Mark PILKINGTON	Wal	70	66	69	70	275	-5	15067.00	9362.05
	Brett RUMFORD	Aus	68	70	69	68	275	-5	15067.00	9362.05
27	Anders FORSBRAND	Swe	65	70	70	71	276	-4	11375.00	7067.98
	Eduardo ROMERO	Arg	67	73	68	68	276	-4	11375.00	7067.98
	Philip WALTON	Ire	68	71	68	69	276	-4	11375.00	7067.98
	Richard GREEN	Aus	68	69	70	69	276	-4	11375.00	7067.98
	Hennie WALTERS	SA	69	68	70	69	276	-4	11375.00	7067.98
	Russell CLAYDON	Eng	68	68	68	72	276	-4	11375.00	7067.98
	Diego BORREGO	Sp	69	68	69	70	276	-4	11375.00	7067.98
	Tobias DIER	Ger	69	71	70	66	276	-4	11375.00	7067.98
35	Andrew MARSHALL	Eng	66	71	70	70	277	-3	9620.00	5977.49
	Fredrik ANDERSSON	Swe	68	71	69	69	277	-3	9620.00	5977.49
37	Peter HANSON	Swe	71	65	72	70	278	-2	8840.00	5492.83
	Shaun P WEBSTER	Eng	68	71	65	74	278	-2	8840.00	5492.83
	Jonathan LOMAS	Eng	65	72	69	72	278	-2	8840.00	5492.83
	Robert COLES	Eng	67	69	71	71	278	-2	8840.00	5492.83
41	Mark ROE	Eng	72	67	71	69	279	-1	6890.00	4281.18
	Mark DAVIS	Eng	67	68	77	67	279	-1	6890.00	4281.18
	John SENDEN	Aus	69	68	72	70	279	-1	6890.00	4281.18
	Peter BAKER	Eng	69	68	71	71	279	-1	6890.00	4281.18
	Henrik BJORNSTAD	Nor	72	68	63	76	279	-1	6890.00	4281.18
	Per NYMAN	Swe	68	72	75	64	279	-1	6890.00	4281.18
	Ricardo GONZALEZ	Arg	70	68	69	72	279	-1	6890.00	4281.18
	Ignacio GARRIDO	Sp	68	69	71	71	279	-1	6890.00	4281.18
	Christian CEVAER	Fr	69	71	67	72	279	-1	6890.00	4281.18
	Daren LEE	Eng	64	71	68	76	279	-1	6890.00	4281.18
	Nic HENNING	SA	73	66	70	70	279	-1	6890.00	4281.18
52	Warren BENNETT	Eng	65	73	75	67	280	0	5070.00	3150.30
	Olivier EDMOND	Fr	70	69	71	70	280	0	5070.00	3150.30
	Andrew RAITT	Eng	69	71	72	68	280	0	5070.00	3150.30
	Francois DELAMONTAGNE (AM)	Fr	72	68	71	69	280	0		
56	Ross DRUMMOND	Scot	67	72	72	70	281	1	4108.00	2552.55
	José RIVERO	Sp	68	70	71	72	281	1	4108.00	2552.55
	Gary MURPHY	Ire	70	69	73	69	281	1	4108.00	2552.55
	Jeremy ROBINSON	Eng	67	69	74	71	281	1	4108.00	2552.55
	Olle KARLSSON	Swe	70	69	69	73	281	1	4108.00	2552.55
61	Miguel Angel MARTIN	Sp	71	69	68	74	282	2	3380.00	2100.20
	Gary EVANS	Eng	68	67	76	71	282	2	3380.00	2100.20
	Tomas Jesus MUÑOZ	Sp	69	70	71	72	282	2	3380.00	2100.20
	David PARK	Wal	70	68	74	70	282	2	3380.00	2100.20
	Erol SIMSEK	Ger	67	72	72	71	282	2	3380.00	2100.20
66	Jarrod MOSELEY	Aus	63	75	74	71	283	3	2860.00	1777.09
	Van PHILLIPS	Eng	68	72	72	71	283	3	2860.00	1777.09
	Nicolas JOAKIMIDES	Fr	67	73	68	75	283	3	2860.00	1777.09
69	Garry HOUSTON	Wal	66	71	76	71	284	4	2350.00	1460.20
	Elliot BOULT	NZ	69	70	70	75	284	4	2350.00	1460.20
	Hennie OTTO	SA	69	70	75	70	284	4	2350.00	1460.20
	Jamie SPENCE	Eng	69	70	69	76	284	4	2350.00	1460.20
73	Barry LANE	Eng	71	68	74	72	285	5	1945.50	1208.86
	Justin HOBDAY	SA	67	72	73	73	285	5	1945.50	1208.86
75	Thomas GÖGELE	Ger	69	70	74	73	286	6	1941.00	1206.06
76	Massimo FLORIOLI	It	68	72	72	75	287	7	1938.00	1204.20
77	Michele REALE	It	69	70	78	71	288	8	1935.00	1202.33
78	Trevor IMMELMAN	SA	71	69	77	75	292	12	1929.00	1198.61
	Lionel ALEXANDRE	Fr	69	70	80	73	292	12	1929.00	1198.61
	Chris BENIANS	Eng	69	71	76	76	292	12	1929.00	1198.61

SOURCE
DÉCLARÉE D'INTÉRÊT PUBLIC

Even Keel

THE DE VERE BELFRY, SUTTON COLDFIELD, ENGLAND

Henrik Stenson was, as he put it, "in the bubble" as he came up the last hole on his way to capturing the Benson and Hedges International Open. He was also three ahead of the field. However, those who wanted the final scene to be dripping with drama did not go away disappointed.

Barely had this thoroughly impressive 25 year old holed the winning putt than the sky darkened and there was the mother and father of all thunderstorms. The De Vere Belfry was lit by a combination of camera flashes and lightning.

Of the latter, one bolt completely destroyed a tree in the hotel car park, while another struck the press tent at a time when the winner was trying to belt out his answers above the thunder. Fortunately, no harm was done.

Not much more than an hour after Colin Montgomerie had decreed that The De Vere Belfry could do with a little more rain, the place was awash.

As much as anything, Stenson's success - his 13 under tally saw him win by three from Angel Cabrera and Paul McGinley - was a victory for the European Challenge Tour.

Like Thomas Björn before him, Stenson had graduated to The European Tour by finishing first on this circuit. At the start of 2001, he had struggled with the more extensive travelling but, the moment the tournaments returned to Europe, he had the agreeable sensation that nothing was more than "a pitch shot" away.

On the Challenge Tour, where he won three times, Stenson had learned that he had to be able to put his mistakes behind him. At The De Vere Belfry, he redoubled his efforts on that front, with no finer example than what happened on the ninth and tenth holes in his final round. Though he ran up a bunkered double bogey six at the ninth, he had nothing but positive thoughts in his head as he approached the tenth tee. Not for a moment did he think of protecting his lead.

Drawing on memories of the good shot he had unleashed the day before, he lashed out with his tee-shot. His ball bounded onto the bank to the right of the green from where he went on to hole his highly dangerous pitch for an eagle two.

Paul McGinley

Olle Karlsson

Henrik Stenson

On a final afternoon when Darren Clarke and Montgomerie both made early moves which came to nothing, Cabrera proved to be the main threat. The burly Argentinian, whose massive tee shots were such a wow with the crowd, made back to back birdies at the 15th and 16th to arrive at ten under par to Stenson's 12 under. Then though, the phlegmatic Stenson calmly holed from eight feet at the 16th to put himself virtually out of reach.

Cabrera seemed set to have second place to himself until McGinley made a final thrust at the last. At the start of the week, McGinley, who had shared the first day lead with Stenson after a 66, had said he would do better to have more highs and lows in his season. Much though he enjoyed his reputation for consistency, he knew he would do better on the Official World Golf Ranking were he to alternate, say, between missed cuts and top three finishes. "I'm not complaining," he said, "but that's how it is."

On the Sunday, McGinley dropped back when he pulled his tee shot into the water at the eighth. However, this determined character clung fast to the leaderboard and, when it came to the 18th, he holed a left-to-right 15 footer to capture a share of Cabrera's second place. It was precisely what he wanted.

Shot of the Week

All week, word spread about Angel Cabrera's mammoth hitting, with open-mouthed locals pacing out some of his most hefty strikes. On Sunday, when it came to the 538 yards third hole, the general consensus of opinion was that the Argentinian's drive worked out at 375 yards. "They talk about the long arm of the law but this is something else," said a special constable on crowd control.

Thomas Björn 1-2-3!

It is not merely in the matter of having won the Challenge Tour that Stenson is to be compared with Björn. He has a touch of the same on-course class, walking tall between shots and looking wholly in control. There was no slouching of the shoulders when a putt missed any more than there was any danger of his getting carried away when things were going well. From start to finish, he stayed on an even keel.

Desvonde Botes

"It just goes to show," said Montgomerie, when weighing things up at the end of his day, "that winning the Challenge Tour is not to be sniffed at. It's as tough as its opposite number in the States. Good luck to Henrik."

Curtis Strange, the American Ryder Cup Captain who had accepted an invitation to play at The De Vere Belfry in order to do some reconnaissance work on behalf of his team, missed the cut and was not around on the last day.

With The 34th Ryder Cup Matches in mind, he would doubtless have been more than a little interested in the result, with particular reference to the fact that the winner had never clapped eyes on The De Vere Belfry before the week of the tournament. That information would have served as confirmation he had made the right decision in not asking his men to make a special trip to the venue in advance of The Matches.

Back at The De Vere Belfry, those who followed Montgomerie in paying fulsome tribute to the young Swede included Mark James, who was in fine form and doing duty as a commentator rather than a player. "Henrik is better than I was when I played in my first Ryder Cup," maintained James.

Even without the thunder and lightning, Henrik Stenson would have made his mark.

Lewine Mair

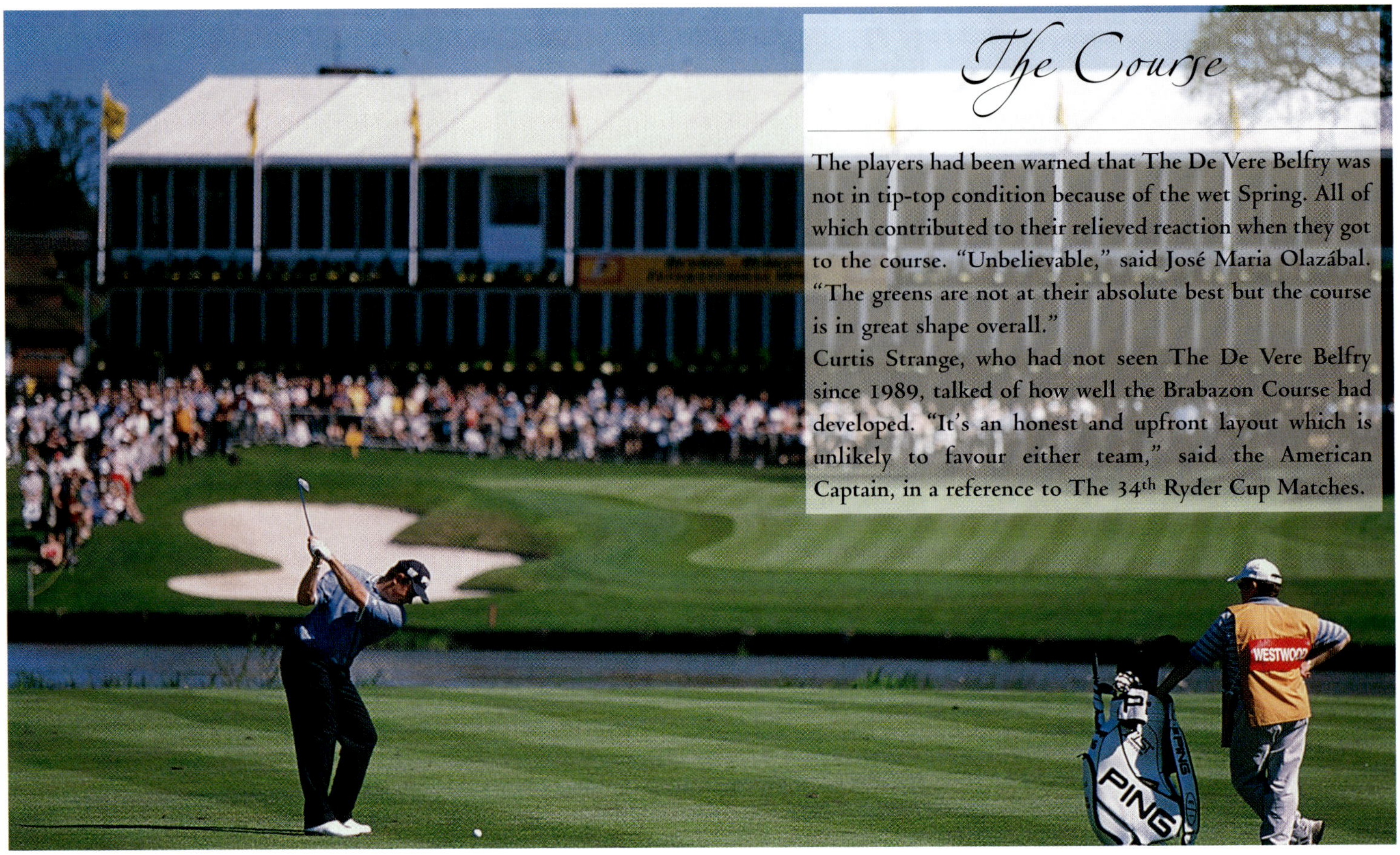

The Course

The players had been warned that The De Vere Belfry was not in tip-top condition because of the wet Spring. All of which contributed to their relieved reaction when they got to the course. "Unbelievable," said José Maria Olazábal. "The greens are not at their absolute best but the course is in great shape overall."

Curtis Strange, who had not seen The De Vere Belfry since 1989, talked of how well the Brabazon Course had developed. "It's an honest and upfront layout which is unlikely to favour either team," said the American Captain, in a reference to The 34th Ryder Cup Matches.

THE DE VERE BELFRY, SUTTON COLDFIELD, ENGLAND, 10-13 MAY, 2001, PAR 72, 7118 YARDS, 6509 METRES

Pos.	Name		Rd1	Rd2	Rd3	Rd4	Total	Par	Prize Money Euro	£
1	Henrik STENSON	Swe	66	68	71	70	275	-13	267917.62	166660.00
2	Paul MCGINLEY	Ire	66	72	70	70	278	-10	139625.50	86855.00
	Angel CABRERA	Arg	70	70	69	69	278	-10	139625.50	86855.00
4	Olle KARLSSON	Swe	69	71	68	73	281	-7	80378.50	50000.00
5	Desvonde BOTES	SA	69	69	72	72	282	-6	68160.97	42400.00
6	Richard GREEN	Aus	72	70	70	71	283	-5	56264.95	35000.00
7	Eduardo ROMERO	Arg	70	74	66	74	284	-4	37231.32	23160.00
	David HOWELL	Eng	69	70	73	72	284	-4	37231.32	23160.00
	Raphaël JACQUELIN	Fr	68	74	72	70	284	-4	37231.32	23160.00
	Thomas BJÖRN	Den	69	68	75	72	284	-4	37231.32	23160.00
	Retief GOOSEN	SA	71	68	74	71	284	-4	37231.32	23160.00
12	Colin MONTGOMERIE	Scot	73	69	71	72	285	-3	24354.69	15150.00
	Ian GARBUTT	Eng	72	70	72	71	285	-3	24354.69	15150.00
	Phillip PRICE	Wal	70	74	67	74	285	-3	24354.69	15150.00
	Jorge BERENDT	Arg	75	67	70	73	285	-3	24354.69	15150.00
	Patrik SJÖLAND	Swe	69	73	71	72	285	-3	24354.69	15150.00
	Nick DOUGHERTY (AM)	Eng	72	72	70	71	285	-3		
	Paul CASEY	Eng	72	73	71	69	285	-3	24354.69	15150.00
19	Padraig HARRINGTON	Ire	68	72	76	70	286	-2	18547.34	11537.50
	Richard S JOHNSON	Swe	73	71	74	68	286	-2	18547.34	11537.50
	Jarrod MOSELEY	Aus	70	69	72	75	286	-2	18547.34	11537.50
	Johan RYSTRÖM	Swe	72	70	75	69	286	-2	18547.34	11537.50
	Diego BORREGO	Sp	68	73	74	71	286	-2	18547.34	11537.50
	Paul LAWRIE	Scot	70	71	74	71	286	-2	18547.34	11537.50
	Brett RUMFORD	Aus	72	71	71	72	286	-2	18547.34	11537.50
	Aaron BADDELEY	Aus	69	72	69	76	286	-2	18547.34	11537.50
27	Jeev Milkha SINGH	Ind	72	69	71	75	287	-1	14548.51	9050.00
	José Manuel LARA	Sp	72	73	69	73	287	-1	14548.51	9050.00
	José Maria OLAZÁBAL	Sp	67	75	72	73	287	-1	14548.51	9050.00
	Sven STRÜVER	Ger	74	66	75	72	287	-1	14548.51	9050.00
	Miguel Angel JIMÉNEZ	Sp	72	70	71	74	287	-1	14548.51	9050.00
	Peter MITCHELL	Eng	76	69	69	73	287	-1	14548.51	9050.00
	Darren CLARKE	N.Ire	69	76	68	74	287	-1	14548.51	9050.00
	Robert COLES	Eng	70	73	74	70	287	-1	14548.51	9050.00
35	Costantino ROCCA	It	73	71	74	70	288	0	11413.75	7100.00
	José RIVERO	Sp	72	67	76	73	288	0	11413.75	7100.00
	Mark MCNULTY	Zim	70	74	73	71	288	0	11413.75	7100.00
	Elliot BOULT	NZ	68	73	77	70	288	0	11413.75	7100.00
	Nick O'HERN	Aus	70	75	71	72	288	0	11413.75	7100.00
	Russell CLAYDON	Eng	71	68	74	75	288	0	11413.75	7100.00
	Markus BRIER	Aut	73	72	71	72	288	0	11413.75	7100.00
42	David GILFORD	Eng	68	73	73	75	289	1	8680.88	5400.00
	Steve WEBSTER	Eng	71	73	69	76	289	1	8680.88	5400.00
	Anthony WALL	Eng	69	72	76	72	289	1	8680.88	5400.00
	Peter BAKER	Eng	71	71	75	72	289	1	8680.88	5400.00
	Henrik BJORNSTAD	Nor	72	72	71	74	289	1	8680.88	5400.00
	Robert KARLSSON	Swe	71	73	72	73	289	1	8680.88	5400.00
	Jonathan LOMAS	Eng	72	72	70	75	289	1	8680.88	5400.00
	Dean ROBERTSON	Scot	71	70	72	76	289	1	8680.88	5400.00
	Henrik NYSTROM	Swe	70	70	71	78	289	1	8680.88	5400.00
	Stephen GALLACHER	Scot	69	74	72	74	289	1	8680.88	5400.00
52	Jean-Francois REMESY	Fr	71	70	73	76	290	2	6269.52	3900.00
	Soren KJELDSEN	Den	71	74	72	73	290	2	6269.52	3900.00
	Paul EALES	Eng	73	72	73	72	290	2	6269.52	3900.00
	Francisco CEA	Sp	70	72	72	76	290	2	6269.52	3900.00
	Marco BERNARDINI	It	73	70	73	74	290	2	6269.52	3900.00
57	Eamonn DARCY	Ire	75	67	75	74	291	3	4684.92	2914.29
	Bernhard LANGER	Ger	72	69	73	77	291	3	4684.92	2914.29
	Ian WOOSNAM	Wal	71	69	74	77	291	3	4684.92	2914.29
	Marc FARRY	Fr	70	75	69	77	291	3	4684.92	2914.29
	Fredrik HENGE	Swe	70	72	74	75	291	3	4684.92	2914.29
	Jean VAN DE VELDE	Fr	72	73	74	72	291	3	4684.92	2914.29
	Lee WESTWOOD	Eng	73	68	76	74	291	3	4684.92	2914.29
64	Jean HUGO	SA	69	76	73	74	292	4	3777.79	2350.00
	Pierre FULKE	Swe	75	68	77	72	292	4	3777.79	2350.00
	Ricardo GONZALEZ	Arg	71	70	80	71	292	4	3777.79	2350.00
	Graeme STORM	Eng	76	68	73	75	292	4	3777.79	2350.00
68	Peter HANSON	Swe	73	72	75	73	293	5	2999.65	1865.95
	Gregory HAVRET	Fr	72	72	71	78	293	5	2999.65	1865.95
	Stephen DODD	Wal	73	72	77	71	293	5	2999.65	1865.95
	Nicolas VANHOOTEGEM	Bel	68	73	76	76	293	5	2999.65	1865.95
	David LYNN	Eng	72	73	74	74	293	5	2999.65	1865.95
73	Santiago LUNA	Sp	72	73	73	76	294	6	2405.00	1496.05
	Carl SUNESON	Sp	74	70	73	77	294	6	2405.00	1496.05
	Greg OWEN	Eng	72	72	75	75	294	6	2405.00	1496.05
76	Steen TINNING	Den	75	68	79	74	296	8	2399.00	1492.31
77	Gary EMERSON	Eng	69	73	83	73	298	10	2396.00	1490.45
78	David CARTER	Eng	74	70	77	80	301	13	2393.00	1488.58

DEUTSCHE BANK - SAP OPEN TPC OF EUROPE

Pretty Cool

ST LEON-ROT, HEIDELBERG, GERMANY

Inevitably, it was the Tiger Woods show on and off the course at St Leon-Rot, a flat course close to the old and attractive German city of Heidelberg. From the moment he arrived, patiently answering his local inquisitors on race, rules and Ryder Cups, until he sank his final putt in a four shot win, he was the star of the Deutsche Bank - SAP Open TPC of Europe.

There was hardly a spare hotel bed for miles around as people travelled from all over the country to see the Great One in action although they were held up for seven hours on the opening day as overnight rain swamped the course.

When play finally began, preferred lies were the order of the day which meant that Michael Campbell's stunning opening 62 would not count as a course record which remains at 65. It did, however, set Campbell off on an impressive run which left Woods somewhere back in the pack until his weekend charge thrilled all those who craned their necks to get a glimpse of the renowned Tiger genius.

With the delay, it took until Saturday evening to get the tournament back on schedule but the climax was worth the wait. Woods shot 69 on that first, rain-sodden day after having a spat with some over-enthusiastic German photographers who downed tools for two holes before realising the futility of it all. They were also missing Campbell's astonishing run. After 12 holes his card showed six threes and six fours. A two followed but it was so dark when play finished for the day around 9pm that it was difficult to read the scoreboard.

His 62 was the lowest of his career and his form continued into the second round with more immaculate golf and a 65 although his re-arranged tee time was 6pm. By the time he had completed his round he was ten shots ahead of Woods and one London bookmaker was said to have offered 14/1 against Tiger winning the tournament.

Campbell was out in front, six shots ahead of Eduardo Romero, but the question was whether Woods could close the gap. He went into the third round ten shots off the pace set by Campbell before people recalled that in the 1998 Johnnie Walker Classic in Thailand he had trailed Ernie Els by 11 but went on to win.

Søren Kjeldsen

Peter O'Malley

Shot of the Week

Tiger Woods's seven iron that flew straight into the hole from 175 yards at the 13th in the final round. He had a six iron in his hand, the wind dropped and he changed to a seven. He described it: "I aimed it right with a nice high draw and all of a sudden it disappeared. The crowd went nuts around the green and that's when I knew it was in the hole."

As an interesting aside, Darren Clarke arrived at the course so convinced that he would miss the cut when he returned, five over par with seven holes to play, that he had checked out of his hotel and sent for his private aircraft which was waiting for him on the runway. His golf took off instead and a run of five birdies and an eagle meant he covered the back nine in 29 to make it comfortably.

When the third round got under way on Saturday afternoon, Woods knew he had to start a charge. Four birdies and an eagle in a front nine of 30 were more than declarations of intent. He was on the move. Romero held his nerve with a 66 but Campbell suddenly found trouble.

He double bogeyed the 12th and was in the water at the 16th for bogey. His 73 dropped him to joint second alongside Woods whose magnificent 63 was a perfect exhibition of his temperament, technique and vision.

The three of them went out together on the final day in what was to be a gripping climax to a tournament that rose above the disappointment of the sodden state of the course in the early part of the week.

Few people knew that Woods had broken his driver on the practice ground after his third round. The shaft had broken at the neck and

Richard Green

Andrew Coltart

he did not have a spare. Frantic phone calls were made to professionals and club-makers all over Germany in the hunt for a X100 steel shaft. Graphite varieties were plentiful but Tiger prefers steel.

In the end he located young Australian professional Adam Scott, who was also playing in the tournament, and using the same clubs. He had a spare driver with him. Tiger used it to such good effect that his final round of 66 gave him a four shot win over the valiant Campbell (70) while Romero (77) tumbled back through the field.

It was not Scott's driver that had them talking as Woods moved towards the first prize of 450,000 euro (£278,000), but the shot he holed from 175 yards on the par four, 396 yard 13th for an eagle two.

He said: "I enjoy coming here. I enjoy playing all round the world. It's fun. I am young in my career. It's awfully nice to play in different places. You get to meet a lot of new people and that's one of the things I really cherish. It's pretty cool."

He made a lot of new friends in Germany.

James Mossop

The Course

A parkland course with ten fours, four threes and four fives. The fairways were flat, average width and cut to 9mm. Tee shots were extremely important as the rough was cut at 94mm. There were lakes and ditches and an island green at the par four seventh.

ST LEON-ROT, HEIDELBERG, GERMANY, 17-20 MAY, 2001, PAR 72, 7207 YARDS, 6587 METRES

Pos.	Name		Rd1	Rd2	Rd3	Rd4	Total	Par	Prize Money Euro	£
1	Tiger WOODS	USA	69	68	63	66	266	-22	450000.00	278024.91
2	Michael CAMPBELL	NZ	62	65	73	70	270	-18	300000.00	185349.94
3	Søren KJELDSEN	Den	70	67	69	65	271	-17	152005.00	93913.73
	Peter O'MALLEY	Aus	71	68	63	69	271	-17	152005.00	93913.73
5	Padraig HARRINGTON	Ire	70	69	64	70	273	-15	96660.00	59719.75
	Andrew COLTART	Scot	68	69	68	68	273	-15	96660.00	59719.75
	Mikael LUNDBERG	Swe	69	69	69	66	273	-15	96660.00	59719.75
8	Nick O'HERN	Aus	69	69	66	70	274	-14	63990.00	39535.14
	Henrik STENSON	Swe	71	68	63	72	274	-14	63990.00	39535.14
10	Richard GREEN	Aus	68	69	69	69	275	-13	48397.50	29901.58
	Colin MONTGOMERIE	Scot	70	66	69	70	275	-13	48397.50	29901.58
	Paul MCGINLEY	Ire	69	65	72	69	275	-13	48397.50	29901.58
	John BICKERTON	Eng	69	67	73	66	275	-13	48397.50	29901.58
14	Eduardo ROMERO	Arg	66	67	66	77	276	-12	37305.00	23048.27
	Peter BAKER	Eng	71	70	68	67	276	-12	37305.00	23048.27
	Miguel Angel JIMÉNEZ	Sp	69	69	68	70	276	-12	37305.00	23048.27
	Phillip PRICE	Wal	71	70	66	69	276	-12	37305.00	23048.27
	Ricardo GONZALEZ	Arg	73	67	68	68	276	-12	37305.00	23048.27
	Retief GOOSEN	SA	72	68	64	72	276	-12	37305.00	23048.27
20	Warren BENNETT	Eng	68	70	67	73	278	-10	30982.50	19142.02
	Greg TURNER	NZ	71	71	69	67	278	-10	30982.50	19142.02
	Angel CABRERA	Arg	69	70	68	71	278	-10	30982.50	19142.02
	Peter LONARD	Aus	70	71	68	69	278	-10	30982.50	19142.02
24	Darren FICHARDT	SA	71	69	70	69	279	-9	27675.00	17098.53
	Thomas LEVET	Fr	74	67	72	66	279	-9	27675.00	17098.53
	Darren CLARKE	N.Ire	76	67	69	67	279	-9	27675.00	17098.53
	Gustavo ROJAS	Arg	66	72	69	72	279	-9	27675.00	17098.53
28	Miguel Angel MARTIN	Sp	69	70	69	72	280	-8	22500.00	13901.25
	Ian WOOSNAM	Wal	66	72	73	69	280	-8	22500.00	13901.25
	Justin ROSE	Eng	70	69	73	68	280	-8	22500.00	13901.25
	Paul EALES	Eng	68	71	66	75	280	-8	22500.00	13901.25
	Ernie ELS	SA	66	71	72	71	280	-8	22500.00	13901.25
	Mathias GRÖNBERG	Swe	69	68	72	71	280	-8	22500.00	13901.25
	Greg OWEN	Eng	68	70	72	70	280	-8	22500.00	13901.25
	Patrik SJÖLAND	Swe	71	70	70	69	280	-8	22500.00	13901.25
	Daren LEE	Eng	70	68	69	73	280	-8	22500.00	13901.25
37	Mark MCNULTY	Zim	69	73	68	71	281	-7	17820.00	11009.79
	Peter MITCHELL	Eng	74	67	73	67	281	-7	17820.00	11009.79
	Robert KARLSSON	Swe	71	71	69	70	281	-7	17820.00	11009.79
	Paul LAWRIE	Scot	72	70	69	70	281	-7	17820.00	11009.79
	Dean ROBERTSON	Scot	69	68	72	72	281	-7	17820.00	11009.79
	Lucas PARSONS	Aus	66	75	68	72	281	-7	17820.00	11009.79
43	Anders HANSEN	Den	74	69	70	69	282	-6	15120.00	9341.64
	Carl SUNESON	Sp	67	76	70	69	282	-6	15120.00	9341.64
	Niclas FASTH	Swe	74	69	71	68	282	-6	15120.00	9341.64
	Adam SCOTT	Aus	74	68	70	70	282	-6	15120.00	9341.64
47	Bernhard LANGER	Ger	72	71	70	70	283	-5	12690.00	7840.30
	Anthony WALL	Eng	72	71	69	71	283	-5	12690.00	7840.30
	Steen TINNING	Den	70	70	68	75	283	-5	12690.00	7840.30
	Søren HANSEN	Den	70	73	66	74	283	-5	12690.00	7840.30
	Andrew RAITT	Eng	70	69	75	69	283	-5	12690.00	7840.30
52	Malcolm MACKENZIE	Eng	71	69	69	75	284	-4	9990.00	6172.15
	John SENDEN	Aus	70	71	72	71	284	-4	9990.00	6172.15
	Jarrod MOSELEY	Aus	72	71	68	73	284	-4	9990.00	6172.15
	Ian GARBUTT	Eng	73	70	70	71	284	-4	9990.00	6172.15
	Lee WESTWOOD	Eng	66	71	70	77	284	-4	9990.00	6172.15
57	Jean-Francois REMESY	Fr	75	66	75	69	285	-3	7695.00	4754.23
	José Maria OLAZÁBAL	Sp	70	71	71	73	285	-3	7695.00	4754.23
	Olivier EDMOND	Fr	71	67	71	76	285	-3	7695.00	4754.23
	Jarmo SANDELIN	Swe	70	69	70	76	285	-3	7695.00	4754.23
	Christopher HANELL	Swe	70	73	70	72	285	-3	7695.00	4754.23
	Tobias DIER	Ger	71	71	74	69	285	-3	7695.00	4754.23
63	Marc FARRY	Fr	70	70	73	73	286	-2	6210.00	3836.74
	Brian DAVIS	Eng	70	69	71	76	286	-2	6210.00	3836.74
	Jamie SPENCE	Eng	71	71	72	72	286	-2	6210.00	3836.74
	Gary ORR	Scot	71	71	71	73	286	-2	6210.00	3836.74
	David PARK	Wal	73	69	75	69	286	-2	6210.00	3836.74
68	Diego BORREGO	Sp	71	72	73	71	287	-1	5265.00	3252.89
	Christian CÉVAËR	Fr	72	69	75	71	287	-1	5265.00	3252.89
70	Eamonn DARCY	Ire	71	72	74	71	288	0	4342.33	2682.84
	Des SMYTH	Ire	74	69	71	74	288	0	4342.33	2682.84
	Alex CEJKA	Ger	73	68	73	74	288	0	4342.33	2682.84
73	Emanuele CANONICA	It	72	71	69	77	289	1	4042.50	2497.59
	Thomas BJÖRN	Den	67	75	71	76	289	1	4042.50	2497.59
75	Mikko ILONEN	Fin	71	72	72	77	292	4	4038.00	2494.81

Theatre of Dreams

WENTWORTH CLUB, SURREY, ENGLAND

No event on The European Tour glitters more than the Volvo PGA Championship. This shiny, happy week is no accident of course. It is the result of a sensational amount of hard work by everyone at The European Tour headquarters that are situated conveniently behind the castellated clubhouse and an equal amount of effort by Wentworth Club's dedicated team led by the always amiable, eternally vigilant, Managing Director Julian Small for whom no task is too large, no detail irrelevant.

Shot of the Week

It was only natural that Andrew Oldcorn's mind wandered back to Druids Glen in 1996 as he played the 72nd hole at Wentworth Club. On that occasion, he needed a four to win the Murphy's Irish Open but took a six. This time he stood over his third shot - a delicate pitch from a divot mark in the dropping zone - and played it with great finesse to eight feet, setting up the winning putt. With that stroke, Ireland became a distant memory.

Chris Kennedy (front left) and his greenkeeping team share the spotlight with champion Andrew Oldcorn and one young student of the game!

This attention to the small print oozes throughout the Volvo PGA Championship from the way the grass is cross-cut under the careful eye of Golf Course Manager Chris Kennedy through to the tented village where the nice Moët & Chandon people rub shoulders and pop corks with the folk from Langan's restaurant and where a visit to the Victor Chandler betting arena may be offset if necessary by a trip through the revolutionary Pfizer Men's Health Initiative. Eating, drinking, betting and then staying alive has never been made more accessible.

It is thus a seriously class act but then this always has been the way with the Volvo PGA Championship. Just glance at the names on the trophy, a long and eloquent homage to the great and the good of the grand, old European game. In the fifties there was Peter Alliss and Dai Rees, in the sixties we welcomed winners like Bernard Gallacher and Peter Townsend, the seventies greeted Neil Coles, Nick Faldo, Tony Jacklin, Peter Oosterhuis and Arnold Palmer among others, the eighties gave us the likes of Seve Ballesteros, Bernhard Langer and Ian Woosnam while the last decade of the 20th Century endorsed the abiding quality of Colin Montgomerie and José Maria Olazábal.

And now there is a new name, but a reassuringly familiar face, to add to this bouquet of stars. Andrew Steven Oldcorn was nobody's idea of a potential winner of this title when the week began, as it ended, in a blaze of sunshine but then even he had not considered seriously the prospect of victory in this Surrey heartland. Making the cut and making a decent cheque had been the height of Oldcorn's ambition when he strode to the tee for Friday's opening round.

Yes, he had dreamed of lifting the beautiful, silver trophy high into a balmy May sky but despite his successes in the 1993 Turespaña Masters Open de Andalucia and the 1995 DHL Jersey Open, the last few years had been hard for the man who was raised briefly in Bolton before becoming a born-again Scot when his parents moved north to Edinburgh. At 41 there was reason to suspect that Oldcorn's future was mostly behind him, that the years and illness had taken too much of a toll and that this season was to be a struggle merely to retain his card.

Yet when it all ended it was this most amiable of men who walked, half in triumph, half in clear, if delighted, embarrassment, 42 paces across the 18th green to receive the trophy and to pocket a cheque for 544,521 euro (£333,330) which was more than a third of his career earnings since joining The European Tour in 1983. And it was Oldcorn who then delivered a speech of such spontaneous grace it is difficult not to believe that beneath the fairytale the reality was that he had been preparing for this moment for a very, very long time.

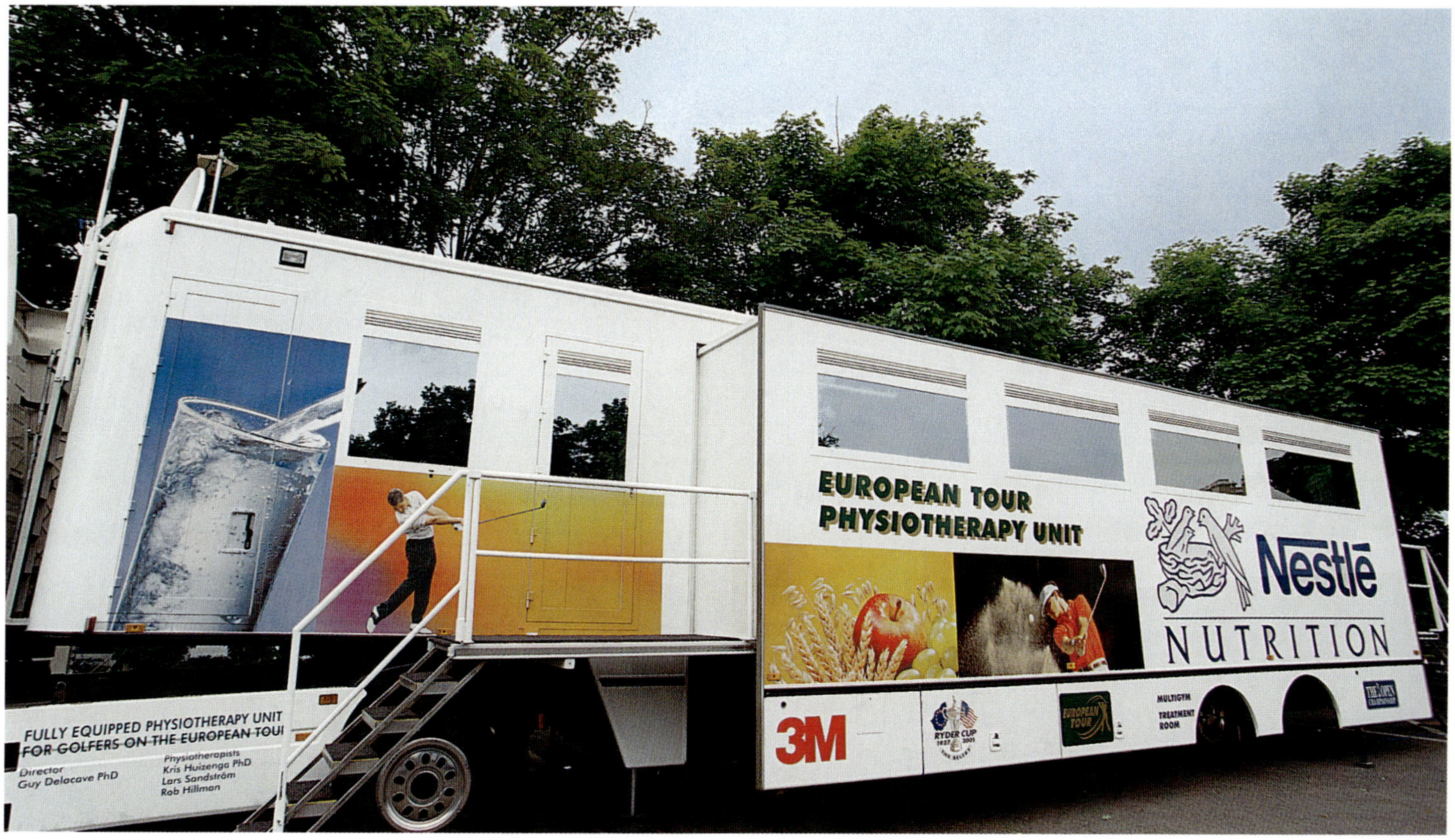

Colin Montgomerie

The Course

Harry Colt designed and built some of the finest courses in England but the challenge of Wentworth Club's West Course remains his signature effort. Its length, 7050 yards, on top of its undulating contours, means that this is a challenge tough enough to please even the most masochistic and ambitious of golfers.

Behind him on the grass the men who filled second and third places, Angel Cabrera and Nick Faldo, grinned happily at a golfer whose real riches lie in the long queue of people who simply like him a lot.

A month earlier Cabrera had led the Masters Tournament at Augusta National briefly just six days after victory at home in the Open de Argentina. Faldo, of course, has won three Masters titles and three Open Championships but the genuine delight each of these competitors showed towards Oldcorn was reassuring in these often shallow sporting times. For each there had been much to savour over the week. Cabrera's opening 63 had equalled the course record, the stocky man with the constantly bemused look overpowering even the West Course with his length and accuracy off the tee.

Faldo, meanwhile, had returned home, linked up once more with caddie Fanny Sunesson and reignited his game and his thirst for the Big Moments that send adrenalin surging through a man's body like a river of fire. Yet despite these heroics it was Oldcorn who prevailed. In so doing he set behind him forever the desperate thought that when the final, defining holes arrived in a big tournament he too often ran for cover.

Angel Cabrera

Nick Faldo and caddie Fanny Sunesson

VOLVO
PGA CHAMPIONSHIP

Lee Westwood and wife Laurae

On Saturday evening as he contemplated a halfway lead in a Championship that he knew could change his life he admitted that he could not quite believe the low number of putts taken in this second round - it was 20 - and that he was not quite sure how he was going to react over the closing stretch. "It rankles with me that I haven't made the most of a lot of good situations," he said disarmingly. "The worst was in 1996 when I led with two holes to go and gifted it to Monty instead. It took me two long years to get over that one. Can I do it now? Well, this is the biggest title I can win outside the Open itself so I've certainly got the desire."

Hmmm, we thought, though naturally no-one hummed it. Twenty-four hours later Oldcorn had answered his own question emphatically and positively, his third round 69 by far the best of his life, his 54 hole lead adding up to a reassuring five shots, his instant answer to the occasional mistake that Sunday a shot of blistering, reconstituting brilliance.

It was an attitude he took with him into a glorious final day. In front of record crowds he surveyed the dramatic progress being made by Faldo whose 67 revived memories of his historic last day stalking of Greg Norman at Augusta National in 1996. Although the lead was reduced and there was the odd stumble, Andrew Oldcorn remained upright and in control of a suddenly steely nerve. This was his

moment and he refused to allow it to slip by. It was compelling theatre as well as ultimately the most human of stories centred round a man whose career had been threatened terminally by the onset of myalgic encephalomyelitis (ME).

Back in those dark days he often had to crawl painfully up to bed in the middle of a bright afternoon. Now here he was marching briskly across that 18th green to a trophy, a cheque and a speech that said all the right things and included the thought that he hoped his success would be an inspiration to all the other chorus line players on the circuit. And behind him as he spoke, someone began to whistle 'Fairytales can come true...'

Bill Elliott

Andrew Oldcorn takes centre-stage flanked by Gerry Keaney (left), Managing Director, Volvo Car UK Limited, and Mel Pyatt, President & CEO, Volvo Event Management

Michael Campbell

WENTWORTH CLUB, SURREY, ENGLAND, 25-28 MAY, 2001, PAR 72, 7050 YARDS, 6445 METRES

Pos.	Name		Rd1	Rd2	Rd3	Rd4	Total	Par	Prize Money Euro	£
1	Andrew OLDCORN	Scot	66	66	69	71	272	-16	544521.20	333330.00
2	Angel CABRERA	Arg	63	71	72	68	274	-14	363014.20	222220.03
3	Nick FALDO	Eng	72	66	70	67	275	-13	204524.20	125199.99
4	Phillip PRICE	Wal	65	69	72	71	277	-11	138745.40	84933.34
	Mathias GRÖNBERG	Swe	71	69	72	65	277	-11	138745.40	84933.34
	Michael CAMPBELL	NZ	70	70	67	70	277	-11	138745.40	84933.34
7	Vijay SINGH	Fiji	73	65	70	70	278	-10	98014.80	60000.00
8	Peter BAKER	Eng	67	72	75	65	279	-9	73402.20	44933.34
	Darren CLARKE	N.Ire	72	69	68	70	279	-9	73402.20	44933.34
	Gary ORR	Scot	74	67	69	69	279	-9	73402.20	44933.34
11	José Maria OLAZÁBAL	Sp	72	68	67	73	280	-8	56304.05	34466.66
	Steve WEBSTER	Eng	67	68	72	73	280	-8	56304.05	34466.66
	Dean ROBERTSON	Scot	68	68	75	69	280	-8	56304.05	34466.66
14	John SENDEN	Aus	71	67	72	71	281	-7	48027.25	29400.00
	Niclas FASTH	Swe	69	68	69	75	281	-7	48027.25	29400.00
	Simon DYSON	Eng	68	72	72	69	281	-7	48027.25	29400.00
17	Richard GREEN	Aus	73	68	70	71	282	-6	41492.93	25400.00
	Anthony WALL	Eng	70	70	72	70	282	-6	41492.93	25400.00
	Colin MONTGOMERIE	Scot	73	69	69	71	282	-6	41492.93	25400.00
	Paul LAWRIE	Scot	69	68	72	73	282	-6	41492.93	25400.00
21	Ian WOOSNAM	Wal	71	68	73	71	283	-5	35938.76	22000.00
	Anders HANSEN	Den	71	70	72	70	283	-5	35938.76	22000.00
	Stephen LEANEY	Aus	70	64	74	75	283	-5	35938.76	22000.00
	Gary EMERSON	Eng	70	69	71	73	283	-5	35938.76	22000.00
	Mikael LUNDBERG	Swe	67	72	70	74	283	-5	35938.76	22000.00
26	Raphaël JACQUELIN	Fr	69	68	74	73	284	-4	30547.95	18700.00
	Thomas LEVET	Fr	72	71	72	69	284	-4	30547.95	18700.00
	Peter O'MALLEY	Aus	69	71	71	73	284	-4	30547.95	18700.00
	Paul MCGINLEY	Ire	66	74	73	71	284	-4	30547.95	18700.00
	Ian GARBUTT	Eng	71	71	70	72	284	-4	30547.95	18700.00
	Diego BORREGO	Sp	72	70	69	73	284	-4	30547.95	18700.00
32	Søren KJELDSEN	Den	71	66	72	76	285	-3	24643.72	15085.71
	Justin ROSE	Eng	72	69	73	71	285	-3	24643.72	15085.71
	Joakim HAEGGMAN	Swe	68	73	74	70	285	-3	24643.72	15085.71
	Greg OWEN	Eng	69	74	68	74	285	-3	24643.72	15085.71
	Markus BRIER	Aut	72	71	71	71	285	-3	24643.72	15085.71
	Andrew COLTART	Scot	68	69	71	77	285	-3	24643.72	15085.71
	Adam SCOTT	Aus	70	69	74	72	285	-3	24643.72	15085.71
39	Henrik STENSON	Swe	76	66	71	73	286	-2	20256.39	12400.00
	Ernie ELS	SA	70	72	68	76	286	-2	20256.39	12400.00
	Rolf MUNTZ	Hol	71	67	74	74	286	-2	20256.39	12400.00
	Thomas BJÖRN	Den	68	69	72	77	286	-2	20256.39	12400.00
	Henrik NYSTROM	Swe	69	72	72	73	286	-2	20256.39	12400.00
	Christopher HANELL	Swe	72	71	72	71	286	-2	20256.39	12400.00
45	Eamonn DARCY	Ire	72	71	71	73	287	-1	15028.94	9200.00
	Des SMYTH	Ire	70	68	75	74	287	-1	15028.94	9200.00
	Padraig HARRINGTON	Ire	67	75	69	76	287	-1	15028.94	9200.00
	Carlos RODILES	Sp	69	70	78	70	287	-1	15028.94	9200.00
	Steen TINNING	Den	70	73	73	71	287	-1	15028.94	9200.00
	Jonathan LOMAS	Eng	72	67	73	75	287	-1	15028.94	9200.00
	Nicolas VANHOOTEGEM	Bel	69	71	72	75	287	-1	15028.94	9200.00
	David LYNN	Eng	72	71	75	69	287	-1	15028.94	9200.00
	Patrik SJÖLAND	Swe	70	73	74	70	287	-1	15028.94	9200.00
	John BICKERTON	Eng	69	71	76	71	287	-1	15028.94	9200.00
55	Paul BROADHURST	Eng	69	74	73	72	288	0	10781.63	6600.00
	David HIGGINS	Ire	72	71	74	71	288	0	10781.63	6600.00
	Alastair FORSYTH	Scot	67	73	75	73	288	0	10781.63	6600.00
58	Miguel Angel MARTIN	Sp	69	70	75	75	289	1	9148.05	5600.00
	Damian MCGRANE	Ire	68	72	70	79	289	1	9148.05	5600.00
	Nick O'HERN	Aus	66	71	78	74	289	1	9148.05	5600.00
	Søren HANSEN	Den	71	70	73	75	289	1	9148.05	5600.00
	Raymond RUSSELL	Scot	72	69	76	72	289	1	9148.05	5600.00
63	Warren BENNETT	Eng	71	68	76	75	290	2	7677.83	4700.00
	Jean HUGO	SA	72	70	75	73	290	2	7677.83	4700.00
	Emanuele CANONICA	It	71	70	72	77	290	2	7677.83	4700.00
	Peter LONARD	Aus	71	71	72	76	290	2	7677.83	4700.00
67	Robert KARLSSON	Swe	72	70	73	76	291	3	6534.32	4000.00
	Alex CEJKA	Ger	73	70	75	73	291	3	6534.32	4000.00
	Pierre FULKE	Swe	71	70	79	71	291	3	6534.32	4000.00
70	Gary EVANS	Eng	71	71	77	74	293	5	5962.57	3650.00
71	Jarmo SANDELIN	Swe	71	72	73	78	294	6	4901.00	3000.16
72	Jeev Milkha SINGH	Ind	76	67	76	80	299	11	4898.00	2998.32

OPERATIONAL EXCELLENCE
VOLVO

Magnifique!

WOBURN GOLF AND COUNTRY CLUB, MILTON KEYNES, ENGLAND

Nobody can tell us whether the bookies cleaned up on Napoleon at Waterloo, but Victor Chandler were certainly not complaining when another fighting Frenchman, Thomas Levet, won the Battle of Woburn after a thrilling four-way sudden-death shoot-out on the magnificent new Marquess Course.

And while the sponsors might, in publicity terms, have preferred a bigger name to win their British Masters, Victor Chandler, the bookmakers, were deliriously happy that an unconsidered 125-1 chance headed back to Paris with their much-augmented 345,080 euro (£208,330) winner's cheque.

The only significant bet on the 32 year old doctor's son whose only previous win had been in the 1998 Cannes Open, came when the play-off, also involving Mathias Grönberg, David Howell and Robert Karlsson cut to two men, Grönberg and Levet. Some shrewd cookie stepped in with an £8,000 wager at 13-8. Levet obliged with a stunning six iron ten feet above the cup at the 176 yards 17th hole and sank the left-to-right putt.

Then, with true Gallic exuberance, he raced round the circumference of the green in a Hale Irwin-style lap of honour, high-fiving everyone as he celebrated by far the biggest victory of his career.

Ninety four years on, he became the first Frenchman to win a pukka tournament in Britain since Arnaud Massy's Open Championship at Hoylake in 1907 - and wasn't he just in seventh heaven. A "Unbelievable, unbelievable", he kept repeating. "To win outside France for the first time - and in such a big tournament! I thought it might be my lucky day when I found a marker beside my bag when I finished my final round. On it was written 'Bringing You the Luck of the Irish with the Blarney Stone'. As my caddie, Owen Craig, comes from Ireland, I thought it might be a sign that I was meant to win."

David Howell

Robert Karlsson

"It is a very good and beautiful golf course. I think they have done a very good job on the design. It is one of the top new courses I have played."

Mathias Grönberg

Levet had already had Lady Luck on his side when his hooked drive at the 72nd hole hit a spectator's handbag, breaking a bottle of French perfume in the process, and came to rest in a good lie in the rough. "Without that, I might have finished behind a tree and not been able to make four," conceded the new champion.

As his victory followed two similarly unlikely champions at The De Vere Belfry and Wentworth Club on The 2001 European Tour International Schedule in 150-1 chances Henrik Stenson and Andrew Oldcorn, Levet was asked how many members of The European Tour were actually capable of winning. "Most of them," came the reply. "Technically, they can all win; mentally, that is the barrier."

Levet got his own mind straight for the play-off by talking with sports psychologist Jos Vanstiphout as he waited for the others to finish. Levet said: "He told me to play it simple, to uncomplicate my mind, make myself calm and remember my good shots, not my bad ones."

That advice paid off when Levet missed a simple-looking five-foot birdie putt for outright victory on the first extra hole, the 459 yard 18th, after he had just hit "my best shot of the week", a three iron

The Course

Many hands make nice work! From Peter Alliss, Clive Clark and Alex Hay through to Ross McMurray at European Tour Design, The Marquess has taken its time evolving, but the wait has been well worth it. Considering the dreadful winter, the new course, more American in style than its Woburn neighbours, was turned out looking a picture and received glowing compliments from the professionals.

pin-high from the left rough.

"I told myself that, even if I missed it, I would still be better off because it would reduce my opposition from three to just one because Howell and Karlsson had made bogeys," said Levet. "Dwelling on the positive instead of the negative after such a terrible putt kept me in a winning frame of mind, and I holed two much harder ones, one to stay alive and one to win, after that mistake."

So a tournament that had started with favourite Colin Montgomerie reducing the easier front nine to just 30 shots and proclaiming "this is a great course and it has got my name on it. It is perfect for my game," ended as nobody foresaw, with the big names, Darren Clarke, Lee Westwood and Montgomerie as the supporting act while others moved centre stage.

Karlsson set the first day pace with a 66 and he was joined in the lead at halfway by Howell, whose second round 65 turned out to be the low round of a week when the weather gods were especially kind and the spectacular new venue, following the switch from the neighbouring Duke's Course, lived up to all expectations.

"It's a fabulous venue. I have heard praise from caddies, spectators and players alike. It is a very, very good golf course. I think we have a real jewel, a real gem. It is a big tournament venue, exceptional with a big finish – driver, four iron at 16, five iron at 17 and driver, four iron at 18."

Colin Montgomerie

The charges expected from Montgomerie and Westwood, both six adrift at this stage, never really came, although Europe's Number One threatened to take a hand with a 67 in round three that hauled him into fourth place. But a frustrating last round left the stage clear for an Englishman, a Frenchman and two Swedes to fight it out.

It was the Englishman, the 1999 Dubai Desert Classic winner Howell who held the call going into the last day one ahead on 15 under 201, at which stage it was hard to believe that 14 under would make the play-off. But with players finding the wind difficult to gauge and the course presenting a stiff challenge, scoring soared and while Grönberg holed out of a bunker at the fifth on the way to four straight birdies, he could not keep it up.

Meanwhile Howell, after falling to as many as four behind, made a superb late rally which gained him a play-off spot. Karlsson, needing to play the last five holes in one over to win, slipped up at the 14th and 16th and eventually needed to bravely hole a 12 footer at the last to earn a second bite of the cherry.

Howell and Karlsson dropped out with bogeys at the first extra hole, where Grönberg had to get up and down to force Levet to hole his short birdie putt. With so much going on around him, it must have seemed a lifetime for the Frenchman to wait his turn, and the putt did not do him justice. His next two did, though, and after 75 holes nobody could begrudge him "la victoire."

For a man who had been a 25-1 outsider at the start of the final round and 4-1 outsider of four when it came to the shoot-out, it was a day he will never forget. And so ended Victor Chandler's third British Masters sponsorship, this time with a new June date, an immaculate new course and a huge hike in prize money from 1,324,256 euro (£800,000) to 2,082,918 euro (£1.25 million). After the victories of long-shots Bob May, Gary Orr and Thomas Levet, cynics would say they can well afford it!

Lee Westwood

Shot of the Week

The 200 yards three iron from the left rough from Thomas Levet that nestled up to the cup on the first play-off hole. True, the winner spoiled the script by missing the five footer for a winning birdie but in the circumstances it was exceptional, and it put him in the driving seat. "My best shot of the week," said Levet. "Even though I followed it with a terrible putt, it still meant I had only one player left to beat."

WOBURN GOLF AND COUNTRY CLUB, MILTON KEYNES, ENGLAND, 31 MAY - 3 JUNE, 2001, PAR 72, 7214 YARDS, 6597 METRES

Pos.	Name		Rd1	Rd2	Rd3	Rd4	Total	Par	Prize Money Euro	£
1	Thomas LEVET	Fr	69	69	67	69	274	-14	345079.90	208330.00
2	David HOWELL	Eng	68	65	68	73	274	-14	154394.00	93210.01
	Robert KARLSSON	Swe	66	67	69	72	274	-14	154394.00	93210.01
	Mathias GRÖNBERG	Swe	69	70	67	68	274	-14	154394.00	93210.01
5	Olle KARLSSON	Swe	71	70	68	69	278	-10	87789.73	53000.00
6	Ricardo GONZALEZ	Arg	70	73	67	69	279	-9	67291.66	40625.00
	Niclas FASTH	Swe	74	69	66	70	279	-9	67291.66	40625.00
8	Anthony WALL	Eng	70	68	69	73	280	-8	49071.14	29625.00
	Lee WESTWOOD	Eng	69	70	67	74	280	-8	49071.14	29625.00
10	Roger WESSELS	SA	70	68	72	71	281	-7	41410.25	25000.00
11	Malcolm MACKENZIE	Eng	70	70	66	76	282	-6	35681.83	21541.67
	Fredrik JACOBSON	Swe	70	71	75	66	282	-6	35681.83	21541.67
	Erol SIMSEK	Ger	68	73	73	68	282	-6	35681.83	21541.67
14	Mark MOULAND	Wal	70	73	72	68	283	-5	27563.70	16640.63
	Ian WOOSNAM	Wal	69	73	72	69	283	-5	27563.70	16640.63
	Warren BENNETT	Eng	70	72	72	69	283	-5	27563.70	16640.63
	Sven STRÜVER	Ger	68	73	71	71	283	-5	27563.70	16640.63
	Richard GREEN	Aus	73	71	70	69	283	-5	27563.70	16640.63
	Jean HUGO	SA	72	72	70	69	283	-5	27563.70	16640.63
	Rolf MUNTZ	Hol	72	70	70	71	283	-5	27563.70	16640.63
	Adam SCOTT	Aus	67	74	71	71	283	-5	27563.70	16640.63
22	Mark MCNULTY	Zim	70	66	76	72	284	-4	22154.48	13375.00
	Greg TURNER	NZ	70	72	73	69	284	-4	22154.48	13375.00
	Stephen LEANEY	Aus	72	72	73	67	284	-4	22154.48	13375.00
	Justin ROSE	Eng	70	70	73	71	284	-4	22154.48	13375.00
	Peter MITCHELL	Eng	72	69	74	69	284	-4	22154.48	13375.00
27	John SENDEN	Aus	71	69	78	67	285	-3	18427.56	11125.00
	Colin MONTGOMERIE	Scot	68	71	74	72	285	-3	18427.56	11125.00
	Thomas BJÖRN	Den	69	75	69	72	285	-3	18427.56	11125.00
	David PARK	Wal	72	71	71	71	285	-3	18427.56	11125.00
	John BICKERTON	Eng	69	73	72	71	285	-3	18427.56	11125.00
	David CARTER	Eng	76	66	72	71	285	-3	18427.56	11125.00
	Paul CASEY	Eng	71	69	69	76	285	-3	18427.56	11125.00
34	Sandy LYLE	Scot	69	72	72	73	286	-2	14493.59	8750.00
	Brian DAVIS	Eng	70	74	66	76	286	-2	14493.59	8750.00
	Nick O'HERN	Aus	69	70	72	75	286	-2	14493.59	8750.00
	Steen TINNING	Den	72	72	71	71	286	-2	14493.59	8750.00
	Alex CEJKA	Ger	71	71	71	73	286	-2	14493.59	8750.00
	Peter O'MALLEY	Aus	71	71	71	73	286	-2	14493.59	8750.00
	Jorge BERENDT	Arg	70	71	72	73	286	-2	14493.59	8750.00
	Greg OWEN	Eng	68	74	73	71	286	-2	14493.59	8750.00
42	Mark ROE	Eng	73	70	72	72	287	-1	11801.92	7125.00
	David GILFORD	Eng	72	72	71	72	287	-1	11801.92	7125.00
	Ian GARBUTT	Eng	71	73	72	71	287	-1	11801.92	7125.00
	Darren CLARKE	N.Ire	70	72	71	74	287	-1	11801.92	7125.00
	Michael CAMPBELL	NZ	74	70	69	74	287	-1	11801.92	7125.00
47	Sam TORRANCE	Scot	72	72	66	78	288	0	9524.36	5750.00
	Fredrik HENGE	Swe	70	72	74	72	288	0	9524.36	5750.00
	Gary EVANS	Eng	74	69	73	72	288	0	9524.36	5750.00
	Markus BRIER	Aut	72	72	70	74	288	0	9524.36	5750.00
	Andrew COLTART	Scot	70	68	75	75	288	0	9524.36	5750.00
	Christopher HANELL	Swe	74	70	76	68	288	0	9524.36	5750.00
53	Peter FOWLER	Aus	71	69	77	72	289	1	7453.85	4500.00
	Patrik SJÖLAND	Swe	71	73	69	76	289	1	7453.85	4500.00
	Dean ROBERTSON	Scot	72	70	70	77	289	1	7453.85	4500.00
	Simon DYSON	Eng	73	71	71	74	289	1	7453.85	4500.00
57	Des SMYTH	Ire	72	72	71	75	290	2	5590.38	3375.00
	Ian POULTER	Eng	72	70	74	74	290	2	5590.38	3375.00
	Carlos RODILES	Sp	72	70	76	72	290	2	5590.38	3375.00
	Per HAUGSRUD	Nor	72	71	72	75	290	2	5590.38	3375.00
	Jarrod MOSELEY	Aus	73	71	74	72	290	2	5590.38	3375.00
	Jeremy ROBINSON	Eng	72	72	71	75	290	2	5590.38	3375.00
	Thomas GÖGELE	Ger	70	72	73	75	290	2	5590.38	3375.00
	Russell CLAYDON	Eng	73	70	69	78	290	2	5590.38	3375.00
	David LYNN	Eng	69	74	73	74	290	2	5590.38	3375.00
66	Andrew OLDCORN	Scot	71	73	74	73	291	3	4451.60	2687.50
	Massimo SCARPA	It	72	71	76	72	291	3	4451.60	2687.50
68	Marco BERNARDINI	It	68	74	79	71	292	4	4141.02	2500.00
69	Costantino ROCCA	It	72	70	73	78	293	5	3933.97	2375.00
70	Elliot BOULT	NZ	73	71	70	81	295	7	3793.18	2290.00
71	Neil CHEETHAM	Eng	73	71	73	79	296	8	3106.00	1875.14
72	Darren FICHARDT	SA	74	68	80	75	297	9	3103.00	1873.33
73	Eamonn DARCY	Ire	68	75	77	78	298	10	3100.00	1871.52
	Tony JOHNSTONE	Zim	72	72	76	78	298	10	3100.00	1871.52

Red Hot

MARRIOTT FOREST OF ARDEN HOTEL, WARWICKSHIRE, ENGLAND

Colin Montgomerie spared himself a lot of extra pain in more ways than one when he ended his involvement in The Compass Group English Open just three holes into the second round.

Montgomerie's withdrawal was designed to avoid further discomfort from the lower back problems that had forced him to miss the Wednesday Pro-Am, and which had seen him plunge to five over par before he bowed out.

Adam Scott

But his early departure also meant he did not have to endure the anguish of seeing Peter O'Malley serve up an unwelcome reminder of the incredible scoring spree that had allowed him to pip the Scot for the 1992 Scottish Open title.

On that occasion, O'Malley covered the final five holes at Gleneagles in an incredible seven under par to claim his first European Tour title. He also won the 1995 Benson and Hedges International Open, but had to wait six years for his third success on The European Tour International Schedule. But just two weeks short of his 36th birthday, he showed he still had the ability to produce a hot streak at just the right time.

Raphaël Jacquelin

O'Malley, descended from Irish ancestors as his name suggests, was expected to prove a prolific winner on The European Tour after finishing runner-up to Mark James in his first event, the 1989 Dubai Desert Classic. Two European Tour victories in addition to others in New Zealand in 1995 and his native Australia in 1998 gave him cause to celebrate but his win-rate was not as prolific as some observers had predicted.

He said: "The last few years I felt I've put myself in position to win tournaments and haven't done it. The key has been my putting, but the confidence I got from playing well in Germany a few weeks ago where I finished third really helped me. I played well coming down the stretch and finished everything off nicely.

"I guess I was thinking about the way I played to beat Colin, even though it was quite a while ago now. It was a similar kind of streak. You get into a phase where you know you are going to hit good shots and score well, and that's how it was again today. Certainly, the run from the eighth to the 14th was similar sort of golf."

The crowds who gathered at the Marriott Forest of Arden Hotel had come to expect an Australian triumph - but it was 20 year old Adam Scott who seemed likely to provide it. He took a two shot lead into the final round, and was installed as a red-hot favourite to add to his victory in the Alfred Dunhill Championship in South Africa earlier in the year. But he never really recovered from the blow of dropping three shots in the first six holes, and a one over par 73 eventually dropped him to third place.

Playing partner Raphaël Jacquelin took advantage of Scott's frustration, and a couple of early birdies saw him transform a two shot deficit into a two shot lead just before the turn.

Jean Hugo

The Course

Defending champion Darren Clarke said he had never seen the Marriott Forest of Arden Hotel course in better shape, and it proved an excellent test of golf. There were plenty of birdie opportunities, but the watery 16th and the 18th - one of the toughest par threes on the Tour - again proved troublesome.

Shot of the Week

Peter O'Malley was in no doubt about the shot that set him on his way to the title - the curling 60 footer he holed for an eagle at the 12th in the final round. O'Malley estimated that it broke between five and six feet from the left of the cup, and he admitted he would have been happy to leave himself a tap-in birdie. But he had his putter raised when his ball was still four feet short, recognising it was destined for the hole.

But O'Malley was just beginning to slip into overdrive, and he burned up the course between the eighth and 12th holes. He grabbed three birdies and a stunning eagle to join Jacquelin on 12 under par, and hit the front on his own with yet another birdie at the 14th.

His French rival drew level with a rare birdie at the tricky 16th, but he still had to negotiate the long par three final hole, the scene of so much drama over the years.

Jacquelin's tee shot found the bunker, and he splashed out to ten feet to leave himself an awkward putt to force a play-off. But his ball rolled agonisingly past the hole, and O'Malley was able to pocket a cheque for 223,373 euro (£133,330), his biggest pay day so far.

David Facey

Paul Lawrie

MARRIOTT FOREST OF ARDEN HOTEL, WARWICKSHIRE, ENGLAND, 7-10 JUNE, 2001, PAR 72, 7182 YARDS, 6567 METRES

Pos.	Name		Rd1	Rd2	Rd3	Rd4	Total	Par	Prize Money Euro	£
1	Peter O'MALLEY	Aus	70	69	70	66	275	-13	223373.10	133330.01
2	Raphaël JACQUELIN	Fr	73	67	66	70	276	-12	148904.20	88879.99
3	Adam SCOTT	Aus	67	70	67	73	277	-11	83901.03	50080.00
4	Jean HUGO	SA	70	68	68	73	279	-9	67013.60	40000.00
5	Steve WEBSTER	Eng	73	69	73	66	281	-7	44363.00	26480.00
	Darren CLARKE	N.Ire	74	72	67	68	281	-7	44363.00	26480.00
	Lee WESTWOOD	Eng	77	67	68	69	281	-7	44363.00	26480.00
	Retief GOOSEN	SA	75	71	65	70	281	-7	44363.00	26480.00
9	Ian POULTER	Eng	72	71	69	70	282	-6	30022.09	17920.00
10	Paul MCGINLEY	Ire	73	69	70	71	283	-5	26805.44	16000.00
11	Greg OWEN	Eng	77	70	66	71	284	-4	24661.01	14720.00
12	Jorge BERENDT	Arg	72	72	73	68	285	-3	21209.80	12660.00
	Massimo SCARPA	It	70	69	74	72	285	-3	21209.80	12660.00
	David LYNN	Eng	74	70	70	71	285	-3	21209.80	12660.00
	Paul CASEY	Eng	73	72	72	68	285	-3	21209.80	12660.00
16	Roger CHAPMAN	Eng	75	70	69	72	286	-2	16810.84	10034.29
	Jeremy ROBINSON	Eng	75	67	71	73	286	-2	16810.84	10034.29
	Ian GARBUTT	Eng	72	77	69	68	286	-2	16810.84	10034.29
	Paul LAWRIE	Scot	70	77	69	70	286	-2	16810.84	10034.29
	Raymond RUSSELL	Scot	76	69	68	73	286	-2	16810.84	10034.29
	John BICKERTON	Eng	79	70	64	73	286	-2	16810.84	10034.29
	Alastair FORSYTH	Scot	73	72	68	73	286	-2	16810.84	10034.29
23	Costantino ROCCA	It	69	73	73	72	287	-1	14340.91	8560.00
	Anthony WALL	Eng	70	75	69	73	287	-1	14340.91	8560.00
	Marco BERNARDINI	It	68	72	69	78	287	-1	14340.91	8560.00
26	Andrew OLDCORN	Scot	67	76	73	72	288	0	12330.50	7360.00
	David GILFORD	Eng	74	71	73	70	288	0	12330.50	7360.00
	Justin ROSE	Eng	72	67	70	79	288	0	12330.50	7360.00
	Peter BAKER	Eng	77	68	71	72	288	0	12330.50	7360.00
	Jonathan LOMAS	Eng	71	78	71	68	288	0	12330.50	7360.00
	Stephen DODD	Wal	72	70	73	73	288	0	12330.50	7360.00
	Francisco CEA	Sp	72	74	70	72	288	0	12330.50	7360.00
33	Barry LANE	Eng	74	74	72	69	289	1	10521.14	6280.00
	Tobias DIER	Ger	73	71	73	72	289	1	10521.14	6280.00
35	David HOWELL	Eng	69	76	72	73	290	2	9515.93	5680.00
	Anders HANSEN	Den	77	71	75	67	290	2	9515.93	5680.00
	Dennis EDLUND	Swe	77	69	71	73	290	2	9515.93	5680.00
	Phillip PRICE	Wal	74	75	70	71	290	2	9515.93	5680.00
	Stephen GALLACHER	Scot	74	71	72	73	290	2	9515.93	5680.00
40	David J RUSSELL	Eng	76	70	70	75	291	3	8309.69	4960.00
	Warren BENNETT	Eng	73	74	75	69	291	3	8309.69	4960.00
	Steen TINNING	Den	72	73	70	76	291	3	8309.69	4960.00
	Nic HENNING	SA	73	71	74	73	291	3	8309.69	4960.00
44	Mark MCNULTY	Zim	70	76	72	74	292	4	6835.39	4080.00
	Brian DAVIS	Eng	73	74	73	72	292	4	6835.39	4080.00
	Nick O'HERN	Aus	73	76	72	71	292	4	6835.39	4080.00
	Carl SUNESON	Sp	75	73	75	69	292	4	6835.39	4080.00
	Gary EVANS	Eng	74	69	72	77	292	4	6835.39	4080.00
	David CARTER	Eng	74	73	73	72	292	4	6835.39	4080.00
	David HIGGINS	Ire	76	73	71	72	292	4	6835.39	4080.00
51	Peter HANSON	Swe	74	71	73	75	293	5	5361.09	3200.00
	Peter MITCHELL	Eng	71	73	73	76	293	5	5361.09	3200.00
	Johan RYSTRÖM	Swe	71	75	74	73	293	5	5361.09	3200.00
	Mark PILKINGTON	Wal	76	70	73	74	293	5	5361.09	3200.00
55	Greg TURNER	NZ	72	75	75	72	294	6	4422.90	2640.00
	Roger WESSELS	SA	73	73	72	76	294	6	4422.90	2640.00
	Gary ORR	Scot	76	71	75	72	294	6	4422.90	2640.00
58	Gordon BRAND JNR.	Scot	76	73	71	75	295	7	3819.78	2280.00
	Sandy LYLE	Scot	77	72	74	72	295	7	3819.78	2280.00
	Philip WALTON	Ire	75	72	76	72	295	7	3819.78	2280.00
	Paolo QUIRICI	Swi	73	74	74	74	295	7	3819.78	2280.00
62	Wayne RILEY	Aus	78	71	74	74	297	9	3350.68	2000.00
	Peter FOWLER	Aus	73	71	74	79	297	9	3350.68	2000.00
	Hennie OTTO	SA	71	73	77	76	297	9	3350.68	2000.00
65	Marc FARRY	Fr	74	66	81	77	298	10	2755.93	1645.00
	Stephen LEANEY	Aus	71	77	73	77	298	10	2755.93	1645.00
	Paul BROADHURST	Eng	76	73	77	72	298	10	2755.93	1645.00
	Gary EMERSON	Eng	73	74	74	77	298	10	2755.93	1645.00
	Bradley DREDGE	Wal	72	76	74	76	298	10	2755.93	1645.00
	Francis VALERA	Sp	77	72	72	77	298	10	2755.93	1645.00
71	Tony JOHNSTONE	Zim	77	71	75	76	299	11	2005.50	1197.07
	Graham RANKIN	Scot	72	73	74	80	299	11	2005.50	1197.07
	Andrew MARSHALL	Eng	74	74	74	77	299	11	2005.50	1197.07
	Neil CHEETHAM	Eng	76	71	75	77	299	11	2005.50	1197.07
75	Wei-Tze YEH	Taiwan	73	74	75	78	300	12	1998.00	1192.59
76	Robert COLES	Eng	75	72	77	77	301	13	1995.00	1190.80

European Tour Hospitality
Masters of Golf Hospitality
Golf hospitality provides the perfect combination of informality and serious sport, in a beautifully relaxed setting. Entertain your valued clients at a leading golf event and generate new business, build goodwill and give your enterprise a distinctive edge.
Let European Tour Hospitality manage your event with an unrivalled degree of professionalism and experience. European Tour Hospitality is a joint venture set up between the PGA European Tour and the corporate hospitality business of Compass Group to offer you official hospitality for a number of world-class golf events.
Before entertaining your clients at a top sports event, talk to the key players in golf hospitality. Contact our corporate hospitality sales team for immediate attention:
0845 30 50 900
European Tour Hospitality
Queen's Wharf
Queen Caroline Street
London W6 9RJ
Tel outside UK: +44 (0) 20 8600 2506
Fax: +44 (0) 20 8841 9749
Email: eth@compass-group.co.uk
EUROPEAN TOUR
OFFICIAL HOSPITALITY
Volvo PGA Championship, Victor Chandler British Masters, The Compass Group English Open, The Open Championship,
World Golf Championships-American Express Championship.

Absolutely Amazing

SOUTHERN HILLS COUNTRY CLUB, TULSA, OKLAHOMA, USA

Retief Goosen thoroughly deserved the accolade of "Sportstar of the Year 2001", awarded by David Walsh of The Sunday Times following the end of the 101st United States Open, as he basked shyly in the glory of finishing ahead of all the best golfers in the world.

For this was the moment when Goosen, born in Pietersburg, a beer and rugby town in South Africa, not only demonstrated his world-class skills but also his superb resilience. He led from start to finish but then on the very last green contrived to take three putts from 12 feet. Yet 24 hours later in Tulsa, he returned to the superb Southern Hills Country Club to triumph in the 18 hole play-off against Mark Brooks.

OOSEN
CLUB

It was a magnificent victory for Goosen and a huge fillip for The European Tour as he followed in the footsteps of compatriots Ernie Els and Gary Player onto the US Open Roll of Honour. It was a victory, too, for his control from tee to green and for a clinical display with the putter. And it was a victory which took the total number of Major Championship victories by European Tour Members to 26 since Seve Ballesteros won the Open Championship in 1979.

After the glories of Pebble Beach and Tiger Woods's rampant win in the Millennium US Open, Southern Hills Country Club was always going to struggle to get the 21st century off with a bang. How hot and how humid were the main concerns, while the imperious form of Woods going into the Championship, allied to his string of four consecutive Majors, had all but stifled debate as to who might win.

In the event, one almighty storm on the first afternoon cleared away days of hot, steamy weather and the remainder of the Championship, whilst still hot, was played under cloudless skies. That, coupled with the inability of Woods to sort out the intricacies of the tree-lined fairways and the small, quirky greens, gave us a Championship few had anticipated.

In truth, Woods, from his first pushed tee shot, never looked comfortable. An opening 74 left him eight shots off the lead and the anticipated charge from the back never materialised. When he did look like getting going he fell at the ninth, an innocuous uphill par four of only 374 yards. Twice at the weekend it cost him a five, and that after a six on the first day.

Sergio Garcia

Colin Montgomerie

The Course

Southern Hills Country Club was a pleasant surprise in many ways. Emboldened by the success of Pinehurst No 2 two years previously, the USGA had left the course pretty well to look after itself. Fairways were wider than usual and the rough sufficiently short to tempt players. Almost every hole was a dogleg, and with tall trees lining the fairways, tee shots in particular had to be shaped.

At the halfway stage there were just ten players on par or better. Within that elite group were David Duval and Phil Mickelson who, with Woods for once not in the running, had their best chance of picking up that elusive first Major victory. Sergio Garcia was there too, confident after having won his first US PGA Tour title three weeks previously. Leading the field, though, were the only two men who had managed to put together significant birdie runs over the first couple of days.

Mark Brooks

Goosen had found six birdies in his first ten holes in round one. A couple had gone by the time he finished, but nevertheless he still held the first round lead with a 66. His second round 70 was a fine exercise in consolidation. Brooks, the winner five years previously of the US PGA Championship, joined him on four under. He had finished his first round with a six, but started the second with five birdies in six holes and went on to post a 64. J.L. Lewis, after two 68's, was also tied for the lead.

By Saturday night, the number of those below par had dwindled to six, all between three and five under. Duval and Lewis had gone, but Garcia and Mickelson remained, the sextet being made up of Stewart Cink, the only player to beat par all three days, and Rocco Mediate. The one distinguishing feature of all their play was an ability to keep their scores intact over the difficult closing holes. Goosen, in particular, struggled with his approach play but salvaged a level par back nine of 35 with only 11 putts to tie with Cink at five under - one ahead of Brooks, Garcia and Mediate and two in front of Mickelson

On Sunday, the first to fall by the wayside were Garcia and Mickelson. The Spaniard is still learning and will come again, but on a US Open course more forgiving than most, Mickelson was again frustrated – this time by a closing 75.

Mediate also fell back, dropping a couple of shots after the turn and ending in fourth place. So it came down to three, and with a bogey here, a birdie there, Brooks, Cink and Goosen all arrived on the 18th tee five under par. Brooks played first, being in the penultimate group, and three putts from 40 feet looked to have ruined his chances.

Next up, Cink missed the green left and could not get down in two. He rushed his second putt from 18 inches, a miss that at the time seemed only to have cost him a share of second place. Goosen's second shot had surely settled it; a superb six iron to 12 feet and two putts from there for the title. But the formality became a nightmare when not just the first putt missed, but the one back as well. Indeed the third putt was longer than the second, yet somehow Goosen got it in.

Steadfastly the USGA have refused to countenance sudden-death or limited holes solutions for its premier Championship and so it was that Brooks and Goosen, not to mention thousands of helpers and attendant media and officials, returned on the Monday to sort the matter out.

Indeed, the USGA's hand may have been strengthened, since few would have fancied Goosen to pick himself up after the horrors of those few minutes on the 18th green to win that same evening. As it was he came out revived the following day and, five ahead after 12 holes, he retained his composure over the closing stretch.

Goosen said: "I certainly had to work hard for the win. It was a long week, and it felt like a year out there. But I played pretty solid all week and the putter was warm in places, except for Sunday afternoon. What can I say? Well this is absolutely amazing!"

Of course it was fair that Walsh should also point out that those three putts on the 18th late on Sunday afternoon could have destroyed what had been a good, if far from fulfilled, career. Goosen, however, had for two years increased his mental strength by working with Jos Vanstiphout, who investigated sports psychology in California. Vanstiphout had impressed on Goosen: "Walk, talk and think like a champion and you become a champion." Before Goosen teed off in the play-off, Vanstiphout simply told his pupil: "I trust you, buddy."

Goosen, of course, trusted himself and triumphed.

Bruce Critchley

Shot of the Week

Retief Goosen's five foot putt on the 18th green in the play-off. Twenty four hours earlier Goosen faltered on that green - the five footer expelled all demons and gave him a 70 to the 72 of Mark Brooks.

SOUTHERN HILLS COUNTRY CLUB, TULSA, OKLAHOMA, USA, 14-17 JUNE, 2001, PAR 70, 6973 YARDS, 6376 METRES

Pos.	Name		Rd1	Rd2	Rd3	Rd4	Total	Par	Prize Money Euro	Prize Money £
1	Retief GOOSEN	SA	66	70	69	71	276	-4	1058198.60	651371.50
2	Mark BROOKS	USA	72	64	70	70	276	-4	623161.40	383585.44
3	Stewart CINK	USA	69	69	67	72	277	-3	382491.77	235441.85
4	Rocco MEDIATE	USA	71	68	67	72	278	-2	266639.00	164128.97
5	Tom KITE	USA	73	72	72	64	281	1	203305.82	125144.39
	Paul AZINGER	USA	74	67	69	71	281	1	203305.82	125144.39
7	Davis LOVE III	USA	72	69	71	70	282	2	147174.26	90592.75
	Vijay SINGH	Fiji	74	70	74	64	282	2	147174.26	90592.75
	Angel CABRERA	Arg	70	71	72	69	282	2	147174.26	90592.75
	Phil MICKELSON	USA	70	69	68	75	282	2	147174.26	90592.75
	Kirk TRIPLETT	USA	72	69	71	70	282	2	147174.26	90592.75
12	Tiger WOODS	USA	74	71	69	69	283	3	107858.66	66392.13
	Sergio GARCIA	Sp	70	68	68	77	283	3	107858.66	66392.13
	Michael ALLEN	USA	77	68	67	71	283	3	107858.66	66392.13
	Matt GOGEL	USA	70	69	74	70	283	3	107858.66	66392.13
16	David DUVAL	USA	70	69	71	74	284	4	88579.45	54524.86
	Scott HOCH	USA	73	73	69	69	284	4	88579.45	54524.86
	Chris DIMARCO	USA	69	73	70	72	284	4	88579.45	54524.86
19	Corey PAVIN	USA	70	75	68	72	285	5	74574.78	45904.32
	Chris PERRY	USA	72	71	73	69	285	5	74574.78	45904.32
	Mike WEIR	Can	67	76	68	74	285	5	74574.78	45904.32
22	Scott VERPLANK	USA	71	71	73	71	286	6	64447.83	39670.70
	Thomas BJÖRN	Den	72	69	73	72	286	6	64447.83	39670.70
24	Steve LOWERY	USA	71	73	72	71	287	7	49997.54	30775.86
	Joe DURANT	USA	71	74	70	72	287	7	49997.54	30775.86
	Mark CALCAVECCHIA	USA	70	74	73	70	287	7	49997.54	30775.86
	Hal SUTTON	USA	70	75	71	71	287	7	49997.54	30775.86
	Tom LEHMAN	USA	76	68	69	74	287	7	49997.54	30775.86
	Olin BROWNE	USA	71	74	71	71	287	7	49997.54	30775.86
30	Padraig HARRINGTON	Ire	73	70	71	74	288	8	35337.96	21752.19
	Jesper PARNEVIK	Swe	73	73	74	68	288	8	35337.96	21752.19
	Dean WILSON	USA	71	74	72	71	288	8	35337.96	21752.19
	Bob ESTES	USA	70	72	75	71	288	8	35337.96	21752.19
	Steve JONES	USA	73	73	72	70	288	8	35337.96	21752.19
	Gabriel HJERTSTEDT	Swe	72	74	70	72	288	8	35337.96	21752.19
	Darren CLARKE	N.Ire	74	71	71	72	288	8	35337.96	21752.19
	Bob MAY	USA	72	72	69	75	288	8	35337.96	21752.19
	Bryce MOLDER (Am)	USA	75	71	68	74	288	8		
	J.L. LEWIS	USA	68	68	77	75	288	8	35337.96	21752.19
40	Bernhard LANGER	Ger	71	73	71	74	289	9	28139.86	17321.42
	Tim HERRON	USA	71	74	73	71	289	9	28139.86	17321.42
	Briny BAIRD	USA	71	72	70	76	289	9	28139.86	17321.42
	Shaun MICHEEL	USA	73	70	75	71	289	9	28139.86	17321.42
44	Fred FUNK	USA	78	68	71	73	290	10	22081.07	13591.95
	Toshimitsu IZAWA	USA	69	74	74	73	290	10	22081.07	13591.95
	Brandel CHAMBLEE	USA	72	71	71	76	290	10	22081.07	13591.95
	Jeff MAGGERT	USA	69	73	72	76	290	10	22081.07	13591.95
	Duffy WALDORF	USA	75	68	69	78	290	10	22081.07	13591.95
	Kevin SUTHERLAND	USA	73	72	73	72	290	10	22081.07	13591.95
	Tom BYRUM	USA	74	72	72	72	290	10	22081.07	13591.95
51	Eduardo ROMERO	Arg	74	72	72	73	291	11	17677.79	10881.52
52	Loren ROBERTS	USA	69	76	69	78	292	12	15477.91	9527.39
	Colin MONTGOMERIE	Scot	71	70	77	74	292	12	15477.91	9527.39
	Mark WIEBE	USA	73	72	74	73	292	12	15477.91	9527.39
	Bob TWAY	USA	75	71	72	74	292	12	15477.91	9527.39
	Hale IRWIN	USA	67	75	74	76	292	12	15477.91	9527.39
	José COCERES	Arg	70	73	75	74	292	12	15477.91	9527.39
	Scott DUNLAP	USA	74	70	73	75	292	12	15477.91	9527.39
	Brandt JOBE	USA	77	68	71	76	292	12	15477.91	9527.39
	Frank LICKLITER	USA	75	71	70	76	292	12	15477.91	9527.39
	Jimmy WALKER	USA	79	66	74	73	292	12	15477.91	9527.39
62	Jim FURYK	USA	70	70	71	82	293	13	13454.41	8281.83
	Dudley HART	USA	71	73	74	75	293	13	13454.41	8281.83
	Richard ZOKOL	Can	72	71	74	76	293	13	13454.41	8281.83
	Tim PETROVIC	USA	74	71	75	73	293	13	13454.41	8281.83
66	Ernie ELS	SA	71	74	77	72	294	14	12190.45	7503.80
	Peter LONARD	Aus	76	69	70	79	294	14	12190.45	7503.80
	Dan FORSMAN	USA	75	71	77	71	294	14	12190.45	7503.80
	David TOMS	USA	71	71	77	75	294	14	12190.45	7503.80
	Harrison FRAZAR	USA	73	73	76	72	294	14	12190.45	7503.80
	David PEOPLES	USA	73	73	72	76	294	14	12190.45	7503.80
72	Nick FALDO	Eng	76	70	74	75	295	15	11179.28	6881.38
	Franklin LANGHAM	USA	75	71	75	74	295	15	11179.28	6881.38
74	Anthony KANG	Rep.Kor	74	72	77	73	296	16	10420.90	6414.56
	Mathias GRÖNBERG	Swe	74	69	74	79	296	16	10420.90	6414.56
	Gary ORR	Scot	74	72	74	76	296	16	10420.90	6414.56
	Thongchai JAIDEE	Thai	73	73	72	78	296	16	10420.90	6414.56
78	Jim MCGOVERN	USA	71	73	77	76	297	17	9788.34	6025.19
79	Stephen GANGLUFF	USA	74	72	78	77	301	21	9529.66	5865.96

We are Family

DE VERE SLALEY HALL, NORTHUMBERLAND, ENGLAND

It was worth waiting for, according to Andrew Coltart, as he kept The Great North Open title in the family after surviving the demons in a mini final round crisis. Last year, brother-in-law Lee Westwood lifted the title, then named the Compaq European Grand Prix, but Westwood's interest this time around ended when he missed the halfway cut and it was the 31 year old Scot who pocketed the 217,209 euro (£133,330) cheque and took home The Great North Open crown.

Coltart started the final day with a three shot lead over Bradley Dredge and Jamie Spence but he wobbled around Slaley's own notorious Amen Corner, dropping shots at the eighth and ninth, and found himself trailing as Paul Casey, Stephen Gallacher, Daren Lee and Dredge all made determined moves.

But Coltart birdied both the par five 11th and 12th, showing enormous resolve, and it all came down to the Scot having to make par on Slaley's treacherous 18th to finish one ahead of Casey and Gallacher after Dredge stumbled to a double-bogey six on the last.

Dredge had looked a possible winner as he was tied with Coltart on 11 under par playing the last but his tee shot drifted on the wind, hit a spectator on the shoulder and ricocheted into an awful lie leaving him no chance of reaching the green in two. All he could do was lay up and his third was too bold, running through the green on to the bank at the back from where he was faced with a lightning-fast chip, which rolled past and he two-putted for a six to slide into a tie for third place.

Coltart, having hit his tee shot on the 18th slightly right, was able to view Dredge's frustrating finish.

Bradley Dredge

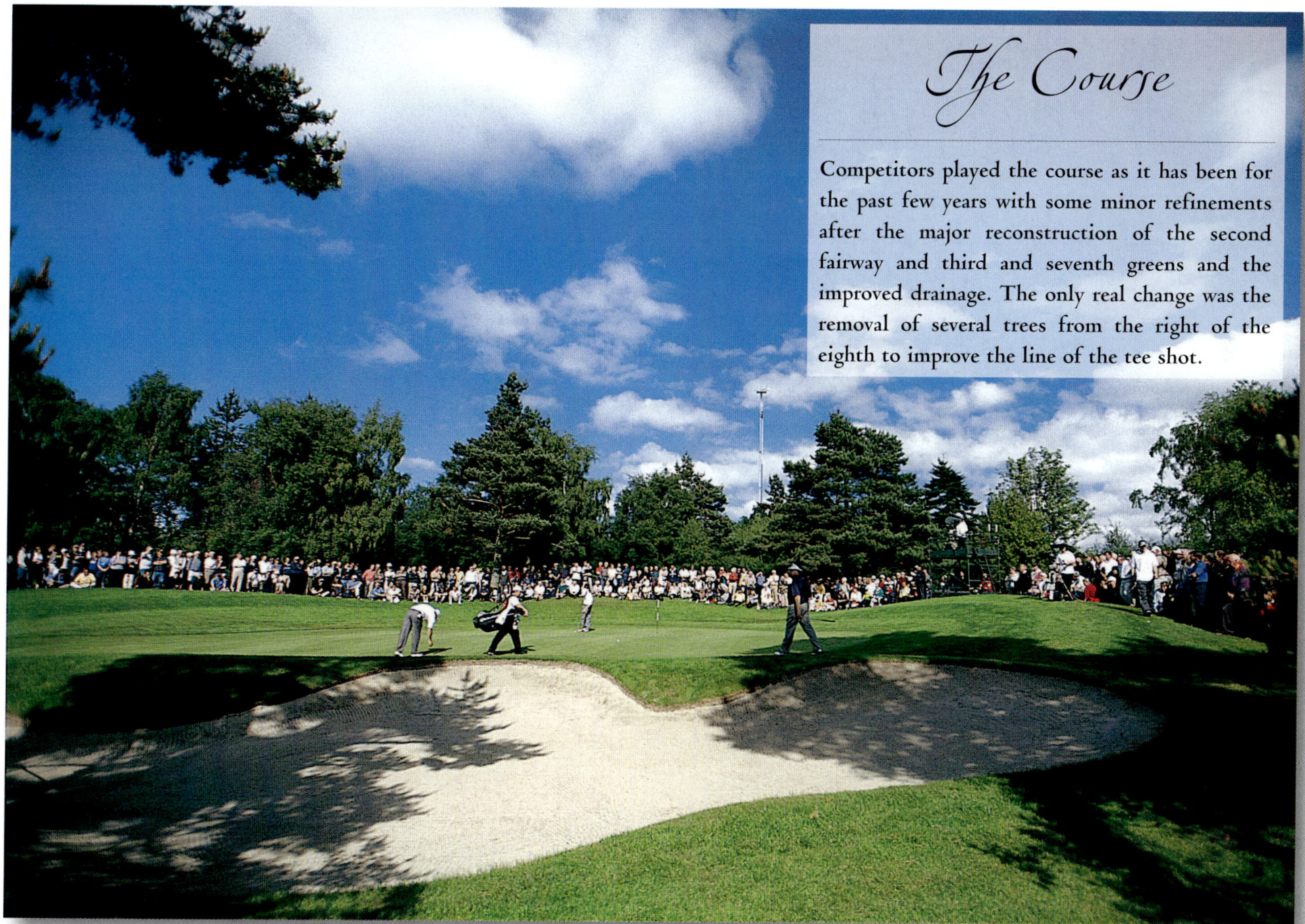

The Course

Competitors played the course as it has been for the past few years with some minor refinements after the major reconstruction of the second fairway and third and seventh greens and the improved drainage. The only real change was the removal of several trees from the right of the eighth to improve the line of the tee shot.

Daren Lee

Carlos Rodiles

"I was watching what happened on the 18th and I was trying not to get distracted," said Coltart. "You look at the faces of some of the guys who are very successful and they don't let anything deflect from the job in hand.

"It's one of the hardest holes to finish with par in Europe. There are a lot of pitfalls down that 463 yards par four hole. I was trying to focus on the next shot in hand when in the past I would have gone away and started panicking about how I was going to swing it.

"That would have been disastrous, I think. I managed to stay fairly focused and pulled it off."

Coltart knew he needed par to win and put a good swing on his approach to hit the back of the green from where he two putted to take his first title on The European Tour International Schedule since the 1998 Qatar Masters.

"It's been a while since I won in Qatar and it can be very difficult to try and find the self belief when you've got very little to try and justify it," said Coltart. "I'm almost doubly delighted that it was pretty horrible and that I managed to keep my head and keep my patience, stay fairly focused and get the job done."

There was no shortage of top quality golf with a new course record and a clutch of scores in the 60s over the Hunting course which was in pristine condition. They included a 66 from 26 year old Londoner Daren Lee in the first round to take him two shots clear of Coltart and Spence with Westwood taking 81.

Shot of the Week

Italian Michele Reale hit a superb seven iron for a hole in one at the 184 yards 17th - he won a Renault Mégane.

Westwood missed the cut by nine shots after a second round 74 and made it clear he was chucking the clubs in the garage and going on a week's holiday. He was still able to joke: "When I came off the course and looked down at my card over the last eight holes, it reminded me of the telephone number for the vets in Worksop!"

Dredge's second round 67 took him into a tie for the lead with Coltart, who posted a second successive 68 as Lee slipped back with 74, with Casey one shot back after a 66. The highlight of the second round was Olle Karlsson's 65 to equal the course record jointly held by Ross Drummond, Colin Montgomerie and David Park.

Karlsson, who considers himself an adopted Geordie because his fiancee Andrea Gray is from Sunderland, had quite an entourage of local golfers because he now lives in Belsay just north of Newcastle, but he remained joint holder of the Slaley record only a matter of hours as Richard Green shaved one off it on the Friday evening with a 64.

Stephen Gallacher

Erol Simsek

Green birdied six in a row from the sixth. "It was fantastic," said the 1997 Dubai Desert Classic winner. "It was one of those days when the putter was red hot and and I was thinking birdie and nothing else on every hole."

Coltart took a real grip on the title on the Saturday with a third round 69 to establish a three shot lead over Dredge and Spence and admitted he would be disappointed if he let the opportunity of his second European Tour title slip from his grasp on the Sunday. He didn't.

"I wouldn't have thought it would be more than 300 rounds of golf until I won again after winning in Qatar but I only have myself to blame for getting in my own way," said Coltart afterwards. "I do think this is my best win because it wasn't pretty. I've heard that people have said it is easier to win when you're playing well and what you have to try and do is win when you're playing poorly. I managed to scramble it around and knock it off, so that gives me a lot of heart and lot of pride."

Alan Hedley

Brian Davis

DE VERE SLALEY HALL, NORTHUMBERLAND, ENGLAND, 21-24 JUNE, 2001, PAR 72, 7088 YARDS, 6481 METRES

Pos.	Name		Rd1	Rd2	Rd3	Rd4	Total	Par	Prize Money Euro	£
1	Andrew COLTART	Scot	68	68	69	72	277	-11	217209.20	133330.00
2	Stephen GALLACHER	Scot	76	67	67	68	278	-10	113190.60	69480.02
	Paul CASEY	Eng	71	66	72	69	278	-10	113190.60	69480.02
4	Steve WEBSTER	Eng	73	68	71	67	279	-9	55346.30	33973.34
	Bradley DREDGE	Wal	69	67	72	71	279	-9	55346.30	33973.34
	Daren LEE	Eng	66	74	69	70	279	-9	55346.30	33973.34
7	Ian POULTER	Eng	73	68	73	66	280	-8	39098.64	24000.00
8	Peter FOWLER	Aus	71	71	70	69	281	-7	23632.96	14506.67
	Jamie SPENCE	Eng	68	70	70	73	281	-7	23632.96	14506.67
	Gregory HAVRET	Fr	73	68	70	70	281	-7	23632.96	14506.67
	Soren HANSEN	Den	71	70	72	68	281	-7	23632.96	14506.67
	Andrew BEAL	Eng	72	69	68	72	281	-7	23632.96	14506.67
	Christophe POTTIER	Fr	76	69	70	66	281	-7	23632.96	14506.67
	Dean ROBERTSON	Scot	73	70	69	69	281	-7	23632.96	14506.67
	Lucas PARSONS	Aus	71	69	69	72	281	-7	23632.96	14506.67
	Scott GARDINER	Aus	69	71	69	72	281	-7	23632.96	14506.67
17	Justin ROSE	Eng	70	70	72	70	282	-6	16855.86	10346.67
	Gary EVANS	Eng	70	74	69	69	282	-6	16855.86	10346.67
	Fredrik JACOBSON	Swe	73	69	69	71	282	-6	16855.86	10346.67
20	Warren BENNETT	Eng	72	71	69	71	283	-5	14753.22	9056.00
	Richard GREEN	Aus	75	64	72	72	283	-5	14753.22	9056.00
	Carlos RODILES	Sp	72	70	73	68	283	-5	14753.22	9056.00
	Jean HUGO	SA	75	71	68	69	283	-5	14753.22	9056.00
	Brett RUMFORD	Aus	74	71	66	72	283	-5	14753.22	9056.00
25	Gordon BRAND JNR.	Scot	70	74	69	71	284	-4	12185.74	7480.00
	Roger CHAPMAN	Eng	69	72	72	71	284	-4	12185.74	7480.00
	Elliot BOULT	NZ	74	70	69	71	284	-4	12185.74	7480.00
	Marcello SANTI	It	72	72	72	68	284	-4	12185.74	7480.00
	Per NYMAN	Swe	72	72	70	70	284	-4	12185.74	7480.00
	Olle KARLSSON	Swe	74	65	72	73	284	-4	12185.74	7480.00
	Jonathan LOMAS	Eng	73	70	71	70	284	-4	12185.74	7480.00
	Nicolas VANHOOTEGEM	Bel	72	66	72	74	284	-4	12185.74	7480.00
33	Andrew OLDCORN	Scot	69	72	71	73	285	-3	9666.05	5933.33
	Greg TURNER	NZ	69	74	73	69	285	-3	9666.05	5933.33
	Paul NILBRINK	Swe	75	71	70	69	285	-3	9666.05	5933.33
	Henrik BJORNSTAD	Nor	73	72	68	72	285	-3	9666.05	5933.33
	Robin BYRD	USA	73	71	71	70	285	-3	9666.05	5933.33
	Carl WATTS	Eng	73	71	73	68	285	-3	9666.05	5933.33
39	Mark ROE	Eng	72	70	75	69	286	-2	7950.06	4880.00
	David GILFORD	Eng	73	70	73	70	286	-2	7950.06	4880.00
	Garry HOUSTON	Wal	74	70	69	73	286	-2	7950.06	4880.00
	Fredrik HENGE	Swe	76	69	68	73	286	-2	7950.06	4880.00
	Nicolas COLSAERTS	Bel	71	73	69	73	286	-2	7950.06	4880.00
	Massimo SCARPA	It	73	71	68	74	286	-2	7950.06	4880.00
	Roger WESSELS	SA	71	75	70	70	286	-2	7950.06	4880.00
	Nick DOUGHERTY (AM)	Eng	70	73	72	71	286	-2		
47	Peter BAKER	Eng	70	71	77	69	287	-1	6777.10	4160.00
	Greg OWEN	Eng	72	70	72	73	287	-1	6777.10	4160.00
49	Mats LANNER	Swe	74	68	71	75	288	0	5864.80	3600.00
	Barry LANE	Eng	76	69	74	69	288	0	5864.80	3600.00
	Scott DRUMMOND	Scot	75	71	74	68	288	0	5864.80	3600.00
	Francis VALERA	Sp	76	70	70	72	288	0	5864.80	3600.00
	Erol SIMSEK	Ger	74	69	74	71	288	0	5864.80	3600.00
54	John WADE	Aus	74	67	76	72	289	1	4561.51	2800.00
	Marc PENDARIES	Fr	71	71	74	73	289	1	4561.51	2800.00
	Hennie OTTO	SA	74	71	71	73	289	1	4561.51	2800.00
	Francisco CEA	Sp	75	70	71	73	289	1	4561.51	2800.00
	David CARTER	Eng	74	68	70	77	289	1	4561.51	2800.00
59	Brian DAVIS	Eng	75	71	74	70	290	2	3714.37	2280.00
	Shaun P WEBSTER	Eng	71	73	72	74	290	2	3714.37	2280.00
	Michael ARCHER	Eng	75	71	75	69	290	2	3714.37	2280.00
	Richard BLAND	Eng	72	70	72	76	290	2	3714.37	2280.00
63	Mark JAMES	Eng	74	71	76	70	291	3	3193.06	1960.00
	Ross MCFARLANE	Eng	74	71	71	75	291	3	3193.06	1960.00
	Craig HAINLINE	USA	73	73	71	74	291	3	3193.06	1960.00
	Simon DYSON	Eng	72	68	77	74	291	3	3193.06	1960.00
67	Jeremy ROBINSON	Eng	70	73	75	74	292	4	2671.74	1640.00
	David LYNN	Eng	75	70	74	73	292	4	2671.74	1640.00
	Mark PILKINGTON	Wal	71	73	74	74	292	4	2671.74	1640.00
	Iain PYMAN	Eng	74	72	74	72	292	4	2671.74	1640.00
71	Mattias NILSSON	Swe	73	70	74	76	293	5	2174.90	1335.02
	Massimo FLORIOLI	It	75	70	74	74	293	5	2174.90	1335.02
73	Gordon J BRAND	Eng	71	74	77	73	295	7	1952.00	1198.20
74	David ORR	Scot	72	71	79	76	298	10	1949.00	1196.36
75	Paul EALES	Eng	74	71	80	78	303	15	1946.00	1194.52

Special Bond

FOTA ISLAND GOLF CLUB, CORK, IRELAND

Before his arrival by the banks of the River Lee in Co Cork, where killer whales frolicked in the harbour and white-handed gibbons from the wildlife park that adjoins the course's fourth fairway screeched incessantly for food, many had wondered if Colin Montgomerie had forgotten the art of winning.

Not since his Volvo PGA Championship victory at Wentworth Club 13 months previously had Montgomerie savoured a win on The European Tour. Some had even cruelly suggested that the player might be better off keeping his clubs in the locker-room and concentrating on his burgeoning golf course design business instead.

On the practice range on Thursday, just before he headed out for his first round, a final piece in the jigsaw fell into place that allowed the Montgomerie swing of old to return. "I just found something that hadn't been there in the timing," he was to explain on Sunday evening, not long after ending his tournament winning drought with his 25th win on The European Tour. It was also his third Murphy's Irish Open success, which only served to confirm the suspicion that the Scot has managed to establish a special bond with the Irish golfing public who greeted his arrival onto the 72nd green as if he were a prodigal son returning home.

What made the reception from the huge galleries all the more genuine was that among those left in his wake were two of Ireland's home-grown heroes, Darren Clarke and Padraig Harrington - who produced a brace of final round 64s to tie for the runners-up position with Sweden's Niclas Fasth, who shot a superb 63. Yet, an indication of how awesome Montgomerie's play had been for the four days of the championship was that he finished five strokes ahead of his nearest pursuers.

From the start, Montgomerie had stated his intent. On the eve of the tournament, he had said, rather boldly: "The best I can do now is win .... and here I am." In the first round, he was as good as his word as he finished off with a 210 yards five iron second shot from a downhill stance to the 507 yards 18th hole that ended up four feet from the hole. He rolled in the eagle putt for a course record eight

Barry Lane

Niclas Fasth

The Course

It's rare that a course receives near universal praise from all of the players, but that was the case at Fota Island. Located on an island in the Lee estuary that is also home to a wildlife park, the course was originally designed by Peter McEvoy and Christy O'Connor Jnr but was re-designed by Jeff Howes in 1999 to bring the extensive water and magnificent trees on the parkland terrain more into play.

Padraig Harrington

under par 63 and, even at that stage, Montgomerie must have felt he could have walked across the pond that separated the final green from the recorder's hut rather than undertake the circuitous 200 yards walk around by the clubhouse.

So it was that Montgomerie went into day two with a two stroke lead over the chasing pair of Irish veteran Eamonn Darcy and Sweden's Fredrik Henge. By day's end, Montgomerie was still at the head of the field, but with a different chasing pack. The Scot had to work extremely hard for a second round 69 and England's Anthony Wall - expressing some appreciation for the fact that the following galleries actually knew him by name - moved into second place on his own with a second successive 67, while Thomas Björn moved into a four-way tie for third.

The Irish challenge had apparently evaporated. Harrington, who had expressed mild concern about his participation in the build-up because of a wrist injury which he first sustained as a teenager playing Gaelic football, was a distant 21st, and Clarke was among those who narrowly survived on the cut mark which fell at level par.

Over the weekend, however, Clarke exploded into life. Part of the reason for his transformation he attributed to renewing acquaintances with the Belgian sports psychologist Jos Vanstiphout in mid-tournament, switching his mental guidance away from US-

Mathias Grönberg

based Bob Rotella. On the Saturday and Sunday, nobody played better golf that Clarke who was 13 under par for those two days, not sufficient to trouble Montgomerie, but enough to give him a career-best Murphy's Irish Open finish.

Montgomerie, though, continued on his merry way. Rather surprisingly, in all his career wins in the past, the Scottish player had never managed to lead on his own after all four rounds. By Saturday evening, after a third round 68, Montgomerie had stretched his lead to three shots. Now, the chief pursuer was Australian Adam Scott, who had a promise for the leader. "I want to chase him down, it makes me want to play even better," said Scott. To which Montgomerie retorted: "If I was him, I would be chasing down whoever is leading as well. I'm there, and I have been for an awful long time in Europe, to be shot at - and it is a position I have got used to and coped quite well with in the past."

Again, Montgomerie was as good as his word on a final day when the crowds reached an estimated 40,000 and a carnival atmosphere pervaded. With the sun shining, and hardly a breath of wind, the

Costantino Rocca

champion finished off his tournament with a 66 for an 18 under par aggregate of 266. "That was one of the most important, if not the most important win of my career," he insisted. Indeed, as he trooped behind a local pipe and drum band who serenaded him with a melody of Scottish tunes on his way to collect the Waterford Crystal trophy, it was almost possible to see the weight lift from those hefty shoulders of his.

As for the Irish? When Clarke and Harrington met for the first time after their closing 64s, Harrington extended a congratulatory hand to his compatriot. "We nearly did it. If we could have got rid of the other, it would have been nearly perfect," he said with a cheeky grin. "Yeh, it would have been," replied Clarke with a smile. But, not for the first time on The European Tour, the duo had discovered that Montgomerie - once he gets into a winning position - is a hard man to shift.

Philip Reid

Steve Webster

Shot of the Week

The 18th hole at Fota Island is a par five measuring 507 yards and is a true risk hole. In Thursday's first round, Colin Montgomerie hit a drive of almost 300 yards and was left with a second shot of 210 yards off a downhill stance. Using a five iron, his approach finished four feet from the pin, and he rolled in the eagle putt. "That gave me a huge boost for the rest of the week," he admitted.

Darren Clarke

FOTA ISLAND GOLF CLUB, CORK, IRELAND, 28 JUNE - 1 JULY, 2001, PAR 71, 6927 YARDS, 6334 METRES

Pos.	Name		Rd1	Rd2	Rd3	Rd4	Total	Par	Prize Money Euro	Prize Money £
1	Colin MONTGOMERIE	Scot	63	69	68	66	266	-18	266660.00	161618.00
2	Padraig HARRINGTON	Ire	67	72	68	64	271	-13	119310.00	72311.72
	Darren CLARKE	N.Ire	70	72	65	64	271	-13	119310.00	72311.72
	Niclas FASTH	Swe	68	71	69	63	271	-13	119310.00	72311.72
5	Thomas BJÖRN	Den	66	69	72	66	273	-11	67840.00	41116.65
6	Gary EMERSON	Eng	68	70	67	69	274	-10	48000.00	29091.97
	Robert KARLSSON	Swe	71	69	67	67	274	-10	48000.00	29091.97
	Adam SCOTT	Aus	68	69	66	71	274	-10	48000.00	29091.97
9	David HOWELL	Eng	68	70	71	66	275	-9	29173.33	17681.45
	Barry LANE	Eng	68	67	72	68	275	-9	29173.33	17681.45
	Ian POULTER	Eng	69	69	71	66	275	-9	29173.33	17681.45
	Steen TINNING	Den	69	68	72	66	275	-9	29173.33	17681.45
	Thomas LEVET	Fr	68	67	72	68	275	-9	29173.33	17681.45
	Andrew COLTART	Scot	67	71	69	68	275	-9	29173.33	17681.45
15	Gordon BRAND JNR.	Scot	68	69	71	68	276	-8	21632.00	13110.78
	Ian WOOSNAM	Wal	73	69	70	64	276	-8	21632.00	13110.78
	Steve WEBSTER	Eng	67	71	72	66	276	-8	21632.00	13110.78
	Anthony WALL	Eng	67	67	71	71	276	-8	21632.00	13110.78
	Justin ROSE	Eng	70	70	69	67	276	-8	21632.00	13110.78
20	Mark MOULAND	Wal	71	70	67	69	277	-7	17866.67	10828.68
	Marc FARRY	Fr	72	65	71	69	277	-7	17866.67	10828.68
	John SENDEN	Aus	67	70	71	69	277	-7	17866.67	10828.68
	Ian GARBUTT	Eng	70	71	69	67	277	-7	17866.67	10828.68
	Gary EVANS	Eng	66	70	73	68	277	-7	17866.67	10828.68
	Massimo SCARPA	It	67	73	67	70	277	-7	17866.67	10828.68
26	Gregory HAVRET	Fr	69	71	69	69	278	-6	15440.00	9357.92
	Christophe POTTIER	Fr	70	69	72	67	278	-6	15440.00	9357.92
	Peter LONARD	Aus	73	68	71	66	278	-6	15440.00	9357.92
	Carl PETTERSSON	Swe	68	72	72	66	278	-6	15440.00	9357.92
30	Phillip PRICE	Wal	75	65	73	66	279	-5	13280.00	8048.78
	Jorge BERENDT	Arg	68	73	71	67	279	-5	13280.00	8048.78
	Paul LAWRIE	Scot	71	66	72	70	279	-5	13280.00	8048.78
	David LYNN	Eng	71	65	75	68	279	-5	13280.00	8048.78
	Raymond RUSSELL	Scot	71	69	71	68	279	-5	13280.00	8048.78
35	Søren KJELDSEN	Den	69	73	72	66	280	-4	10720.00	6497.21
	Stephen LEANEY	Aus	71	70	70	69	280	-4	10720.00	6497.21
	Andrew BEAL	Eng	70	70	68	72	280	-4	10720.00	6497.21
	Jonathan LOMAS	Eng	72	70	70	68	280	-4	10720.00	6497.21
	Ignacio GARRIDO	Sp	68	72	68	72	280	-4	10720.00	6497.21
	Gary ORR	Scot	72	69	70	69	280	-4	10720.00	6497.21
	Dean ROBERTSON	Scot	67	70	73	70	280	-4	10720.00	6497.21
	John BICKERTON	Eng	67	72	69	72	280	-4	10720.00	6497.21
	Simon DYSON	Eng	70	72	69	69	280	-4	10720.00	6497.21
44	Sandy LYLE	Scot	68	72	70	71	281	-3	8640.00	5236.55
	Costantino ROCCA	It	70	72	70	69	281	-3	8640.00	5236.55
	Peter O'MALLEY	Aus	71	70	69	71	281	-3	8640.00	5236.55
	Stephen DODD	Wal	69	72	71	69	281	-3	8640.00	5236.55
48	Jean-Francois REMESY	Fr	69	73	69	71	282	-2	7040.00	4266.82
	Fredrik HENGE	Swe	65	70	70	77	282	-2	7040.00	4266.82
	Henrik BJORNSTAD	Nor	66	74	67	75	282	-2	7040.00	4266.82
	Paul MCGINLEY	Ire	69	73	66	74	282	-2	7040.00	4266.82
	Henrik NYSTRÖM	Swe	70	72	71	69	282	-2	7040.00	4266.82
	Mikael LUNDBERG	Swe	69	72	73	68	282	-2	7040.00	4266.82
54	Peter FOWLER	Aus	73	69	70	71	283	-1	5600.00	3394.06
	Warren BENNETT	Eng	72	67	72	72	283	-1	5600.00	3394.06
	Sven STRÜVER	Ger	67	74	68	74	283	-1	5600.00	3394.06
57	Raphaël JACQUELIN	Fr	68	71	73	72	284	0	4880.00	2957.68
	Francisco CEA	Sp	70	71	72	71	284	0	4880.00	2957.68
59	Darren LEE	Eng	70	70	73	72	285	1	4640.00	2812.22
60	Andrew OLDCORN	Scot	73	69	73	71	286	2	4320.00	2618.28
	Fredrik JACOBSON	Swe	70	72	70	74	286	2	4320.00	2618.28
	Wei-Tze YEH	Taiwan	72	70	75	69	286	2	4320.00	2618.28
63	Eamonn DARCY	Ire	65	75	72	75	287	3	4000.00	2424.33
64	Carlos RODILES	Sp	71	71	74	72	288	4	3680.00	2230.38
	Raul BALLESTEROS	Sp	70	71	74	73	288	4	3680.00	2230.38
	Erol SIMSEK	Ger	68	72	73	75	288	4	3680.00	2230.38
67	Thomas GÖGELE	Ger	70	72	72	75	289	5	3280.00	1987.95
	Marco BERNARDINI	It	72	70	69	78	289	5	3280.00	1987.95
69	Patrik SJÖLAND	Swe	73	68	70	80	291	7	3040.00	1842.49
70	Graham RANKIN	Scot	70	70	74	81	295	11	2930.00	1775.82

Strolling Home

THE K CLUB, STRAFFAN, DUBLIN, IRELAND

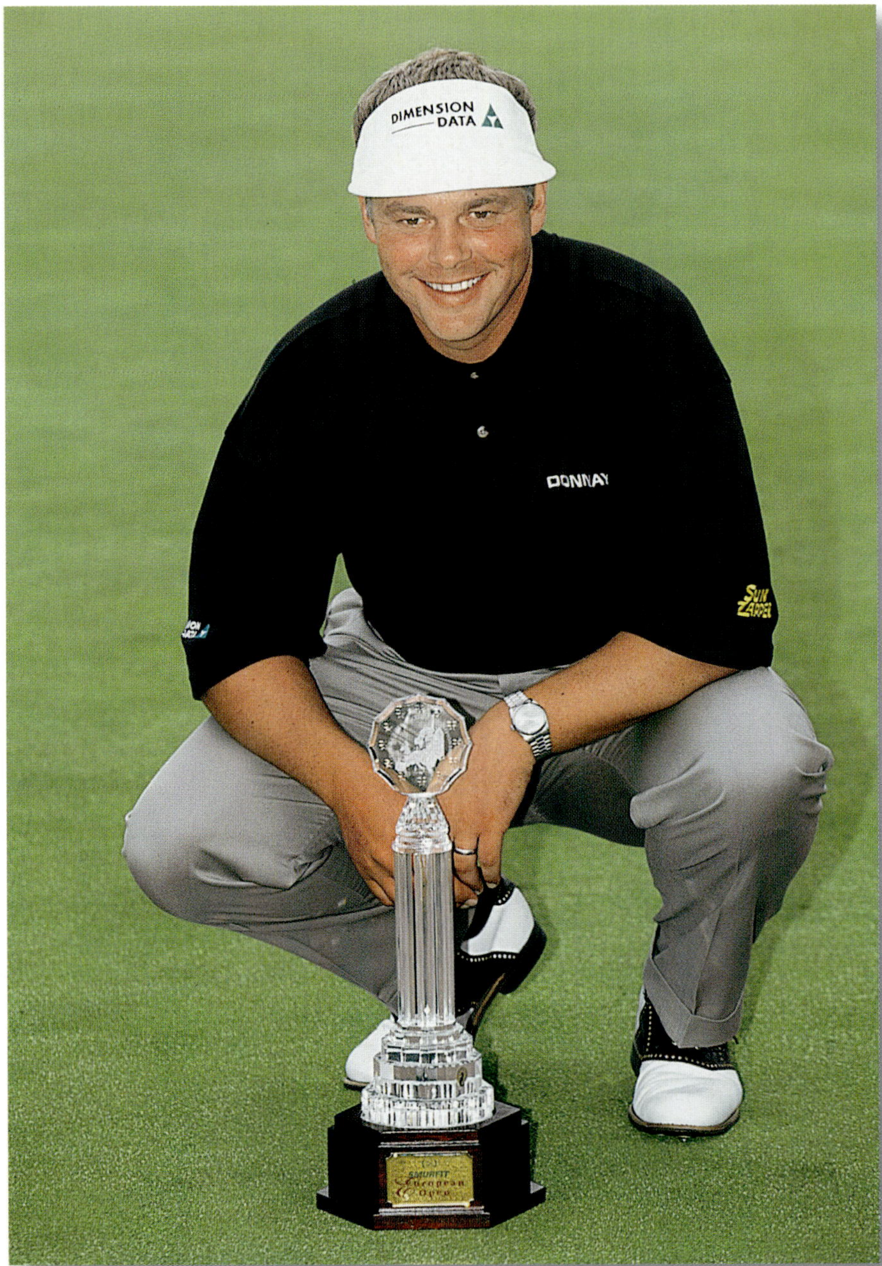

The trilogy of tournaments that form the overture to the Open Championship is the most prestigious and lucrative mid-summer run on The European Tour International Schedule. Apart from the cumulative prize fund of a handsome 8.6 million euro, (£5.2 million) the Smurfit European Open was flanked by two National Championships, the Murphy's Irish Open at Fota Island and The Scottish Open at Loch Lomond, but the one in the middle was the one that mattered most to Ireland and the Irish.

Shot of the Week

There were three holes in one but the accolade goes to winner Darren Clarke. He made triple bogey at the 17th hole in the third round and was through the back of the 18th in a poor lie in the rough. He was just 25 feet from the hole with little green to play with but he finessed the most delicate of lob shots to four feet for a closing birdie. "That was the most important shot of the tournament for me," said the champion.

For 19 years the Irish public and their professionals had longed for a home victory. Twenty four Tour championships had passed since John O'Leary won the Carrolls Irish Open on the world-renowned Portmarnock links in 1982. In the intervening years several top class professionals chased the dream but the fervent hopes, the great expectations of a couple of generations of ever-enthusiastic Irish fans, continued to fall on barren ground.

Then along came Darren Clarke. "Big D" from Dungannon in the County of Tyrone has a God-given talent and a man-driven desire to succeed. In unison, they make a powerful combination but sometimes the mind gets in the way and blurs the focus. But on this occasion he had all the ingredients for a champion's cocktail. He had proved before that he is capable of challenging and conquering the very best in the world, like in California when he beat Paul Azinger, Mark O'Meara, Thomas Björn, Hal Sutton, David Duval and finally, Tiger Woods in the 2000 WGC - Accenture Match Play.

"The win at La Costa was great. It was fantastic. But this is better," said Clarke. "For a lot of reasons this is the most important victory of my career. I have won all around the world but never at home. To come back and win at home in front of a home crowd means everything. The crowds were fantastic." It was more than just a victory. It was authoritative, emphatic and it was comfortable. "I've been close before, like two years ago here at The K Club when I led and lost. I felt embarrassed walking on to the 18th green then but today I felt proud and relieved. It was a wonderful feeling."
He certainly savoured the atmosphere generated by a record

Miguel Angel Martin

Padraig Harrington

attendance for the championship of almost 28,000. He paused for a moment at the edge of the 18th green to reflect on his achievement, confident in the knowledge that he could not be overtaken by the players behind. His final round 66 brought him from three shots behind to three shots ahead of a truly international field. A revitalised Ian Woosnam, another home hero in Padraig Harrington and the Great Dane, Thomas Björn, shared second place.

Victory came as no surprise. Darren's talent was never in doubt. It was only a matter of time before all the pieces fitted neatly in place. Patience was the name of the game and he would be the first to admit that it is a game he finds hard to play. "I have been playing well for some time without getting the reward," he said. "There were times when it was frustrating but I remained patient. Last week at Fota Island I came from the cut line to shoot 129 the last two rounds to finish second and this week I'm 15 under which is pretty good on a course as difficult as this."

The K Club had certainly been toughened since he shot 60 two years earlier and by the time The Ryder Cup Matches come around in 2006 it will present a real challenge. But, it says much for the quality and strength in depth on The European Tour that 14 nationalities from four continents were represented among the top 20 finishers. They included South Africa's Retief Goosen, who was making his first competitive appearance since winning the US Open Championship.

Henrik Bjornstad

Trevor Immelman

Five players shared the first round lead and it was interesting to note their countries of origin. Henrik Bjornstad from Norway, Michael Campbell from New Zealand, Maarten Lafeber from Holland, Mikael Lundberg from Sweden and Massimo Scarpa from Italy. Lundberg remained at the top for three rounds but fell away on the final day and only Bjornstad of the original quintet remained to contend and took a share of sixth place.

Clarke had to pass Jarmo Sandelin, Bjornstad, Harrington and Lundberg to take the lead on the last day. He made his move early with birdies at the fourth, fifth and sixth but he needed a little divine intervention at the last of these. His six iron second was heading for potential disaster to the left of the green when the ball ran up the trunk of a tree and rolled back to ten feet from the hole. He then dropped his only shot of the day at the seventh but from there on he took complete control of affairs with further birdies at the eighth, ninth and 11th. He played flawless golf and only Harrington got within two shots on the back nine. But he three putted the 13th and by the time Clarke registered his final birdie at the 16th it was only a matter of strolling home.

Apart from Clarke, the happiest man on that bright Sunday afternoon was Björn, or more correctly his wife, Pernilla. Dublin Jewellers, Appleby, donated a diamond, valued at IR£100,000, for the first professional to reach 14 under for The K Club's par fives. The Dane eagled the 16th and 18th in a final round of 67 to carry off the booty.

So ended 19 years of foreign domination of Tour events in Ireland and, in a special moment, John O'Leary was the first to toast Darren Clarke, suitably, with a couple of pints of Guinness. The title had come home at last.

Colm Smith

The Course

The Arnold Palmer-designed course will host The 2006 Ryder Cup Matches and to this end nothing is being spared to present as fine and as fair a test possible. The K Club was opened in 1993 and has improved and matured almost beyond recognition with a tree planting programme designed to make it a fitting challenge for the world's best players.

THE K CLUB, STRAFFAN, DUBLIN, IRELAND, 5-8 JULY, 2001, PAR 72, 7227 YARDS, 6607 METRES

Pos.	Name		Rd1	Rd2	Rd3	Rd4	Total	Par	Prize Money Euro	£
1	Darren CLARKE	N.Ire	68	68	71	66	273	-15	553727.80	333330.00
2	Ian WOOSNAM	Wal	69	66	73	68	276	-12	247751.40	149140.02
	Padraig HARRINGTON	Ire	70	67	69	70	276	-12	247751.40	149140.02
	Thomas BJÖRN	Den	73	71	65	67	276	-12	247751.40	149140.02
5	Mark MOULAND	Wal	70	71	68	68	277	-11	140869.80	84800.02
6	Henrik BJORNSTAD	Nor	67	68	70	73	278	-10	107978.00	65000.00
	Retief GOOSEN	SA	69	70	73	66	278	-10	107978.00	65000.00
8	Bernhard LANGER	Ger	71	70	69	69	279	-9	71265.48	42900.00
	Phillip PRICE	Wal	70	72	70	67	279	-9	71265.48	42900.00
	Ricardo GONZALEZ	Arg	69	70	70	70	279	-9	71265.48	42900.00
	Dean ROBERTSON	Scot	70	72	69	68	279	-9	71265.48	42900.00
12	Miguel Angel MARTIN	Sp	71	71	67	71	280	-8	48257.86	29050.00
	Costantino ROCCA	It	70	69	69	72	280	-8	48257.86	29050.00
	Raphaël JACQUELIN	Fr	70	70	72	68	280	-8	48257.86	29050.00
	Richard GREEN	Aus	70	70	70	70	280	-8	48257.86	29050.00
	Thomas LEVET	Fr	72	68	69	71	280	-8	48257.86	29050.00
	Mathias GRÖNBERG	Swe	68	70	73	69	280	-8	48257.86	29050.00
	Paul LAWRIE	Scot	70	72	68	70	280	-8	48257.86	29050.00
	Daren LEE	Eng	70	70	71	69	280	-8	48257.86	29050.00
20	Colin MONTGOMERIE	Scot	68	72	69	72	281	-7	38650.59	23266.67
	Gary EVANS	Eng	73	67	72	69	281	-7	38650.59	23266.67
	Paul CASEY	Eng	69	68	71	73	281	-7	38650.59	23266.67
23	Sven STRÜVER	Ger	75	70	69	68	282	-6	33556.24	20200.00
	Stephen LEANEY	Aus	71	69	71	71	282	-6	33556.24	20200.00
	Trevor IMMELMAN	SA	74	68	70	70	282	-6	33556.24	20200.00
	Robert KARLSSON	Swe	72	70	69	71	282	-6	33556.24	20200.00
	Roger WESSELS	SA	69	72	69	72	282	-6	33556.24	20200.00
	Jarmo SANDELIN	Swe	69	71	65	77	282	-6	33556.24	20200.00
	Michael CAMPBELL	NZ	67	70	71	74	282	-6	33556.24	20200.00
30	David HOWELL	Eng	69	71	71	72	283	-5	28074.28	16900.00
	Anders HANSEN	Den	74	68	71	70	283	-5	28074.28	16900.00
	Olle KARLSSON	Swe	72	73	69	69	283	-5	28074.28	16900.00
	Christopher HANELL	Swe	72	72	70	69	283	-5	28074.28	16900.00
34	Anders FORSBRAND	Swe	73	72	66	73	284	-4	23921.28	14400.00
	Marc FARRY	Fr	70	75	70	69	284	-4	23921.28	14400.00
	Maarten LAFEBER	Hol	67	72	73	72	284	-4	23921.28	14400.00
	Angel CABRERA	Arg	71	73	66	74	284	-4	23921.28	14400.00
	Andrew COLTART	Scot	72	71	69	72	284	-4	23921.28	14400.00
	Mikael LUNDBERG	Swe	67	65	72	80	284	-4	23921.28	14400.00
40	Mark ROE	Eng	72	72	71	70	285	-3	20266.64	12200.00
	Jonathan LOMAS	Eng	76	69	71	69	285	-3	20266.64	12200.00
	Peter O'MALLEY	Aus	71	73	72	69	285	-3	20266.64	12200.00
	Massimo SCARPA	It	67	71	73	74	285	-3	20266.64	12200.00
	Brett RUMFORD	Aus	68	77	73	67	285	-3	20266.64	12200.00
45	Eamonn DARCY	Ire	75	69	72	70	286	-2	16279.76	9800.00
	John SENDEN	Aus	71	74	70	71	286	-2	16279.76	9800.00
	Søren HANSEN	Den	71	69	70	76	286	-2	16279.76	9800.00
	Joakim HAEGGMAN	Swe	72	72	70	72	286	-2	16279.76	9800.00
	Rolf MUNTZ	Hol	71	71	71	73	286	-2	16279.76	9800.00
	Peter LONARD	Aus	73	71	71	71	286	-2	16279.76	9800.00
	Niclas FASTH	Swe	69	75	68	74	286	-2	16279.76	9800.00
52	Brian DAVIS	Eng	70	70	72	75	287	-1	11960.64	7200.00
	Stephen DODD	Wal	73	72	68	74	287	-1	11960.64	7200.00
	Markus BRIER	Aut	73	70	70	74	287	-1	11960.64	7200.00
	Raymond RUSSELL	Scot	72	73	68	74	287	-1	11960.64	7200.00
	Alastair FORSYTH	Scot	70	75	75	67	287	-1	11960.64	7200.00
	Scott GARDINER	Aus	74	70	70	73	287	-1	11960.64	7200.00
58	Eduardo ROMERO	Arg	72	72	70	74	288	0	9468.84	5700.00
	Greg TURNER	NZ	71	74	73	70	288	0	9468.84	5700.00
	Steen TINNING	Den	72	73	71	72	288	0	9468.84	5700.00
	Greg OWEN	Eng	70	69	71	78	288	0	9468.84	5700.00
62	Santiago LUNA	Sp	72	73	71	73	289	1	7807.64	4700.00
	Warren BENNETT	Eng	70	73	74	72	289	1	7807.64	4700.00
	Ian GARBUTT	Eng	71	69	73	76	289	1	7807.64	4700.00
	Lee WESTWOOD	Eng	71	74	73	71	289	1	7807.64	4700.00
	Stephen GALLACHER	Scot	74	69	74	72	289	1	7807.64	4700.00
	Adam SCOTT	Aus	75	70	71	73	289	1	7807.64	4700.00
68	Gordon BRAND JNR.	Scot	71	73	71	75	290	2	5488.84	3304.14
	Jean-Francois REMESY	Fr	71	72	75	72	290	2	5488.84	3304.14
	Jamie SPENCE	Eng	71	74	70	75	290	2	5488.84	3304.14
	Gregory HAVRET	Fr	76	68	72	74	290	2	5488.84	3304.14
	Olivier EDMOND	Fr	71	73	71	75	290	2	5488.84	3304.14
	Alex CEJKA	Ger	72	71	73	74	290	2	5488.84	3304.14
	Des TERBLANCHE	SA	70	72	74	74	290	2	5488.84	3304.14
	Alan MCLEAN	Scot	73	71	71	75	290	2	5488.84	3304.14
76	Damien MCGRANE	Ire	73	72	72	74	291	3	4964.50	2988.50
	Paul BROADHURST	Eng	78	67	68	78	291	3	4964.50	2988.50
	Nicolas VANHOOTEGEM	Bel	73	72	71	75	291	3	4964.50	2988.50
	Simon DYSON	Eng	73	69	75	74	291	3	4964.50	2988.50
80	Roger CHAPMAN	Eng	75	70	66	81	292	4	4955.50	2983.08
	Paul EALES	Eng	71	72	74	75	292	4	4955.50	2983.08
82	Steve WEBSTER	Eng	72	69	79	73	293	5	4948.00	2978.57
	David CARTER	Eng	72	73	69	79	293	5	4948.00	2978.57
	Wei-Tze YEH	Taiwan	73	70	77	73	293	5	4948.00	2978.57
85	Richard S JOHNSON	Swe	74	71	75	74	294	6	4942.00	2974.96
86	David GILFORD	Eng	75	69	74	77	295	7	4937.50	2972.25
	Marco BERNARDINI	It	74	70	74	77	295	7	4937.50	2972.25
88	Gary EMERSON	Eng	71	73	72	80	296	8	4933.00	2969.54
89	Wayne RILEY	Aus	75	70	77	79	301	13	4930.00	2967.73
90	Ian POULTER	Eng	71	74	78	79	302	14	4927.00	2965.93
91	Stephen SCAHILL	NZ	71	73	76	83	303	15	4924.00	2964.12

JEFFERSON
SMURFIT
GROUP plc

Going Low

LOCH LOMOND GOLF CLUB, GLASGOW, SCOTLAND

If the air of quiet determination surrounding Retief Goosen when he arrived at Loch Lomond appeared surprisingly intense for a man who had just won the US Open a few weeks earlier, and could have been forgiven for lazing around on a beach, the South African came into The Scottish Open at Loch Lomond with a point to prove.

Although this softly spoken, unassuming South African is unlikely ever to be confused with Mr Angry, he was disappointed and surprised that so much of the media coverage of his victory at Southern Hills Country Club concentrated on the short missed putt which led to a play-off with Mark Brooks.

"I wanted to prove to myself that I could be a winner again," he said. "Guys like Paul Lawrie and Mark Brooks won Majors and haven't won since. It meant a lot to show the people who thought I was lucky in Tulsa to go out and win another great title."

The return of the 3.6 million euro (£2.2 million) Scottish Open, which last featured on The European Tour International Schedule at Carnoustie in 1996, gave Goosen an opportunity to become champion of the oldest golfing nation in the world as well as the biggest in the space of a month.

Always at ease on the course designed by Tom Weiskopf and Jay Morrish - he set the course record in 1997 - Goosen was keen to follow once more in the foosteps of his countryman and friend Ernie Els, the two time US Open champion who won at Loch Lomond the previous summer.

"I had the feeling that I was going to go low," he revealed later. "You've got to like a course to play it well and I think this design is great. Some courses you never get comfortable with, others you just blend into."

The blending process began for Goosen on a sodden morning when play was delayed by four hours. Although the unavoidable decision to allow the players to lift and clean was deemed "legalised cheating" by Tom Lehman, Goosen ignored the driech weather as he compiled an opening score of 62 which was a masterpiece of flawless iron play.

Michael Hoey

Jesper Parnevik

During his opening 12 holes, the South African made seven birdies, one eagle and seemed on course to break 60. "I really thought he was going to shoot 59 or 58," recalled playing companion Gary Orr. "It was the best golf I have ever seen anyone play."

While his momentum was halted by a bogey six at the 13th, Goosen was still able to sign for 62 and open up a three shot lead over Elliot Boult, Jarrod Moseley, and Adam Scott.

With the first round still to be completed on Friday morning, Goosen didn't reach the halfway mark of the Championship until 9pm. By late evening, the temperature had dropped and most of the crowds had gone home.

It produced a slightly unreal atmosphere and one which prevented Goosen matching the previous day's brilliance. On the positive side, he eliminated careless mistakes and got in with a 69, two shots better than Scott, the talented young Australian coached by Butch Harmon.

Also on the leaderboard by this stage was John Daly. The former Open and US PGA Champion was to finish in the top three for the first time at any event since winning at St Andrews in 1995.

Fredrik Jacobson

Shot of the Week

There were any number of contenders in Retief Goosen's 62 deserving of this accolade. At the sixth hole, he was stuck behind a tree and smashed an iron left of the branches before the ball faded back onto the fairway. At the seventh he demonstrated his versatility by hitting a draw from a downslope around trees leaving the ball to curve onto the green as if guided by radar. Best of all, though, was a majestic five iron into a gusting wind at the tenth which landed four feet from the hole.

Mark Mouland

Having installed a practice pitching area in the back garden of his home, Daly's game was also in better shape than it had been for years. A reformed character, the former alcoholic and gambler quipped: "Now I get up in the morning at the same time I used to come home..."

Much to the delight of the large crowds who braved the elements, Daly added a superb 66 in the third round. He felt at home on a course where generous fairways presented the chance to grip it and rip it with the driver.

Colin Montgomerie, another former winner on a course with a history of distinguished champions, reckons Loch Lomond is very much a second shot lay-out. This notion was confirmed on Saturday when Goosen followed up a piercing drive at the par five 13th with a stunning approach to 20 feet before holing the putt for eagle.

A ridiculously unflustered 66 gave the leader a three shot advantage going into the last day which was never threatened. At last the weather took a turn for the better and a glimpse of sunshine served as a welcome reminder that the entire summer in Scotland is not spent sheltering under an umbrella.

The Course

In spite of torrential rain, Loch Lomond held up superbly and produced a test of golf deserving of one of the strongest fields of the year on The European Tour. Although they won't be seen at their best until this summer the 18 new greens built at a cost of £650,000 already look like a shrewd investment, as did the 20,000 tons of sand used to bolster the fairways.

The improvement in overhead conditions - the Amateur champion Michael Hoey went round in 64 - made Goosen wonder if he might need to card 67 or 66 to win.

In fact, the challengers were never able to make the South African feel uncomfortable. Thomas Björn, the first winner at Loch Lomond, came closest with a 67 for 271 and second place on his own. "But you have to take your hat off to Retief," said the Dane. "Everyone knows what a good player he is, now he's moved into a different class."

Goosen, 71 for 268, was so far in front that he was able to allow himself the luxury of finding sand at the last two holes and still take home the first prize of 610,998 euro (£366,660).

"It was pretty impressive to watch," noted six times Major winner Nick Faldo. "Retief's ball striking was awesome. If that's the way the game is going to be played in the 21st century, then I might have to seek new employment !"

Mike Aitken

Jamie Spence

LOCH LOMOND GOLF CLUB, GLASGOW, SCOTLAND, 12-15 JULY, 2001, PAR 71, 7050 YARDS, 6446 METRES

Pos.	Name		Rd1	Rd2	Rd3	Rd4	Total	Par	Prize Money Euro	£
1	Retief GOOSEN	SA	62	69	66	71	268	-16	610998.54	366660.00
2	Thomas BJÖRN	Den	68	67	69	67	271	-13	407332.36	244440.00
3	Barry LANE	Eng	70	65	69	68	272	-12	174137.70	104500.00
	Paul MCGINLEY	Ire	68	67	67	70	272	-12	174137.70	104500.00
	John DALY	USA	68	68	66	70	272	-12	174137.70	104500.00
	Adam SCOTT	Aus	65	68	67	72	272	-12	174137.70	104500.00
7	Darren CLARKE	N.Ire	69	67	68	69	273	-11	109981.70	66000.00
8	Jesper PARNEVIK	Swe	71	69	65	70	275	-9	86885.57	52140.00
	Mathias GRÖNBERG	Swe	73	70	65	67	275	-9	86885.57	52140.00
10	José COCERES	Arg	69	72	69	66	276	-8	73321.16	44000.00
11	Michael HOEY (AM)	N.Ire	71	71	71	64	277	-7		
	Greg OWEN	Eng	72	68	68	69	277	-7	65255.83	39160.00
	Brett RUMFORD	Aus	73	65	71	68	277	-7	65255.83	39160.00
14	Sergio GARCIA	Sp	69	69	69	71	278	-6	51848.53	31114.28
	Søren HANSEN	Den	72	71	64	71	278	-6	51848.53	31114.28
	Geoff OGILVY	Aus	69	73	69	67	278	-6	51848.53	31114.28
	Fredrik JACOBSON	Swe	69	70	68	71	278	-6	51848.53	31114.28
	Niclas FASTH	Swe	67	71	66	74	278	-6	51848.53	31114.28
	Tom LEHMAN	USA	70	66	74	68	278	-6	51848.53	31114.28
	Daren LEE	Eng	70	67	73	68	278	-6	51848.53	31114.28
21	José Maria OLAZÁBAL	Sp	70	73	65	71	279	-5	40379.01	24231.43
	Anders HANSEN	Den	69	71	70	69	279	-5	40379.01	24231.43
	Ian POULTER	Eng	69	72	71	67	279	-5	40379.01	24231.43
	Ricardo GONZALEZ	Arg	74	69	68	68	279	-5	40379.01	24231.43
	Peter LONARD	Aus	69	71	71	68	279	-5	40379.01	24231.43
	John BICKERTON	Eng	72	69	71	67	279	-5	40379.01	24231.43
	Simon DYSON	Eng	69	73	68	69	279	-5	40379.01	24231.43
28	Greg CHALMERS	Aus	70	66	75	69	280	-4	31568.83	18944.44
	Steve WEBSTER	Eng	69	70	69	72	280	-4	31568.83	18944.44
	Anthony WALL	Eng	67	70	70	73	280	-4	31568.83	18944.44
	Carlos RODILES	Sp	68	73	69	70	280	-4	31568.83	18944.44
	Colin MONTGOMERIE	Scot	70	67	69	74	280	-4	31568.83	18944.44
	Richard S JOHNSON	Swe	73	70	67	70	280	-4	31568.83	18944.44
	Johan RYSTRÖM	Swe	73	69	68	70	280	-4	31568.83	18944.44
	Angel CABRERA	Arg	68	74	70	68	280	-4	31568.83	18944.44
	Dean ROBERTSON	Scot	73	69	70	68	280	-4	31568.83	18944.44
37	Jeev Milkha SINGH	Ind	71	71	70	69	281	-3	25662.40	15400.00
	Sven STRÜVER	Ger	73	69	66	73	281	-3	25662.40	15400.00
	Justin ROSE	Eng	67	70	72	72	281	-3	25662.40	15400.00
	Carl PETTERSSON	Swe	69	71	68	73	281	-3	25662.40	15400.00
41	Nick FALDO	Eng	70	73	69	70	282	-2	21996.35	13200.00
	Raphaël JACQUELIN	Fr	70	67	76	69	282	-2	21996.35	13200.00
	Miguel Angel JIMÉNEZ	Sp	70	72	68	72	282	-2	21996.35	13200.00
	Peter O'MALLEY	Aus	72	71	69	70	282	-2	21996.35	13200.00
	David LYNN	Eng	68	75	67	72	282	-2	21996.35	13200.00
	David CARTER	Eng	70	69	72	71	282	-2	21996.35	13200.00
47	Warren BENNETT	Eng	71	68	75	69	283	-1	18696.89	11220.00
	John SENDEN	Aus	69	72	73	69	283	-1	18696.89	11220.00
	Colin GILLIES	Scot	69	69	72	73	283	-1	18696.89	11220.00
50	Thomas LEVET	Fr	72	67	72	73	284	0	16497.26	9900.00
	Jarrod MOSELEY	Aus	65	75	68	76	284	0	16497.26	9900.00
	Christian CËVAÉR	Fr	70	73	73	68	284	0	16497.26	9900.00
53	Emanuele CANONICA	It	71	70	71	73	285	1	13931.02	8360.00
	Ian GARBUTT	Eng	68	74	72	71	285	1	13931.02	8360.00
	Andrew COLTART	Scot	72	70	73	70	285	1	13931.02	8360.00
	Erol SIMSEK	Ger	69	74	70	72	285	1	13931.02	8360.00
57	Gary ORR	Scot	69	71	72	74	286	2	11731.38	7040.00
	Michael CAMPBELL	NZ	71	68	74	73	286	2	11731.38	7040.00
59	David HOWELL	Eng	70	69	72	76	287	3	10814.87	6490.00
	Peter BAKER	Eng	72	69	73	73	287	3	10814.87	6490.00
61	Andrew OLDCORN	Scot	71	69	78	70	288	4	9898.36	5940.00
	Thomas GÖGELE	Ger	68	70	78	72	288	4	9898.36	5940.00
	Diego BORREGO	Sp	72	67	72	77	288	4	9898.36	5940.00
64	Andrew MCLARDY	SA	71	70	75	73	289	5	8981.84	5390.00
	Jamie SPENCE	Eng	73	70	72	74	289	5	8981.84	5390.00
66	Stephen SCAHILL	NZ	73	69	75	73	290	6	8431.93	5060.00
67	Greg NORMAN	Aus	68	71	74	78	291	7	8065.33	4840.00
68	Mark MOULAND	Wal	70	67	78	77	292	8	7698.72	4620.00
69	Sandy LYLE	Scot	72	70	74	78	294	10	7332.12	4400.00
70	Bradley DREDGE	Wal	73	69	76	77	295	11	6965.51	4180.00
71	Bernhard LANGER	Ger	70	69	W/D		139	-3	6698.89	4020.00

L'esprit Moët & Chandon
BRUT IMPÉRIAL
MOËT & CHANDON
CHAMPAGNE
Official Supplier to the PGA European Tour

Spontaneous Grace

ROYAL LYTHAM & ST ANNES, LYTHAM ST ANNES, ENGLAND

He looked very different when he walked back on to the 18th green ... younger, somehow smaller, certainly much, much more vulnerable. Yet all David Duval had done was to remove his trademark shades, extricate himself from his cap and show us the slow, long burn that is his smile. Oh, and he had just won the 130th Open Championship.

Not just won it, not scraped it, not fluked it. He had won it thanks partly to a golf swing to die for but mostly because this much misunderstood man has the character, the resilience and the relentless ambition that carries a player towards the really big titles. It helps him to stay in control when the even bigger moments arrive and every instinct screams at you to throw away the clubs and find something at least slightly less nerve-shredding to do for a living.

There were many fine memories from this Open at Royal Lytham & St Annes, much to savour for even peripheral fans, never mind connoisseurs of the grand, old game but none compared with the way Duval, the hard man, allowed the paying public and the attendant television cameras to glimpse at last the decent bloke who has always lived behind his golfing disguise.

He did so as he walked towards the centre of this final green to acknowledge the cheers. At least this is what he intended. What he did as the noise cascaded around him was to cuddle the Claret Jug in his arms like some puppy while he read intensely the history of the game as inscribed on the base, a testament to glory that now ended with his name as Champion.

David Duval

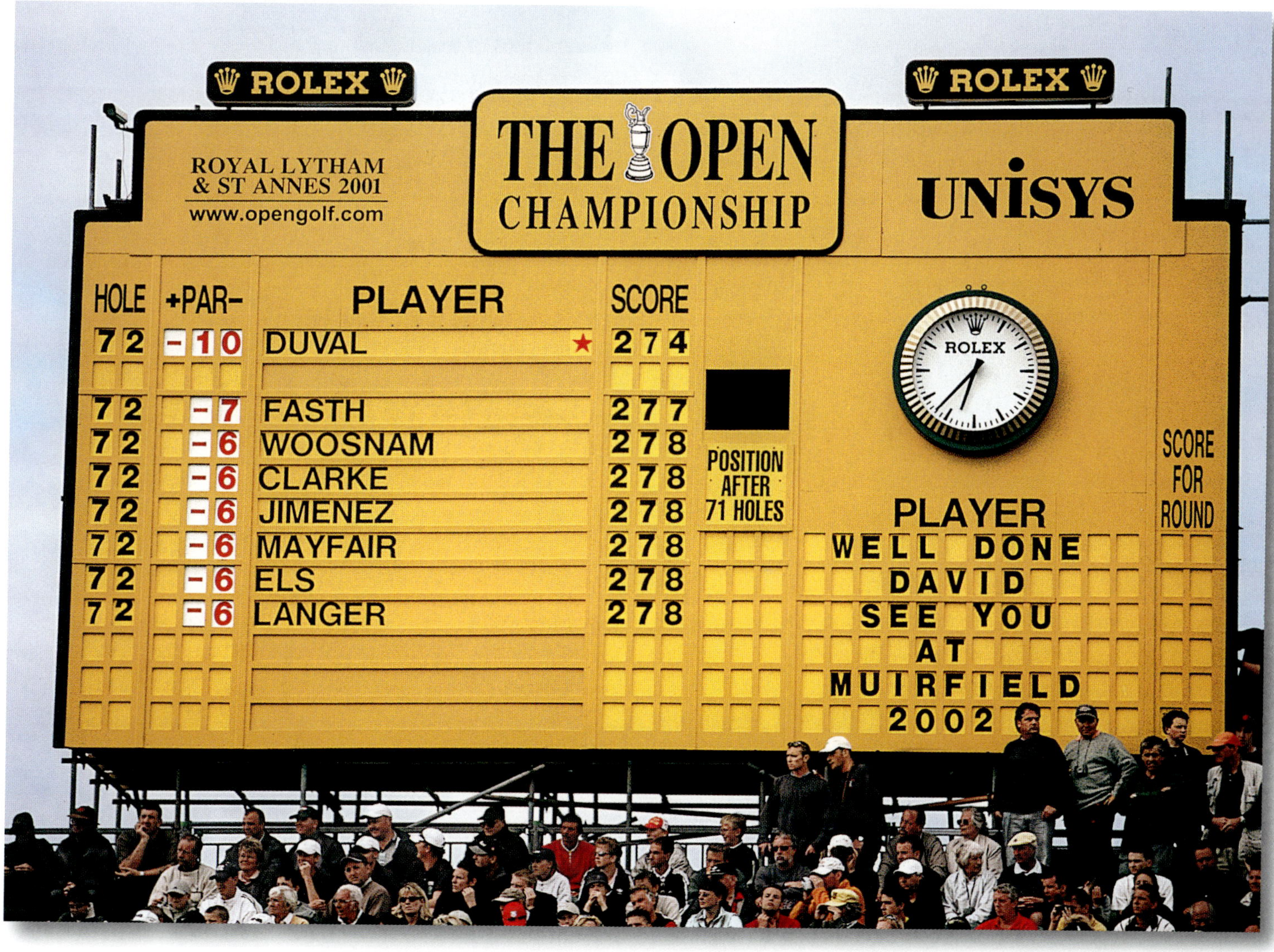

And suddenly Duval was lost again in his own inner world, reliving no doubt the long, lonely months he had spent playing golf on his own as he sought solace following the death of his older brother. Twenty years ago as a nine year old his world had caved in when Brent Duval died from aplastic anaemia. David gave his own bone marrow in a last, desperate attempt to stave off the inevitable but when this failed, he retreated within himself and took his immature anger out on a golf course.

Niclas Fasth

Winning the Open does not make up for this time but it suddenly, thrillingly, gave some real meaning to Duval's life. This knowledge gleamed on his face as he picked up a microphone and giggled: "So waddya wanna know," into a balmy Lancashire sky before constructing a speech of spontaneous grace that endorsed the day just as much as his final round had filled it with brilliance.

What a last day it had been. After three rounds the leaderboard was as packed as a Northern Line tube train on a Friday evening. Players of all types were hanging on to contention like commuters defending their space against all-comers. At least 20 such players were within a couple of shots of the lead on that Sunday morning, the lead itself split four ways at six under par between Alex Cejka, Bernhard Langer, Ian Woosnam and Duval. One stroke behind came a clutch of players including Darren Clarke and Colin Montgomerie.

Colin Montgomerie

Miguel Angel Jiménez

Shot of the Week

At 29 years of age Greg Owen is still waiting to make his mark on the professional game. Affable, sufficiently talented to comfortably make a very decent living on The European Tour, the Mansfield golfer is the first to offer up a smile on the greyest of days but has yet to make it past the finishing line before anyone else. This was to be the case at Lytham but he still managed a supreme moment in the limelight when he holed his second shot at the 542 yards 11th hole during the third round. After his drive, Owen had 240 yards left to the pin and selected a three iron. It was a good choice, his ball sweeping brightly away before rolling towards the hole and that rarest of birds, an albatross. He was one of no fewer than 22 European Tour Members to have top 30 finishes.

Montgomerie, still searching for the Major title that would embroider his already glittering curriculum vitae, had roared out of the blocks at Lytham. His opening 65, six under par, was a round of velvety smoothness and high emotion as the Scot rode a magic carpet offered up by galleries who were desperate to support the man who has represented Europe so wonderfully over the last decade.

Having bonded with the crowd and fed off the excitement, Montgomerie tried to create Groundhog Day. He told the parking attendant to reserve the space he had occupied on Thursday, ordered up a repeat sausage sandwich before going out again and insisted on sitting on the same side of the Press Officer for his subsequent interviews. Sadly, this cunning plan did not work and he never again found the inspiration he had enjoyed so effortlessly over those first 18 holes.

Montgomerie's closing 72 and the share of 13th place it offered was a huge disappointment after a week that had begun so vividly. Downsides also for Clarke, who suddenly lost his way over the toughest closing stretch in Championship golf, and for Langer, who never quite got in touch with his A-game on Sunday.

If these Europeans were left to mull over a lot of 'what ifs', then Woosnam had to digest a memory that will linger darkly in his mind for ever more. An opening birdie on Sunday had trumpeted the Welshman's intent as he re-ignited the form that once made him a Masters Tournament champion, but the dramatic discovery on the next tee that he had 15 clubs in his bag struck like a thunderbolt out of an otherwise cloudless sky.

Sergio Garcia

We really know
the score

Poor Woosnam was incandescent with rage and disappointment as referee John Paramor confirmed that he must absorb a two stroke penalty. Understandably, he bogeyed two holes shortly thereafter though it was to his eternal credit that he recovered sufficiently to finish on level par 71 for a share of third place. It was an undeniable fact though that this cruellest of accidents effectively destroyed what may have been the sternest of challenges to Duval's supremacy on the day.

Bernhard Langer

The American, however, could do nothing about that. All he could do was to react to his own game and to what his many rivals were doing. Niclas Fasth, the winner of The European Tour Qualifying School in 1996, produced the performance of a lifetime to emphasise his huge potential and underline his Ryder Cup credentials. The 29 year old displayed a cool nerve under the full glare of the world's spotlight as he put together a closing 67 which would set the target at seven under par.

Duval, with the defending champion, Tiger Woods, unable to mount a challenge, knew, as he edged ahead of Fasth, that this was now his moment but he remained aware that he was still vulnerable as a galaxy of world class golfers, including a courageously resurgent Woosnam, snapped at his heels. Indeed by the end, and for the first time since the inception of The European Tour, nine European Tour Members had enjoyed top ten finishes with Fasth runner-up; Ernie Els, Miguel Angel Jiménez, Clarke, Langer and Woosnam sharing third place with Billy Mayfair, and Sergio Garcia, Mikko Ilonen and Jesper Parnevik tying ninth with Kevin Sutherland.

Duval, however, was in front, composed, and able to progress sensibly rather than sensationally over the final four holes, a barbed-wire stretch of golf that can ruin a card in a few seconds of poor focus. His was the ultimate professional performance. His was the joy. When, finally, he holed the winning putt, he paused to look up into the Fylde heavens, and smiled at last.

Bill Elliott

David Dixon

The Course

Royal Lytham & St Annes is the most removed of links, the Irish Sea lapping at least a mile away at its closest point, but the old girl's reputation as an outstanding Open Championship venue was endorsed hugely in 2001. At 6,905 yards Lytham is short by modern standards but the fact that no player managed four rounds under 70 proved that brilliant conditioning and the strategic placing of bunkers can still offer an effective barricade to modern club and ball development.

ROYAL LYTHAM & ST ANNES, LYTHAM ST ANNES, ENGLAND, 19-22 JULY, 2001, PAR 71, 6905 YARDS, 6314 METRES

Pos.	Name		Rd1	Rd2	Rd3	Rd4	Total	Par	Prize Money Euro	£
1	David DUVAL	USA	69	73	65	67	274	-10	984756.02	600000.00
2	Niclas FASTH	Swe	69	69	72	67	277	-7	590853.61	360000.00
3	Bernhard LANGER	Ger	71	69	67	71	278	-6	232511.84	141666.67
	Ian WOOSNAM	Wal	72	68	67	71	278	-6	232511.84	141666.67
	Miguel Angel JIMÉNEZ	Sp	69	72	67	70	278	-6	232511.84	141666.67
	Billy MAYFAIR	USA	69	72	67	70	278	-6	232511.84	141666.67
	Ernie ELS	SA	71	71	67	69	278	-6	232511.84	141666.67
	Darren CLARKE	N.Ire	70	69	69	70	278	-6	232511.84	141666.67
9	Sergio GARCIA	Sp	70	72	67	70	279	-5	104630.33	63750.00
	Jesper PARNEVIK	Swe	69	68	71	71	279	-5	104630.33	63750.00
	Mikko ILONEN	Fin	68	75	70	66	279	-5	104630.33	63750.00
	Kevin SUTHERLAND	USA	75	69	68	67	279	-5	104630.33	63750.00
13	Des SMYTH	Ire	74	65	70	71	280	-4	65752.98	40062.50
	Loren ROBERTS	USA	70	70	70	70	280	-4	65752.98	40062.50
	Raphaël JACQUELIN	Fr	71	68	69	72	280	-4	65752.98	40062.50
	Colin MONTGOMERIE	Scot	65	70	73	72	280	-4	65752.98	40062.50
	Billy ANDRADE	USA	69	70	70	71	280	-4	65752.98	40062.50
	Vijay SINGH	Fiji	70	70	71	69	280	-4	65752.98	40062.50
	Alex CEJKA	Ger	69	69	69	73	280	-4	65752.98	40062.50
	Retief GOOSEN	SA	74	68	67	71	280	-4	65752.98	40062.50
21	Nick PRICE	Zim	73	67	68	73	281	-3	53340.95	32500.00
	Davis LOVE III	USA	73	67	74	67	281	-3	53340.95	32500.00
23	Greg OWEN	Eng	69	68	72	73	282	-2	50058.43	30500.00
	Michael CAMPBELL	NZ	71	72	71	68	282	-2	50058.43	30500.00
25	Eduardo ROMERO	Arg	70	68	72	73	283	-1	45134.65	27500.00
	Tiger WOODS	USA	71	68	73	71	283	-1	45134.65	27500.00
	Bob ESTES	USA	74	70	73	66	283	-1	45134.65	27500.00
	Joe OGILVIE	USA	69	68	71	75	283	-1	45134.65	27500.00
29	Barry LANE	Eng	70	72	72	70	284	0	41031.50	25000.00
30	Stewart CINK	USA	71	72	72	70	285	1	35287.09	21500.00
	Justin ROSE	Eng	69	72	74	70	285	1	35287.09	21500.00
	Scott VERPLANK	USA	71	72	70	72	285	1	35287.09	21500.00
	Phillip PRICE	Wal	74	69	71	71	285	1	35287.09	21500.00
	Nicolas VANHOOTEGEM	Bel	72	68	70	75	285	1	35287.09	21500.00
	Phil MICKELSON	USA	70	72	72	71	285	1	35287.09	21500.00
	David DIXON (Am)	Eng	70	71	70	74	285	1		
37	Padraig HARRINGTON	Ire	75	66	74	71	286	2	26752.54	16300.00
	Dudley HART	USA	74	69	69	74	286	2	26752.54	16300.00
	Toru TANIGUCHI	Jpn	72	69	72	73	286	2	26752.54	16300.00
	Andrew COLTART	Scot	75	68	70	73	286	2	26752.54	16300.00
	Frank LICKLITER	USA	71	71	73	71	286	2	26752.54	16300.00
42	Mark O'MEARA	USA	70	69	72	76	287	3	22157.01	13500.00
	Steve STRICKER	USA	71	69	72	75	287	3	22157.01	13500.00
	Richard GREEN	Aus	71	70	72	74	287	3	22157.01	13500.00
	JP HAYES	USA	69	71	74	73	287	3	22157.01	13500.00
	Paul LAWRIE	Scot	72	70	69	76	287	3	22157.01	13500.00
47	Brad FAXON	USA	68	71	74	75	288	4	17444.25	10628.57
	Peter LONARD	Aus	72	70	74	72	288	4	17444.25	10628.57
	Robert ALLENBY	Aus	73	71	71	73	288	4	17444.25	10628.57
	Lee WESTWOOD	Eng	73	70	71	74	288	4	17444.25	10628.57
	Chris DIMARCO	USA	68	74	72	74	288	4	17444.25	10628.57
	Adam SCOTT	Aus	73	71	70	74	288	4	17444.25	10628.57
	Matt GOGEL	USA	73	70	71	74	288	4	17444.25	10628.57
54	José Maria OLAZÁBAL	Sp	69	74	73	73	289	5	14677.55	8942.85
	Paul CURRY	Eng	72	71	71	75	289	5	14677.55	8942.85
	Mark CALCAVECCHIA	USA	72	70	72	75	289	5	14677.55	8942.85
	Carlos Daniel FRANCO	Par	71	71	73	74	289	5	14677.55	8942.85
	Paul MCGINLEY	Ire	69	72	72	76	289	5	14677.55	8942.85
	Duffy WALDORF	USA	70	73	69	77	289	5	14677.55	8942.85
	Rory SABBATINI	SA	70	69	76	74	289	5	14677.55	8942.85
61	Stuart APPLEBY	Aus	69	75	72	74	290	6	13950.71	8500.00
62	Gordon BRAND JNR.	Scot	70	72	75	74	291	7	13786.58	8400.00
	Brandel CHAMBLEE	USA	72	69	74	76	291	7	13786.58	8400.00
	Pierre FULKE	Swe	69	67	72	83	291	7	13786.58	8400.00
65	Neil CHEETHAM	Eng	72	72	73	78	295	11	13622.46	8300.00
66	Alexandre BALICKI	Fr	69	75	75	77	296	12	13499.37	8225.00
	Thomas LEVET	Fr	72	72	77	75	296	12	13499.37	8225.00
68	David SMAIL	NZ	71	72	76	79	298	14	13376.27	8150.00
69	Sandy LYLE	Scot	72	71	77	81	301	17	13253.18	8075.00
	Scott HENDERSON	Scot	75	69	81	76	301	17	13253.18	8075.00

Job Done

NOORDWIJKSE GOLF CLUB, NOORDWIJK, THE NETHERLANDS

No one doubted Bernhard Langer's resolve and resilience even before he bounced back to win the German Masters seven days after missing "that" putt to retain The Ryder Cup at Kiawah Island in 1991.

His powers of recovery, his courage and his ability to get the job done are legendary and never were they more eloquently demonstrated than by his victory - after four long years without a win - in The TNT Open on the seaside links of Noordwijkse.

After playing in nine successive Ryder Cups, three of them on winning sides, Langer was deeply disappointed when Mark James failed to hand him one of his Captain's picks in 1999. Typically there was no whingeing - simply a determination to be back at The De Vere Belfry for The 34th Ryder Cup Matches.

Langer highlighted an outstanding run of form on the US Tour with his sixth place in the Masters Tournament at Augusta National, where he collected the Green Jacket in 1985 and 1993.

Following an eighth place in the Smurfit European Open, his joint third place finish in the Open Championship at Royal Lytham & St Annes confirmed that he would be the man to beat as he sought a third TNT Open crown. He occupied 14th place in The Ryder Cup qualifying table and was well aware that a 38th European Tour victory and a repeat of his 1992 triumph in Noordwijkse, worth 300,000 euro (£182,917), would almost guarantee his Cup berth.

At the very least his target was to do sufficiently well to ensure he would be among the top 12 in The European Ryder Cup Ranking after the US PGA Championship to gain entry into the World Golf Championships - NEC Invitational a week later. Langer also felt it would hugely help the cause of European Team Captain Sam Torrance if he earned one of the ten automatic places.

He was convinced he could win: "Everything in the bag, clubs, ball, is new this year and it's made a big difference. I'm hitting it much more solidly. In 1999 I finished many times between ninth and 20th. This year I've had a lot more top tens."

All that remained for Langer, who was feeling the strain physically and mentally of battling it out with David Duval in the Open Championship having had to withdraw with back problems after opening up 70, 69 at Loch Lomond, was to get the job done before taking a well earned fortnight's holiday.

With the likes of Darren Clarke, Ernie Els (also joint third at Royal Lytham & St Annes) and Lee Westwood on parade it would be no walk in the park.

Stephen Leaney

Warren Bennett

An opening 69 left him five shots adrift of surprise leader Niels Boysen, a 27 year old Dutch amateur who had missed the cut on his previous nine outings in the championship. But two subsequent 67s hoisted him within a single stroke of English pacesetter Warren Bennett, who had missed most of the 2000 season recovering from pneumonia and undergoing extensive treatment for damaged nerves and bones in his neck.

So effectively had Bennett taken advantage of a European Tour medical exemption, finishing second in the Caltex Singapore Masters and adding six more top 20 finishes, that his 2002 card was already assured. Langer knew there was much to do before it would be mission accomplished.

He had displayed signs of frustration after dropping three shots in a row following a spectacular 30 to the turn on day two and confessed: "It's human nature - I don't do that often. It's a thinking mans course. You have to position the ball to be able to attack the pins. It's not one of those courses that's 7,300 yards long and the person who hits it 320 yards wins."

Bennett, a young man with the 6ft 3in stature and straight-backed bearing of a guardsman, refused to go quietly. A birdie three at the tenth doubled his last round lead to two. Both eagled the 11th and after Langer birdied the 13th he did well to drop only one shot after his one bad drive at the 14th.

Anders Hansen

The Course

The Noordwijkse links is ranked among the top 20 courses in Europe. Designed by Frank Pennink with the help of sketches by club secretary Paul de Jong and opened in 1971 to replace the old nine hole layout, the course undulates dramatically between high sand dunes and is distinctive by having trees on the fifth, sixth and seventh.

Shot of the Week

The hole in one with a wedge at the 154 yards 12th snapped up on day one by Russell Claydon. Claydon won a Lancia Lybra saloon worth around £20,000 and admitted: "It's great news because my Volvo is currently in the body shop after a lorry collided with it on the A11."

Ian Garbutt

It was Bennett's turn to display his bravery when he matched Langer's birdie from four feet with one from 12 feet at the 15th, but the man who followed five European Challenge Tour victories in 1998 by winning the 1999 Scottish PGA Championship had no answer to the birdie threes from 12 feet and 30 feet at the 16th and short 17th that saw Langer draw level.

They parred the last, Langer getting home in 30 for 66 and Bennett in 31 for 67 for 15 below par 269 totals, that left them four clear of Miguel Angel Jiménez in third place.

Bennett, 14 years Langer's junior, finally succumbed at the first play-off hole - the 18th - and confessed: "Bernhard played like the champion he's been for over 20 years."

Langer was delighted: "I've been close to winning a few times since 1997 but somebody always rose to the challenge and nipped in on me. I played my best golf over the last five holes, which proves I can hit good shots under the highest pressure."

It is a quality that was not lost on Torrance, who phoned minutes later to congratulate the German after watching the action on television.

Gordon Richardson

NOORDWIJKSE GOLF CLUB, NOORDWIJK, THE NETHERLANDS, 26-29 JULY, 2001, PAR 71, 6751 YARDS, 6173 METRES

Pos.	Name		Rd1	Rd2	Rd3	Rd4	Total	Par	Prize Money Euro	£
1	Bernhard LANGER	Ger	69	67	67	66	269	-15	300000.00	182917.91
2	Warren BENNETT	Eng	68	67	67	67	269	-15	200000.00	121945.27
3	Miguel Angel JIMÉNEZ	Sp	71	65	71	66	273	-11	112680.00	68703.97
4	Barry LANE	Eng	71	67	66	70	274	-10	76440.00	46607.48
	Anders HANSEN	Den	69	67	75	63	274	-10	76440.00	46607.48
	Raymond RUSSELL	Scot	68	68	69	69	274	-10	76440.00	46607.48
7	Greg TURNER	NZ	68	65	71	71	275	-9	49500.00	30181.45
	Ricardo GONZALEZ	Arg	67	65	75	68	275	-9	49500.00	30181.45
9	Andrew OLDCORN	Scot	70	65	72	69	276	-8	36480.00	22242.82
	Padraig HARRINGTON	Ire	67	67	71	71	276	-8	36480.00	22242.82
	Stephen LEANEY	Aus	71	67	70	68	276	-8	36480.00	22242.82
12	Ian GARBUTT	Eng	69	71	71	66	277	-7	29970.00	18273.50
	Ernie ELS	SA	68	70	75	64	277	-7	29970.00	18273.50
14	Raphaël JACQUELIN	Fr	68	71	69	70	278	-6	24870.00	15163.89
	Peter BAKER	Eng	66	68	74	70	278	-6	24870.00	15163.89
	Henrik BJORNSTAD	Nor	73	64	72	69	278	-6	24870.00	15163.89
	Roger WINCHESTER	Eng	72	66	72	68	278	-6	24870.00	15163.89
	Peter O'MALLEY	Aus	73	68	69	68	278	-6	24870.00	15163.89
	Gary EVANS	Eng	69	71	69	69	278	-6	24870.00	15163.89
20	Steve WEBSTER	Eng	71	69	71	68	279	-5	20655.00	12593.90
	Bradley DREDGE	Wal	70	70	71	68	279	-5	20655.00	12593.90
	Dean ROBERTSON	Scot	66	68	72	73	279	-5	20655.00	12593.90
	Scott GARDINER	Aus	68	73	71	67	279	-5	20655.00	12593.90
24	Philip WALTON	Ire	69	68	70	73	280	-4	18180.00	11084.83
	John SENDEN	Aus	69	70	69	72	280	-4	18180.00	11084.83
	Desvonde BOTES	SA	69	70	70	71	280	-4	18180.00	11084.83
	Tomas Jesus MUÑOZ	Sp	74	67	65	74	280	-4	18180.00	11084.83
	Des TERBLANCHE	SA	69	71	74	66	280	-4	18180.00	11084.83
29	Roger CHAPMAN	Eng	70	69	72	70	281	-3	16020.00	9767.82
	Joakim HAEGGMAN	Swe	70	69	71	71	281	-3	16020.00	9767.82
	Michael JONZON	Swe	68	68	76	69	281	-3	16020.00	9767.82
32	Peter FOWLER	Aus	69	71	72	70	282	-2	13387.50	8162.71
	Mark MCNULTY	Zim	71	67	72	72	282	-2	13387.50	8162.71
	Darren FICHARDT	SA	68	66	70	78	282	-2	13387.50	8162.71
	Peter HANSON	Swe	70	69	72	71	282	-2	13387.50	8162.71
	Jamie SPENCE	Eng	69	70	70	73	282	-2	13387.50	8162.71
	Søren HANSEN	Den	70	71	70	71	282	-2	13387.50	8162.71
	Rolf MUNTZ	Hol	71	68	71	72	282	-2	13387.50	8162.71
	Richard STERNE	SA	67	67	73	75	282	-2	13387.50	8162.71
40	Jarrod MOSELEY	Aus	67	73	74	69	283	-1	10980.00	6694.80
	Per NYMAN	Swe	73	67	69	74	283	-1	10980.00	6694.80
	Paul MCGINLEY	Ire	71	70	67	75	283	-1	10980.00	6694.80
	Christian CÉVAËR	Fr	70	67	72	74	283	-1	10980.00	6694.80
	David HIGGINS	Ire	70	71	67	75	283	-1	10980.00	6694.80
45	Gregory HAVRET	Fr	72	69	72	71	284	0	8100.00	4938.78
	Jonathan LOMAS	Eng	70	68	76	70	284	0	8100.00	4938.78
	Stephen DODD	Wal	70	71	72	71	284	0	8100.00	4938.78
	Gary ORR	Scot	71	68	72	73	284	0	8100.00	4938.78
	David PARK	Wal	68	72	74	70	284	0	8100.00	4938.78
	Fredrik ANDERSSON	Swe	71	68	73	72	284	0	8100.00	4938.78
	Andrew COLTART	Scot	66	69	79	70	284	0	8100.00	4938.78
	Daren LEE	Eng	72	68	70	74	284	0	8100.00	4938.78
	John BICKERTON	Eng	70	69	73	72	284	0	8100.00	4938.78
	Alastair FORSYTH	Scot	70	71	71	72	284	0	8100.00	4938.78
	Aaron BADDELEY	Aus	72	69	74	69	284	0	8100.00	4938.78
56	José Manuel CARRILES	Sp	68	72	73	72	285	1	5535.00	3374.84
	Paolo QUIRICI	Swi	67	72	73	73	285	1	5535.00	3374.84
	Darren CLARKE	N.Ire	68	70	73	74	285	1	5535.00	3374.84
	Graeme STORM	Eng	71	68	71	75	285	1	5535.00	3374.84
60	Olle KARLSSON	Swe	67	70	74	75	286	2	4950.00	3018.15
	Mikael LUNDBERG	Swe	67	72	69	78	286	2	4950.00	3018.15
62	Niels BOYSEN (AM)	Hol	64	75	77	71	287	3		
63	Mark ROE	Eng	69	69	73	77	288	4	4500.00	2743.77
	Carl SUNESON	Sp	69	70	76	73	288	4	4500.00	2743.77
	Christophe POTTIER	Fr	68	72	73	75	288	4	4500.00	2743.77
66	Hennie OTTO	SA	71	70	74	74	289	5	3960.00	2414.52
	Joost STEENKAMER	Hol	75	64	75	75	289	5	3960.00	2414.52
	Marco BERNARDINI	It	69	71	72	77	289	5	3960.00	2414.52
69	Eamonn DARCY	Ire	70	71	76	73	290	6	3510.00	2140.14
	Elliot BOULT	NZ	74	63	75	78	290	6	3510.00	2140.14
71	Gordon BRAND JNR.	Scot	72	69	77	73	291	7	3280.00	1999.90

make it as
easy
as possible
hatever you send, all it takes is a single click
tell us what you want to send and when, we
ure it arrives with the greatest possible efficiency.
ether you want to send documents to London
machine parts to Japan, we deliver everything.
Where and whenever you want us to. And to book a
delivery, you don't even have to phone - you can book
it yourself on our website. That's easy, that's TNT. For
more information go to www.tnt.com.
TNT
Global Express, Logistics & Mail

Stuff of Legend

BARSEBÄCK GOLF AND COUNTRY CLUB, MALMO, SWEDEN

One thing became clear during the course of a blessedly sun-dappled four days in early August, and that was that Swedes, almost without challenge, own more knapsacks per capita of the population than any other.

Watching the huge galleries that flocked to the 11th Volvo Scandinavian Masters at Barsebäck was to observe a race utterly dedicated to the abiding principle that the exercise of making the greatest success of watching golf was likely to go to those who had joined in a battle for the survival of the fittest and prevailed in it.

When you're at your furthest point from home at Barsebäck Golf and Country Club, near the beautiful city of Malmo, it requires nothing less than a yomp of SAS proportions to return you to civilisation. But still they did it and, to a man, woman and child, it was well worth the effort.

Those hardy souls who went the distance — and there were almost 104,000 of them during the course of the tournament — were handsomely rewarded for their powers of dedication and endurance. If there was a more titanically-fought event in Europe in 2001, it must have been a real beauty, for this was the stuff of legend.

The eventual fact was that Colin Montgomerie won with a closing 70 for a total of 274, 14 under par, to claim his 26th victory on The European Tour International Schedule. It was his second triumph within a month, following his win in the Murphy's Irish Open at Fota Island at the beginning of July, but there were more sub-plots within the piece than you shake a 63-degree wedge at.

Like, for instance, the marvellous 63 conjured up by Anthony Wall that put him into a three stroke lead after the first round. It was the best round of the 26 year old Londoner's European Tour career and was also the lowest opening round in five Scandinavian Masters at Barsebäck.

Joakim Haeggman

Peter Hedblom

Peter Mitchell

The day before the event started, Montgomerie had made the confirmation of his place in the European Ryder Cup Team his mission statement for the week, and he proved that they had not been empty words by returning a 66 to share second place with Darren Clarke, Søren Hansen and Peter Hedblom. Wall was facing a fight to the death here, and he was the first to admit it.

One of those on 67 after 18 holes was Lee Westwood, showing a welcome return to form after missing four of his previous six cuts. At this stage, Westwood was hovering on the point where the darkness of obscurity was transformed into the bright lights of contention; he would not stay there long.

The aforesaid Lee John Westwood, the defending champion, had his second 67 running on day two to assume, on ten under par, a one stroke lead over Ian Poulter, a feisty and fully fledged Member of the new order in European golf, and Montgomerie.

Poulter was in the frame by the close of play on the third day, as well. As the knapsacks meandered their way round the sylvan splendour of Barsebäck, so Poulter prospered as he put up a score that gave him a share of the lead with Westwood on 13 under par. Montgomerie, meanwhile, was compiling a 69 to stay within touch of the leaders.

The name of another 2001 winner figures prominently on the honours board at Barsebäck. Henrik Stenson won the Club

The Course

The Barsebäck course is a glorious oddity. It has 15 holes that might have been lifted straight out of Berkshire and three that are pure, unadulterated links. The point is that it works. It was set up and prepared beautifully and the players were as one in their approval of it. A hybrid gem.

Jarmo Sandelin

Shot of the Week

Lee Westwood had just bogeyed the fifth hole in the final round and was in trouble deep in the trees on the next. He had virtually no gap through which to thread his recovery, but he produced a stroke of which even Harry Houdini would have been proud, punching a low runner between the trees to within 15 feet from the cup. It would have spoilt the story if he had missed the par putt. He didn't.

Championship four times in the 1990s, but this was not destined to be a week to put the young Swede even more prominently in lights.

Instead, the beam was focused on the final day on Montgomerie and a small handful of opposing suspects. Leading them was the sturdy figure of Westwood. Going into the tournament, Westwood had talked eloquently of the "comfort zone" into which he had sunk and his desire to escape from it. In this week he broke free from the shackles and was the better for it.

Westwood had a final round of 72, a more than decent effort as the wind swirled off the choppy waters of the Oresund that borders three holes at Barsebäck. It was not enough, but that said more about the excellence of Montgomerie than Westwood's own inadequacies.

On the final day, Montgomerie, Poulter and Westwood, the three leading contenders for the title, were two under par between them. Crucially, both strokes were gained by Montgomerie. It was enough to give him another precious battle honour to emblazon on his escutcheon.

Indeed, so dominant was Montgomerie in that final round that he could afford to bogey the last two holes and still win. In the end, he won by only one shot, and it would have been closer still had Westwood birdied one of the last two himself.

The record books will show that the Englishman failed to pick up a shot at the vital time and that Montgomerie came through, even if he wobbled more than he would have liked at the end.

It was a famous victory, a triumph for a dogged master of the game. Others had taken a dart at him and had not delivered the goods. Over a distinguished career, Montgomerie had demonstrated many times that once he got his nose in front, he was the very devil to shake off.

This time, this week in the Swedish sun, was no different. For the umpteenth time, Montgomerie had been put to the test. For the umpteenth time, he had passed it with flying colours.

Mel Webb

Carl Suneson

BARSEBÄCK GOLF AND COUNTRY CLUB, MALMO, SWEDEN, 2-5 AUGUST, 2001, PAR 72, 7323 YARDS, 6695 METRES

Pos.	Name		Rd1	Rd2	Rd3	Rd4	Total	Par	Prize Money Euro	£
1	Colin MONTGOMERIE	Scot	66	69	69	70	274	-14	300000.00	184112.33
2	Ian POULTER	Eng	70	65	68	72	275	-13	156340.00	95947.07
	Lee WESTWOOD	Eng	67	67	69	72	275	-13	156340.00	95947.07
4	Warren BENNETT	Eng	67	70	69	70	276	-12	65664.00	40298.51
	Dennis EDLUND	Swe	69	67	71	69	276	-12	65664.00	40298.51
	Joakim HAEGGMAN	Swe	71	67	70	68	276	-12	65664.00	40298.51
	Jarmo SANDELIN	Swe	68	74	68	66	276	-12	65664.00	40298.51
	Adam SCOTT	Aus	69	72	67	68	276	-12	65664.00	40298.51
9	Peter HANSON	Swe	70	72	66	69	277	-11	35100.00	21541.14
	Søren HANSEN	Den	66	73	68	70	277	-11	35100.00	21541.14
	Peter HEDBLOM	Swe	66	70	68	73	277	-11	35100.00	21541.14
	Thomas BJÖRN	Den	68	72	67	70	277	-11	35100.00	21541.14
13	Fredrik ANDERSSON	Swe	69	71	71	67	278	-10	27660.00	16975.16
	Niclas FASTH	Swe	67	69	72	70	278	-10	27660.00	16975.16
	Michael CAMPBELL	NZ	69	70	70	69	278	-10	27660.00	16975.16
16	Anders FORSBRAND	Swe	72	69	67	71	279	-9	22950.00	14084.59
	Tony JOHNSTONE	Zim	71	69	70	69	279	-9	22950.00	14084.59
	Johan RYSTRÖM	Swe	67	72	71	69	279	-9	22950.00	14084.59
	Olivier EDMOND	Fr	68	74	68	69	279	-9	22950.00	14084.59
	Darren CLARKE	N.Ire	66	70	70	73	279	-9	22950.00	14084.59
	Peter LONARD	Aus	71	68	69	71	279	-9	22950.00	14084.59
22	Roger CHAPMAN	Eng	69	69	72	70	280	-8	19800.00	12151.41
	Raphaël JACQUELIN	Fr	68	75	68	69	280	-8	19800.00	12151.41
	Steve WEBSTER	Eng	71	68	70	71	280	-8	19800.00	12151.41
25	Wayne RILEY	Aus	71	68	71	71	281	-7	17910.00	10991.51
	Thomas LEVET	Fr	67	72	67	75	281	-7	17910.00	10991.51
	Ian GARBUTT	Eng	71	71	69	70	281	-7	17910.00	10991.51
	Pierre FULKE	Swe	68	71	71	71	281	-7	17910.00	10991.51
29	Costantino ROCCA	It	68	72	71	71	282	-6	14965.71	9184.57
	Brian DAVIS	Eng	71	71	69	71	282	-6	14965.71	9184.57
	Anthony WALL	Eng	63	76	71	72	282	-6	14965.71	9184.57
	Jarrod MOSELEY	Aus	70	71	66	75	282	-6	14965.71	9184.57
	Peter O'MALLEY	Aus	70	71	68	73	282	-6	14965.71	9184.57
	Paul LAWRIE	Scot	69	71	65	77	282	-6	14965.71	9184.57
	Carl PETTERSSON	Swe	74	68	70	70	282	-6	14965.71	9184.57
36	David HOWELL	Eng	73	70	66	74	283	-5	11340.00	6959.45
	Jesper PARNEVIK	Swe	71	72	69	71	283	-5	11340.00	6959.45
	Anders HANSEN	Den	71	72	70	70	283	-5	11340.00	6959.45
	Søren KJELDSEN	Den	69	72	71	71	283	-5	11340.00	6959.45
	Fredrik HENGE	Swe	71	69	69	74	283	-5	11340.00	6959.45
	Peter BAKER	Eng	72	70	72	69	283	-5	11340.00	6959.45
	Carl SUNESON	Sp	68	74	72	69	283	-5	11340.00	6959.45
	Alex CEJKA	Ger	73	70	70	70	283	-5	11340.00	6959.45
	Ignacio GARRIDO	Sp	71	71	72	69	283	-5	11340.00	6959.45
	Raymond RUSSELL	Scot	70	74	71	68	283	-5	11340.00	6959.45
	Stephen GALLACHER	Scot	70	70	69	74	283	-5	11340.00	6959.45
47	Desvonde BOTES	SA	71	68	72	73	284	-4	8280.00	5081.50
	Paul BROADHURST	Eng	71	73	69	71	284	-4	8280.00	5081.50
	Per-Ulrik JOHANSSON	Swe	72	72	68	72	284	-4	8280.00	5081.50
	Christian CÉVAËR	Fr	71	69	73	71	284	-4	8280.00	5081.50
	Steven RICHARDSON	Eng	74	66	72	72	284	-4	8280.00	5081.50
	Christopher HANELL	Swe	70	72	72	70	284	-4	8280.00	5081.50
53	Gordon BRAND JNR.	Scot	72	71	72	70	285	-3	6150.00	3774.30
	Mark ROE	Eng	72	71	71	71	285	-3	6150.00	3774.30
	Mark MCNULTY	Zim	70	71	70	74	285	-3	6150.00	3774.30
	Jamie SPENCE	Eng	69	74	70	72	285	-3	6150.00	3774.30
	Gary EVANS	Eng	72	71	72	70	285	-3	6150.00	3774.30
	Bradley DREDGE	Wal	68	74	73	70	285	-3	6150.00	3774.30
59	Ian WOOSNAM	Wal	70	74	73	69	286	-2	4500.00	2761.68
	Marc FARRY	Fr	71	72	71	72	286	-2	4500.00	2761.68
	Richard GREEN	Aus	69	74	70	73	286	-2	4500.00	2761.68
	Steen TINNING	Den	73	71	73	69	286	-2	4500.00	2761.68
	Peter MITCHELL	Eng	72	70	72	72	286	-2	4500.00	2761.68
	Ricardo GONZALEZ	Arg	71	73	75	67	286	-2	4500.00	2761.68
	Fredrik JACOBSON	Swe	71	73	71	71	286	-2	4500.00	2761.68
	Greg OWEN	Eng	73	71	70	72	286	-2	4500.00	2761.68
	David CARTER	Eng	70	70	73	73	286	-2	4500.00	2761.68
68	Hennie OTTO	SA	69	74	74	70	287	-1	3250.00	1994.55
	Henrik BJORNSTAD	Nor	73	70	71	73	287	-1	3250.00	1994.55
	Nicolas COLSAERTS	Bel	71	71	73	72	287	-1	3250.00	1994.55
	Olle KARLSSON	Swe	71	73	73	70	287	-1	3250.00	1994.55
72	Greg TURNER	NZ	72	72	74	70	288	0	2695.50	1654.25
	Carlos RODILES	Sp	72	71	71	74	288	0	2695.50	1654.25
74	Marcus NORGREN	Swe	73	69	74	73	289	1	2683.50	1646.88
	Gregory HAVRET	Fr	67	73	75	74	289	1	2683.50	1646.88
	Roger WINCHESTER	Eng	75	69	69	76	289	1	2683.50	1646.88
	Van PHILLIPS	Eng	70	74	72	73	289	1	2683.50	1646.88
	Stephen SCAHILL	NZ	72	67	73	77	289	1	2683.50	1646.88
	Michael JONZON	Swe	71	70	74	74	289	1	2683.50	1646.88
80	Henrik STENSON	Swe	70	74	74	72	290	2	2673.00	1640.44
81	Des TERBLANCHE	SA	70	72	77	73	292	4	2670.00	1638.60
82	Tomas Jesus MUÑOZ	Sp	70	74	73	76	293	5	2667.00	1636.76
83	Niklas LEMKE (AM)	Swe	72	72	75	75	294	6		

Bumper Haul

THE CELTIC MANOR RESORT, NEWPORT, WALES

By his own admission, Paul McGinley has, in the past, been inclined to fall asleep when the heat of the battle has been at its most intense. With tournaments hanging in the balance, this engaging Dubliner has, to his cost, switched off at the wrong moment.

For example, McGinley can ruefully recall the time when he led José Maria Olazábal by two shots with just two holes to play at the 1994 Turespaña Open Mediterrania - only to lose to the Spaniard in a play-off. As he put it, he took his eye off the ball during a 20 minute hold-up on a par three.

Now, though, McGinley can rest assured that he possesses concentration and resolve to match the best of them after a brave play-off victory over Paul Lawrie and Daren Lee at The Celtic Manor Resort Wales Open. In such situations, it is as much about nerve as skill and the Irishman displayed plenty of both in securing the third European Tour title of his career.

Paul McGinley

What was most significant about the victory was that it was completed with the on-going pressure of Ryder Cup qualification. Almost since the points list began some 11 months earlier, McGinley had found his game under constant scrutiny. Could he sink those key putts at crucial moments? How would he react when the chips were down? Now we know.

When the big questions were asked in the play-off at The Celtic Manor Resort, McGinley had all the answers. And while, ostensibly, his reward for emerging victorious from the extra five holes was the 201,685 euro (£125,000) winner's cheque, it was the bumper haul of Ryder Cup points gained that clearly mattered most.

"There was a huge difference between first and second place in terms of Ryder Cup points and that's what drove me on," he said after the win that consolidated his bid to make Sam Torrance's European Team. "It probably was the most tension-packed situation I've been in. But it was a pressure I felt I could handle and come through. I wasn't overawed by it - I just felt unbelievably determined.

"As my wife said to me on the phone before I went out, it's a bit like penalty kicks in football. Anything can happen and she's so right. Fortunately it fell for me."

Daren Lee

The championship, which ultimately would be cut to 36 holes, got off to a wet start. Only nine players managed to get their opening rounds underway as scheduled before Tournament Director Mike Stewart was forced to suspend play. And as the rain continued to pour throughout the morning, it was no surprise when the players were told at lunchtime not to come back until the following day.

Thankfully, conditions did improve immeasurably overnight. With the sun shining and blue skies all around, The Celtic Manor Resort looked simply magnificent for the Ryder Cup Board, who came to assess Wales's bid to stage the 2010 Matches there. While they took to the skies for a helicopter ride over the site, Gary Orr, Lawrie and McGinley were busy soaring to the top of the leaderboard. All three shot impressive five under par 67s on the 7,324 yards course, which offered no easy birdies.

Lawrie and McGinley kept up their respective challenges during the second round, moving to six under par. And then with darkness beginning to circle the Usk River Valley, Lee joined them in front thanks to a second successive 69. Trailing just a shot behind that trio came the resurgent Swede Anders Forsbrand and two potential Welsh stars of the future, Jamie Donaldson and Mark Pilkington. It was all set up nicely for an enthralling final day.

However, the rain that had so infuriatingly disrupted the first day's play returned to wreak havoc once more, leaving the championship

Paul Lawrie

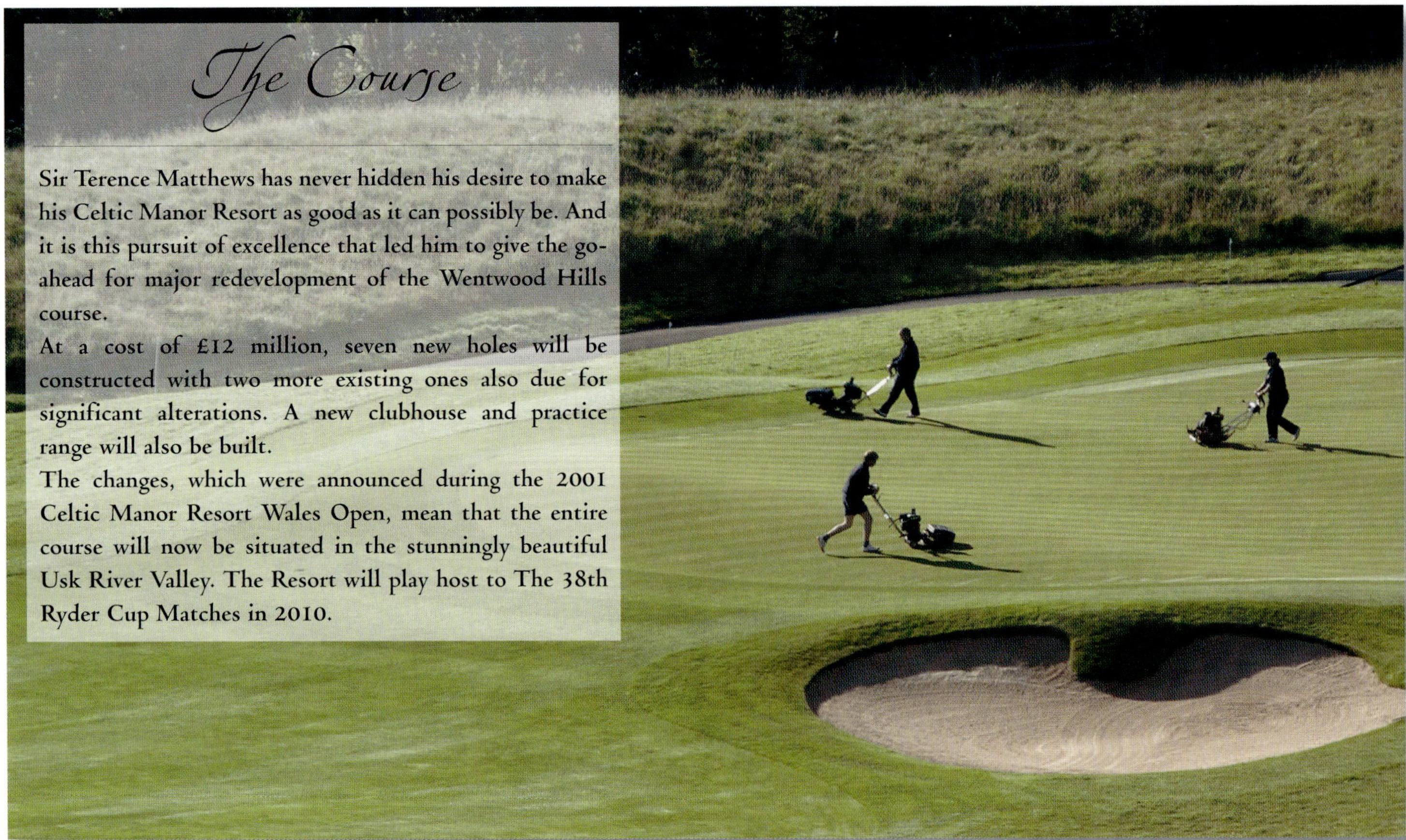

The Course

Sir Terence Matthews has never hidden his desire to make his Celtic Manor Resort as good as it can possibly be. And it is this pursuit of excellence that led him to give the go-ahead for major redevelopment of the Wentwood Hills course.

At a cost of £12 million, seven new holes will be constructed with two more existing ones also due for significant alterations. A new clubhouse and practice range will also be built.

The changes, which were announced during the 2001 Celtic Manor Resort Wales Open, mean that the entire course will now be situated in the stunningly beautiful Usk River Valley. The Resort will play host to The 38th Ryder Cup Matches in 2010.

Shot of the Week

Ian Woosnam's nine iron approach shot on the par four 13th hole in the second round. The home favourite holed out from 136 yards for an eagle two to trigger a colossal roar that seemed to echo for ages around the Valley. "It bounced just past the hole and spun back in," said the crowd-pleasing Welshman.

to be decided by way of a sudden death play-off between the three leaders. It was frustrating, certainly, but Lawrie, Lee and McGinley still managed to produce a thrilling finale in any case.

The scene for the play-off was the 211 yards 12th hole where McGinley almost came to grief with his first shot. He blocked a two iron far to the right before somehow getting up and down to stay alive. At the second time of asking, Lawrie bogeyed the hole leaving Lee and McGinley to go head-to-head.

There was everything for which to play. Lee, for example, had never finished higher than tied fourth on The European Tour. This, then, was his chance to land that elusive first victory.

But McGinley, who confessesd to having daydreamed his way through school, never lost sight of the prize on offer at The Celtic Manor Resort. On the fifth visit to the 12th hole, he focused and refocused before hitting a supreme bunker shot to eight inches to set up the par putt that would bring victory.

Tony Rushmer

Anders Forsbrand

THE CELTIC MANOR RESORT, NEWPORT, WALES, 9-12 AUGUST, 2001, PAR 72, 7324 YARDS, 6698 METRES

Pos.	Name		Rd1	Rd2	Rd3	Rd4	Total	Par	Prize Money Euro	£
1	Paul MCGINLEY	Ire	67	71			138	-6	201685.00	125000.00
2	Paul LAWRIE	Scot	67	71			138	-6	105102.10	65140.00
	Daren LEE	Eng	69	69			138	-6	105102.10	65140.00
4	Anders FORSBRAND	Swe	72	67			139	-5	51389.34	31850.00
	Mark PILKINGTON	Wal	68	71			139	-5	51389.34	31850.00
	Jamie DONALDSON	Wal	68	71			139	-5	51389.34	31850.00
7	Anders HANSEN	Den	72	68			140	-4	36303.30	22500.00
8	Steve WEBSTER	Eng	74	67			141	-3	24020.68	14887.50
	Nick O'HERN	Aus	70	71			141	-3	24020.68	14887.50
	Thomas LEVET	Fr	71	70			141	-3	24020.68	14887.50
	Roger WESSELS	SA	68	73			141	-3	24020.68	14887.50
	Gary ORR	Scot	67	74			141	-3	24020.68	14887.50
	Nic HENNING	SA	73	68			141	-3	24020.68	14887.50
14	Kevin SPURGEON	Eng	72	70			142	-2	16719.69	10362.50
	Sven STRÜVER	Ger	72	70			142	-2	16719.69	10362.50
	Jarrod MOSELEY	Aus	70	72			142	-2	16719.69	10362.50
	Phillip PRICE	Wal	70	72			142	-2	16719.69	10362.50
	Simon DYSON	Eng	73	69			142	-2	16719.69	10362.50
	Scott GARDINER	Aus	69	73			142	-2	16719.69	10362.50
20	Santiago LUNA	Sp	72	71			143	-1	12231.42	7580.77
	Warren BENNETT	Eng	72	71			143	-1	12231.42	7580.77
	Søren KJELDSEN	Den	70	73			143	-1	12231.42	7580.77
	John SENDEN	Aus	72	71			143	-1	12231.42	7580.77
	Graham RANKIN	Scot	68	75			143	-1	12231.42	7580.77
	Ian POULTER	Eng	71	72			143	-1	12231.42	7580.77
	Jean HUGO	SA	72	71			143	-1	12231.42	7580.77
	Jeremy ROBINSON	Eng	73	70			143	-1	12231.42	7580.77
	Jonathan LOMAS	Eng	73	70			143	-1	12231.42	7580.77
	Ignacio GARRIDO	Sp	72	71			143	-1	12231.42	7580.77
	Simon HURD	Eng	69	74			143	-1	12231.42	7580.77
	David HIGGINS	Ire	73	70			143	-1	12231.42	7580.77
	Alastair FORSYTH	Scot	72	71			143	-1	12231.42	7580.77
33	Andrew OLDCORN	Scot	69	75			144	0	7752.27	4804.69
	Mark ROE	Eng	70	74			144	0	7752.27	4804.69
	Marc FARRY	Fr	71	73			144	0	7752.27	4804.69
	Mark MCNULTY	Zim	77	67			144	0	7752.27	4804.69
	Trevor IMMELMAN	SA	72	72			144	0	7752.27	4804.69
	Justin ROSE	Eng	71	73			144	0	7752.27	4804.69
	Fredrik HENGE	Swe	72	72			144	0	7752.27	4804.69
	Roger WINCHESTER	Eng	68	76			144	0	7752.27	4804.69
	Per NYMAN	Swe	72	72			144	0	7752.27	4804.69
	Alex CEJKA	Ger	74	70			144	0	7752.27	4804.69
	Des TERBLANCHE	SA	77	67			144	0	7752.27	4804.69
	David LYNN	Eng	69	75			144	0	7752.27	4804.69
	Michael JONZON	Swe	70	74			144	0	7752.27	4804.69
	John BICKERTON	Eng	71	73			144	0	7752.27	4804.69
	Paul CASEY	Eng	74	70			144	0	7752.27	4804.69
	Carl PETTERSSON	Swe	74	70			144	0	7752.27	4804.69
49	Ian WOOSNAM	Wal	73	72			145	1	4162.78	2580.00
	Jeev Milkha SINGH	Ind	75	70			145	1	4162.78	2580.00
	Barry LANE	Eng	71	74			145	1	4162.78	2580.00
	Anthony WALL	Eng	72	73			145	1	4162.78	2580.00
	Dennis EDLUND	Swe	72	73			145	1	4162.78	2580.00
	Thomas GÖGELE	Ger	70	75			145	1	4162.78	2580.00
	Olivier EDMOND	Fr	75	70			145	1	4162.78	2580.00
	Gary EVANS	Eng	72	73			145	1	4162.78	2580.00
	Jorge BERENDT	Arg	74	71			145	1	4162.78	2580.00
	Tomas Jesus MUÑOZ	Sp	70	75			145	1	4162.78	2580.00
	Markus BRIER	Aut	72	73			145	1	4162.78	2580.00
	Fredrik ANDERSSON	Swe	72	73			145	1	4162.78	2580.00
	David CARTER	Eng	70	75			145	1	4162.78	2580.00
	Stephen GALLACHER	Scot	74	71			145	1	4162.78	2580.00
	Marco BERNARDINI	It	73	72			145	1	4162.78	2580.00
	Craig WILLIAMS (AM)	Wal	74	71			145	1		
65	Wayne RILEY	Aus	70	76			146	2	2107.99	1306.49
	Gary MURPHY	Ire	71	75			146	2	2107.99	1306.49
	Maarten LAFEBER	Hol	72	74			146	2	2107.99	1306.49
	Richard GREEN	Aus	73	73			146	2	2107.99	1306.49
	Marcus HIGLEY	Eng	70	76			146	2	2107.99	1306.49
	Garry HOUSTON	Wal	73	73			146	2	2107.99	1306.49
	Desvonde BOTES	SA	73	73			146	2	2107.99	1306.49
	Simon D. HURLEY	Eng	75	71			146	2	2107.99	1306.49
	Andrew BEAL	Eng	74	72			146	2	2107.99	1306.49
	Massimo SCARPA	It	74	72			146	2	2107.99	1306.49
	Steven RICHARDSON	Eng	74	72			146	2	2107.99	1306.49
	Sion E BEBB	Wal	72	74			146	2	2107.99	1306.49
	Stephen SCAHILL	NZ	72	74			146	2	2107.99	1306.49
	Bradley DREDGE	Wal	73	73			146	2	2107.99	1306.49
	David PARK	Wal	72	74			146	2	2107.99	1306.49
	Jarmo SANDELIN	Swe	71	75			146	2	2107.99	1306.49
	Erol SIMSEK	Ger	72	74			146	2	2107.99	1306.49

EUROPEAN GOLF DESIGN

porting Club Berlin, Nick Faldo Course
German Open 1998-1999

PGA Golf de Catalunya
Open De España 2000

Marquess Course, Woburn G&CC
Victor Chandler British Masters 2001

Celtic Manor Resort
Home of the 2010 Ryder Cup Matches

Courageous Decision

ATLANTA ATHLETIC CLUB, ATLANTA, GEORGIA, USA

It is one of golf's idiosyncracies that the US PGA Championship, the last of the game's four annual Major Championships, throws up more lesser known players as winners than any of the Major Championships. Not always and not often but sometimes. Mark Brooks was a surprise in 1996, and so was John Daly in 1991 because he was the ninth alternate for the event. How many men would have backed Wayne Grady to win in 1990?

Equally, though, David Toms would win his first Major Championship by one stroke, holding off Phil Mickelson with a resolution it was not thought he possessed. He would not have been in many people's list of possible winners prior to the Championship unfolding at the Atlanta Athletic Club. Little-known and self-effacing, Toms had been on Tour since 1989 and won only five times. Furthermore, the 34 year old, a moderately long hitter, would never have been expected to have been able to cope with a long course that in the 18th had one of the longest par fours in Championship history. Officially said to be 490 yards, it was played from a point at least ten yards further back. With hindsight we should have known that far from disqualifying Toms from winning the Championship, this had the opposite effect, making him more qualified.

At first, in the steaming heat of the south, no one was really looking much beyond David Duval, who had blossomed in character and appeal after his win in the Open Championship the previous month. Duval was photographed without his sun glasses on the eve of this event, and suddenly it became clear that not only did he sound a changed man, talking relaxedly and more easily about golf, but he looked a different man too, smiling. The eyes are the window to the soul and now Duval's sunglasses were removed it was possible to see that his soul seemed to be happy, laughing.

Phil Mickelson

Which was more than could be said for Tiger Woods. The defending champion, having become the complete golfer by winning a fourth Major Championship in a row at Augusta National in April, revealed on the eve of the Championship that he was bidding to become the *compleat* angler too. He spoke about fishing as warmly as he once did about golf. His mind did not seem to be on golf, which it probably wasn't as he had not played a 72 hole tournament since the Open Championship. It was revealing when Woods struggled badly to make the halfway cut, birdieing two of his last four holes to survive to the last two rounds. People tapped the sides of their noses and nodded sagely. Tiger is not the player he was, they said, and on this evidence they were right. Woods would finish joint 29th, equalling his worst finish in a Major Championship as a professional.

Jesper Parnevik

It was left to Mickelson to make the routine challenge by One of The Game's Great Players. Old Leftie, lolloping around with that distinctive gait, talked up a good fight in the days leading up to the Championship. Mickelson, many felt, was finally ready to win that first Major Championship that had eluded him so often hitherto. Mickelson, 31, had been in contention at the Masters Tournament in April and the US Open in June. On six previous occasions Mickelson started the final round of a Major Championship within two strokes of the leader and failed to break par, scoring an average of 72.43. This time Mickelson's final round was one stroke better than that of Toms, a 68 to a 69. What was bad for Mickelson was that for the second time in three years a rival had laid up on the 72nd hole and beaten him. Payne Stewart did it in the US Open at Pinehurst in 1999.

It was Toms's week. There had been a portent of this on the Saturday when he holed out on the 15th with a five wood. On Sunday he and Mickelson played together, the only two golfers to have broken 200 for three rounds, and Toms never lost the lead though Mickelson occasionally tied him for it. After 14 holes, Toms was leading by two strokes. He was outdriven but not outplayed. On the 15th, where Toms had holed in one 24 hours earlier, Mickelson chipped in for a birdie and Toms bogeyed. The two were tied as they reached the 16th tee.

The Course

A tree-lined, long course of 7,213 yards with a par of 70 that included a par four of 490 yards, the 18th. The club was made famous by Bobby Jones, the legendary amateur, who was a member of the Atlanta Athletic Club when it was on other premises in the 1920s and 1930s. In 1976 Jerry Pate won the US Open at the present AAC and five years later Larry Nelson won the 1981 US PGA Championship at the same venue. Despite its length, there were 146 rounds in the 60s.

José Maria Olazábal

If this was to be his moment, then surely Mickelson would take it. To his 19 Tour victories would now be added his first Major Championship. But no. He hit his tee shot into the trees and three-putted. Toms, meanwhile, parred and when he was faced with laying up on the 18th or going for glory with a wood, he took the courageous decision. He knew Mickelson, who was yards further up the fairway, could reach the green comfortably with a mid-iron second shot. And just as certainly, he knew that if he hit a wood his ball might land on the green, hop through and leave him a delicate chip back down the green with a pond waiting the other side of the putting surface. Toms hit a pitching wedge nearly 100 yards down the fairway, followed by a shot with a lob wedge to ten feet from the hole. When Mickelson missed his 25 foot putt for birdie, Toms coolly sank his putt. Victory for the unfancied. A typical US PGA Championship.

John Hopkins

Shingo Katayama

Shot of the Week

The hole in one by Toms on the 15th on Saturday, the first player to make an ace in a Major Championship and go on to win. Toms used a five wood for this shot on the 243 yards hole, his ball bouncing three times before smacking the flagstick and falling out of sight. It was also the longest hole in one ever hit in a Major Championship.

Phillip Price

ATLANTA ATHLETIC CLUB, ATLANTA, GEORGIA, USA, 16-19 AUGUST, 2001, PAR 70, 7213 YARDS, 6596 METRES

Pos.	Name		Rd1	Rd2	Rd3	Rd4	Total	Par	Prize Money Euro	Prize Money £
1	David TOMS	USA	66	65	65	69	265	-15	1046978.00	655783.48
2	Phil MICKELSON	USA	66	66	66	68	266	-14	628634.40	393750.45
3	Steve LOWERY	USA	67	67	66	68	268	-12	395972.50	248020.71
4	Mark CALCAVECCHIA	USA	71	68	66	65	270	-10	248881.00	155888.71
	Shingo KATAYAMA	Jpn	67	64	69	70	270	-10	248881.00	155888.71
6	Billy ANDRADE	USA	68	70	68	66	272	-8	195749.10	122609.10
7	Jim FURYK	USA	70	64	71	69	274	-6	170395.00	106728.34
	Scott VERPLANK	USA	69	68	70	67	274	-6	170395.00	106728.34
	Scott HOCH	USA	68	70	69	67	274	-6	170395.00	106728.34
10	David DUVAL	USA	66	68	67	74	275	-5	136465.10	85476.06
	Justin LEONARD	USA	70	69	67	69	275	-5	136465.10	85476.06
	Kirk TRIPLETT	USA	68	70	71	66	275	-5	136465.10	85476.06
13	Steve FLESCH	USA	73	67	70	66	276	-4	105891.00	66325.72
	Jesper PARNEVIK	Swe	70	68	70	68	276	-4	105891.00	66325.72
	Ernie ELS	SA	67	67	70	72	276	-4	105891.00	66325.72
16	Stuart APPLEBY	Aus	66	70	68	73	277	-3	79045.37	49510.73
	Mike WEIR	Can	69	72	66	70	277	-3	79045.37	49510.73
	Dudley HART	USA	66	68	73	70	277	-3	79045.37	49510.73
	José COCERES	Arg	69	68	73	67	277	-3	79045.37	49510.73
	Robert ALLENBY	Aus	69	67	73	68	277	-3	79045.37	49510.73
	Chris DIMARCO	USA	68	67	71	71	277	-3	79045.37	49510.73
22	Mark O'MEARA	USA	72	63	70	73	278	-2	49536.52	31027.62
	Shigeki MARUYAMA	Jpn	68	72	71	67	278	-2	49536.52	31027.62
	Paul AZINGER	USA	68	67	69	74	278	-2	49536.52	31027.62
	Paul MCGINLEY	Ire	68	72	71	67	278	-2	49536.52	31027.62
	Briny BAIRD	USA	70	69	72	67	278	-2	49536.52	31027.62
	J Brian GAY	USA	70	68	69	71	278	-2	49536.52	31027.62
	Charles HOWELL III	USA	71	67	69	71	278	-2	49536.52	31027.62
29	Greg NORMAN	Aus	70	68	71	70	279	-1	32927.80	20624.60
	Tiger WOODS	USA	73	67	69	70	279	-1	32927.80	20624.60
	Nick PRICE	Zim	71	67	71	70	279	-1	32927.80	20624.60
	Kyoung-Ju CHOI	RepKor	66	68	72	73	279	-1	32927.80	20624.60
	Bob TWAY	USA	69	69	71	70	279	-1	32927.80	20624.60
	Carlos Daniel FRANCO	Par	67	72	71	69	279	-1	32927.80	20624.60
	Niclas FASTH	Swe	66	69	72	72	279	-1	32927.80	20624.60
	Christopher SMITH	USA	69	71	68	71	279	-1	32927.80	20624.60
37	José Maria OLAZÁBAL	Sp	71	70	68	71	280	0	23489.90	14713.10
	Fred COUPLES	USA	70	69	70	71	280	0	23489.90	14713.10
	Davis LOVE III	USA	71	67	65	77	280	0	23489.90	14713.10
	Bob ESTES	USA	67	65	75	73	280	0	23489.90	14713.10
	Angel CABRERA	Arg	69	69	70	72	280	0	23489.90	14713.10
	Andrew COLTART	Scot	67	72	71	70	280	0	23489.90	14713.10
	Retief GOOSEN	SA	69	70	66	75	280	0	23489.90	14713.10
44	Andrew OLDCORN	Scot	73	67	74	67	281	1	15939.57	9983.88
	Greg CHALMERS	Aus	68	70	69	74	281	1	15939.57	9983.88
	Jerry KELLY	USA	69	67	72	73	281	1	15939.57	9983.88
	Hal SUTTON	USA	67	71	73	70	281	1	15939.57	9983.88
	Kenny PERRY	USA	68	70	71	72	281	1	15939.57	9983.88
	Lee WESTWOOD	Eng	71	68	68	74	281	1	15939.57	9983.88
	Rick SCHULLER	USA	68	70	72	71	281	1	15939.57	9983.88
51	Nick FALDO	Eng	67	74	71	70	282	2	12688.74	7947.70
	Ian WOOSNAM	Wal	71	70	73	68	282	2	12688.74	7947.70
	Joe DURANT	USA	68	71	72	71	282	2	12688.74	7947.70
	Vijay SINGH	Fiji	73	68	70	71	282	2	12688.74	7947.70
	Scott DUNLAP	USA	69	72	70	71	282	2	12688.74	7947.70
	Tom PERNICE	USA	69	69	74	70	282	2	12688.74	7947.70
	Chris RILEY	USA	68	71	73	70	282	2	12688.74	7947.70
	Frank LICKLITER	USA	71	69	71	71	282	2	12688.74	7947.70
59	Brad FAXON	USA	66	70	74	73	283	3	11912.73	7461.64
	Stewart CINK	USA	68	72	71	72	283	3	11912.73	7461.64
	Phillip PRICE	Wal	68	69	76	70	283	3	11912.73	7461.64
	Grant WAITE	NZ	64	74	73	72	283	3	11912.73	7461.64
63	Skip KENDALL	USA	72	67	73	72	284	4	11521.24	7216.43
	Thomas BJÖRN	Den	67	71	73	73	284	4	11521.24	7216.43
	Jonathan KAYE	USA	67	68	78	71	284	4	11521.24	7216.43
66	Tom WATSON	USA	69	70	76	70	285	5	11129.74	6971.21
	Steve STRICKER	USA	75	65	75	70	285	5	11129.74	6971.21
	Robert DAMRON	USA	68	73	71	73	285	5	11129.74	6971.21
	Rocco MEDIATE	USA	71	65	73	76	285	5	11129.74	6971.21
70	Fred FUNK	USA	66	74	71	75	286	6	10878.06	6813.56
	Scott MCCARRON	USA	69	67	73	77	286	6	10878.06	6813.56
72	John HUSTON	USA	67	68	75	77	287	7	10794.17	6761.02
73	Bob MAY	USA	71	70	76	74	291	11	10738.24	6725.99
74	Paul STANKOWSKI	USA	67	71	76	79	293	13	10682.31	6690.95
75	Steve PATE	USA	71	69	71	83	294	14	10626.38	6655.92
76	Colin MONTGOMERIE	Scot	71	69	74	DISQ	214	4	2237.13	1401.25

Hungry Soul

SLIEVE RUSSELL HOTEL GOLF & COUNTRY CLUB, CO. CAVAN, IRELAND

When Bernhard Langer was struggling to break through on The European Tour, it was a case of pre-qualifying on a Monday but pack your bags for the following week if you were unsuccessful and on to the next tournament. If you made it and qualified, there was your chance to build a career and make a card.

For his 2001 counterpart Tobias Dier, the struggle was no less acute, even if the accommodation was rather more sumptuous.

The German had to overcome 155 hungry souls from The European Tour and the European Challenge Tour, searching for their own little acre of Nirvana - a Tour card in one fell swoop, an automatic exemption for a year.

That is what this event, the North West of Ireland Open, brought for the 24 year old biochemistry graduate from Nürnberg. Dier certainly found the right formula again at the course he loves, Slieve Russell Hotel Golf & Country Club, where he had shot a course record 65 the previous year.

Langer would have been proud of the way his fellow countryman refused to lose sight of his dream. And in some way the double Masters champion did have a little to do with the determined victory by Dier.

Feeling that the man who had placed Germany on the world golfing map would be loath to take any interest in a young player who had decided his chemistry of life would be on the fairways and not in the laboratory, Dier had never approached Langer for any help. When he did, though, during the months leading up to his maiden success, he was delighted to find his compatriot was more than willing to advise. Dier practised with Langer and learned how to think his way better around a golf course.

That stood him in good stead as he fended off all-comers to achieve his dream and set his career on its way.

Jesus Maria Arruti

Stephen Dodd

While Dier was glad of advice from a two-times Masters Tournament champion, then the first round leader on a day bedevilled by lightning and heavy rain on an already wet course, Jesus Maria Arruti, was happy to reveal he had done the same. José Maria Olazábal was Arruti's mentor at San Sebastian. The Spaniard was a soul hungry to get back to The European Tour and, perhaps, meet up with his illustrious compatriot again. His 65, not a record because of preferred lies, ruled the day. But Dier lurked only a stroke behind.

After a foggy start to the second round, there was another player starving for long overdue success, who made his mark and put himself on the way to at last achieving it. Stephen Dodd emerged from the mists of a 12 year professional career shrouded in disappointment. The 1989 Amateur Champion had had little success since his heady victory over Craig Cassells at Royal Birkdale and his triumphant appearance in the Great Britain and Ireland Walker Cup team at Peachtree, Atlanta, Georgia. But Dodd had carried on improving, he felt. And this was his finest year, could it be his finest hour?

It looked as though Dodd would carry the day but three birdies in the midst of his back nine took Dier to the fore, a stroke ahead of Dodd, with his fellow Welshman Mark Pilkington carrying his form on from The Celtic Manor Resort the previous week to contend again.

The third round was again all about a stunning late run. Dier separated himself from Dodd by three strokes as he finished with an exhilarating three birdies to take a commanding lead into the final round. The previous year Dier, on his way to fourth place, had led briefly with eight holes to go. This time there was no faltering and with another telling run of three birdies in five holes to the turn, the tournament looked all over bar the shouting as Dier built his lead to four strokes.

That was reckoning without a few understandable nerves by Dier and Dodd's determination. When the pair stood on the last there was only a stroke between them in Dier's favour. This was no time for faint hearts, and both men produced expert drives, both found the green, Dier 25 feet away; Dodd only 15 feet. A putt up to inches by the German, a narrow miss by the Welshman.

One hungry soul, at least, had been fed.

Norman Dabell

Shot of the Week

With the nerves understandably jangling, only a stroke now between himself and playing companion Stephen Dodd, Tobias Dier knew he could make no mistakes after both had split the fairway on the 72nd hole. In best Christy O'Connor Jnr fashion, the German reached for his two iron and produced the unwavering 220 yards approach to 25 feet which, with two putts, ensured the birdie on the last that would secure success.

The Course

The spectacular Slieve Russell Hotel Golf & Country Club layout, designed by one of Ireland's most notable architects, Patrick Merrigan, had on its best bib and tucker when the weather decided to intervene. But Sean Quinn's 7,061 yards, par 72 brainchild, in Co. Cavan, close to the border with Ulster, took its punishment from the elements admirably and its valleys, embroidered with lakes and ponds, provided a beautifully manicured test.

Mark Pilkington

SLIEVE RUSSELL HOTEL GOLF & COUNTRY CLUB, CO. CAVAN, IRELAND, 16-19 AUGUST, 2001, PAR 72, 7061 YARDS, 6449 METRES

Pos.	Name		Rd1	Rd2	Rd3	Rd4	Total	Par	Prize Money Euro	Prize Money £
1	Tobias DIER	Ger	66	68	66	71	271	-17	58330.00	36535.49
2	Stephen DODD	Wal	67	68	68	69	272	-16	38880.00	24352.82
3	Mark PILKINGTON	Wal	68	69	69	68	274	-14	21910.00	13723.51
4	Mattias ELIASSON	Swe	67	70	72	68	277	-11	16170.00	10128.22
	James HEPWORTH	Eng	68	69	72	68	277	-11	16170.00	10128.22
6	Peter HANSON	Swe	75	65	67	71	278	-10	8796.67	5509.87
	Domingo HOSPITAL	Sp	70	69	73	66	278	-10	8796.67	5509.87
	Peter HEDBLOM	Swe	71	67	70	70	278	-10	8796.67	5509.87
	David HIGGINS	Ire	69	71	69	69	278	-10	8796.67	5509.87
	Andreas LJUNGGREN	Swe	72	71	66	69	278	-10	8796.67	5509.87
	Graeme STORM	Eng	69	73	70	66	278	-10	8796.67	5509.87
12	Robert Jan DERKSEN	Hol	68	68	69	74	279	-9	5418.00	3393.61
	Kenneth FERRIE	Eng	70	68	73	68	279	-9	5418.00	3393.61
	Jesus Maria ARRUTI	Sp	65	72	70	72	279	-9	5418.00	3393.61
	Johan SKOLD	Swe	71	69	69	70	279	-9	5418.00	3393.61
	Joakim RASK	Swe	71	72	68	68	279	-9	5418.00	3393.61
17	Christian CÉVAËR	Fr	74	69	67	70	280	-8	4620.00	2893.78
	Jamie DONALDSON	Wal	69	69	72	70	280	-8	4620.00	2893.78
19	Niels KRAAIJ	Hol	72	71	71	67	281	-7	3808.00	2385.17
	Damien MCGRANE	Ire	70	70	72	69	281	-7	3808.00	2385.17
	Grant DODD	Aus	68	70	75	68	281	-7	3808.00	2385.17
	Graham RANKIN	Scot	71	70	70	70	281	-7	3808.00	2385.17
	Renaud GUILLARD	Fr	76	68	67	70	281	-7	3808.00	2385.17
	Trevor IMMELMAN	SA	71	71	70	69	281	-7	3808.00	2385.17
	Jeremy ROBINSON	Eng	73	71	68	69	281	-7	3808.00	2385.17
	Johan RYSTRÖM	Swe	71	73	67	70	281	-7	3808.00	2385.17
	Andrew RAITT	Eng	74	68	67	72	281	-7	3808.00	2385.17
	Michael JONZON	Swe	68	70	71	72	281	-7	3808.00	2385.17
29	Klas ERIKSSON	Swe	72	69	71	70	282	-6	3010.00	1885.34
	Gary MURPHY	Ire	72	70	73	67	282	-6	3010.00	1885.34
	Kalle BRINK	Swe	72	70	71	69	282	-6	3010.00	1885.34
	Gary EVANS	Eng	72	72	68	70	282	-6	3010.00	1885.34
	Matthew BLACKEY	Eng	70	69	71	72	282	-6	3010.00	1885.34
34	Peter FOWLER	Aus	72	71	74	66	283	-5	2590.00	1622.27
	Euan LITTLE	Scot	74	70	68	71	283	-5	2590.00	1622.27
	Simon D. HURLEY	Eng	71	71	70	71	283	-5	2590.00	1622.27
	Raimo SJÖBERG	Swe	72	71	73	67	283	-5	2590.00	1622.27
38	Greig HUTCHEON	Scot	68	72	74	70	284	-4	2275.00	1424.97
	Alberto BINAGHI	It	71	70	71	72	284	-4	2275.00	1424.97
	Philip GOLDING	Eng	74	69	70	71	284	-4	2275.00	1424.97
	Mattias NILSSON	Swe	72	68	73	71	284	-4	2275.00	1424.97
	Didier DE VOOGHT	Bel	74	70	67	73	284	-4	2275.00	1424.97
43	Des SMYTH	Ire	72	72	72	69	285	-3	1890.00	1183.82
	Robin BYRD	USA	73	68	72	72	285	-3	1890.00	1183.82
	Miles TUNNICLIFF	Eng	72	71	71	71	285	-3	1890.00	1183.82
	Gianluca BARUFFALDI	It	72	68	74	71	285	-3	1890.00	1183.82
	Robert COLES	Eng	74	70	71	70	285	-3	1890.00	1183.82
	Birgir HAFTHORSSON	Ice	72	72	72	69	285	-3	1890.00	1183.82
49	Paul NILBRINK	Swe	72	71	69	74	286	-2	1470.00	920.75
	Craig HAINLINE	USA	72	70	71	73	286	-2	1470.00	920.75
	Chris GANE	Eng	75	67	69	75	286	-2	1470.00	920.75
	Dennis EDLUND	Swe	69	69	75	73	286	-2	1470.00	920.75
	Simon KHAN	Eng	73	66	76	71	286	-2	1470.00	920.75
	Alan MCLEAN	Scot	71	73	72	70	286	-2	1470.00	920.75
55	Knud STORGAARD	Den	70	72	73	72	287	-1	1065.00	667.07
	Michele REALE	It	70	70	71	76	287	-1	1065.00	667.07
	Federico BISAZZA	It	75	69	69	74	287	-1	1065.00	667.07
	Gianluca PIETROBONO	It	71	71	77	68	287	-1	1065.00	667.07
	Carlos LARRAIN	Ven	74	68	73	72	287	-1	1065.00	667.07
	Sebastien DELAGRANGE	Fr	70	74	72	71	287	-1	1065.00	667.07
	Nic HENNING	SA	71	73	68	75	287	-1	1065.00	667.07
62	Eric CARLBERG	Swe	70	74	70	74	288	0	822.50	515.18
	Patrik GOTTFRIDSON	Swe	71	73	72	72	288	0	822.50	515.18
	Marcello SANTI	It	73	69	72	74	288	0	822.50	515.18
	José ROMERO	Sp	71	71	74	72	288	0	822.50	515.18
	Francis HOWLEY	Ire	75	68	75	70	288	0	822.50	515.18
	Simon WAKEFIELD	Eng	69	71	73	75	288	0	822.50	515.18
68	Pasi PURHONEN	Fin	74	67	74	74	289	1	682.50	427.49
	Ian HUTCHINGS	SA	75	68	72	74	289	1	682.50	427.49
70	Andrew MARSHALL	Eng	67	74	74	75	290	2	554.00	347.00
	Mads VIBE-HASTRUP	Den	71	70	78	71	290	2	554.00	347.00
	Wolfgang HUGET	Ger	70	72	73	75	290	2	554.00	347.00
	Thomas NORRET	Den	73	70	76	71	290	2	554.00	347.00
74	Jorge BERENDT	Arg	72	72	72	75	291	3	511.50	320.38
	Dominique NOUAILHAC	Fr	70	71	74	76	291	3	511.50	320.38
	John MELLOR	Eng	75	67	74	75	291	3	511.50	320.38
	Kariem BARAKA	Ger	73	70	77	71	291	3	511.50	320.38
78	Mårten OLANDER	Swe	73	71	79	69	292	4	501.00	313.81
	Garry HOUSTON	Wal	74	70	76	72	292	4	501.00	313.81
	Stuart LITTLE	Eng	70	74	75	73	292	4	501.00	313.81
81	John DIGNAM	Ire	69	75	74	75	293	5	493.50	309.11
	David DIXON	Eng	71	71	77	74	293	5	493.50	309.11
83	Marco BERNARDINI	It	72	69	72	82	295	7	489.00	306.29
84	Roger WINCHESTER	Eng	73	70	78	75	296	8	486.00	304.41
85	Andrew BUTTERFIELD	Eng	75	68	80	74	297	9	483.00	302.53
86	Philip WALTON	Ire	71	71	RETD		142	-2		

Mystical Presence

FIRESTONE COUNTRY CLUB, AKRON, OHIO, USA

The sudden-death play-off is a relatively modern invention. Time was when tournaments were tied and the protagonists returned to play 18 (they still insist on this anachronistic tradition in the US Open Championship, not that Retief Goosen will ever complain) or even more improbably, 36 holes, to determine a winner.

However sport, by its very competitive nature, tends to demand a victor and a vanquished, and by the most convenient and time-conserving resolution, namely the penalty shoot-out in soccer, the tie-break in tennis and, of course, the play-off in golf.

Tiger Woods had contested play-offs before he shook hands with Jim Furyk after 72 holes had failed to separate the two American Ryder Cup players in the third consecutive World Golf Championships NEC Invitational to be held at Firestone Country Club in Akron, Ohio. Neither was Furyk a stranger to this peculiar form of white-knuckle torture at the conclusion of a long, hard week at the office.

When the dust settled on regulation play in the 2001 WGC - NEC Invitational, Furyk and Woods still had some unfinished business to conduct. They had tied on 268, 12 under par, and sudden-death was imminent.

Not a play-off in the style of the Open Championship (four holes) or the US PGA Championship (three holes). This was do or die; the title decided by a flash of genius or a split second's lack of concentration. Little did the residents of Akron realise they were about to witness a towering duel between two players who did not comprehend the meaning of surrender.

Pierre Fulke

Tiger Woods and Jim Furyk

Ian Poulter

Tin Cup had a more plausible plot line. Harry Houdini's legendary powers of escapology seemed ineffectual compared to the outrageous stunts pulled by Messrs Furyk and Woods.

This was sporting theatre of the purest kind. Not life or death. Rather, life or sudden-death. Woods, who had won the first two WGC - NEC Invitationals (the second by a margin of 11 strokes) girded his loins for the shoot-out buoyed by a record of five wins and a lone defeat in his six play-offs. Furyk boasted a more tentative record of one win and two losses.

Then began a contest within a contest which will live long in the memory. Furyk, having left his ball in the bunker at the first extra hole (the 18th), holed out from the sand for an improbable par, leaving Woods to sink a five footer to stay alive. We should have known at that moment that some kind of mystical presence was at work.

Woods countered by sinking a par putt of 20 feet from a collar of rough at the next (the 17th) with Furyk half that distance away in birdie range and even closer to the one million greenbacks on offer. He missed and the hole was halved. The World Number One sprayed his drive as the players headed back down the 18th, but conjured up a glorious pitch and run to three feet to rescue his par. Still no winner.

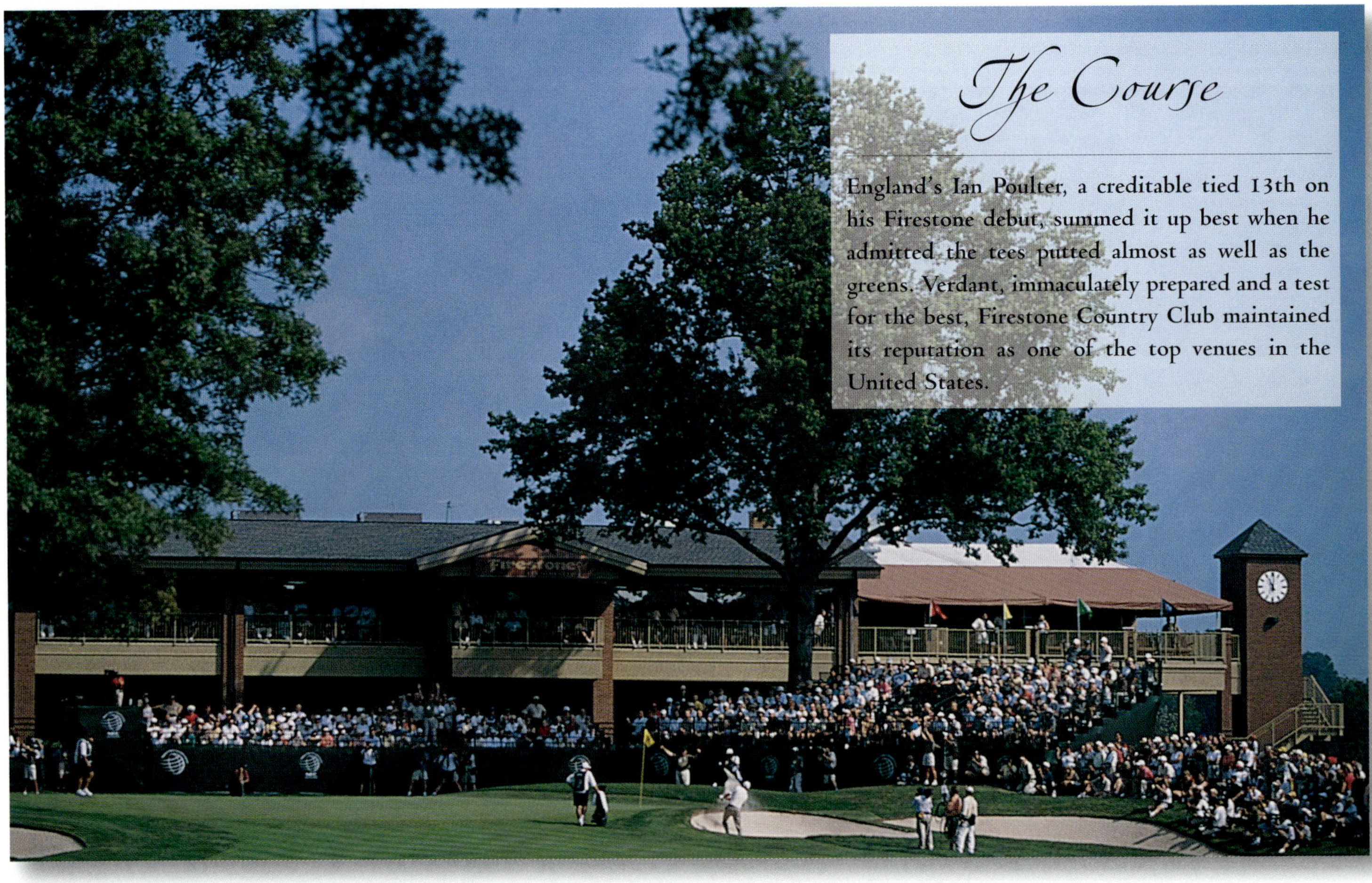

The Course

England's Ian Poulter, a creditable tied 13th on his Firestone debut, summed it up best when he admitted the tees putted almost as well as the greens. Verdant, immaculately prepared and a test for the best, Firestone Country Club maintained its reputation as one of the top venues in the United States.

Colin Montgomerie

Shot of the Week

Jim Furyk looked down and out, a forlorn figure in a cavernous bunker at the 18th, the first play-off hole. He knew the only way to prolong the tournament was to gather his thoughts and hole the next one. He did just that, and the marathon play-off was able to continue for another six glorious holes.

The fourth hole was positively routine, with two-putt pars, but the sense of drama had heightened to fever pitch. For the fourth time on the same day Woods played the 18th for play-off hole number five, and his demise seemed imminent as the ball came to rest behind a tree. Woods, though, is nothing if not resilient, taking a line-of-sight relief and threading a shot to the apron and wedging to three feet. Furyk, buried in a front trap, extricated himself with the most delicate of shots and watched the contours of the green deliver the ball two feet away from the pin. Still 'all square' and so it remained at the sixth additional hole.

The end, when it came, was mercifully swift. Furyk, under the hanging limbs of a pine tree, hacked his way to the fairway and chopped his third near the front of the green. Woods cast his mind back 12 months. Then, in the gathering gloom and amid the clicking of cigarette lighters used to illuminate the 18th green backdrop, he deposited an eight iron two feet away.

This time his ball soared into the stratosphere with radar vision and landed even closer. An appropriately epic conclusion to a memorable play-off. It meant Woods had won his last six starts in the State of Ohio, three WGC - NEC Invitationals sitting comfortably alongside his three successive Memorial Tournament wins.

It was his 29th victory and in so doing he became the first player on the US PGA Tour to win two tournaments three times in a row since Gene Sarazen in the 1920s. He also became the first player to win more than $25 million in a career.

"I was lucky to come out on top," he said graciously. "A lot of different scenarios could have happened where I would not have won. But it was a lot of fun just to be involved in this - win or lose. Neither of us was prepared to give an inch and it's fun to be tested to your absolute limit."

Europe also played a commendable role in the tournament, as Phillip Price had done 12 months previously. Darren Clarke, on a roll since finishing second in the Murphy's Irish Open winning the Smurfit European Open, and coming close in the Open Championship, shot 66-68-68-69 to finish three behind the principals. Colin Montgomerie came fourth a further two strokes behind.

But this was the day when sudden-death made a tournament come to life. Play-offs don't really get much better.

Gordon Simpson

Darren Clarke

FIRESTONE COUNTRY CLUB, AKRON, OHIO, USA, 23-26 AUGUST, 2001, PAR 70, 7139 YARDS, 6527 METRES

Pos.	Name		Rd1	Rd2	Rd3	Rd4	Total	Par	Prize Money Euro	£
1	Tiger WOODS	USA	66	67	66	69	268	-12	1091096.00	691324.04
2	Jim FURYK	USA	65	66	66	71	268	-12	545547.90	345661.96
3	Darren CLARKE	N.Ire	66	68	68	69	271	-9	409160.90	259246.45
4	Colin MONTGOMERIE	Scot	66	71	66	70	273	-7	327328.70	207397.15
5	Stuart APPLEBY	Aus	70	64	70	70	274	-6	220037.60	139416.96
	Davis LOVE III	USA	68	68	70	68	274	-6	220037.60	139416.96
	Paul AZINGER	USA	67	70	65	72	274	-6	220037.60	139416.96
8	Ernie ELS	SA	67	70	66	72	275	-5	160936.60	101970.26
	Phil MICKELSON	USA	67	66	70	72	275	-5	160936.60	101970.26
10	Retief GOOSEN	SA	72	69	64	71	276	-4	142933.50	90563.40
11	Bernhard LANGER	Ger	69	67	68	73	277	-3	129294.90	81921.91
	Hal SUTTON	USA	69	71	67	70	277	-3	129294.90	81921.91
13	Stewart CINK	USA	69	67	70	72	278	-2	109655.10	69478.04
	Ian POULTER	Eng	67	72	69	70	278	-2	109655.10	69478.04
	Vijay SINGH	Fiji	68	68	69	73	278	-2	109655.10	69478.04
	David TOMS	USA	68	70	70	70	278	-2	109655.10	69478.04
17	Padraig HARRINGTON	Ire	68	66	73	72	279	-1	90560.95	57379.88
	Scott VERPLANK	USA	69	71	70	69	279	-1	90560.95	57379.88
	Pierre FULKE	Swe	73	71	65	70	279	-1	90560.95	57379.88
20	Carlos Daniel FRANCO	Par	68	71	68	73	280	0	79649.99	50466.64
21	Scott HOCH	USA	71	70	69	71	281	1	72012.32	45627.38
	Niclas FASTH	Swe	74	67	68	72	281	1	72012.32	45627.38
23	Steve ELKINGTON	Aus	73	68	73	68	282	2	63283.55	40096.78
	Robert ALLENBY	Aus	68	67	75	72	282	2	63283.55	40096.78
25	Mike WEIR	Can	69	70	71	73	283	3	57828.07	36640.16
26	Paul MCGINLEY	Ire	68	73	71	72	284	4	55645.88	35257.52
27	David DUVAL	USA	69	69	72	75	285	5	53463.69	33874.87
28	Phillip PRICE	Wal	70	71	74	71	286	6	51281.50	32492.22
29	Loren ROBERTS	USA	72	70	67	79	288	8	48008.21	30418.25
	Nick PRICE	Zim	71	70	71	76	288	8	48008.21	30418.25
31	Shigeki MARUYAMA	Jpn	68	75	73	73	289	9	41461.64	26270.31
	Thomas BJÖRN	Den	66	79	73	71	289	9	41461.64	26270.31
	Michael CAMPBELL	NZ	71	71	75	72	289	9	41461.64	26270.31
	Notah BEGAY III	USA	77	71	72	69	289	9	41461.64	26270.31
35	Greg NORMAN	Aus	65	71	74	80	290	10	36006.16	22813.69
36	Miguel Angel JIMÉNEZ	Sp	70	72	74	76	292	12	33823.97	21431.04
	Mark CALCAVECCHIA	USA	72	69	72	79	292	12	33823.97	21431.04
38	Kirk TRIPLETT	USA	70	70	69	DISQ	209	-1	28368.49	17974.42
	Lee WESTWOOD	Eng	70	78	WD		148	8	28368.49	17974.42

Bigger & Better

THE GLENEAGLES HOTEL, AUCHTERARDER, SCOTLAND

Sometimes, you just know. Sometimes, you can tell right away. Sometimes, it's just plain obvious.

So it is with Paul Casey. When the two-time English Amateur champion, Walker Cup player and All-American at Arizona State turned professional in November 2000, he was hailed - understandably with such a pedigree - as the latest "can't miss" prospect in world golf.

Alex Cejka

And, for once, the pundits got it dead right. From his European Tour debut at the Benson and Hedges International Open, Casey was clearly a young man on the up. After tying for 12th place that week at The De Vere Belfry, the 24 year old racked up three more top 20 finishes - highlighted by a runners-up spot in The Great North Open at De Vere Slaley Hall - in his next nine events. A coveted European Tour card was his after only five appearances.

Jamie Donaldson

Shot of the Week

Uphill and into the prevailing wind, not many players could reach the 568 yards final hole in two shots on the third day of the Gleneagles Scottish PGA Championship. But Paul Casey could. And did. At a time when most players were coming up 40 yards short of the putting surface, Casey pitched his three wood approach in the middle of the green. Awesome hitting.

Which brought Casey to The PGA Centenary Course at The Gleneagles Hotel for the 1.6 million euro (£1 million) Gleneagles Scottish PGA Championship and what, in only his 11th European Tour start, would turn out to be his maiden victory as a professional.

As you'd expect, too, he won it in the style of the young Tony Jacklin he puts so many in mind of. Pushed all the way to the final green by a brave performance from Germany's Alex Cejka, Casey was forced to birdie two of the last three holes to secure a single shot win. Indeed, the climax could not have been closer.

Playing alongside his closest challenger in the final group, Casey held a slender one shot advantage with three holes to play. A birdie at the par five 16th from the long-hitting Englishman - he covered the 543 yards with two mighty blows - doubled the difference between the two, but Cejka was far from finished. Casey's advantage was back to one shot when the three time Tour winner made a 25 foot putt of his own for a two at the short 17th.

With all to play for up the 18th, both men - not surprisingly - came up short with their second shots to the uphill, into the wind 568

Gary Murphy

Nick Dougherty

yards par five. Then, after watching Cejka pitch to within two yards of the flag, Casey answered the call with a shot of his own that was almost as good, his ball finishing eight feet from the cup. Crucially, though, he was putting uphill.

Moments later, it was all over. Casey, knowing he had his putt for certain victory, rolled it in, dead centre. That Cejka followed him in was immaterial to the final result. For Casey, it all added up to a final round of 69, three under par, and a 72 hole aggregate of 274. Cejka, of course, was on 275, with another Englishman, David Howell, third on 277.

Significantly, within minutes of collecting the striking crystal trophy and a cheque for 263,034 euro (£166,660), Casey was already looking ahead to bigger and better things.

"The goal is to get into the top 15 in the Volvo Order of Merit by the end of the year so I still have a lot to play for," he said. "I still have a long way to go and I hope to be here for a long time. But I'm looking at the big plan and that is to play in the best events in the world.

"I'm already looking forward to next year and my focus is solely on Europe. I'd like to play a couple of things in America, but the emphasis is still in Europe."

Casey's reluctance to commit to the United States is perhaps understandable. Although managed by Arizona-based Gaylord Sports - and coached by CBS commentator Peter Kostis - he initially found it hard to secure sponsors invites to PGA Tour events when he turned professional. In the two starts he did get at the AT&T National Pro-Am and the Honda Classic he missed the cut.

So now Casey is adding his growing presence to European Tour events. In so doing, he is just one of an ever increasing band of fresh-faced Englishmen - Warren Bennett and Justin Rose are others who spring to mind - looking to make their mark.

Indeed, another such young man made his professional debut at The Gleneagles Hotel. Nineteen year old Nick Dougherty, who two weeks earlier had played such a crucial part in Great Britain & Ireland's retention - for the first time ever - of the Walker Cup on American soil, shot 285 and finished tied for 37th.

But it was Casey's week. The first win of his career. But, not, too many will wager, the last.

John Huggan

Christian Cévaër

The Course

Open for play only eight years, The PGA Centenary Course has already positioned itself as the modern alternative to the fabled Kings and Queens courses at The Gleneagles Hotel. At 7,060 yards it is also a test for even the best, especially when the wind blows across the undulating landscape.

Søren Kjeldsen

THE GLENEAGLES HOTEL, AUCHTERARDER, SCOTLAND, 23-26 AUGUST, 2001, PAR 72, 7060 YARDS, 6456 METRES

Pos.	Name		Rd1	Rd2	Rd3	Rd4	Total	Par	Prize Money Euro	£
1	Paul CASEY	Eng	69	69	67	69	274	-14	263034.50	166660.00
2	Alex CEJKA	Ger	71	67	66	71	275	-13	175361.60	111110.00
3	David HOWELL	Eng	70	71	66	70	277	-11	98799.70	62600.00
4	Gary EVANS	Eng	66	67	77	68	278	-10	67023.87	42466.67
	Christian CÉVAËR	Fr	72	71	69	66	278	-10	67023.87	42466.67
	Carl PETTERSSON	Swe	75	66	70	67	278	-10	67023.87	42466.67
7	Peter HANSON	Swe	74	64	69	72	279	-9	38430.88	24350.00
	Jonathan LOMAS	Eng	66	74	70	69	279	-9	38430.88	24350.00
	Des TERBLANCHE	SA	73	70	70	66	279	-9	38430.88	24350.00
	Stephen GALLACHER	Scot	67	71	69	72	279	-9	38430.88	24350.00
11	Mark MOULAND	Wal	65	70	73	72	280	-8	24643.56	15614.29
	Andrew OLDCORN	Scot	70	67	73	70	280	-8	24643.56	15614.29
	Des SMYTH	Ire	71	71	68	70	280	-8	24643.56	15614.29
	Justin ROSE	Eng	67	71	68	74	280	-8	24643.56	15614.29
	Peter O'MALLEY	Aus	68	72	70	70	280	-8	24643.56	15614.29
	Stephen SCAHILL	NZ	69	74	69	68	280	-8	24643.56	15614.29
	David HIGGINS	Ire	67	71	70	72	280	-8	24643.56	15614.29
18	Roger CHAPMAN	Eng	72	70	70	69	281	-7	19294.35	12225.00
	Gary MURPHY	Ire	68	69	70	74	281	-7	19294.35	12225.00
	Roger WESSELS	SA	69	72	68	72	281	-7	19294.35	12225.00
	Paul LAWRIE	Scot	75	69	69	68	281	-7	19294.35	12225.00
22	Malcolm MACKENZIE	Eng	75	66	70	71	282	-6	16414.01	10400.00
	Mark ROE	Eng	73	71	69	69	282	-6	16414.01	10400.00
	Greg TURNER	NZ	69	67	75	71	282	-6	16414.01	10400.00
	Paul BROADHURST	Eng	68	69	73	72	282	-6	16414.01	10400.00
	Johan RYSTRÖM	Swe	72	69	67	74	282	-6	16414.01	10400.00
	David LYNN	Eng	69	70	72	71	282	-6	16414.01	10400.00
	Simon DYSON	Eng	69	70	69	74	282	-6	16414.01	10400.00
29	Robert KARLSSON	Swe	70	69	70	74	283	-5	13336.38	8450.00
	Stephen DODD	Wal	73	70	70	70	283	-5	13336.38	8450.00
	Ian GARBUTT	Eng	70	72	70	71	283	-5	13336.38	8450.00
	Nicolas VANHOOTEGEM	Bel	73	65	69	76	283	-5	13336.38	8450.00
	Jarmo SANDELIN	Swe	72	66	72	73	283	-5	13336.38	8450.00
	Jamie DONALDSON	Wal	69	71	71	72	283	-5	13336.38	8450.00
35	Peter FOWLER	Aus	66	68	78	72	284	-4	11679.20	7400.00
	Carlos RODILES	Sp	69	67	75	73	284	-4	11679.20	7400.00
37	Mark JAMES	Eng	72	71	70	72	285	-3	9785.27	6200.00
	Sam TORRANCE	Scot	68	74	70	73	285	-3	9785.27	6200.00
	Brian DAVIS	Eng	72	72	69	72	285	-3	9785.27	6200.00
	Anthony WALL	Eng	69	74	70	72	285	-3	9785.27	6200.00
	Jamie SPENCE	Eng	71	68	72	74	285	-3	9785.27	6200.00
	Russell CLAYDON	Eng	70	72	74	69	285	-3	9785.27	6200.00
	Rolf MUNTZ	Hol	69	72	74	70	285	-3	9785.27	6200.00
	Andrew RAITT	Eng	73	67	72	73	285	-3	9785.27	6200.00
	Dean ROBERTSON	Scot	72	69	73	71	285	-3	9785.27	6200.00
	Nick DOUGHERTY	Eng	70	74	70	71	285	-3	9785.27	6200.00
47	Ross DRUMMOND	Scot	71	72	71	72	286	-2	7575.70	4800.00
	Søren KJELDSEN	Den	71	68	71	76	286	-2	7575.70	4800.00
	Trevor IMMELMAN	SA	71	73	70	72	286	-2	7575.70	4800.00
	Colin GILLIES	Scot	74	66	70	76	286	-2	7575.70	4800.00
51	Wayne RILEY	Aus	69	72	72	74	287	-1	6155.25	3900.00
	Warren BENNETT	Eng	67	75	72	73	287	-1	6155.25	3900.00
	David PARK	Wal	73	70	70	74	287	-1	6155.25	3900.00
	Mark PILKINGTON	Wal	72	69	74	72	287	-1	6155.25	3900.00
	Raymond RUSSELL	Scot	71	70	68	78	287	-1	6155.25	3900.00
56	Eamonn DARCY	Ire	73	69	73	73	288	0	4766.38	3020.00
	Anders FORSBRAND	Swe	68	70	80	70	288	0	4766.38	3020.00
	Shaun P WEBSTER	Eng	70	72	74	72	288	0	4766.38	3020.00
	Olivier EDMOND	Fr	68	74	73	73	288	0	4766.38	3020.00
	Robert ARNOTT	Scot	74	66	71	77	288	0	4766.38	3020.00
61	Brian MARCHBANK	Scot	75	69	71	74	289	1	4103.50	2600.00
	Desvonde BOTES	SA	71	70	74	74	289	1	4103.50	2600.00
	Daren LEE	Eng	72	71	74	72	289	1	4103.50	2600.00
64	Santiago LUNA	Sp	71	72	74	73	290	2	3551.11	2250.00
	Garry HOUSTON	Wal	74	70	71	75	290	2	3551.11	2250.00
	John SENDEN	Aus	72	70	70	78	290	2	3551.11	2250.00
	Olle KARLSSON	Swe	72	72	73	73	290	2	3551.11	2250.00
68	David GILFORD	Eng	74	70	74	73	291	3	3014.50	1910.00
	Graham RANKIN	Scot	74	70	73	74	291	3	3014.50	1910.00
	Mathias GRÖNBERG	Swe	73	71	75	72	291	3	3014.50	1910.00
71	Sandy LYLE	Scot	72	71	75	74	292	4	2365.50	1498.79
	Jean HUGO	SA	73	71	72	76	292	4	2365.50	1498.79
73	Neil CHEETHAM	Eng	74	70	72	77	293	5	2361.00	1495.94
74	Gregory HAVRET	Fr	69	73	75	77	294	6	2356.50	1493.09
	Paul EALES	Eng	70	74	78	72	294	6	2356.50	1493.09
76	Roger WINCHESTER	Eng	73	70	79	73	295	7	2352.00	1490.24
77	Craig HAINLINE	USA	72	72	75	77	296	8	2347.50	1487.39
	Søren HANSEN	Den	74	69	77	76	296	8	2347.50	1487.39
	Van PHILLIPS	Eng	75	69	77	75	296	8	2347.50	1487.39

Victor Chandler
COMPASS GROUP English Open
7th-10th JUNE 2001
FOREST OF ARDEN
THE WALES OPEN
FRIDAY 14th APRIL 2000
DAILY DRAWSHEET
VOLVO PGA CHAMPIONSHIP
25th - 28th MAY 2001
WENTWORTH CLUB VIRGINIA WATER SURREY

The European Tour Yearbook 2001
The European Tour Yearbook 2002

BMW INTERNATIONAL OPEN

Driving Force

GOLFCLUB MÜNCHEN NORD-EICHENRIED, MUNICH, GERMANY

Munich, the Bavarian capital, had much to contemplate during the first weekend of September. The sheer scale of the 5-1 defeat inflicted upon Germany's national football team by England in the city's Olympic Stadium was one sporting shock.

That John Daly should emerge from the Golfclub München Nord - Eichenried, in the leafy suburb of Eichenried, as the winner of the BMW International Open was almost as big a surprise.

For more than half a decade the American's turbulent private life had attracted far more headlines than his golfing prowess. However, having re-married just weeks before his trip to Germany and foresworn the demon alcohol, Daly produced four stunning rounds of golf.

Had it not been for heavy overnight rain on two successive days which forced Tour Officials to permit lifting and cleaning early in the tournament, his final total of 261, 27 under par, would have gone into the record books for equalling the Tour's lowest return against par over 72 holes.

Furthermore his performance in the fourth round when he wore down and finally overhauled the overnight leader Padraig Harrington to take the 300,000 euro (£189,352) first prize was a testament to Daly's new found determination to re-establish himself as a golfing force.

The final pairing were left in a compelling head to head battle when Thomas Björn's challenge faltered with a double bogey at the first hole. And the fact that each of the two combatants had their own compelling reasons for seeking victory downgraded a subplot further back in the field where the chase was on for 11th hour Ryder Cup points.

Christopher Hanell

The Course

Golfclub München Nord-Eichenried has matured superbly over the years. Only precisely struck approaches to the deceptive and much praised greens set up birdie opportunities. Water hazards add to the challenge of this parkland test.

Markus Brier

Though the holder of two Major titles, Daly was seeking his first tournament win anywhere in the world to end a barren run stretching back to his 1995 Open Championship triumph at St Andrews. Harrington, meanwhile, was anxious to convert a growing reputation for high class consistency into titles.

After shooting 63 in the second round and a 62 in the third, Harrington, already the runner up in five previous tournaments in 2001 and looking to go one better, held onto his one stroke overnight advantage through the first nine.

But Daly drew level with a birdie at the 13th and eventually the tournament was settled in classic match play style at the 568 yards par five 18th. With little run on the fairway, its length played into the American's powerful hands, if he found the fairway which he did.

Harrington, by contrast, was pushing his three wood to its very limits with a 284 yards approach, and, losing control at impact, he found the water on the right. Though Harrington got up and down with his second ball for a par, Daly, having seen his rival's shot, bailed out to the left with his second, and chipped beautifully to six inches. He was ahead for the first time all day.

Relieved to end his six year victory drought Daly said later: "There was a time two years back when I asked myself whether I wanted to go on or find something else to do. But when golf has been your whole life since the age of four there's nothing else you can do.

Eduardo Romero

John Daly

Shot of the Week

José Maria Olazábal's second round 235 yards one iron into the hole for the first albatross of his professional career at the par five 11th.

"There's no one I need to thank for this victory, no coach or mental expert. Over the past two years I have surrounded myself with wonderful friends and a wonderful wife and I can pat myself on the back and say I have won this one on my own."

For Harrington there was only one consolation. Having celebrated his 30th birthday during the tournament he flew home to Dublin and a surprise present – a radio controlled car - from his wife Caroline.

A vehicle of a much grander marque, however, was heading for the home in Chazay D'Azerques, France, of Raphaël Jacquelin. His hole in one during the second round at the 17th was rewarded with an £82,000 BMW Z8 sports car which made him the envy of the many thousands of spectators who toured the sponsor's spectacular display stands during the week.

But where there was happiness there was also heartbreak. The tournament was the last available opportunity for several players to win an automatic place in the 2001 European Ryder Cup Team.

The hopes of Miguel Angel Jiménez and Ian Poulter evaporated when they missed the cut and though Phillip Price also took no further part after two rounds, he held onto the tenth qualifying position.

On the Sunday night after the presentation ceremony, Sam Torrance the Ryder Cup Captain, strolled into the media centre to announce that Spain's Sergio Garcia and Sweden's Jesper Parnevik would be his two wild card picks for The De Vere Belfry.

There had been speculation that he might prefer José Maria Olazábal to Parnevik or even the young Englishman Paul Casey, playing in his first season on The European Tour. Torrance, however, had clearly decided that two shocks in one weekend were quite sufficient for the city of Munich.

Graham Otway

Jorge Berendt

GOLFCLUB MÜNCHEN NORD-EICHENRIED, MUNICH, GERMANY, 30 AUGUST - 2 SEPTEMBER, 2001, PAR 72, 6914 YARDS, 6321 METRES

Pos.	Name		Rd1	Rd2	Rd3	Rd4	Total	Par	Prize Money Euro	£
1	John DALY	USA	63	64	68	66	261	-27	300000.00	189352.10
2	Padraig HARRINGTON	Ire	69	63	62	68	262	-26	200000.00	126234.73
3	Thomas LEVET	Fr	70	66	64	68	268	-20	112680.00	71120.65
4	Raymond RUSSELL	Scot	68	66	66	69	269	-19	76440.00	48246.92
	Dean ROBERTSON	Scot	64	69	69	67	269	-19	76440.00	48246.92
	Christopher HANELL	Swe	71	65	66	67	269	-19	76440.00	48246.92
7	Sergio GARCIA	Sp	67	67	69	67	270	-18	46440.00	29311.71
	Justin ROSE	Eng	67	69	68	66	270	-18	46440.00	29311.71
	Paul CASEY	Eng	69	67	69	65	270	-18	46440.00	29311.71
10	Søren KJELDSEN	Den	65	70	71	65	271	-17	33360.00	21055.95
	Paul MCGINLEY	Ire	70	66	68	67	271	-17	33360.00	21055.95
	David CARTER	Eng	69	66	68	68	271	-17	33360.00	21055.95
13	José Maria OLAZáBAL	Sp	70	62	70	70	272	-16	27660.00	17458.26
	Raphaël JACQUELIN	Fr	68	67	70	67	272	-16	27660.00	17458.26
	Colin MONTGOMERIE	Scot	69	69	68	66	272	-16	27660.00	17458.26
16	Bernhard LANGER	Ger	67	69	69	68	273	-15	23364.00	14746.74
	Warren BENNETT	Eng	69	68	69	67	273	-15	23364.00	14746.74
	Peter O'MALLEY	Aus	71	67	66	69	273	-15	23364.00	14746.74
	Thomas BJÖRN	Den	65	67	65	76	273	-15	23364.00	14746.74
	Carl PETTERSSON	Swe	66	69	70	68	273	-15	23364.00	14746.74
21	Alex CEJKA	Ger	69	66	69	70	274	-14	20610.00	13008.49
	Ricardo GONZALEZ	Arg	67	68	69	70	274	-14	20610.00	13008.49
23	Sandy LYLE	Scot	69	71	71	65	276	-12	18180.00	11474.74
	Stephen DODD	Wal	69	70	69	68	276	-12	18180.00	11474.74
	Fredrik JACOBSON	Swe	68	66	68	74	276	-12	18180.00	11474.74
	Fredrik ANDERSSON	Swe	69	68	69	70	276	-12	18180.00	11474.74
	Retief GOOSEN	SA	68	69	68	71	276	-12	18180.00	11474.74
	Mikael LUNDBERG	Swe	72	68	70	66	276	-12	18180.00	11474.74
	Adam SCOTT	Aus	67	64	77	68	276	-12	18180.00	11474.74
30	Greg TURNER	NZ	69	70	71	67	277	-11	14477.14	9137.59
	Anders HANSEN	Den	69	69	70	69	277	-11	14477.14	9137.59
	Steen TINNING	Den	74	66	69	68	277	-11	14477.14	9137.59
	Johan RYSTRÖM	Swe	67	70	70	70	277	-11	14477.14	9137.59
	Russell CLAYDON	Eng	70	70	72	65	277	-11	14477.14	9137.59
	Paul LAWRIE	Scot	70	70	69	68	277	-11	14477.14	9137.59
	Stephen GALLACHER	Scot	67	70	68	72	277	-11	14477.14	9137.59
37	Mark MOULAND	Wal	68	68	70	72	278	-10	11340.00	7157.51
	Ian WOOSNAM	Wal	69	67	71	71	278	-10	11340.00	7157.51
	Barry LANE	Eng	69	69	70	70	278	-10	11340.00	7157.51
	John SENDEN	Aus	68	67	70	73	278	-10	11340.00	7157.51
	Gregory HAVRET	Fr	68	70	70	70	278	-10	11340.00	7157.51
	Jorge BERENDT	Arg	69	67	71	71	278	-10	11340.00	7157.51
	Robert COLES	Eng	72	66	68	72	278	-10	11340.00	7157.51
	Markus BRIER	Aut	72	68	70	68	278	-10	11340.00	7157.51
	Brett RUMFORD	Aus	68	68	69	73	278	-10	11340.00	7157.51
46	Desvonde BOTES	SA	70	70	69	70	279	-9	8460.00	5339.73
	Carl SUNESON	Sp	72	68	70	69	279	-9	8460.00	5339.73
	Roger WESSELS	SA	66	70	72	71	279	-9	8460.00	5339.73
	Gary ORR	Scot	68	69	71	71	279	-9	8460.00	5339.73
	Mikko ILONEN	Fin	71	68	68	72	279	-9	8460.00	5339.73
	Alastair FORSYTH	Scot	68	66	74	71	279	-9	8460.00	5339.73
	Nick DOUGHERTY	Eng	71	68	68	72	279	-9	8460.00	5339.73
53	Maarten LAFEBER	Hol	72	68	71	69	280	-8	6017.14	3797.86
	Richard GREEN	Aus	63	69	75	73	280	-8	6017.14	3797.86
	Joakim HAEGGMAN	Swe	67	71	71	71	280	-8	6017.14	3797.86
	Robert KARLSSON	Swe	70	68	71	71	280	-8	6017.14	3797.86
	Ignacio GARRIDO	Sp	68	72	71	69	280	-8	6017.14	3797.86
	Stephen SCAHILL	NZ	71	66	71	72	280	-8	6017.14	3797.86
	Graeme STORM	Eng	71	69	68	72	280	-8	6017.14	3797.86
60	Andrew OLDCORN	Scot	67	69	70	75	281	-7	4500.00	2840.28
	Eduardo ROMERO	Arg	71	67	71	72	281	-7	4500.00	2840.28
	Peter MITCHELL	Eng	68	70	72	71	281	-7	4500.00	2840.28
	Greg OWEN	Eng	69	67	74	71	281	-7	4500.00	2840.28
	David PARK	Wal	68	71	74	68	281	-7	4500.00	2840.28
	Niclas FASTH	Swe	67	71	71	72	281	-7	4500.00	2840.28
	John BICKERTON	Eng	67	68	72	74	281	-7	4500.00	2840.28
67	Tony JOHNSTONE	Zim	66	71	72	73	282	-6	3246.17	2048.90
	Marc FARRY	Fr	67	67	75	73	282	-6	3246.17	2048.90
	Brian DAVIS	Eng	68	68	74	72	282	-6	3246.17	2048.90
	Trevor IMMELMAN	SA	70	69	69	74	282	-6	3246.17	2048.90
	Pierre FULKE	Swe	69	71	72	70	282	-6	3246.17	2048.90
	David LYNN	Eng	70	69	70	73	282	-6	3246.17	2048.90
73	Jonathan LOMAS	Eng	66	71	74	72	283	-5	2694.00	1700.38
74	Søren HANSEN	Den	68	70	78	68	284	-4	2691.00	1698.49
75	Mark JAMES	Eng	72	67	74	72	285	-3	2688.00	1696.59
76	Jarmo SANDELIN	Swe	69	71	70	76	286	-2	2685.00	1694.70
77	Andrew COLTART	Scot	69	71	74	73	287	-1	2682.00	1692.81
78	Sven STRÜVER	Ger	71	69	76	73	289	1	2679.00	1690.91
79	Patrik SJÖLAND	Swe	74	66	78	76	294	6	2676.00	1689.02

Champagne Shower

CRANS-SUR-SIERRE, CRANS MONTANA, SWITZERLAND

For the second year in succession there was the incongruous sight of a uni-cyclist wearing an Argentine football shirt wheeling around to an Alpine background in celebration of a golfing triumph. This time the whimsical display was for Ricardo Gonzalez, a former caddie, who won the Omega European Masters at spectacular Crans-sur-Sierre with golf to match the surroundings, winning by three shots, having led from start to finish.

Søren Hansen

His final putt on the 18th produced more celebrations of Formula One nature when his compatriots Jorge Berendt and last year's winner Eduardo Romero sprayed him with champagne before he had left the green to sign and present his card.

From day one and his opening 65 it seemed that victory in the most picturesque setting on The European Tour would be his. His nerve held, he smiled readily and it seemed nothing could trouble him as he added rounds of 67-68-68 for a 16 under par total of 268.

There were challenges along the way from a variety of players but as the champagne shower hit Gonzalez, the Dane, Søren Hansen, was in second place three shots behind with Gary Orr and former Masters champion, Craig Stadler, a further two shots back.

It was the first win by Gonzalez on The European Tour after graduating from the European Challenge Tour where his last victory came in the Tusker Kenya Open in 1998.

At Crans-sur-Sierre, however, Gonzalez was able to say: "Nothing compares to this."

Gary Orr

Henrik Nystrom

His opening 65 was the foundation of a four round score that saw him collect 250,000 euro(£156,616) and climb the Volvo Order of Merit table. He boomed his drives beyond the 300 yards mark, taking advantage of the thin-air, high-altitude assistance but also showed an impressively deft touch around the greens with his putting and chipping. Such control and class stayed with him through to the end of Sunday afternoon.

That first round with five birdies and an eagle three at the 14th put him one ahead of a pack of five players - Thomas Björn, Gordon Brand Jnr., Thomas Gögele, Henrik Nystrom and Dean Robertson.

Could he stay there? Absolutely. The 31 year old from the North of Argentina refused to be fazed and by the end of the second day he had retained his lead though his closest challengers, a shot behind, were now former Ryder Cup player David Gilford and Scotland's Orr.

Gonzalez had one hiccup but recovered admirably. He was well off target with his shot to the 11th, missing the green by a considerable distance, but he holed a magnificent putt after chipping to 20 feet. His steady progress was briefly overshadowed on Saturday morning when Björn withdrew because of a shoulder injury. The Dane went back to London for a scan and treatment and Gonzalez picked up where he had left off.

David Gilford

The Course

Ten miles above the small Swiss town of Sierre but well below the snowline of the Alps, this is an undulating parkland course with a par of 71. The ball flies further than normal at altitude but accuracy remains a key as there are some tight, fir-tree lined fairways and cannily placed traps. It is the most picturesque venue on The European Tour.

Patience was a virtue added to long driving and neat chipping as he increased his lead going into the final round to be two shots ahead of Stephen Scahill of New Zealand with Greg Owen and Hansen, three shots off the lead, also challenging. A run of four birdies in five holes from the 12th had put Owen in contention.

Sunday, however, was a glorious walk for Gonzalez beneath those towering peaks that had received a fresh covering of snow overnight, though the sun blessed those who turned out to watch, even if warm clothing was required.

Three birdies on his front nine kept his eye on the prize while his rivals looked at him and the leaderboard and probably concluded that his form was unstoppable. Gonzalez is built like a chunky, middleweight boxer. He has an indomitable spirit and a sense of purpose which indicated, clearly, that nothing was going to keep him from his winner's cheque.

After he had collected, still damp from the champagne shower, he was barely able to contain his national pride as he said: "This is a major victory, especially for Argentina. To be on The European Tour and have the first win means a great deal to me. It's a great honour to follow in Eduardo's footsteps. Everyone looks to him, to Vincente Fernandez and Roberto de Vicenzo and every player wants to be like them."

Back in his home town of Formosa, they were probably celebrating as joyfully as the small party in Switzerland. The ex-caddie, who paid six visits to the Qualifying School before graduating from the Challenge Tour, made sure that the hills were alive with the sound of Argentines having Sunday night fun.

James Mossop

Shot of the Week

Ricardo Gonzalez's drive of 330 yards on the difficult par five 15th which set up an eagle that put him two shots clear of the field. At the time four players had been tied on 11 under par. His tee shot left him 180 yards from the green, enabling him to float in a seven iron to 15 feet which he holed. He never looked back.

David Carter

CRANS-SUR-SIERRE, CRANS MONTANA, SWITZERLAND, 6-9 SEPTEMBER, 2001, PAR 71, 6857 YARDS, 6239 METRES

Pos.	Name		Rd1	Rd2	Rd3	Rd4	Total	Par	Prize Money Euro	£
1	Ricardo GONZALEZ	Arg	65	67	68	68	268	-16	250000.00	156616.09
2	Søren HANSEN	Den	70	65	68	68	271	-13	166660.00	104406.55
3	Craig STADLER	USA	69	69	67	68	273	-11	84450.00	52904.92
	Gary ORR	Scot	67	66	71	69	273	-11	84450.00	52904.92
5	Fredrik JACOBSON	Swe	68	71	65	70	274	-10	63600.00	39843.13
6	Stephen SCAHILL	NZ	67	67	68	74	276	-8	48750.00	30540.14
	Greg OWEN	Eng	68	67	68	73	276	-8	48750.00	30540.14
8	Gordon BRAND JNR.	Scot	66	71	71	69	277	-7	35550.00	22270.81
	Peter FOWLER	Aus	69	71	69	68	277	-7	35550.00	22270.81
10	Eduardo ROMERO	Arg	72	67	71	68	278	-6	27800.00	17415.71
	David GILFORD	Eng	67	66	72	73	278	-6	27800.00	17415.71
	Raphaël JACQUELIN	Fr	68	70	72	68	278	-6	27800.00	17415.71
13	Francis VALERA	Sp	69	72	67	71	279	-5	23050.00	14440.00
	Markus BRIER	Aut	69	67	70	73	279	-5	23050.00	14440.00
	Jamie DONALDSON	Wal	71	72	66	70	279	-5	23050.00	14440.00
16	Greg TURNER	NZ	67	71	71	71	280	-4	18814.29	11786.48
	Stephen LEANEY	Aus	67	71	72	70	280	-4	18814.29	11786.48
	Jeremy ROBINSON	Eng	70	72	70	68	280	-4	18814.29	11786.48
	Peter O'MALLEY	Aus	68	71	67	74	280	-4	18814.29	11786.48
	Ernie ELS	SA	71	72	68	69	280	-4	18814.29	11786.48
	Lee WESTWOOD	Eng	70	69	69	72	280	-4	18814.29	11786.48
	Steven O'HARA	Scot	74	64	71	71	280	-4	18814.29	11786.48
23	Mark MOULAND	Wal	69	72	72	68	281	-3	14250.00	8927.12
	Barry LANE	Eng	72	69	69	71	281	-3	14250.00	8927.12
	Brian DAVIS	Eng	68	71	71	71	281	-3	14250.00	8927.12
	José Manuel CARRILES	Sp	73	68	70	70	281	-3	14250.00	8927.12
	Paul EALES	Eng	68	69	70	74	281	-3	14250.00	8927.12
	Joakim HAEGGMAN	Swe	71	68	73	69	281	-3	14250.00	8927.12
	David PARK	Wal	69	71	70	71	281	-3	14250.00	8927.12
	Fredrik ANDERSSON	Swe	68	70	70	73	281	-3	14250.00	8927.12
	Dean ROBERTSON	Scot	66	70	74	71	281	-3	14250.00	8927.12
	David CARTER	Eng	73	67	69	72	281	-3	14250.00	8927.12
	Adam SCOTT	Aus	69	69	72	71	281	-3	14250.00	8927.12
34	Justin ROSE	Eng	69	69	72	72	282	-2	11250.00	7047.72
	Mathias GRÖNBERG	Swe	70	72	68	72	282	-2	11250.00	7047.72
	Christopher HANELL	Swe	69	71	70	72	282	-2	11250.00	7047.72
37	Sam TORRANCE	Scot	72	71	71	69	283	-1	9450.00	5920.09
	Gary MURPHY	Ire	69	69	72	73	283	-1	9450.00	5920.09
	Elliot BOULT	NZ	70	72	71	70	283	-1	9450.00	5920.09
	Thomas GÖGELE	Ger	66	75	71	71	283	-1	9450.00	5920.09
	Johan RYSTRÖM	Swe	69	74	69	71	283	-1	9450.00	5920.09
	Alex CEJKA	Ger	70	72	69	72	283	-1	9450.00	5920.09
	David LYNN	Eng	68	70	73	72	283	-1	9450.00	5920.09
	David HIGGINS	Ire	71	70	71	71	283	-1	9450.00	5920.09
	Paul CASEY	Eng	76	67	65	75	283	-1	9450.00	5920.09
46	Nick FALDO	Eng	70	72	70	72	284	0	7050.00	4416.57
	Marc FARRY	Fr	70	70	71	73	284	0	7050.00	4416.57
	Trevor IMMELMAN	SA	70	69	72	73	284	0	7050.00	4416.57
	Miguel Angel JIMÉNEZ	Sp	73	68	73	70	284	0	7050.00	4416.57
	Olle KARLSSON	Swe	71	69	70	74	284	0	7050.00	4416.57
	Emanuele CANONICA	It	70	72	70	72	284	0	7050.00	4416.57
	Van PHILLIPS	Eng	69	69	74	72	284	0	7050.00	4416.57
53	Mark JAMES	Eng	71	70	71	73	285	1	5250.00	3288.94
	Santiago LUNA	Sp	71	70	69	75	285	1	5250.00	3288.94
	Warren BENNETT	Eng	68	69	74	74	285	1	5250.00	3288.94
	Shaun P WEBSTER	Eng	69	71	69	76	285	1	5250.00	3288.94
	Stephen GALLACHER	Scot	71	69	74	71	285	1	5250.00	3288.94
58	Sandy LYLE	Scot	72	70	71	73	286	2	4125.00	2584.17
	Jean HUGO	SA	72	68	74	72	286	2	4125.00	2584.17
	Russell CLAYDON	Eng	72	71	72	71	286	2	4125.00	2584.17
	Christian CÉVAËR	Fr	71	71	72	72	286	2	4125.00	2584.17
	Henrik NYSTROM	Swe	66	73	75	72	286	2	4125.00	2584.17
	Graeme STORM	Eng	71	72	68	75	286	2	4125.00	2584.17
64	Roger CHAPMAN	Eng	72	70	71	74	287	3	3300.00	2067.33
	David HOWELL	Eng	71	72	73	71	287	3	3300.00	2067.33
	Anders HANSEN	Den	73	69	70	75	287	3	3300.00	2067.33
	Roger WINCHESTER	Eng	71	71	76	69	287	3	3300.00	2067.33
	Ian GARBUTT	Eng	72	69	73	73	287	3	3300.00	2067.33
69	Carlos RODILES	Sp	71	72	70	75	288	4	2850.00	1785.42
70	Wayne RILEY	Aus	74	67	73	75	289	5	2495.00	1563.03
	Gary EMERSON	Eng	71	72	71	75	289	5	2495.00	1563.03
72	Ignacio GARRIDO	Sp	67	72	75	76	290	6	2247.00	1407.67
73	Maarten LAFEBER	Hol	72	71	77	71	291	7	2241.00	1403.91
	Peter MITCHELL	Eng	71	71	71	78	291	7	2241.00	1403.91
	Nic HENNING	SA	72	66	74	79	291	7	2241.00	1403.91
76	Seve BALLESTEROS	Sp	72	71	76	74	293	9	2235.00	1400.15
77	Philip WALTON	Ire	68	73	74	80	295	11	2232.00	1398.27
78	Massimo SCARPA	It	70	73	78	77	298	14	2229.00	1396.39
79	Kim FELTON	Aus	70	73	77	79	299	15	2226.00	1394.51

Mark of Respect

BELLERIVE COUNTRY CLUB, ST LOUIS, MISSOURI, USA

September 11, 2001 will live long in the memory as a date with infamy. The haunting images of the crumbling twin towers of the World Trade Centre in New York confronted a horrified world with the stark reality of terrorism.

That appalling tragedy, and the consequent anguish and sorrow of the families and friends of the victims, transfixed the global population in a manner seldom, if ever, witnessed in peacetime.

In the circumstances, the game of golf became an irrelevance. After all, what is a mere game in the context of that atrocity? One day changed people's lives for ever and in that climate of confusion, the swift decision to cancel the third World Golf Championships-American Express Championship was universally applauded.

The European Tour, in conjunction with the other Members of the International Federation of PGA Tours, concurred. As a mark of respect to the victims, the WGC-American Express Championship was cancelled along with several other tournaments in the United States and Europe. The US PGA Tour pledged an immediate $2 million to the relief efforts in a devastated New York City and The Pentagon.

The seismic tremors felt by the devastation in New York and Washington, and Pennsylvania, where another hijacked jet crashed, created a ripple effect in every State, and none less so than in Missouri and at Bellerive Country Club, where many of the world's leading professional golfers were assembling in readiness for the WGC-American Express Championship.

One picture is worth a thousand words, and there can be no doubting the sheer horror in the expressive face of World Number One, Tiger Woods, when he was informed that two hijacked airliners had smashed into the Twin Towers. Hand covering his mouth, those famous almond eyes registered the shock and numbness experienced

Bellerive Country Club

Mount Juliet Golf Club, Thomastown, Co. Kilkenny, will host the 2002 WGC-American Express Championship

Equally surreal was the shot of Justin Leonard working on the range. In the background, the giant television screen bearing the American Express Championship banner and the logos from the six Members of the International Federations of PGA Tours, contained not stirring images of great golfing achievements, but the concerned, sombre face of US President George W. Bush.

Clearly, the playing of a golf tournament was imprudent. The American Express headquarters, close to the World Trade Centre, was badly damaged and employees of the company had been lost in the disaster.

European Ryder Cup player, Jesper Parnevik, was located in the nearby Plaza Hotel in New York City involved in a photo shoot when the planes struck with brutal force. The Swede headed for Central Park, where he sheltered for several hours before returning to the hotel.

Parnevik will not easily forget the morning of September 11, 2001. Nor will millions of other innocents who had never seen or even heard of the World Trade Centre. It was a time to reflect and to pay respects to those who lost their lives.

Gordon Simpson

Sting in the Tail

SAINT-NOM-LA-BRETÈCHE, PARIS, FRANCE

Mark Roe is the sort of person who can raise a smile in the most difficult of circumstances. He was, therefore, just what the Trophée Lancôme ordered at a time when everyone - not least sensitive sponsors - remained deeply affected by the terrorist attacks in the United States the previous week. "We are all quite flat," Colin Montgomerie had said in his capacity as unofficial spokesman of The European Tour. "There is a lot less laughter in the locker room, a lot less joviality between players and caddies. The dinner conversation is less jocular."

Jean Hugo

Jonathan Lomas

Then Roe was stung by a wasp towards the end of his first round. He suffered a reaction, of course. Someone sidelined by injury for 20 months after walking the dog, a springer spaniel at that, was not going to settle for a bite whose legacy would be nothing more than a red mark and an itch.

Roe's left wrist swelled to three times its normal size, prompting a worry that the inflammation would spread to his fingers and necessitate withdrawal. In an attempt to prevent that, he held his left arm across his chest, as if in a sling, between shots for the whole of his second round. He looked ridiculous, as he later admitted, but cared not a jot as a second 66 gave him the halfway lead.

He did not smell so good either, having decided that balsamic vinegar contained magical healing qualities.

His sudden emergence in a season of modest achievement and at a time when lying a lowly 131st in the Volvo Order of Merit afforded everyone the opportunity to tell their favourite Mark Roe story.

Some opted for the time he resolved an on/off television dispute with a hotel roommate by taking a pair of scissors to a power cable; others preferred the occasion he poured a bowl of spaghetti over the head of fellow professional Russell Claydon who, contrary to popular belief, did not react by eating every strand; the aforementioned shaggy dog story took a bit of beating, though.

Malcolm Mackenzie

"I am hoping I get bitten on the other wrist before tomorrow," Roe joked as he looked at a leader board showing himself ten under par. But as his wrist recovered his golf relapsed. The weekend saw him slide back into the pack.

Advance preparations had been for 'le weekend' without precedent, the first professional appearance in France of Tiger Woods. However, the World Number One decided that in the wake of the Twin Tower tragedy he had neither the stomach for competition nor the appetite for international travel.

If his absence left a hole, then who better to fill it than Sergio Garcia. The Spaniard had proved himself a poet as well as an artist when describing the minute's silence held at noon on the first day as a mark of respect for the victims of the attrocities.

"It was as if the sky was crying," Garcia said. "It had stopped. But as soon as the silence began it started raining again."

It was raining birdies wherever Retief Goosen squelched on a sodden opening day, seven in a row from the fourth for the US Open Champion, just one short of an European record shared by, among others, Seve Ballesteros, Darren Clarke, Mark O'Meara and Ian Woosnam.

John Bickerton

The Course

Set in rolling countryside on lush parkland the combined test that Saint-Nom-La-Bretèche comes up with from the best of its two courses demands total concentration through to the finishing hole - a downhill par three - because of the pond which menaces the right edge of the green and the left hand bunker which narrows the target area. Many titles have been won and lost here over the years.

Diego Borrego

Jarrod Moseley

With three previous victories in France, Goosen had acquired a reputation for being something of a Gallic specialist. And he looked like collecting a fourth title for most of the event, not least when four strokes to the good with only four holes remaining.

Had this been the Open Championship, the official engraver would have already been following the mantra of his English teacher in putting 'i' before 'e' on the Claret Jug. But faced with a typical birdie onslaught by the tumultuous Garcia, Goosen lost by a single stroke in one of those extraordinary U-turns after which the victor and the vanquished are left equally stunned.

Garcia's brilliance, however, had produced his first victory on The European Tour for two years, though he considered it little consolation for the postponement of The Ryder Cup Matches which had been scheduled for the following week.

Once again his poetic bent materialised. He likened that to having the 'honey taken away from his lips.'

Goosen ought to have known the feeling.

Alan Fraser

Shot of the Week

Sergio Garcia's four iron at the 209 yards par three 72nd hole. It is a tough tee shot at any time, with a bunker to the left and water to the right, but the Spaniard applied the pressure by hitting his to ten feet. Game, set and match.

SAINT-NOM-LA-BRETÈCHE, PARIS, FRANCE, 20-23 SEPTEMBER, 2001, PAR 71, 6903 YARDS, 6311 METRES

Pos.	Name		Rd1	Rd2	Rd3	Rd4	Total	Par	Prize Money Euro	£
1	Sergio GARCIA	Sp	68	65	68	65	266	-18	239782.49	150000.00
2	Retief GOOSEN	SA	64	71	65	67	267	-17	159855.00	100000.00
3	Jean HUGO	SA	66	68	69	66	269	-15	90062.30	56340.00
4	Gary EMERSON	Eng	66	70	66	69	271	-13	71934.75	45000.00
5	Niclas FASTH	Swe	69	66	66	71	272	-12	61000.67	38160.00
6	Raphaël JACQUELIN	Fr	68	71	68	66	273	-11	46757.59	29250.00
	Anthony WALL	Eng	68	65	70	70	273	-11	46757.59	29250.00
8	Ian WOOSNAM	Wal	68	71	69	66	274	-10	32322.68	20220.00
	Trevor IMMELMAN	SA	70	72	67	65	274	-10	32322.68	20220.00
	Henrik NYSTROM	Swe	70	66	69	69	274	-10	32322.68	20220.00
11	Steve WEBSTER	Eng	66	68	71	70	275	-9	24793.51	15510.00
	Phillip PRICE	Wal	70	67	66	72	275	-9	24793.51	15510.00
	Adam SCOTT	Aus	69	70	65	71	275	-9	24793.51	15510.00
14	Mark MOULAND	Wal	75	67	69	65	276	-8	19877.97	12435.00
	Sven STRÜVER	Ger	69	68	70	69	276	-8	19877.97	12435.00
	Shaun P WEBSTER	Eng	67	68	69	72	276	-8	19877.97	12435.00
	David LYNN	Eng	70	71	64	71	276	-8	19877.97	12435.00
	Andrew COLTART	Scot	66	71	66	73	276	-8	19877.97	12435.00
	Graeme STORM	Eng	71	65	69	71	276	-8	19877.97	12435.00
20	Richard S JOHNSON	Swe	70	72	67	68	277	-7	16736.82	10470.00
	Greg OWEN	Eng	68	70	73	66	277	-7	16736.82	10470.00
	John BICKERTON	Eng	68	71	71	67	277	-7	16736.82	10470.00
23	Malcolm MACKENZIE	Eng	69	70	70	69	278	-6	14530.82	9090.00
	Paul EALES	Eng	69	70	69	70	278	-6	14530.82	9090.00
	Russell CLAYDON	Eng	68	73	69	68	278	-6	14530.82	9090.00
	Jonathan LOMAS	Eng	69	71	70	68	278	-6	14530.82	9090.00
	Markus BRIER	Aut	73	66	67	72	278	-6	14530.82	9090.00
	Dean ROBERTSON	Scot	69	71	66	72	278	-6	14530.82	9090.00
	David CARTER	Eng	72	67	68	71	278	-6	14530.82	9090.00
30	Mark ROE	Eng	66	66	75	72	279	-5	11401.66	7132.50
	Mark MCNULTY	Zim	71	68	68	72	279	-5	11401.66	7132.50
	Jarrod MOSELEY	Aus	71	71	70	67	279	-5	11401.66	7132.50
	Per NYMAN	Swe	74	67	73	65	279	-5	11401.66	7132.50
	Jorge BERENDT	Arg	69	68	68	74	279	-5	11401.66	7132.50
	Christian CÉVAËR	Fr	73	67	67	72	279	-5	11401.66	7132.50
	Angel CABRERA	Arg	72	68	67	72	279	-5	11401.66	7132.50
	Gary ORR	Scot	66	73	71	69	279	-5	11401.66	7132.50
38	Santiago LUNA	Sp	71	68	68	73	280	-4	9351.52	5850.00
	Thomas LEVET	Fr	68	72	71	69	280	-4	9351.52	5850.00
	Emanuele CANONICA	It	72	67	71	70	280	-4	9351.52	5850.00
	Diego BORREGO	Sp	70	71	69	70	280	-4	9351.52	5850.00
	Fredrik ANDERSSON	Swe	71	68	70	71	280	-4	9351.52	5850.00
43	José RIVERO	Sp	71	71	67	72	281	-3	7768.95	4860.00
	Graham RANKIN	Scot	69	72	68	72	281	-3	7768.95	4860.00
	Joakim HAEGGMAN	Swe	69	71	70	71	281	-3	7768.95	4860.00
	Van PHILLIPS	Eng	70	68	72	71	281	-3	7768.95	4860.00
	Brett RUMFORD	Aus	70	72	69	70	281	-3	7768.95	4860.00
	Scott GARDINER	Aus	66	73	70	72	281	-3	7768.95	4860.00
49	Peter HANSON	Swe	71	68	69	74	282	-2	6186.39	3870.00
	Peter BAKER	Eng	67	72	71	72	282	-2	6186.39	3870.00
	Jeremy ROBINSON	Eng	71	69	75	67	282	-2	6186.39	3870.00
	Massimo SCARPA	It	69	72	67	74	282	-2	6186.39	3870.00
	Robert COLES	Eng	67	70	69	76	282	-2	6186.39	3870.00
54	Eduardo ROMERO	Arg	67	72	69	75	283	-1	4412.00	2760.00
	Jean VAN DE VELDE	Fr	70	69	71	73	283	-1	4412.00	2760.00
	Carl SUNESON	Sp	69	72	72	70	283	-1	4412.00	2760.00
	Robert KARLSSON	Swe	67	72	72	72	283	-1	4412.00	2760.00
	Bradley DREDGE	Wal	71	71	70	71	283	-1	4412.00	2760.00
	Fredrik JACOBSON	Swe	71	67	68	77	283	-1	4412.00	2760.00
	Erol SIMSEK	Ger	69	72	70	72	283	-1	4412.00	2760.00
	Mikael LUNDBERG	Swe	66	73	73	71	283	-1	4412.00	2760.00
	Simon DYSON	Eng	69	68	70	76	283	-1	4412.00	2760.00
63	Gordon BRAND JNR.	Scot	71	69	71	73	284	0	3524.81	2205.00
	Andrew OLDCORN	Scot	71	67	72	74	284	0	3524.81	2205.00
65	Barry LANE	Eng	72	69	71	73	285	1	2954.65	1848.33
	Maarten LAFEBER	Hol	71	71	72	71	285	1	2954.65	1848.33
	Stephen LEANEY	Aus	70	72	69	74	285	1	2954.65	1848.33
	Garry HOUSTON	Wal	69	68	76	72	285	1	2954.65	1848.33
	Peter MITCHELL	Eng	71	71	70	73	285	1	2954.65	1848.33
	Ian GARBUTT	Eng	73	69	73	70	285	1	2954.65	1848.33
71	Raymond RUSSELL	Scot	75	67	69	75	286	2	2156.50	1349.04
	Carl PETTERSSON	Swe	70	71	68	77	286	2	2156.50	1349.04
73	Olivier DAVID	Fr	71	71	69	76	287	3	2152.00	1346.22
74	David GILFORD	Eng	68	73	72	75	288	4	2149.00	1344.34
75	Nicolas COLSAERTS	Bel	68	73	73	76	290	6	2146.00	1342.47
76	David HOWELL	Eng	71	71	74	76	292	8	2141.50	1339.65
	Olivier EDMOND	Fr	73	69	75	75	292	8	2141.50	1339.65
78	Marc PENDARIES	Fr	73	69	76	77	295	11	2137.00	1336.84

No Retirement Plans

GUT LÄRCHENHOF, COLOGNE, GERMANY

When golf's "old firm" of Bernhard Langer and Pete Coleman manufactured their fourth victory in the Linde German Masters at Gut Lärchenhof, Cologne, it was about as big a surprise as Manchester United winning the Premiership.

For the 44 year old German, co-promoter of the event with brother Erwin, and his 60 year old English caddie, it was their 11th European Tour victory on German soil, including five German Opens.

In all it was Langer's 39th European Tour triumph and 38 of those have come in tandem with former British Rail electrician Coleman, who caused consternation in the caddie ranks in Cologne when he solemnly announced his boss, a devout Christian, had, on charitable grounds, agreed that lots would henceforward be drawn each week to decide who got Bernhard's bag.

He was joking, of course. After 20 golden years as Langer's helpmate and friend he knows a good thing when he sees one.

Fredrik Jacobson

Langer's 450,000 euro (£278,711) pay cheque, the biggest of his European Tour career, nudged his official earnings total nearer the ten million euro mark following his TNT Open victory and Open Championship third place.

A caddie's cut adds up to a princely sum and the greying but still spritely Coleman has no retirement plans.

Langer declared before the off that he was playing his best golf for three years, despite a four week lay-off. But a runaway, his latest Linde German Masters win was not.

When he managed to persuade John Daly to become the first American player to leave his country to compete since the New York and Washington terror attacks by offering him a lift from Memphis in his private jet, he knew the big man would be a crowd puller following his brilliant BMW International Open success in September.

He also knew he was making a rod for his own back. Daly, who followed his Munich win - his first since the Open Championship at St Andrews in 1995 - with fourth place in the Canadian Open, looked a solid bet to complete a Deutsche double. He would go oh so close.

After his almost flawless second day 64 Langer, with $1.6 million American winnings under his belt after finishing runner-up in the

John Daly

St Jude Classic and third in The Players Championship, had a two stroke lead, and the question seemed not whether he would win but by how many.

But Daly had plans for the weekend, racing to a 64 of his own on Saturday to move within three strokes of his German host, whose last hole birdie for a 68 and 17 below par 199 squeezed him to a single shot advantage over Swede Fredrik Jacobson, Australian Stephen Leaney and England's Greg Owen, who followed an opening 65 with rounds of 68 and 67.

Predictably Daly staged a typical Sunday surge by going out in 33. Langer, though, reached the turn in 32, helped by a 40 foot two at the eighth. Briefly it was young Jacobson, twice a Tour runner up the previous summer, who looked the man most likely as he moved to within a stroke of Langer at 20 under par. When Langer at last made a mistake by missing a three foot birdie opportunity at the 12th, it was Daly who pounced with a 30 foot eagle at the 13th and birdies at the 15th and 16th.

So when Langer uncharacteristically pushed his second towards the lake at the 17th, with Daly facing a 15 footer on the 18th for another birdie, a play-off looked a distinct possibility. But Langer's luck was in as his ball stuck in the wet grass six inches short of the water and he got up and down for a cheeky par.

Roger Chapman

The Course

Sited some 20 minutes along the autobahn from Cologne this essentially flat Jack Nicklaus layout has water on many holes, big lakes crucially coming into play to the right of the ninth and 17th and to the left of the 18th.

Shot of the Week

Following his worst shot of the week - a push from mid fairway towards the lake at the 71st - it has to be Bernhard Langer's semi blind pitch from a soggy lie in the rough six inches short of the water up over a bank to within five feet of the flag to scramble an audacious par four and preserve the two stroke cushion which enabled him to play the last as a bogey five.

Daly missed and Langer was able to enjoy the luxury of a shrewdly plotted bogey five via rough and sand at the last to squeeze out a 67 and 22 under par 266 for a one stroke win over the American and the gutsy Jacobson, who had chipped in for a two at 16.

Daly, who finished 64-65 and was 20 under par for his last 45 holes, had warned Langer was a hard man to catch once he got his nose in front. So it proved.

A closing 66 earned Roger Chapman a share of fourth place on 269 with the rapidly improving Owen, who revealed he would work on strengthening a troublesome back with martial arts expert Ron Cuthbert in the winter months.

US Open Champion Retief Goosen shared tenth place on 273 to stretch his lead at the top of the Volvo Order of Merit to 708,547 euro (£438,846) over Darren Clarke, who ended four behind.

But it was Herr Langer, moving up behind Clarke in third place in the table, and faithful caddie Coleman who ruled the roost in Cologne.

Gordon Richardson

Rolf Muntz

GUT LÄRCHENHOF, COLOGNE, GERMANY, 4-7 OCTOBER, 2001, PAR 72, 7289 YARDS, 6662 METRES

Pos.	Name		Rd1	Rd2	Rd3	Rd4	Total	Par	Prize Money Euro	£
1	Bernhard LANGER	Ger	67	64	68	67	266	-22	450000.00	278711.98
2	Fredrik JACOBSON	Swe	67	66	67	67	267	-21	234510.00	145246.10
	John DALY	USA	71	67	64	65	267	-21	234510.00	145246.10
4	Roger CHAPMAN	Eng	67	69	67	66	269	-19	124740.00	77258.96
	Greg OWEN	Eng	65	68	67	69	269	-19	124740.00	77258.96
6	Gary ORR	Scot	70	67	66	67	270	-18	87750.00	54348.84
	David LYNN	Eng	68	66	68	68	270	-18	87750.00	54348.84
8	Ian WOOSNAM	Wal	69	68	66	68	271	-17	63990.00	39632.84
	Paul MCGINLEY	Ire	70	67	68	66	271	-17	63990.00	39632.84
10	Robert KARLSSON	Swe	67	69	69	68	273	-15	46980.00	29097.53
	Gary EVANS	Eng	71	65	66	71	273	-15	46980.00	29097.53
	Roger WESSELS	SA	67	70	65	71	273	-15	46980.00	29097.53
	Raymond RUSSELL	Scot	71	67	67	68	273	-15	46980.00	29097.53
	Retief GOOSEN	SA	68	68	67	70	273	-15	46980.00	29097.53
15	Marc FARRY	Fr	72	65	66	71	274	-14	37260.00	23077.35
	Steve WEBSTER	Eng	70	68	65	71	274	-14	37260.00	23077.35
	Ian POULTER	Eng	67	69	67	71	274	-14	37260.00	23077.35
	Colin MONTGOMERIE	Scot	70	70	68	66	274	-14	37260.00	23077.35
19	Anders FORSBRAND	Swe	73	69	64	69	275	-13	31050.00	19231.13
	Padraig HARRINGTON	Ire	70	67	67	71	275	-13	31050.00	19231.13
	Barry LANE	Eng	68	70	68	69	275	-13	31050.00	19231.13
	Peter O'MALLEY	Aus	69	70	66	70	275	-13	31050.00	19231.13
	Markus BRIER	Aut	70	70	65	70	275	-13	31050.00	19231.13
	Michael CAMPBELL	NZ	72	68	68	67	275	-13	31050.00	19231.13
25	Trevor IMMELMAN	SA	68	72	69	67	276	-12	25650.00	15886.58
	Miguel Angel JIMÉNEZ	Sp	68	69	68	71	276	-12	25650.00	15886.58
	Jean HUGO	SA	70	72	68	66	276	-12	25650.00	15886.58
	Roger WINCHESTER	Eng	68	70	72	66	276	-12	25650.00	15886.58
	Van PHILLIPS	Eng	68	69	72	67	276	-12	25650.00	15886.58
	Niclas FASTH	Swe	72	69	68	67	276	-12	25650.00	15886.58
	Paul CASEY	Eng	72	69	67	68	276	-12	25650.00	15886.58
32	Warren BENNETT	Eng	68	66	71	72	277	-11	19800.00	12263.33
	Anders HANSEN	Den	70	68	70	69	277	-11	19800.00	12263.33
	Søren KJELDSEN	Den	70	67	72	68	277	-11	19800.00	12263.33
	Stephen LEANEY	Aus	67	66	67	77	277	-11	19800.00	12263.33
	Pierre FULKE	Swe	67	70	69	71	277	-11	19800.00	12263.33
	Darren CLARKE	N.Ire	68	67	71	71	277	-11	19800.00	12263.33
	Rolf MUNTZ	Hol	70	71	70	66	277	-11	19800.00	12263.33
	Jarmo SANDELIN	Swe	67	69	70	71	277	-11	19800.00	12263.33
	Mikko ILONEN	Fin	69	67	72	69	277	-11	19800.00	12263.33
41	Mark MCNULTY	Zim	68	72	70	68	278	-10	15930.00	9866.40
	John SENDEN	Aus	66	72	68	72	278	-10	15930.00	9866.40
	Carl SUNESON	Sp	70	69	68	71	278	-10	15930.00	9866.40
	Ricardo GONZALEZ	Arg	66	70	73	69	278	-10	15930.00	9866.40
	David CARTER	Eng	73	68	67	70	278	-10	15930.00	9866.40
46	David HOWELL	Eng	70	70	69	70	279	-9	11340.00	7023.54
	Maarten LAFEBER	Hol	72	68	72	67	279	-9	11340.00	7023.54
	Anthony WALL	Eng	71	69	70	69	279	-9	11340.00	7023.54
	Justin ROSE	Eng	72	66	68	73	279	-9	11340.00	7023.54
	Henrik STENSON	Swe	67	69	73	70	279	-9	11340.00	7023.54
	Jean VAN DE VELDE	Fr	73	68	67	71	279	-9	11340.00	7023.54
	Jonathan LOMAS	Eng	69	68	71	71	279	-9	11340.00	7023.54
	Ian GARBUTT	Eng	74	65	70	70	279	-9	11340.00	7023.54
	Mathias GRÖNBERG	Swe	67	74	69	69	279	-9	11340.00	7023.54
	Paul LAWRIE	Scot	71	70	67	71	279	-9	11340.00	7023.54
	Wolfgang HUGET	Ger	70	68	70	71	279	-9	11340.00	7023.54
	Nick DOUGHERTY	Eng	69	72	66	72	279	-9	11340.00	7023.54
58	Jean-Francois REMESY	Fr	68	70	72	70	280	-8	7830.00	4849.59
	Thomas LEVET	Fr	71	71	69	69	280	-8	7830.00	4849.59
	Lucas PARSONS	Aus	69	70	69	72	280	-8	7830.00	4849.59
61	Santiago LUNA	Sp	71	69	70	71	281	-7	6480.00	4013.45
	Des SMYTH	Ire	71	71	72	67	281	-7	6480.00	4013.45
	Brian DAVIS	Eng	67	74	69	71	281	-7	6480.00	4013.45
	Alex CEJKA	Ger	74	67	67	73	281	-7	6480.00	4013.45
	Ignacio GARRIDO	Sp	72	70	70	69	281	-7	6480.00	4013.45
	Henrik NYSTROM	Swe	65	73	70	73	281	-7	6480.00	4013.45
	Stephen GALLACHER	Scot	72	70	72	67	281	-7	6480.00	4013.45
68	Tony JOHNSTONE	Zim	71	71	71	69	282	-6	5265.00	3260.93
	José Maria OLAZáBAL	Sp	69	71	68	74	282	-6	5265.00	3260.93
70	Jochen LUPPRIAN	Ger	70	70	70	73	283	-5	4220.40	2613.95
	Marcel SIEM	Ger	72	70	71	70	283	-5	4220.40	2613.95
	Massimo SCARPA	It	72	68	74	69	283	-5	4220.40	2613.95
	Andrew COLTART	Scot	72	69	72	70	283	-5	4220.40	2613.95
	Nick CASSINI	USA	73	68	70	72	283	-5	4220.40	2613.95
75	Lee WESTWOOD	Eng	72	70	69	73	284	-4	4036.50	2500.05
	Adam SCOTT	Aus	70	71	73	70	284	-4	4036.50	2500.05
77	Emanuele CANONICA	It	70	71	71	73	285	-3	4032.00	2497.26
78	Darren FICHARDT	SA	68	74	75	69	286	-2	4027.50	2494.47
	Gary EMERSON	Eng	71	71	70	74	286	-2	4027.50	2494.47
80	Gordon BRAND JNR.	Scot	70	69	73	75	287	-1	4023.00	2491.69
81	Mark JAMES	Eng	72	70	72	80	294	6	4020.00	2489.83

Opportunity and Incentive

CANNES MOUGINS, CANNES, FRANCE

As a tournament it might have taken a mere two weeks to organise but, for Jorge Berendt, victory in the Cannes Open had been eight years in the making.

Ever since losing to David Gilford in a play-off for the Portuguese Open in 1993, the softly-spoken 37 year old from Buenos Aires had worked on his game, largely away from the limelight, but all the while dreaming of glory.

As with fellow countrymen Angel Cabrera, José Coceres and Ricardo Gonzalez, Berendt's first golfing experience had been as a caddie but although he had long since laid down the bag, he had yet to follow in their spikemarks and pick up a winner's cheque on The European Tour.

However, all that changed at the end of a glorious week on the Côte d'Azur as Berendt triumphed at last, and in doing so pocketed 92,500 euro (£57,319).

Having seen the scheduled Estoril Open cancelled at the 11th hour by the tournament promoters, Berendt et al seemed set for a week at home until The European Tour, with the assistance of the International Sports Management group and Cannes Mougins Golf and Country Club, stepped in. From scratch and within a fortnight, the Cannes Open - last played in 1998 when Thomas Levet claimed his maiden European Tour victory - had been resurrected, a truly wonderful effort from all concerned.

"We really must thank everyone involved because to put a tournament on so quickly is fantastic," said Levet, desperate for another victory to please his growing legion of French fans, ignited by his inspirational victory four months earlier in the Victor Chandler British Masters at Woburn.

"I saw it at the Trophée Lancôme," he explained. "I was out early in the morning and even then I had a big crowd with me, so it shows the news of my success is getting to the public, people are following what I do."

Jean Van de Velde

Andrew Marshall

The Gallic galleries again turned out for Levet, who would eventually finish tied for third with Spain's Santiago Luna and young Englishman Andrew Marshall.

They also rolled up for compatriot Jean Van de Velde, back in his native land to help complete his required number of tournaments on The European Tour International Schedule as well as attempting to make enough money to ensure his playing privileges for 2002.

Neither disappointed, Levet carding 69 and Van de Velde 70, but the opening day belonged to Lucas Parsons, whose flawless ten under par 62 was only denied a share of the nine year old course record by the fact that preferred lies were in operation.

The Australian took a two shot lead into the second round but a 73 saw him slip back and he never again threatened the top ten, his place in pole position at the halfway stage being taken by Warren Bennett. A second consecutive 66 gave the 30 year old Englishman a one shot lead over Henrik Bjornstad, who suddenly found himself attracting a few more supporters than that with which he started the week, Berendt and Marshall.

Although Bjornstad is a charming young man, the reason had rather more to do with the appearance of 12 year old Jack Sorrell, the son of Cannes Mougins professional Richard Sorrell, as a trolley puller for the Norwegian after his local caddie failed to show on the first tee.

Santiago Luna

How much local knowledge the schoolboy imparted before being replaced for the weekend is unclear but perhaps Bjornstad should have stuck with him, for he carded a 68 on the Friday, as opposed to 70 and 71 over the weekend.

Weekends in France are a time for the family and a barbeque in the warm autumnal sunshine must have seemed a perfect idea for la famille whose house backs onto the opening stretch of the Cannes Mougins golf course. Not so thrilled were the players who had to cough and splutter their way through the charcoal fumes but, ironically, the incident succinctly summed up the challenge of the man who would go on to be champion.

Berendt's third round smouldered in the early stages, the flames were fanned with birdies at the fourth, sixth, eighth and tenth before his challenge truly ignited with an audacious eagle two at the 438 yards 12th, courtesy of a holed nine iron from 137 yards.

"I didn't feel as confident with my swing today as I had done the previous couple of days," he admitted magnanimously before adding with delicious understatement, "But the 12th was a big break for me."

It gave the Argentinian a two shot lead going into the last round with Bennett and Marshall his closest pursuers. If he was to crack, it would surely be in the nervy early stages, but Berendt played as if he had been in that position all his life.

Patrik Sjöland

An immaculate front nine featured three birdies in a row from the fourth and when he trundled home an eight footer for another birdie on the 12th to move three shots clear, the question in most minds was: Who would be second? For a while it looked like Bennett until a poor drive at the last and a flirtation with the clubhouse wall cost him a double bogey six and, simultaneously, even a place in the top five.

In the end the runners-up slot went to Van de Velde, who pushed hard with four birdies in a row from the sixth and an eagle three at the 16th, but could not find another birdie in the final two holes to exert real pressure on the leader.

Berendt came to the last and, for the first time, looked at the scoreboards to clarify exactly what he needed to do. What greeted him was the classic situation. Standing 20 under par with Van de Velde at 19, he required a par four to win. Having seen his drive catch the rough, Berendt's second flew from the long grass off the back of the putting surface. It left him his least favourite shot but he composed himself and played it to perfection, pitching to three feet from where he calmly found the bottom of the cup.

The putt prompted scenes reminiscent of a month earlier when his good friend Gonzalez had claimed his maiden victory in the Omega

Johan Ryström

The Course

At 6830 yards, Cannes Mougins is one of the shorter courses played on The European Tour International Schedule but its defence came via the compact and undulating greens which demanded precision and accuracy from all approach shots. Set in idyllic, wooded surroundings on the Côte d'Azur, the warm autumnal sunshine which blessed all four days made playing conditions a delight. Considering the short time Cannes Mougins had to prepare for the tournament, the overall condition of the course was remarkable and drew praise from all quarters.

Shot of the Week

Jorge Berendt's spectacular eagle two on the 438 yards 12th hole in the third round. Five months earlier at St Leon-Rot, World Number One Tiger Woods holed his second shot at the par four 13th in the final round of the Deutsche Bank - SAP Open TPC of Europe, a wonder stroke which proved the catalyst for his victory - and it was the same for the Argentinian. The perfectly struck 137 yards nine iron shot helped Berendt take a two stroke lead into the final round and gave him belief that perhaps, at last, his time had come to win. It had.

Warren Bennett

European Masters at Crans-sur-Sierre. In France, as in Switzerland, everyone on the 18th green ended up drenched in champagne.

Berendt was delighted. "To be talked of now in the same breath as the other Argentinian golfers who have won in Europe is absolutely unbelievable," he said.

Van de Velde, who secured his card, was delighted. "I am happy because I have a job next year and I will not be tempted to return to America," he said.

And The European Tour was delighted, because from the ashes of Estoril had risen the phoenix of Cannes. At the beginning of the season, Executive Director Ken Schofield had talked of The Tour's desire, at all times, to give its Members both playing opportunity and incentive. Through the staging of the Cannes Open, there was no greater example of that.

Scott Crockett

CANNES MOUGINS, CANNES, FRANCE, 11- 14 OCTOBER, 2001, PAR 72, 6830 YARDS, 6246 METRES

Pos.	Name		Rd1	Rd2	Rd3	Rd4	Total	Par	Prize Money Euro	£
1	Jorge BERENDT	Arg	67	66	67	68	268	-20	92500.00	57319.55
2	Jean VAN DE VELDE	Fr	70	66	68	65	269	-19	61660.00	38208.90
3	Santiago LUNA	Sp	70	66	68	68	272	-16	28675.00	17769.06
	Thomas LEVET	Fr	69	66	69	68	272	-16	28675.00	17769.06
	Andrew MARSHALL	Eng	65	68	69	70	272	-16	28675.00	17769.06
6	Warren BENNETT	Eng	66	66	70	71	273	-15	16650.00	10317.52
	Johan RYSTRÖM	Swe	67	71	69	66	273	-15	16650.00	10317.52
	Ignacio GARRIDO	Sp	69	67	67	70	273	-15	16650.00	10317.52
9	Henrik BJORNSTAD	Nor	65	68	70	71	274	-14	12432.00	7703.75
10	Shaun P WEBSTER	Eng	68	72	67	68	275	-13	9948.38	6164.72
	Paul EALES	Eng	67	70	68	70	275	-13	9948.38	6164.72
	Fredrik ANDERSSON	Swe	70	68	67	70	275	-13	9948.38	6164.72
	Matthew BLACKEY	Eng	69	70	66	70	275	-13	9948.38	6164.72
14	Raphaël JACQUELIN	Fr	69	65	71	71	276	-12	7992.00	4952.41
	Carl SUNESON	Sp	68	67	71	70	276	-12	7992.00	4952.41
	Bradley DREDGE	Wal	68	67	71	70	276	-12	7992.00	4952.41
	David PARK	Wal	64	75	71	66	276	-12	7992.00	4952.41
18	Van PHILLIPS	Eng	67	69	69	72	277	-11	6682.20	4140.76
	Lucas PARSONS	Aus	62	73	72	70	277	-11	6682.20	4140.76
	Richard STERNE	SA	71	71	68	67	277	-11	6682.20	4140.76
	Steven O'HARA	Scot	67	69	71	70	277	-11	6682.20	4140.76
	Martin MARITZ	SA	71	69	68	69	277	-11	6682.20	4140.76
23	Jeremy ROBINSON	Eng	66	76	71	65	278	-10	5772.00	3576.74
	Roger WINCHESTER	Eng	69	69	68	72	278	-10	5772.00	3576.74
	José ROMERO	Sp	70	68	71	69	278	-10	5772.00	3576.74
	Roger WESSELS	SA	66	70	73	69	278	-10	5772.00	3576.74
	Paddy GRIBBEN	Ire	71	69	67	71	278	-10	5772.00	3576.74
28	Wayne RILEY	Aus	66	69	75	69	279	-9	4696.69	2910.40
	Garry HOUSTON	Wal	71	68	68	72	279	-9	4696.69	2910.40
	Tomas Jesus MUÑOZ	Sp	71	71	67	70	279	-9	4696.69	2910.40
	Des TERBLANCHE	SA	72	68	72	67	279	-9	4696.69	2910.40
	Robert COLES	Eng	68	70	73	68	279	-9	4696.69	2910.40
	David HIGGINS	Ire	70	72	69	68	279	-9	4696.69	2910.40
	Simon DYSON	Eng	71	67	71	70	279	-9	4696.69	2910.40
	David DIXON	Eng	69	69	70	71	279	-9	4696.69	2910.40
36	Lionel ALEXANDRE	Fr	68	69	70	73	280	-8	3940.50	2441.81
	Fredrik HENGE	Swe	67	68	74	71	280	-8	3940.50	2441.81
	Gregory HAVRET	Fr	72	70	70	68	280	-8	3940.50	2441.81
39	Anders FORSBRAND	Swe	68	74	71	68	281	-7	3163.50	1960.33
	Mark MOULAND	Wal	71	67	69	74	281	-7	3163.50	1960.33
	Marc FARRY	Fr	71	70	71	69	281	-7	3163.50	1960.33
	Jean-Francois REMESY	Fr	69	70	71	71	281	-7	3163.50	1960.33
	Thomas GÖGELE	Ger	73	67	71	70	281	-7	3163.50	1960.33
	Stephen DODD	Wal	67	71	71	72	281	-7	3163.50	1960.33
	Mark PILKINGTON	Wal	68	69	75	69	281	-7	3163.50	1960.33
	Frédéric CUPILLARD	Fr	70	67	72	72	281	-7	3163.50	1960.33
	Daren LEE	Eng	69	69	73	70	281	-7	3163.50	1960.33
	Christopher HANELL	Swe	71	69	72	69	281	-7	3163.50	1960.33
	Scott GARDINER	Aus	68	70	68	75	281	-7	3163.50	1960.33
50	Peter FOWLER	Aus	72	69	71	70	282	-6	2386.50	1478.84
	Nicolas VANHOOTEGEM	Bel	71	69	70	72	282	-6	2386.50	1478.84
	Henrik NYSTROM	Swe	72	69	71	70	282	-6	2386.50	1478.84
53	Emanuele CANONICA	It	71	68	71	73	283	-5	1998.00	1238.10
	Nicolas KALOUGUINE	Fr	71	71	71	70	283	-5	1998.00	1238.10
	Erol SIMSEK	Ger	70	67	72	74	283	-5	1998.00	1238.10
	Graeme STORM	Eng	70	69	70	74	283	-5	1998.00	1238.10
57	José Manuel CARRILES	Sp	69	73	71	71	284	-4	1637.25	1014.56
	Peter HANSON	Swe	69	71	75	69	284	-4	1637.25	1014.56
	Paul BROADHURST	Eng	70	68	70	76	284	-4	1637.25	1014.56
	Russell CLAYDON	Eng	71	70	73	70	284	-4	1637.25	1014.56
61	Domingo HOSPITAL	Sp	71	71	74	71	287	-1	1443.00	894.19
	Marcello SANTI	It	70	71	71	75	287	-1	1443.00	894.19
	Michele REALE	It	71	69	76	71	287	-1	1443.00	894.19
64	Gary EVANS	Eng	70	67	70	81	288	0	1304.25	808.21
	Alastair FORSYTH	Scot	69	72	74	73	288	0	1304.25	808.21
66	Gustavo ROJAS	Arg	72	69	70	78	289	1	1221.00	756.62
67	Robin BYRD	USA	72	67	75	76	290	2	1165.50	722.23
68	Olivier EDMOND	Fr	70	72	72	77	291	3	1110.00	687.83
69	Patrik SJÖLAND	Swe	72	69	81	71	293	5	1054.50	653.44
70	Bertrand CORNUT	Fr	71	70	76	78	295	7	1018.00	630.82

Proud Moment

WENTWORTH CLUB, SURREY, ENGLAND

Not since Denmark's footballers received an 11th hour call to play in the 1992 European Championships - and promptly went out and won it - has a late entry made such a thrilling sporting impact as Ian Woosnam did in winning his third Cisco World Match Play Championship title at Wentworth Club by beating Retief Goosen, Colin Montgomerie, Lee Westwood then Padraig Harrington in the final.

Woosnam was one of four of Europe's eternal heroes - Seve Ballesteros, Nick Faldo and Sam Torrance were the others - called in when the repercussions from the dreadful events of September 11 led to leading players from North America not being prepared to leave their families and cross the Atlantic. Some critics claimed their inclusion devalued the tournament, others that the event had lost its glamour and relevance and was more akin to an exhibition match.

Padraig Harrington and caddie Dave McNeilly

No one, however, appeared to have told the thousands of enthusiastic fans who once again poured on to the famous West Course for the annual autumn classic, and were rewarded with record scoring and drama filled contests.

How much did it mean to the players? You just had to witness Woosnam's sheer exuberant delight at ending a four year winless drought that stretched back to the Volvo PGA Championship of May, 1997, or share the almost speechless desolation of Harrington as he was forced to accept his seventh runners-up spot of the season. Even collecting the 193,651 euro (£120,000) cheque and knowing he had contributed to one of the greatest matches in the Championship's illustrious 38 year history seemed scant consolation.

Sam Torrance

The records fell faster than the autumn leaves on that final Sunday on the West Course as Harrington and Woosnam produced a morning round of stunningly sustained brilliance. Between them they posted 21 birdies in 18 holes and were an eclectic 56 (16 under par) to record best ever figures for the Championship.

Harrington was round in a record equalling 61 and was only two up on Woosnam, who scored 64 after sprinting from out of the blocks with seven successive birdies from the second to go to the turn in a record-breaking 28 (one better than Tony Jacklin against

It would have shattered a lesser opponent, but Harrington replied with his own barrage. He birdied seven out of nine holes from the turn to be back in a record equalling 30. It had the huge gallery in raptures and even prompted European Tour Chief Referee John Paramor to describe it as "one of the best matches I have ever seen."

It seemed inconceivable that they could repeat such superhuman heroics in the afternoon. So it proved with the first two holes being won by pars! More birdies, however, were traded and Woosnam, fighting back from three down, maintained his rediscovered smooth as silk action to secure a 2 & 1 victory and collect the winning cheque of 403,440 euro (£250,000).

At 43, Woosnam became not only the oldest Cisco World Match Play champion but also the first player to win in three different decades (having previously triumphed in 1987 and 1990). "When you look at the four players I have beaten this week I have to be especially proud," said the Welshman.

He began with an impressive 4 & 3 first round victory over Goosen, the US Open Champion. The South African twice took the lead in the first four holes, but was never to lead again as Woosnam, with a run of six birdies in ten holes from the ninth, took full control.

The biggest section of a 9,500 opening day crowd opted for the Ballesteros-Torrance match. Ballesteros belied his frustrating recent

Seve Ballesteros

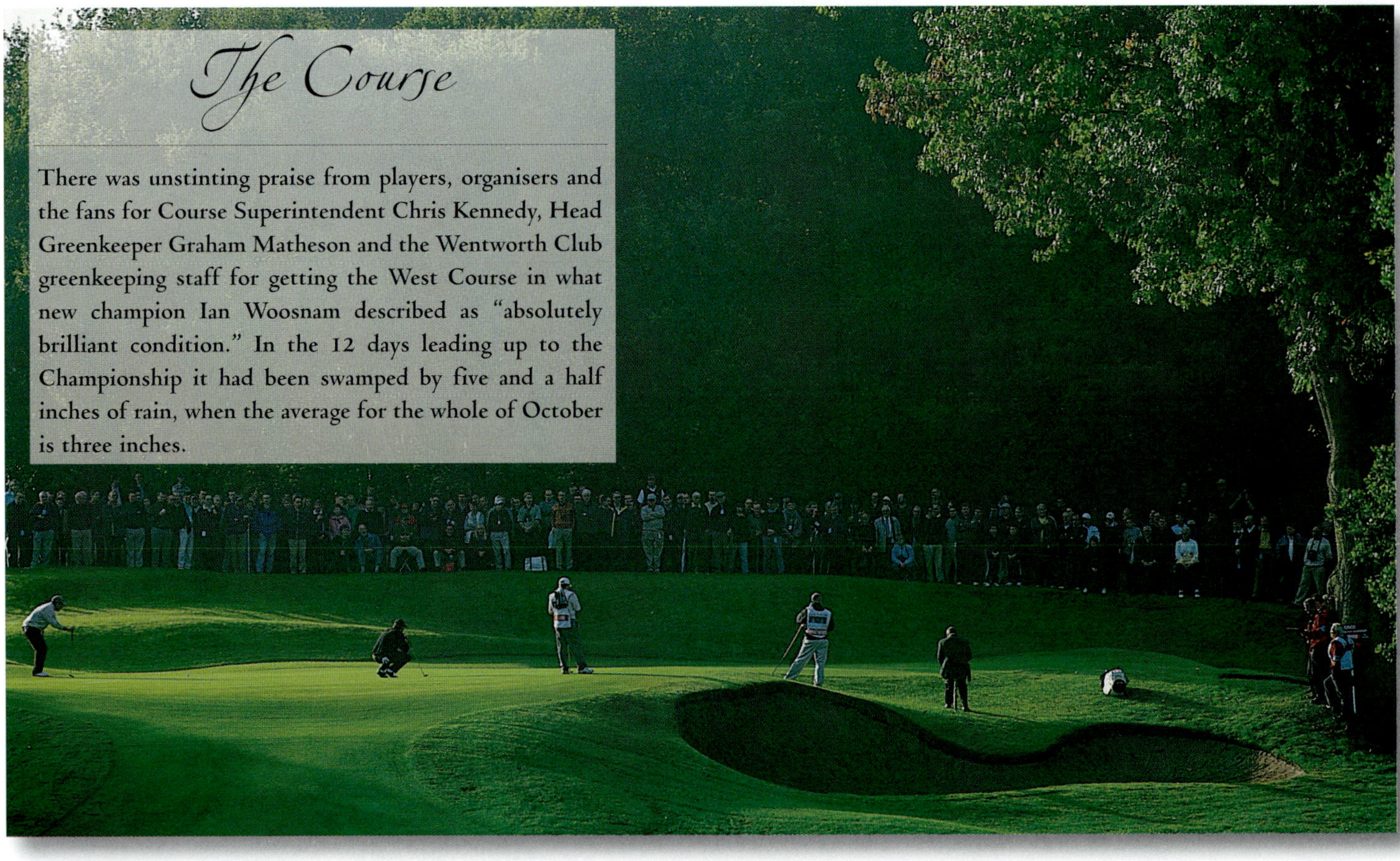

The Course

There was unstinting praise from players, organisers and the fans for Course Superintendent Chris Kennedy, Head Greenkeeper Graham Matheson and the Wentworth Club greenkeeping staff for getting the West Course in what new champion Ian Woosnam described as "absolutely brilliant condition." In the 12 days leading up to the Championship it had been swamped by five and a half inches of rain, when the average for the whole of October is three inches.

form in the morning round by single putting eight greens and claiming seven birdies to be four under at lunch. It was only Torrance's dogged, persistence that meant he was just one behind going into the afternoon round. Sadly for his legion of still adoring fans, it was then that Seve's grip began to falter and he began spending as much time in the trees as the squirrels.

Even then, Ballesteros mounted another fight back before a relieved Torrance sealed a 3 & 2 victory. While Torrance was still celebrating, twice champion Faldo was "devastated" after suffering his biggest ever defeat in this event, crashing 9 & 8 to an inspired Harrington. When they finally shook hands on the 28th green the brilliant young Irishman, who had undergone laser surgery on his eyes just two weeks before, was an impressive 12 under. Faldo, on a course that he knows best and loves the most, was merely on level par.

Thomas Björn looked set to win by an equally impressive margin when he completed the first 14 holes in the morning in figures of seven under to hold a five up lead on Adam Scott. The Australian fought back bravely to cut the deficit to one early in the afternoon before the Dane called on his experience to complete a comfortable 4 & 3 win.

The fairytale continued through the second round for Torrance, at 48, the oldest man in the field. He rolled back the years with an astonishing final hole victory over the second seed Vijay Singh, the favourite with on-site bookmakers Victor Chandler.

Three down after 19 holes Torrance, ranked number 313 in the world, produced an inspired afternoon comeback, making six threes in a row between the 20th and 25th to finish with an approximate 64 and overcome the World Number Five. Meanwhile Torrance's Ryder Cup Vice Captain, Woosnam, created almost as big an upset by outgunning 1999 champion Colin Montgomerie 4 & 3.

Montgomerie began in imperious fashion, drilling a six iron approach to one foot at the first, before the Welshman reacted to be four under after five holes by which time he was ahead. He was never behind again.

Westwood was the only seed to advance. Nevertheless, despite being 14 under, he came desperately close to going out. Indeed, the only time he was ahead in the match with Ryder Cup colleague Björn was when he birdied the 36th hole to win.

Harrington was again the biggest winner, outgunning fellow Irishman Darren Clarke 5 & 4. He was never behind and a burst of five successive birdies was enough to settle it.

The semi finals were played on the most glorious of autumn days and Woosnam responded by crushing Westwood 10 & 9, the second heaviest beating in the history of the event (the biggest being Mark

Mark H McCormack (front row, second from left), Chairman and CEO of the International Management Group and the founder of the World Match Play Championship, and Robert Lloyd, President - EMEA Operations, Senior Vice-President - Cisco Systems Inc. (front row, second from right), gathered on the eve of the 2001 Championship with the players: Back row (left to right): Sam Torrance, Adam Scott, Darren Clarke, Vijay Singh, Nick Faldo, Thomas Björn, Padraig Harrington, Colin Montgomerie and Retief Goosen. Front row (left to right): Ian Woosnam, Lee Westwood and Seve Ballesteros.

O'Meara's 11 & 10 defeat of Singh in 1998).

Westwood, whose see-saw weekend mirrored his entire season, managed just a single birdie all day while Woosnam continued to play incredibly steady golf. Torrance's week-long odyssey finally ended, but not without giving Harrington a real fright.

Torrance was two up after 14 holes but Harrington hit back to win the 16th and 17th and though Torrance stopped the rot with a ten foot putt to halve the 18th the door was beginning to swing open for the Irishman.

He barged right through it with three birdies in the first four holes in the afternoon and though Torrance managed to pull back two of them it was Harrington who accelerated away over the closing stretch.

John Whitbread

WENTWORTH CLUB, SURREY, ENGLAND
11-14 OCTOBER, 2001, PAR 72, 7047 YARDS 6446 METRES

		Euro	Sterling
FIRST ROUND			
Thomas Björn (Den) (8) beat Adam Scott (Aus)	4 & 3	80,688	50,000
Ian Woosnam (Wal) beat Retief Goosen (SA) (5)	4 & 3	80,688	50,000
Padraig Harrington (Ire) (6) beat Nick Faldo (Eng)	9 & 8	80,688	50,000
Sam Torrance (Scot) beat Seve Ballesteros (Sp)	3 & 2	80,688	50,000
SECOND ROUND			
Lee Westwood (Eng) (1) beat Thomas Björn	1 hole	104,894	65,000
Ian Woosnam beat Colin Montgomerie (Scot) (4)	5 & 4	104,894	65,000
Padraig Harrington beat Darren Clarke (N Ire) (3)	5 & 4	104,894	65,000
Sam Torrance beat Vijay Singh (Fiji) (2)	1 hole	104,894	65,000
SEMI-FINALS			
Ian Woosnam beat Lee Westwood	10 & 9	137,169	85,000
Padraig Harrington beat Sam Torrance	4 & 3	137,169	85,000
FINAL			
Ian Woosnam beat Padraig Harrington	2 & 1	403,440	250,000
		193,651	120,000
Total		**1,613,757**	**1,000,000**

Exchange rate: £1 = 1.61376 euro

GEAR
GEAR FOR SPORTS
GEAR for Sports Europe
2 Parsonage Business Park / Horsham West Sussex RH12 4AL
Telephone: (01403) 754585 Fax: (01403) 754748
Email: gear@gearforsports.co.uk www.gearforsportseurope.com
EUROPEAN TOUR

Rock Steady

ST ANDREWS, CARNOUSTIE AND KINGSBARNS, SCOTLAND

If a clue was needed to help answer the question: Who will win the inaugural Dunhill Links Championship, casting ones mind back a couple of years would have provided a strong hint. For when it comes to links golf and severe conditions, there is only one thing to do but send for the man from the Granite City.

Aberdeen is where Paul Lawrie was born and bred. The 32 year old won the Open Championship in 1999 at Carnoustie where the links played as tough as ever and the weather played its part, too. Fast forward two years on and, once again, the weather intervened – it was warm, yes, causing the haar to play havoc, but there was wind and torrential rain too. It is not that Lawrie particularly likes bad weather. "It just doesn't bother me," he said. "I grew up with this."

To win the huge new trophy, Lawrie negotiated the Old Course, Carnoustie and Kingsbarns, and then returned to St Andrews and the Old Course again. The tournament was required to go to the Monday because of the inclement weather which caused several suspensions to play during the week.

Shot of the Week

"Just call me Costantino," Paul Lawrie said. Needing a birdie at the last to beat Ernie Els, Lawrie saw his sand wedge approach from 81 yards spin back off the front of the green into the historic Valley of Sin. It was from there that Costantino Rocca holed a putt to tie with John Daly at the 1995 Open Championship before losing the play-off. Lawrie needed to two putt to force a play-off but saw his putt, from around 40 feet, dive into the hole. "I wasn't thinking about Rocca at all, just trying to make sure I got into the play-off and then it went in," he said.

That Lawrie's victory was sealed with a moment of pure theatre - he holed a monster putt from the Valley of Sin on the 18th to beat Ernie Els by one stroke - was in keeping with a week in which many of the celebrities invited to play in the Pro-Am style tournament were actors. Also in keeping with the week was the reaction of Els after Lawrie sunk his improbable putt: the South African laughed before leaving the recorder's hut then engulfed the Scot in a huge bear hug.

The real heroes of the week were the Rules Officials, greenkeepers and staging crews who managed to get 312 players - 156 professionals each with an amateur partner - on and off the three courses and to their next scheduled tee times. Throughout the tournament there was no denying the camaraderie engendered between the professionals and their amateur partners.

Els had a week to remember playing alongside his father, Neels, while Lawrie was partnered by one of his main sponsors, Martin Gilbert, which proved a relaxing influence for the Scot. Sam Torrance, The Ryder Cup Captain, played with Hugh Grant, the star of many films including Four Weddings and a Funeral, and Notting Hill. They would have made the 20 team cut for the final round but for a bogey at the last at Carnoustie.

The 15 handicap Grant said: "I have never done any acting, either on screen or on stage, that has been as unbelievably frightening as having to tee it up in front of watching spectators and TV cameras. It doesn't come close. Sam was a saint, incredibly supportive. He told me the line, what club to take and a few dirty jokes. It's been a lot of fun. I hope I can be a part of this again."

Johann Rupert, head of the Championship Committee, said that some of the handicapping had been necessarily arbitrary but that "records will be kept for the future." It took some superb golf to win the team event and it was provided by Brett Rumford and his amateur partner, three handicapper Chris Peacock, who birdied the 15th and 16th at St Andrews, a course he has played many times. Being a sergeant air traffic controller at nearby RAF Leuchars and a member of the RAF golf squad, he is even more local than Lawrie and grew up playing all the courses at the Home of Golf.

Ernie Els and father Neels

Darren Clarke and Michael Douglas

Nasser Hussain

Two of the most spectacular rounds of the week were provided by Els and Lawrie. On the first day, Els scored 65 at Carnoustie. He birdied six holes in a row from the turn but his golf on the front nine into the wind was possibly of an even higher quality. Els shared the lead with Brian Davis and the young South African Omar Sandys, who had all the fun of coming up with the round of his career at St Andrews. On Friday Paul McGinley put the finishing touches to a first round of 67 at Kingsbarns before handing in a 64 at St Andrews on the way to a two shot halfway lead ahead of Tony Johnstone and Davis. Lawrie moved alongside McGinley at the head of affairs following round three; Lawrie's 63 at the Old Course being spread over Saturday and Sunday and included a remarkable number of long putts. Els was one shot behind and one ahead of David Howell.

Lawrie went to the turn in 32 in the final round but Els remained a stroke behind until he failed to escape from the Road Hole Bunker on the 17th at the first attempt. He made a bogey five and then rolled in a 20 footer for a birdie at the last just as Lawrie three putted the 17th, setting up the remarkable denouement with the Scot judging the line of the putt out of the Valley of Sin to perfection.

"I had a few chances after the Open Championship to win again," Lawrie said. "But it's so hard to do it. Every player is a good player now. I was not cracking up over not winning, but I wanted to win desperately and maybe I was trying too hard. When you win the Open Championship you can't help but expect to win more tournaments. The Home of Golf is a great place to win, and this is a special victory for me."

Andy Farrell

The Champions ... Pro-Am winners Brett Rumford (centre) and Amateur Chris Peacock (left) with Paul Lawrie

DUNHILL LINKS CHAMPIONSHIP PRO-AM TOP 12

Pos.	Name	Country	Rd1	Rd2	Rd3	Rd4	Total	Par	Prize Money	
									Euro	£ Eqv
1	Brett RUMFORD/Chris PEACOCK	Aus	64	63	62	62	251	-37	55078.18	34440.01
2	Brian DAVIS/Jeremy LAMBOURNE	Eng	61	63	67	61	252	-36	27539.09	17220.00
	Lucas PARSONS/Michael WANG	Aus	64	59	66	63	252	-36	27539.09	17220.00
4	Jamie DONALDSON/Nasser HUSSAIN	Wal	64	61	67	62	254	-34	16523.45	10332.00
5	Wayne SMITH/Mark PRICE	Aus	62	65	65	63	255	-33	11015.64	6888.00
6	Padraig HARRINGTON/Dermot DESMOND	Ire	62	61	70	63	256	-32	5507.82	3444.00
	Ernie ELS/Neels ELS	SA	65	63	63	65	256	-32	5507.82	3444.00
8	David HOWELL/Trevor EVE	Eng	66	64	65	62	257	-31	5507.82	3444.00
	John BICKERTON/Alistair CURRIE	Eng	62	63	66	66	257	-31	5507.82	3444.00
	David DIXON/Steven POSFORD	Eng	64	65	65	63	257	-31	5507.82	3444.00
11	Steve ELKINGTON/Clay WALKER	Aus	59	67	65	67	258	-30	5507.82	3444.00
	Emanuele CANONICA/John ROBINSON	It	63	66	66	63	258	-30	5507.82	3444.00

Sam Torrance and Hugh Grant

Lee Westwood and Samuel L. Jackson

David Howell and caddie Jason Hempleman

The Course

The Old Course was its old familiar self, while at Carnoustie the rough from the 1999 Open Championship had been cut back so the layout was playing as it always used to - tough but fair. Kingsbarns, at 7126 yards, was a newcomer to the professional circuit having opened less than 18 months earlier. The layout, perched above the sea six miles south of St Andrews, received spectacular reviews. Inspired by the Old Course, the fairways are generous and the greens large but precision is still a prerequisite for low scores.

DUNHILL LINKS CHAMPIONSHIP, 18 - 22 OCTOBER, 2001
ST ANDREWS, FIFE, SCOTLAND, PAR 72, 7115 YARDS, 6506 METRES
CARNOUSTIE, ANGUS, SCOTLAND, PAR 72, 7361 YARDS, 6732 METRES
KINGSBARNS, FIFE, SCOTLAND, PAR 72, 7126 YARDS, 6517 METRES

Pos.	Name		Rd1	Rd2	Rd3	Rd4	Total	Par	Prize Money Euro	£
1	Paul LAWRIE	Scot	71	68	63	68	270	-18	881250.90	551040.11
2	Ernie ELS	SA	65	70	68	68	271	-17	587496.90	367357.76
3	David HOWELL	Eng	67	68	69	68	272	-16	330997.80	206970.64
4	Jean HUGO	SA	68	70	69	66	273	-15	264375.30	165312.05
5	Padraig HARRINGTON	Ire	67	67	72	69	275	-13	175016.40	109436.55
	Colin MONTGOMERIE	Scot	71	68	69	67	275	-13	175016.40	109436.55
	Peter O'MALLEY	Aus	71	67	68	69	275	-13	175016.40	109436.55
	Paul CASEY	Eng	69	70	66	70	275	-13	175016.40	109436.55
9	Paul MCGINLEY	Ire	67	64	71	74	276	-12	103106.40	64471.72
	Mathias GRÖNBERG	Swe	68	70	71	67	276	-12	103106.40	64471.72
	Retief GOOSEN	SA	69	69	69	69	276	-12	103106.40	64471.72
	Jamie DONALDSON	Wal	68	66	74	68	276	-12	103106.40	64471.72
13	Brian DAVIS	Eng	65	68	72	72	277	-11	79576.95	49758.92
	Thomas BJÖRN	Den	70	67	71	69	277	-11	79576.95	49758.92
	Mark PILKINGTON	Wal	69	69	71	68	277	-11	79576.95	49758.92
	Brett RUMFORD	Aus	72	67	68	70	277	-11	79576.95	49758.92
17	Justin ROSE	Eng	69	68	74	67	278	-10	63978.81	40005.51
	Wayne SMITH	Aus	71	74	67	66	278	-10	63978.81	40005.51
	Emanuele CANONICA	It	66	74	69	69	278	-10	63978.81	40005.51
	David LYNN	Eng	71	69	69	69	278	-10	63978.81	40005.51
	Greg OWEN	Eng	70	67	72	69	278	-10	63978.81	40005.51
	Patrik SJÖLAND	Swe	71	66	72	69	278	-10	63978.81	40005.51
	Lucas PARSONS	Aus	72	68	69	69	278	-10	63978.81	40005.51
24	Darren CLARKE	N.Ire	72	67	70	70	279	-9	54990.05	34384.90
	John BICKERTON	Eng	69	70	69	71	279	-9	54990.05	34384.90
	David DIXON	Eng	69	70	72	68	279	-9	54990.05	34384.90
27	Jarrod MOSELEY	Aus	67	70	71	72	280	-8	51024.43	31905.22
	Ricardo GONZALEZ	Arg	67	70	72	71	280	-8	51024.43	31905.22
29	Eduardo ROMERO	Arg	70	71	72	68	281	-7	44679.42	27937.73
	Raphaël JACQUELIN	Fr	72	68	74	67	281	-7	44679.42	27937.73
	Miguel Angel JIMÉNEZ	Sp	70	70	69	72	281	-7	44679.42	27937.73
	James KINGSTON	SA	74	67	70	70	281	-7	44679.42	27937.73
	Daren LEE	Eng	68	70	71	72	281	-7	44679.42	27937.73
	David CARTER	Eng	71	73	69	68	281	-7	44679.42	27937.73
35	Anders FORSBRAND	Swe	71	64	76	71	282	-6	35955.04	22482.44
	Barry LANE	Eng	68	72	74	68	282	-6	35955.04	22482.44
	Robert KARLSSON	Swe	70	70	73	69	282	-6	35955.04	22482.44
	Ian GARBUTT	Eng	72	69	68	73	282	-6	35955.04	22482.44
	Ignacio GARRIDO	Sp	67	72	74	69	282	-6	35955.04	22482.44
	Henrik NYSTROM	Swe	70	66	74	72	282	-6	35955.04	22482.44
	Nick DOUGHERTY	Eng	68	68	73	73	282	-6	35955.04	22482.44
	Adam SCOTT	Aus	72	68	75	67	282	-6	35955.04	22482.44
43	Soren KJELDSEN	Den	68	72	71	73	284	-4	29081.28	18184.32
	Jonathan LOMAS	Eng	67	73	72	72	284	-4	29081.28	18184.32
	Graeme STORM	Eng	71	74	70	69	284	-4	29081.28	18184.32
	Brett QUIGLEY	USA	68	69	73	74	284	-4	29081.28	18184.32
	Scott GARDINER	Aus	72	67	75	70	284	-4	29081.28	18184.32
48	Tony JOHNSTONE	Zim	67	66	80	72	285	-3	24322.52	15208.70
	Gary ORR	Scot	75	67	71	72	285	-3	24322.52	15208.70
	Van PHILLIPS	Eng	75	68	69	73	285	-3	24322.52	15208.70
	Fredrik JACOBSON	Swe	73	66	75	71	285	-3	24322.52	15208.70
52	Maarten LAFEBER	Hol	71	74	70	71	286	-2	20092.52	12563.71
	Roger WESSELS	SA	72	69	73	72	286	-2	20092.52	12563.71
	Mikael LUNDBERG	Swe	74	68	72	72	286	-2	20092.52	12563.71
	Simon DYSON	Eng	70	72	71	73	286	-2	20092.52	12563.71
56	Jorge BERENDT	Arg	70	72	73	72	287	-1	16567.52	10359.56
	Peter LONARD	Aus	71	68	76	72	287	-1	16567.52	10359.56
	Markus BRIER	Aut	70	72	69	76	287	-1	16567.52	10359.56
59	Jean-Francois REMESY	Fr	72	74	69	73	288	0	15069.39	9422.79
	Omar SANDYS	SA	65	71	74	78	288	0	15069.39	9422.79
61	Steve WEBSTER	Eng	70	70	75	75	290	2	13747.51	8596.22
	David SMAIL	NZ	70	70	75	75	290	2	13747.51	8596.22
	Jamie SPENCE	Eng	69	74	72	75	290	2	13747.51	8596.22
64	Sam TORRANCE	Scot	69	70	76	76	291	3	12690.01	7934.98
65	Ian WOOSNAM	Wal	71	74	69	RETD	214	-2	11896.89	7439.04
	Arjun ATWAL	Ind	68	72	73	WD	213	-3	11896.89	7439.04
67	Santiago LUNA	Sp	72	72	72		216	0	8609.91	5383.72
	Mark MCNULTY	Zim	75	72	69		216	0	8609.91	5383.72
	Sven STRÜVER	Ger	71	71	74		216	0	8609.91	5383.72
	Anthony WALL	Eng	75	71	70		216	0	8609.91	5383.72
	Bradford VAUGHAN	SA	76	68	72		216	0	8609.91	5383.72
	Henrik STENSON	Swe	72	71	73		216	0	8609.91	5383.72
	Thomas LEVET	Fr	74	67	75		216	0	8609.91	5383.72
	Joakim HAEGGMAN	Swe	71	72	73		216	0	8609.91	5383.72
	Russell CLAYDON	Eng	71	74	71		216	0	8609.91	5383.72
	Phillip PRICE	Wal	71	69	76		216	0	8609.91	5383.72
	Pierre FULKE	Swe	71	66	79		216	0	8609.91	5383.72
	Des TERBLANCHE	SA	74	71	71		216	0	8609.91	5383.72
	Alastair FORSYTH	Scot	74	70	72		216	0	8609.91	5383.72
	Richard STERNE	SA	74	67	75		216	0	8609.91	5383.72

TELEFONICA OPEN DE MADRID

Iconic Status

CLUB DE CAMPO, MADRID, SPAIN

Ernie Els got it right, slap-bang on the button. "We're all very grateful out here," he said. "Woe betide us if the Goose ever finds out how good he is."

The Big Easy made his comment a few years ago when asked to assess his compatriot, Retief Goosen, bearer of the affectionate ornithological sobriquet. Ernie knew, and so did just about everybody else but the man himself, that Goosen was potentially a world-beater.

It took until 2001 for the quiet South African finally to concede that he might, indeed, be pretty handy at the game. Jos Vanstiphout, the Belgian mental coach with whom he had been working for a couple of years, knew that his persuasive words had helped his

Diego Borrego

friend and pupil-client to make a major breakthrough, literally, when he won the US Open Championship in June.

And now, at the end of a four day odyssey round the beautiful and testing acres of Club de Campo on the fringes of Spain's wondrous capital city, the good Retief had put the cap on a season of towering achievement by winning not only the Telefonica Open de Madrid but also the Volvo Order of Merit. Truly, at last, the Goose had laid the golden egg.

The Harry Vardon Trophy that was Goosen's reward for following in the footsteps of Colin Montgomerie and Lee Westwood by becoming The European Tour's top dog is not in itself an impressive piece of hardware. It is a smallish bronze statuette of the legendary Jerseyman who was a member of the fabled Great Triumvirate, along with James Braid and J H Taylor, who dominated golf in the latter years of the 19th Century and the first decade or so of the 20th.

Its iconic status, however, is right up there with the Ashes Urn and, in the game we all love, the Old Claret Jug and The Ryder Cup. And Goosen had won it in the Spanish sunshine on the cusp of November.

It is a truism that no prize is worth winning if it is not hard-won and, even at this late moment on The 2001 European Tour International Schedule, Goosen had to fight every

Steve Webster

inch of the way before he was accorded the acclaim he deserved. The obstacle in his path came in the form of a small, chirpy West Midlander who just would not go away. Even in defeat, this was Steve Webster's finest hour.

It took three holes of agonisingly increasing extra-time tension to settle it. When Goosen finally struck the winning stroke, an eight foot birdie putt on the par three 17th, it was the culmination of a struggle that had never been less than absorbing and one that, at times, had caused the gaze to be averted for fear of breaking the spell.

After he had tied with Goosen on 264, 20 under par, Webster went into sudden-death with nothing in his favour. He had finished second a couple of times in a six year career on The European Tour, but it was his first play-off, while it was Goosen's fourth, two of which he had won. It wouldn't have escaped Webster's attention, either, that Goosen's last experience of extra holes — in that case, 18 of them — had brought him victory over Mark Brooks in the US Open Championship only a few months before.

But still the little Englishman did not capitulate. Indeed, he could and, perhaps, should have finished it all off on the first hole. He was five feet away in two, 15 feet inside his illustrious opponent. Advantage, at that moment, to Webster.

Henrik Nyström

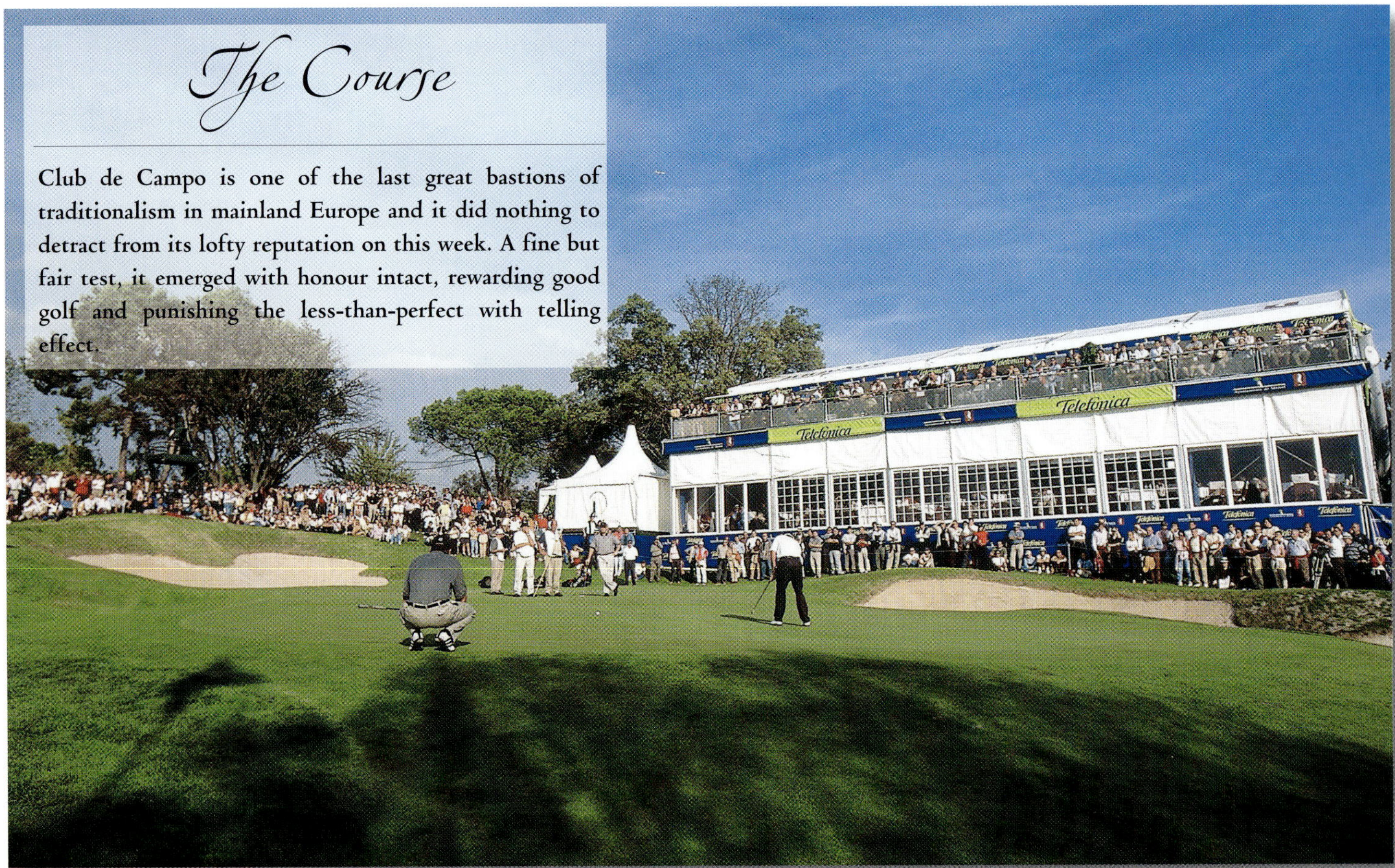

The Course

Club de Campo is one of the last great bastions of traditionalism in mainland Europe and it did nothing to detract from its lofty reputation on this week. A fine but fair test, it emerged with honour intact, rewarding good golf and punishing the less-than-perfect with telling effect.

Shot of the Week

Retief Goosen was under fire as he played the ninth hole of the last round and he was in trouble. He had missed the green to the right and, with a pin positioned tight on the right side, was faced with a tricky shot. However, with no green to work with, he fashioned a lovely little chip that hit the putting surface at precisely the right spot, from where it rolled gently into the hole for an unlikely birdie. It did not win the tournament for him, but it certainly made sure he did not lose it.

Paul Casey

Was it nerves that caused him to miss it? Or was it just a simple misread? On a practice green, he would hole a putt such as this with contemptuous ease. When there was 233,330 euro (£145,904) and a maiden victory riding on it, the apparently simple suddenly became hellishly difficult.

Playing the home hole for the second time, they halved it in par fours, Goosen again leaving his first putt short. Then they moved on to the 167 yards par three 17th which forced a change of strategy and tactics on the part of the protagonists. Now it had to be something other than two iron, wedge, putt for birdie.

It was to be the pivotal moment of the play-off, the tournament, the entire season. It was also, ultimately, what finally separated the man from the boy. Webster left his tee shot short and on the fringe, 18 feet from the hole. Goosen was ten feet closer. Webster missed, Goosen did not.

It was all over, Goosen crowned with many crowns, the Victor Ludorum. It was quite a moment. And he did it in the grandest style possible, too, with a birdie. Who could possibly ask for more?

Mel Webb

Darren Clarke

CLUB DE CAMPO, MADRID, SPAIN, 25-28 OCTOBER 2001, PAR 71, 6957 YARDS, 6362 METRES

Pos.	Name		Rd1	Rd2	Rd3	Rd4	Total	Par	Prize Money Euro	£
1	Retief GOOSEN	SA	66	64	66	68	264	-20	233330.00	145904.20
2	Steve WEBSTER	Eng	68	62	68	66	264	-20	155550.00	97267.38
3	Brian DAVIS	Eng	66	64	73	62	265	-19	78820.00	49287.14
	Diego BORREGO	Sp	69	65	64	67	265	-19	78820.00	49287.14
5	Markus BRIER	Aut	67	68	66	66	267	-17	59360.00	37118.56
6	Jeev Milkha SINGH	Ind	72	67	65	64	268	-16	39340.00	24599.80
	Anders HANSEN	Den	68	69	65	66	268	-16	39340.00	24599.80
	Darren CLARKE	N.Ire	67	69	65	67	268	-16	39340.00	24599.80
	Robert COLES	Eng	66	69	69	64	268	-16	39340.00	24599.80
10	Thomas BJÖRN	Den	68	71	66	64	269	-15	26880.00	16808.40
	Angel CABRERA	Arg	68	69	65	67	269	-15	26880.00	16808.40
12	Richard GREEN	Aus	69	67	65	69	270	-14	22155.00	13853.80
	Van PHILLIPS	Eng	68	67	69	66	270	-14	22155.00	13853.80
	David LYNN	Eng	68	66	68	68	270	-14	22155.00	13853.80
	John BICKERTON	Eng	69	67	68	66	270	-14	22155.00	13853.80
16	José Maria OLAZÁBAL	Sp	69	67	68	67	271	-13	18172.00	11363.18
	Carlos RODILES	Sp	65	70	67	69	271	-13	18172.00	11363.18
	Gary EMERSON	Eng	70	68	68	65	271	-13	18172.00	11363.18
	Phillip PRICE	Wal	66	69	67	69	271	-13	18172.00	11363.18
	Greg OWEN	Eng	67	70	66	68	271	-13	18172.00	11363.18
21	Barry LANE	Eng	66	72	66	68	272	-12	15610.00	9761.13
	Richard S JOHNSON	Swe	73	65	67	67	272	-12	15610.00	9761.13
	Ignacio GARRIDO	Sp	70	67	71	64	272	-12	15610.00	9761.13
	Bradley DREDGE	Wal	70	68	65	69	272	-12	15610.00	9761.13
25	Padraig HARRINGTON	Ire	63	72	69	69	273	-11	13510.00	8447.97
	José Manuel CARRILES	Sp	72	68	69	64	273	-11	13510.00	8447.97
	Fredrik ANDERSSON	Swe	69	65	71	68	273	-11	13510.00	8447.97
	Henrik NYSTROM	Swe	67	67	72	67	273	-11	13510.00	8447.97
	Stephen GALLACHER	Scot	64	70	70	69	273	-11	13510.00	8447.97
	David HIGGINS	Ire	67	62	69	75	273	-11	13510.00	8447.97
31	Des SMYTH	Ire	65	73	67	69	274	-10	11410.00	7134.82
	Miguel Angel JIMÉNEZ	Sp	65	67	70	72	274	-10	11410.00	7134.82
	Ian GARBUTT	Eng	69	71	70	64	274	-10	11410.00	7134.82
	Alastair FORSYTH	Scot	69	67	71	67	274	-10	11410.00	7134.82
35	Eduardo ROMERO	Arg	70	67	72	66	275	-9	10080.00	6303.15
	Maarten LAFEBER	Hol	71	69	68	67	275	-9	10080.00	6303.15
	Roger WINCHESTER	Eng	71	65	72	67	275	-9	10080.00	6303.15
	Carl PETTERSSON	Swe	70	70	67	68	275	-9	10080.00	6303.15
39	Santiago LUNA	Sp	72	68	67	69	276	-8	8540.00	5340.17
	David HOWELL	Eng	70	69	65	72	276	-8	8540.00	5340.17
	Mark MCNULTY	Zim	70	69	69	68	276	-8	8540.00	5340.17
	Peter MITCHELL	Eng	70	69	68	69	276	-8	8540.00	5340.17
	Johan RYSTRÖM	Swe	67	67	71	71	276	-8	8540.00	5340.17
	Emanuele CANONICA	It	70	70	67	69	276	-8	8540.00	5340.17
	Brett RUMFORD	Aus	71	69	66	70	276	-8	8540.00	5340.17
46	Henrik BJORNSTAD	Nor	70	69	72	66	277	-7	7140.00	4464.73
	Thomas GÖGELE	Ger	68	68	73	68	277	-7	7140.00	4464.73
	Stephen DODD	Wal	71	65	72	69	277	-7	7140.00	4464.73
49	Wayne RILEY	Aus	71	67	66	74	278	-6	5740.00	3589.29
	Mark ROE	Eng	67	70	70	71	278	-6	5740.00	3589.29
	Darren FICHARDT	SA	72	68	66	72	278	-6	5740.00	3589.29
	Paul BROADHURST	Eng	72	68	69	69	278	-6	5740.00	3589.29
	Gary ORR	Scot	70	68	68	72	278	-6	5740.00	3589.29
	Matthew BLACKEY	Eng	72	67	72	67	278	-6	5740.00	3589.29
	Nick DOUGHERTY	Eng	71	67	71	69	278	-6	5740.00	3589.29
56	Andrew MARSHALL	Eng	66	68	77	68	279	-5	4620.00	2888.94
57	Juan QUIROS	Sp	70	70	70	70	280	-4	3850.00	2407.45
	Alvaro SALTO	Sp	69	68	73	70	280	-4	3850.00	2407.45
	Marc FARRY	Fr	67	71	71	71	280	-4	3850.00	2407.45
	Henrik STENSON	Swe	71	68	70	71	280	-4	3850.00	2407.45
	Olle KARLSSON	Swe	71	69	70	70	280	-4	3850.00	2407.45
	Rolf MUNTZ	Hol	71	69	72	68	280	-4	3850.00	2407.45
	David PARK	Wal	68	69	74	69	280	-4	3850.00	2407.45
	Paul CASEY	Eng	69	70	72	69	280	-4	3850.00	2407.45
65	Jean-Francois REMESY	Fr	70	68	73	70	281	-3	2940.00	1838.42
	Søren HANSEN	Den	69	69	72	71	281	-3	2940.00	1838.42
	Michele REALE	It	68	70	72	71	281	-3	2940.00	1838.42
	Fernando ROCA	Sp	67	68	76	70	281	-3	2940.00	1838.42
	Graeme STORM	Eng	66	72	73	70	281	-3	2940.00	1838.42
70	Lucas PARSONS	Aus	69	70	70	73	282	-2	2560.00	1600.80
71	Mark PILKINGTON	Wal	70	69	74	72	285	1	2100.00	1313.16
72	Mark JAMES	Eng	69	71	72	80	292	8	2097.00	1311.28

Historic Achievement

IS MOLAS GOLF CLUB, SARDINIA, ITALY

Vive La France! The venue may have been Is Molas on the sunkissed island of Sardinia but at the end of the Atlanet Italian Open it was the French who were celebrating.

While Gregory Havret captured his maiden European Tour title, his compatriot Christian Cévaër also had cause to rejoice as he retained his European Tour card by finishing 115th in the Volvo Order of Merit, taking his season's earnings past the £100,000 mark. It was an historic achievement as for the first time all the leading 115 players won six figure sums, reflecting the growing strength of The European Tour.

At the start of the year few believed that £100,000 could be the target but as 2001 neared its conclusion that milestone became a very real possibility. From the outset, the air was filled with tension as players wrestled with their hopes and fears about securing their

Mark Roe

Shot of the Week

There were two holes in one at Is Molas, both on the 14th, by Raymond Russell and Ian Poulter but the shot of the week goes to Mark Roe's bunker effort at the 15th in the final round which finished just four feet from the hole to set up a birdie four. It was his fifth birdie of the day and helped him to a share of third place, good enough to lift him into the top 115 in the Volvo Order of Merit to secure his European Tour card for 2002.

European Tour card. For many the Atlanet Italian Open was the last event of 2001 and the race to finish in the top 115 in the Volvo Order of Merit was coming right down to the wire. Throughout the week the mathematicians were working overtime to calculate who needed to do what to retain their playing privileges for another year.

Some spectators may have mistaken Havret as one of those mathematicians as his glasses gave him a studious look as he strolled around the clubhouse. But once on the course it became clear that here was a man whose skills lay on the fairways.

Seven years earlier Havret made his debut for the French Amateur team. The venue for that match was Is Molas and the former French Amateur champion was inspired by his return to the course where he first achieved national acclaim, opening with a seven under par 65 and then moving into the halfway lead with a second round of 66. It was the first time the 24 year old had led a European Tour event and he was relishing the experience.

Sven Strüver edged ahead of Havret after a third round 64, but the Frenchman was in his slipstream after a 68 left him one shot off the lead. The German dropped off the pace early on the final day and Bradley Dredge took up the challenge with an eagle and a birdie in the first three holes but a double bogey on the fifth halted him in his tracks. Havret was in front, and three birdies over the back nine completed a round of 69, his fourth successive round in the 60s, for a winning 20 under par total of 268, one stroke clear of Welshman Dredge.

His victory was the first by a Frenchman in the Atlanet Italian Open since The European Tour started in 1972 and for the first time there were two victories by Frenchmen in a season, Havret following Thomas Levet's triumph in the Victor Chandler British Masters. Indeed he was only the fifth French champion on The European Tour after Marc Farry, Jean-Francois Remesy, Jean Van de Velde and Levet.

As the dust settled it became clear he was not the only Frenchman celebrating. Cévaër may have been relatively anonymous in his final position of joint 38th but he had done what he set out to do. At the start of the week he was in 115th position in the Volvo Order of Merit, and the chasing pack were closing in on him. A few weeks earlier people had been congratulating him on retaining his card but as the season neared its end, Cévaër gradually started to slip down the list until his position became the most precarious and sought after of all.

Opening rounds of 69 and 66 provided a solid base but then the pressure started to mount. His last two rounds of 71 and 73 were understandably tense but ultimately good enough. His cheque of 6,400 euro (£3,979) took his season's earnings past the £100,000 milestone and most importantly he remained in 115th position.

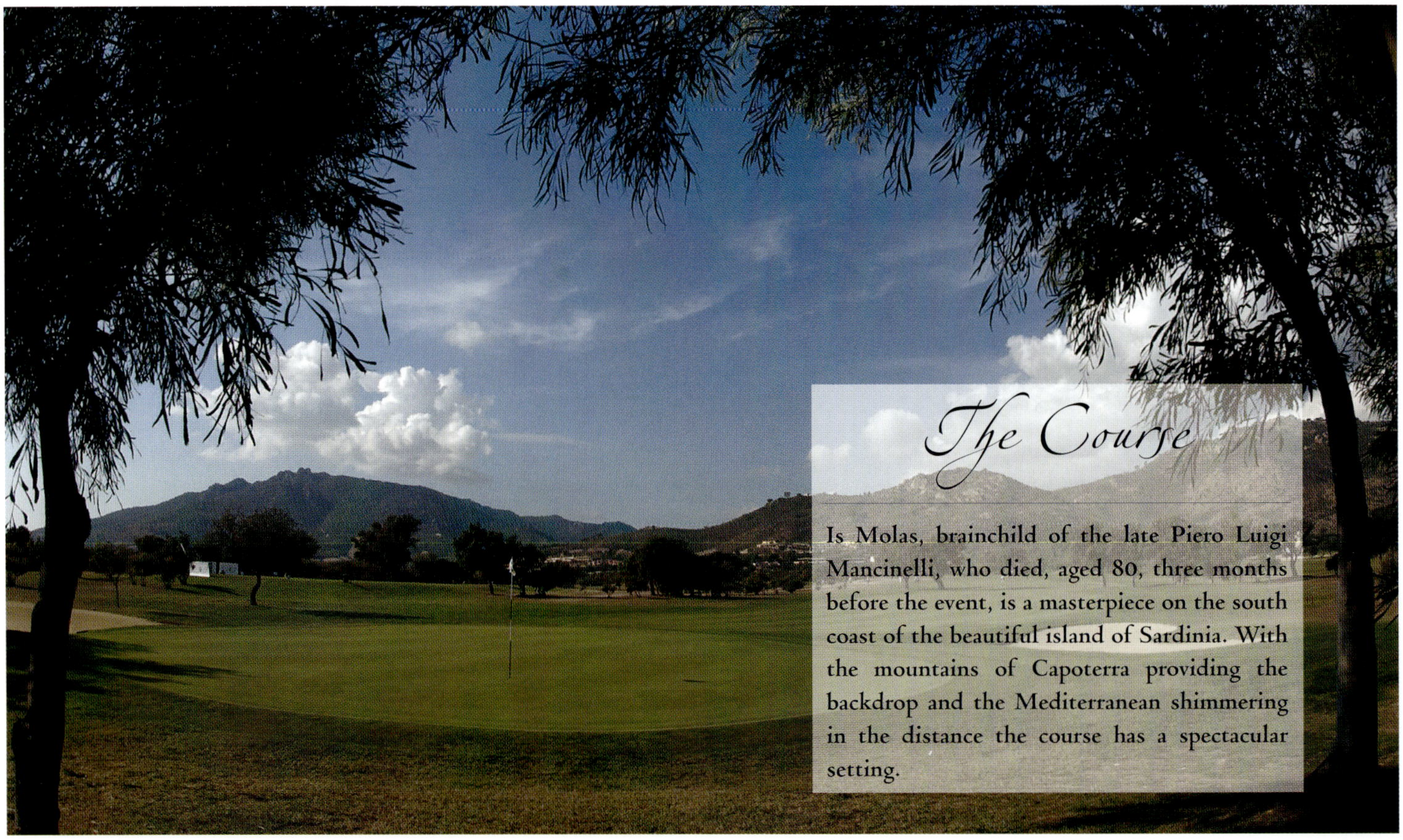

The Course

Is Molas, brainchild of the late Piero Luigi Mancinelli, who died, aged 80, three months before the event, is a masterpiece on the south coast of the beautiful island of Sardinia. With the mountains of Capoterra providing the backdrop and the Mediterranean shimmering in the distance the course has a spectacular setting.

Raymond Russell

There was also joy for Mark Roe, whose 17 year run on The European Tour was in danger of coming to an end as he lay in 131st position entering the tournament. But Roe is a proud man and at the end of a frustrating season he was determined to accentuate the positive. An opening 63, equalling his lowest round in 17 years on Tour, sent pulses racing. When he followed that with rounds of 69 and 73 his chances of climbing into the top 115 looked slim but still possible. He needed a good final round and produced one, a closing 66 earning him a share of third place and lifting him to 111th in the Volvo Order of Merit. His run on The European Tour was extended to an 18th season.

While Roe celebrated, for Shaun Webster it was a case of so near and yet so far. Webster thought it was almost a lost cause to keep his card at the start of the week but suddenly rounds of 70-67 and 66 put him in with a fighting chance. He had to finish first or second to avoid the trip to The European Tour Qualifying School Finals but came up just short, the share of third place not quite enough.

Roe and Webster tied third with Diego Borrego and the defending champion, Ian Poulter, who made a valiant defence of his title with a late charge, holing in one at the 14th on the final day. Havret, however, was home and dry. Vive La France!

Roddy Williams

Bradley Dredge

IS MOLAS GOLF CLUB, SARDINIA, ITALY, 1-4 NOVEMBER, 2001, PAR 72, 7013 YARDS, 6413 METRES

Pos.	Name		Rd1	Rd2	Rd3	Rd4	Total	Par	Prize Money Euro	Prize Money £
1	Gregory HAVRET	Fr	65	66	68	69	268	-20	166660.00	103622.37
2	Bradley DREDGE	Wal	69	66	65	69	269	-19	111110.00	69083.65
3	Mark ROE	Eng	63	69	73	66	271	-17	47500.00	29533.56
	Shaun P WEBSTER	Eng	70	67	66	68	271	-17	47500.00	29533.56
	Ian POULTER	Eng	67	69	68	67	271	-17	47500.00	29533.56
	Diego BORREGO	Sp	70	66	65	70	271	-17	47500.00	29533.56
7	Steve WEBSTER	Eng	68	67	68	69	272	-16	27500.00	17098.37
	Henrik STENSON	Swe	67	70	68	67	272	-16	27500.00	17098.37
9	David HOWELL	Eng	71	66	68	68	273	-15	18820.00	11701.51
	Trevor IMMELMAN	SA	70	67	65	71	273	-15	18820.00	11701.51
	Michele REALE	It	63	73	68	69	273	-15	18820.00	11701.51
	Markus BRIER	Aut	70	66	70	67	273	-15	18820.00	11701.51
	Fredrik ANDERSSON	Swe	65	72	67	69	273	-15	18820.00	11701.51
14	Sven STRÜVER	Ger	66	68	64	76	274	-14	14700.00	9139.86
	Stephen DODD	Wal	70	68	68	68	274	-14	14700.00	9139.86
	Mikko ILONEN	Fin	68	71	66	69	274	-14	14700.00	9139.86
17	Warren BENNETT	Eng	70	71	68	66	275	-13	12283.33	7637.27
	Silvio GRAPPASONNI	It	70	65	69	71	275	-13	12283.33	7637.27
	Richard GREEN	Aus	72	69	66	68	275	-13	12283.33	7637.27
	Anthony WALL	Eng	66	71	72	66	275	-13	12283.33	7637.27
	Jean VAN DE VELDE	Fr	67	65	74	69	275	-13	12283.33	7637.27
	Jonathan LOMAS	Eng	68	72	70	65	275	-13	12283.33	7637.27
23	Santiago LUNA	Sp	69	70	68	69	276	-12	10250.00	6373.03
	Jeremy ROBINSON	Eng	70	68	70	68	276	-12	10250.00	6373.03
	Carl SUNESON	Sp	73	68	69	66	276	-12	10250.00	6373.03
	Nicolas VANHOOTEGEM	Bel	70	69	68	69	276	-12	10250.00	6373.03
	Robert COLES	Eng	72	68	69	67	276	-12	10250.00	6373.03
	Raymond RUSSELL	Scot	66	70	70	70	276	-12	10250.00	6373.03
29	Johan RYSTRÖM	Swe	66	70	71	70	277	-11	8900.00	5533.66
	Gary EVANS	Eng	70	70	66	71	277	-11	8900.00	5533.66
	Patrik SJÖLAND	Swe	69	71	66	71	277	-11	8900.00	5533.66
32	Ronan RAFFERTY	N.Ire	68	69	69	72	278	-10	7650.00	4756.46
	Eduardo ROMERO	Arg	66	70	75	67	278	-10	7650.00	4756.46
	Richard S JOHNSON	Swe	70	70	70	68	278	-10	7650.00	4756.46
	Marcello SANTI	It	68	74	69	67	278	-10	7650.00	4756.46
	Massimo SCARPA	It	70	69	64	75	278	-10	7650.00	4756.46
	Stephen GALLACHER	Scot	67	71	69	71	278	-10	7650.00	4756.46
38	Roger CHAPMAN	Eng	67	69	72	71	279	-9	6400.00	3979.26
	Peter HANSON	Swe	71	66	70	72	279	-9	6400.00	3979.26
	Robin BYRD	USA	68	72	68	71	279	-9	6400.00	3979.26
	Olle KARLSSON	Swe	72	70	66	71	279	-9	6400.00	3979.26
	Christian CÉVAËR	Fr	69	66	71	73	279	-9	6400.00	3979.26
	Lucas PARSONS	Aus	68	71	68	72	279	-9	6400.00	3979.26
44	Stefano SOFFIETTI	It	68	73	68	71	280	-8	5300.00	3295.32
	Henrik BJORNSTAD	Nor	71	68	70	71	280	-8	5300.00	3295.32
	Steven RICHARDSON	Eng	67	73	72	68	280	-8	5300.00	3295.32
	Tony EDLUND	Swe	69	73	70	68	280	-8	5300.00	3295.32
	Peter LONARD	Aus	69	70	69	72	280	-8	5300.00	3295.32
49	Alastair FORSYTH	Scot	70	70	71	70	281	-7	4700.00	2922.27
50	Malcolm MACKENZIE	Eng	70	70	73	69	282	-6	4000.00	2487.04
	Mark MOULAND	Wal	70	71	70	71	282	-6	4000.00	2487.04
	Elliot BOULT	NZ	71	70	74	67	282	-6	4000.00	2487.04
	Roger WINCHESTER	Eng	73	68	70	71	282	-6	4000.00	2487.04
	Angel CABRERA	Arg	72	68	67	75	282	-6	4000.00	2487.04
	Mark PILKINGTON	Wal	69	69	72	72	282	-6	4000.00	2487.04
56	Alessandro TADINI	It	71	69	69	74	283	-5	2966.67	1844.55
	Paul BROADHURST	Eng	70	72	71	70	283	-5	2966.67	1844.55
	Emanuele CANONICA	It	71	70	71	71	283	-5	2966.67	1844.55
	David PARK	Wal	72	67	73	71	283	-5	2966.67	1844.55
	Gianluca PIETROBONO	It	67	70	74	72	283	-5	2966.67	1844.55
	Daren LEE	Eng	72	69	72	70	283	-5	2966.67	1844.55
62	Dennis EDLUND	Swe	70	71	74	69	284	-4	2500.00	1554.40
	Simon HURD	Eng	73	69	72	70	284	-4	2500.00	1554.40
	Luca BERNARDINI	It	70	72	70	72	284	-4	2500.00	1554.40
65	Neil CHEETHAM	Eng	70	70	72	73	285	-3	2250.00	1398.96
	Eduardo DE LA RIVA	Sp	72	68	75	70	285	-3	2250.00	1398.96
67	Paolo TERRENI	It	73	69	71	73	286	-2	1957.50	1217.09
	Stefano REALE	It	71	70	73	72	286	-2	1957.50	1217.09
	Thomas GÖGELE	Ger	70	71	74	71	286	-2	1957.50	1217.09
	Nic HENNING	SA	74	68	70	74	286	-2	1957.50	1217.09
71	Andrea ROMANO (AM)	It	69	71	79	70	289	1		
72	Paul EALES	Eng	73	69	74	75	291	3	1500.00	932.64
	Michele RIGONE (AM)	It	75	67	76	73	291	3		

No Question

MONTECASTILLO HOTEL AND GOLF RESORT, JEREZ, SPAIN

All season long Padraig Harrington had been asking questions of himself. Searching ones. Brutal ones.

He knew he had improved as a golfer. His Volvo Order of Merit and World Ranking positions and his consistency were simple proof of that. But after seven runners-up finishes during the year, what he really wanted to know was whether he was ever going to win again.

Harrington was hoping for a quick answer after losing the Cisco World Match Play Championship final from three up with 12 to play. He was disgusted with himself for that, and was not afraid to say so.

Paul McGinley

The chance to find out came at the Volvo Masters Andalucia at Montecastillo Hotel and Golf Resort, cut to 54 holes because of the high winds that halted play both on Friday and Saturday.

With three holes to play Harrington was in a four way tie for the lead with fellow Irishmen Darren Clarke and Paul McGinley and Australian Adam Scott, who had set the clubhouse target at ten under par with a superb 65. Harrington and McGinley were both on the green at the long 16th in two and two putted for birdies, but Clarke went in the water there and with a bogey six fell out of the race for the 539,074 euro (£333,330) first prize.

So it was down to the two players who had known each other since their schooldays in Dublin, had shared World Cup glory at Kiawah Island in 1997, and who were about to be partners again the following week in Japan. Par fours at the 17th meant the moment of truth came on the final hole, the perfect setting for Harrington to get his answer.

When he stood over a 25 foot putt he was so focused that he had no idea it was for a round of 66 and a 12 under par total of 204. What he did know was that if it went in he would be banishing a lot of the demons which had been preying on him ever since he lost a play-off to Vijay Singh in Malaysia back in February.

Thomas Björn

Adam Scott

Robert Karlsson

Imagine the joy therefore when the putt, travelling at speed, found the target and disappeared. And imagine the celebrations once McGinley, playing in the final group, was unable to find the matching birdie three he needed to force a play-off.

Harrington need question himself no more. He moved to second in the 2001 Volvo Order of Merit standings - one runners-up finish which brought no recriminations. He was in the World's top ten for the first time, and he had the lowest Stroke Average (69.23) of anybody on Tour in the Reuters Performance Data.

In short, a week and a year to remember.

There had been no hint of the weather problems to come for the 3,234,470 euro (£2,000,000) championship when it began in calm, sunny conditions. And nobody enjoyed them more than the 2000 Sir Henry Cotton Rookie of the Year, Ian Poulter. The 25 year old launched his bid for the prestigious title with a 64. The round equalled the lowest of his Tour career and was only one off the course record.

Niclas Fasth

Seniors Tour Guide 2002

The tenth anniversary season on the European Seniors Tour was one of record prize money, increased tournaments and outstanding achievements, and the full story is detailed in the 2002 European Seniors Tour Guide.

In a vintage year, Ian Stanley captured the most prestigious prize when he won The Senior British Open, presented by MasterCard, at Royal County Down, beating a field graced by the presence of golf's "Big Three" – Jack Nicklaus, Arnold Palmer and Gary Player - and the 2002 European Seniors Tour Guide tells it all.

Denis Durnian also enjoyed a year to remember, claiming his maiden European Seniors Tour title in style in The Wales Seniors Open, a performance for which he was rewarded with the largest single first prize in European Seniors Tour history. It moved the Englishman to the top of the Order of Merit in the early part of the season, but find out how the entire race to be Europe's Number One senior golfer unfolded as the Seniors Tour travelled from Barbados to Berlin, Sweden to Spain.

Renowned for the friendly yet intensely competitive nature of tournaments, The European Seniors Tour is now enjoyed by increasing galleries and wider TV audiences worldwide. The facts and figures behind the winning of every tournament throughout the season can be found in the 2002 European Seniors Tour Guide plus biographies, statistics, records and notable achievements. It is a must for all students of the game.

Ordering a copy of the 2002 European Seniors Tour Guide is simple: send a cheque for £12.50 UK and Europe (which includes postage and packaging) or £17.50 for Overseas (which includes postage and packaging), made payable to the PGA European Tour to Emily Doughty, Communications Division, The European Tour, Wentworth Drive, Virginia Water, Surrey GU25 4LX or call +44 1344 840442 with credit card details.

Shot of the Week

How could it be anything other than the 25 foot birdie putt on the last with which Padraig Harrington ended his run of second places. Every putt to win has to be special, but it was not difficult to imagine the joy Harrington felt when he grabbed his third birdie in the last four holes for a 66.

Thomas Levet

Peter O'Malley

VOLVO
for life
JOIN THE ADVENTURE
VOLVO OCEAN RACE PORT STOPOVERS: START SOUTHAMPTON 23/09/2001; CAPE TOWN ETA 23/10/2001, DEPART 11/11/2001; SYDNEY ETA 04/12/2001, DEPART (VIA HOBART) 26/12/2001; AUCKLAND ETA 03/01/2002, DEPART 27/01/2002; RIO DE JANEIRO ETA 19/02/2002, DEPART 09/03/2002; MIAMI ETA 27/03/2002, DEPART 14/04/2002; BALTIMORE ETA 17/04/2002, DEPART ANNAPOLIS 28/04/2002; LA ROCHELLE ETA 11/05/2002, DEPART 25/05/2002; GÖTEBORG ETA 31/05/2002, DEPART 08/06/2002; FINISH KIEL 09/06/2002.
THE VOLVO OCEAN RACE
The 2001-2002 Round The World Volvo Ocean Race is the world's premier sailing competition. It crosses four oceans and stops at ten ports on five continents. Climb aboard and follow the drama live every day on www.VolvoOceanRace.org

Over in north-east Spain, at Pals to be precise, older brother Danny was trying to earn a place in The European Tour Qualifying School. But the Friday was to bring disappointment for both of them. The high winds had kicked up in both places by now, the afternoon gusts reaching 45mph in Jerez. Danny missed out by one and Ian got on a downward slide that he was powerless to halt. Conditions became so bad that the 20 first round leaders were called in on the back nine, but Poulter had fallen back to four under by then and on the resumption the next day, with the flags still bent over, he fell out of contention.

Mathias Grönberg and Clarke scored 67 and 68 respectively on Friday before the weather deteriorated, and McGinley came back on Saturday morning to complete his second round. With a 69 he took the lead on nine under par 135 - two ahead of Grönberg and three in front of Clarke and Harrington, who returned a 71.

The high winds meant that no more play was possible on Saturday, but that took nothing away from the third round which on Sunday became a wonderful finale to the 2001 European Tour season.

Peter Lonard

David Howell

Miguel Angel Jiménez

The Course

The Jack Nicklaus-designed Montecastillo Hotel and Golf Resort, which lies just outside the sherry-producing city of Jerez de la Frontera in south-west Spain, has hosted five Volvo Masters since making its European Tour debut with the 1994 Turespaña Masters Open de Andalucia won by Carl Mason.
At 7069 yards, the par 72 lay-out on hilly terrain builds to an exciting finish with water on the last three holes and the challenge is not just tee-to-green, but on the putting surfaces as well. Padraig Harrington and Paul McGinley both described them as the fastest encountered on the circuit throughout 2001.

That Harrington rose to the occasion, and took himself to another level in the game, was a tribute to his ability to remain composed and focused despite being challenged by an array of talent. Scott completed his wonderful 65, while Clarke and McGinley refused to go away, but Harrington's determination to succeed was to be rewarded. That determination is emphasised by the time he spends on the practice ground and, as one writer explained, he is also intelligent, articulate and courteous, prepared to take as long as is necessary to give the correct answer to a question and prepared to spend as long as it takes to find out the answer. "I am a good learner," he said. "I may be slow, but I learn. I sit back and analyse things and learn from them. I have spent my whole career trying to find out how to improve. Every time I came second I learnt from it."

That Harrington proved, beyond any doubt, for as he won the Volvo Masters Andalucia, and punched the air in joy, so he left no question to be answered.

Mark Garrod

Mathias Grönberg

Padraig Harrington

MONTECASTILLO HOTEL AND GOLF RESORT, JEREZ, SPAIN, 8-11 NOVEMBER, 2001, PAR 72, 7069 YARDS, 6466 METRES

Pos.	Name		Rd1	Rd2	Rd3	Rd4	Total	Par	Prize Money Euro	£
1	Padraig HARRINGTON	Ire	67	71	66		204	-12	539074.60	333329.99
2	Paul MCGINLEY	Ire	66	69	70		205	-11	359383.10	222220.02
3	Adam SCOTT	Aus	67	74	65		206	-10	202478.40	125199.97
4	Robert KARLSSON	Swe	71	68	68		207	-9	137357.60	84933.34
	Mathias GRÖNBERG	Swe	70	67	70		207	-9	137357.60	84933.34
	Darren CLARKE	N.Ire	70	68	69		207	-9	137357.60	84933.34
7	Tony JOHNSTONE	Zim	69	72	67		208	-8	83449.58	51600.00
	Bernhard LANGER	Ger	69	70	69		208	-8	83449.58	51600.00
	Colin MONTGOMERIE	Scot	71	69	68		208	-8	83449.58	51600.00
10	David HOWELL	Eng	69	73	67		209	-7	61455.12	38000.00
	Retief GOOSEN	SA	68	75	66		209	-7	61455.12	38000.00
12	Greg TURNER	NZ	72	70	68		210	-6	50377.02	31150.00
	Gary EVANS	Eng	69	71	70		210	-6	50377.02	31150.00
	Roger WESSELS	SA	70	70	70		210	-6	50377.02	31150.00
	Dean ROBERTSON	Scot	69	72	69		210	-6	50377.02	31150.00
16	José Maria OLAZÁBAL	Sp	69	70	72		211	-5	44312.38	27400.00
	Phillip PRICE	Wal	70	73	68		211	-5	44312.38	27400.00
	Angel CABRERA	Arg	69	73	69		211	-5	44312.38	27400.00
	Peter LONARD	Aus	65	78	68		211	-5	44312.38	27400.00
20	Steve WEBSTER	Eng	70	71	71		212	-4	41077.89	25400.00
21	Søren HANSEN	Den	72	73	68		213	-3	38490.31	23800.00
	Charlie WI	R.Kor	70	72	71		213	-3	38490.31	23800.00
	Niclas FASTH	Swe	72	67	74		213	-3	38490.31	23800.00
24	Ricardo GONZALEZ	Arg	71	76	67		214	-2	34932.38	21600.00
	Paul LAWRIE	Scot	74	73	67		214	-2	34932.38	21600.00
	David LYNN	Eng	71	71	72		214	-2	34932.38	21600.00
27	Nick O'HERN	Aus	69	72	74		215	-1	32021.35	19800.00
	John BICKERTON	Eng	73	75	67		215	-1	32021.35	19800.00
	Carl PETTERSSON	Swe	70	74	71		215	-1	32021.35	19800.00
30	Brian DAVIS	Eng	68	75	73		216	0	29110.32	18000.00
	Miguel Angel JIMÉNEZ	Sp	70	74	72		216	0	29110.32	18000.00
	Michael CAMPBELL	NZ	73	72	71		216	0	29110.32	18000.00
33	Anthony WALL	Eng	72	71	74		217	1	26684.46	16500.00
	Stephen GALLACHER	Scot	70	76	71		217	1	26684.46	16500.00
35	Mark MOULAND	Wal	70	74	74		218	2	21455.38	13266.66
	Barry LANE	Eng	71	75	72		218	2	21455.38	13266.66
	Mark MCNULTY	Zim	69	74	75		218	2	21455.38	13266.66
	Raphaël JACQUELIN	Fr	72	74	72		218	2	21455.38	13266.66
	Søren KJELDSEN	Den	70	75	73		218	2	21455.38	13266.66
	Richard GREEN	Aus	72	71	75		218	2	21455.38	13266.66
	Thomas LEVET	Fr	69	76	73		218	2	21455.38	13266.66
	Jean HUGO	SA	72	72	74		218	2	21455.38	13266.66
	Greg OWEN	Eng	73	76	69		218	2	21455.38	13266.66
44	Pierre FULKE	Swe	73	72	74		219	3	16172.40	10000.00
	Thomas BJÖRN	Den	73	69	77		219	3	16172.40	10000.00
	Fredrik JACOBSON	Swe	73	77	69		219	3	16172.40	10000.00
	Andrew COLTART	Scot	70	76	73		219	3	16172.40	10000.00
	Mikael LUNDBERG	Swe	73	74	72		219	3	16172.40	10000.00
49	Ian POULTER	Eng	64	81	76		221	5	13665.68	8450.00
	Ian GARBUTT	Eng	71	76	74		221	5	13665.68	8450.00
	Paul CASEY	Eng	76	74	71		221	5	13665.68	8450.00
52	Sven STRÜVER	Ger	72	79	71		222	6	12371.89	7650.00
	Anders HANSEN	Den	69	74	79		222	6	12371.89	7650.00
	Lee WESTWOOD	Eng	69	76	77		222	6	12371.89	7650.00
55	Raymond RUSSELL	Scot	70	77	76		223	7	11644.13	7200.00
56	Justin ROSE	Eng	69	83	72		224	8	11158.96	6900.00
	Henrik STENSON	Swe	81	73	70		224	8	11158.96	6900.00
58	Peter O'MALLEY	Aus	77	74	74		225	9	10512.06	6500.00
	Brett RUMFORD	Aus	70	81	74		225	9	10512.06	6500.00
60	Gregory HAVRET	Fr	70	79	77		226	10	10026.89	6200.00
61	Olle KARLSSON	Swe	72	79	76		227	11	9703.44	6000.00
62	Daren LEE	Eng	75	78	75		228	12	9379.99	5800.00
63	Seve BALLESTEROS	Sp	79	80	71		230	14	9137.41	5650.00
64	Ian WOOSNAM	Wal	74	77	DISQ		151	7	8679.19	5366.67
	Warren BENNETT	Eng	72	78	W/D		150	6	8679.19	5366.67
	Gary ORR	Scot	77	80	RTD		157	13	8679.19	5366.67

Unique Flavour

David Duval and Tiger Woods

From Argentina, home of the Tango and Maradona, to Japan, mother country of the Geisha and Sumo Wrestling, the World Golf Championships - EMC[2] World Cup has already stretched the boundaries of professional golf within the first two years under its new format.

The World Cup joined the family of World Golf Championships events in 2000 with EMC[2] taking over the title sponsorship and Buenos Aires Golf Club accepting the honour of becoming the first South American hosts of the new-look WGC-EMC[2] World Cup.

In 2001, it was Japan's turn to experience the unique flavour of the World Golf Championships for the first time at the wonderfully picturesque Taiheiyo Club in Gotemba, nestling cosily in the foothills of Mount Fuji.

Defending the title in Japan, where golf is not so much a hobby as a passion, were the United States, with David Duval and Tiger Woods, hoping to be as perfectly synchronised and choreographed during the four days of intense competition as two of the famous Tango dancers impressing the tourists in the La Boca District of Buenos Aires the previous year.

With the revised fourball and foursomes format employed for the first time, the United States team recorded a 34 under par total of 254, shooting rounds of 61-65-60-68 to win the 2000 edition by three strokes from the local heroes, Angel Cabrera and Eduardo Romero.

The Argentine crowds flocked to the course on the outskirts of Buenos Aires to lend a typically Latin support to the two European Tour champions, who gave their all in pursuit of the title in the country which spawned golfing greats such as Roberto di Vicenzo and Vicente Fernandez.

Angel Cabrera and Eduardo Romero

The Taiheiyo Club, Gotemba, Japan

In the end, Duval and Woods prevailed, thanks mainly to the sublime skills of Duval, who would go on to capture the Open Championship at Royal Lytham & St Annes almost seven months later. Paraguay took third place with Japan - the 2001 hosts - displaying their growing status on the world stage by finishing fourth through the efforts of Shigeki Maruyama and Hidemichi Tanaka.

Unquestionably, the World Golf Championships have become a truly global experience since their launch in February, 1999. They feature the game's leading players competing against one another in a variety of formats. The EMC² World Cup has joined the Accenture Match Play, NEC Invitational and American Express Championship in the World Golf Championships line-up. The events rotate through a variety of outstanding venues worldwide.

Gordon Simpson

Global Success

Peter Lonard

The bar has long since been raised on the expectation of European Tour Members to win "around the world" and Retief Goosen, of course, must take pride of place in 2001 for his outstanding victory in the US Open Championship in Tulsa, Oklahoma.

Nevertheless on his native South African circuit Goosen was compelled to accept a share of second place in the Dimension Data Pro-Am when in February Darren Clarke survived a final hole drama to secure a two shot win at Sun City.

Clarke had demonstrated in 2000 his increasing reputation in global terms when he won the World Golf Championships - Accenture Match Play at La Costa Resort & Spa in Carlsbad, California. "I took a step up by beating a field which had 64 of the world's top 65," he said. "That was big because to beat the players I did (Paul Azinger, Mark O'Meara, Thomas Björn, Hal Sutton, David Duval and Tiger Woods) showed I can do it."

Even so his maturing as a world-class golfer demanded that he advanced his win ratio. So in negotiating the first leg of a million-dollar accumulator in South Africa - he left himself needing another three wins to collect the bonus offered by his backer, Dimension Data, after winning at Sun City - Clarke had good reason to celebrate. "It was the perfect start to the year," said Clarke. "The majority of my game was very good."

This was most certainly the case in the second round when on the testing Gary Player Country Club course he compiled a course record 63. There were to be a couple of banana skins along the way despite Clarke starting his final round with four birdies in his first seven holes to move five ahead of Goosen. He dropped three shots in the next two holes and escaped with a bogey at the par five 18th where his third shot finished in water. Clarke took a drop, hit his fifth shot to ten feet and sank the putt. "It was probably the best six I've ever

made," said Clarke as he enjoyed his customary victory cigar.
His closing 71 for a 14 under par total of 274 gave him his first success in South Africa by two shots from Tjaart van der Walt (66) and Goosen (69), and it was not long before he was celebrating another "first" when this time he won on Japanese soil by capturing the Chunichi Crowns in Togo in late April. This time he emphasised his ability not only to produce the goods in the last round, but also to play his best golf in gruelling conditions.

Clarke became the first European golfer since Severiano Ballesteros in 1991 to win the Chunichi Crowns by defying wind and rain to put together a last round of 67 for a 13 under par total of 267 - four ahead of the Japanese golfers Keiichiro Fukabori and Shinichi Yokota. "It's nice to come along and get my first win here," Clarke said. "Hopefully there's more to come." He came within a whisker of doing exactly that in September when in the Suntory Open at Sobu Country Club he finished joint runner-up to Shingo Katayama of Japan.

Clarke had threatened before to win in Japan. He was runner-up at the 1998 Dunlop Phoenix and lost a three way play-off for the Sumitomo VISA Taiheiyo Masters in 1999. In the Chunichi Crowns tournament he was not about to let victory slip from his grasp as on the Nagoya Club course he birdied three of the last four holes.

Meanwhile Colin Montgomerie, who like Clarke has enjoyed success at Sun City where he won the Nedbank Million Dollar Challenge in 1996, also launched his year in winning style on foreign soil in February when he won the Ericsson Masters on the Huntingdale course in Melbourne, Australia. This was an even better performance than it sounds on face value because Montgomerie had not played since December 6, 2000.

"I wasn't actually going to come down here, but I got a late invite," Montgomerie revealed after his first triumph in Australia. "I went to Houston in American for two days coaching then came here - it's a long way down but I'm glad I came!"

Colin Montgomerie

Darren Clarke

José Coceres

Brett Rumford, who won the Australasian Tour TPC as an amateur in 1999, had become a European Tour Member by coming through the Qualifying School in 2000 and he had high hopes of a first win as a professional in his native Australia when he fired a course record 64 at Huntingdale in the third round to move ahead. Indeed he still had a chance to force a play off at the last when he narrowly missed a chip in for a birdie. Montgomerie, however, once again shown a clean pair of heels to his rivals with a final round of 69 for a ten under par total of 278 which at the end gave him victory by one shot from Nathan Green.

Montgomerie would have enjoyed nothing more than to complete a Masters double at Augusta National in April, although Tiger Woods spoiled that for all by maintaining his incredible momentum in the Majors, but the week after there was to be a win for another European Tour Member on American soil.

José Coceres, winner of the Dubai Desert Classic in 2000, had to come back on the Monday morning when darkness intervened as he played off for the WORLDCOM CLASSIC – The Heritage of Golf in Hilton Head Island, South Carolina. There on a cool morning in front of an unusually large crowd he punched the air in joy after holing a five foot par putt at what was the third extra hole for the title. "This is for my family and my friends and for all Argentineans," he said. "A million thanks!" Victory came in only his tenth start on the US PGA Tour, and it was the first win in America by an Argentine player since Roberto de Vicenzo.

Coceres made it two wins on the US Tour when in October in Florida he held off a late challenge from Davis Love III to win the National Car Rental Golf Classic at Walt Disney World Resort by one shot. Coceres took control with three consecutive birdies from the ninth and led by two until Loves closing birdie.

There was to be another first win in America for a European Tour Member when Sergio Garcia broke through at the MasterCard Colonial in Fort Worth, Texas. Garcia started the final round five shots behind Phil Mickelson, but he powered to a closing 63 to win with a 13 under par total of 267 - two ahead of defending champion Brian Gay and Mickelson. The Spaniard had put himself in the position to win with a six under par outward half of 29, only one shot more than the record 28 carded by both Wayne Levi and Keith Clearwater in 1993. He was still three behind Mickelson but he caught his rival with a 20 foot birdie on the 13th then played stronger down the stretch. Garcia's previous best US PGA Tour performance had been to finish runner-up to Woods in the 1999 US

Sergio Garcia

PGA Championship. "I don't feel like this first win should have taken so much time," he said. "But they always say the first one is the toughest so hopefully I'll start doing some nice things."

Garcia recalled those words some five weeks later as he strolled away with the rain-delayed Buick Classic at the Callaway Gardens Resort in Pine Mountain, Georgia. The tournament was completed on the Monday when Garcia shot a near flawless last round of 67 to tie the Buick Classic record of 16 under 268 and win by three from Scott Hoch. He finished in style by reaching the par five 18th green in two with an iron and two putted for a birdie. "Today it could have been so low," said Garcia. "I played so well." With his win the 21 year old Spaniard became the second youngest player to capture two titles on the US Tour - older only than Woods, who accomplished the feat at 20 years and nine months. What is more he finished the season in sixth place on the US Tour money list following The Tour Championship which was won by Canada's Mike Weir in a play-off with Ernie Els, David Toms and Garcia.

Winning in America has become more of a regular occurrence for Jesper Parnevik. The Swedish golfer, who won The European Tour Qualifying School back in 1988, had four wins on each of The European Tour and the US PGA Tour prior to the start of this year, and he made it five in America when he won the Honda Classic at TPC at Heron Bay, Coral Springs, in Florida, in which state he now lives at Jupiter.

Jesper Parnevik

Zhang Lian-Wei

Parnevik followed opening rounds of 65-67-66 with a closing 72 which proved good enough as with an 18 under par total of 270 he won by one shot from Mark Calcavecchia, Geoff Ogilvy and Craig Perks. Parnevik bogeyed the last hole, but all around him also dropped shots at the 18th, and he confessed: "I'll take it any way I can get it, but I feel more relief than happiness - you never want to win that way." As if to emphasise the point Parnevik had kept the usual victory cigar in its box.

There have been other notable wins by European Tour Members in 2001. Peter Lonard won in his native Australia when he shot 67-67-69-66 to capture the ANZ Championship at Concord, Sydney on the Australasian Tour by one shot from Nathan Green. Zhang Lian-Wei, of China, captured the Macau Open, won by Lee Westwood and Simon Dyson in 1999 and 2000 respectively, at Macau Golf and Country Club. He shot 70-64-71-68 for an 11 under par 273 to win by one shot from Simon Yates in May and four months later also on the Davidoff Tour, Daniel Chopra compiled rounds of 71-69-73-71 for a four under par 284 and a one shot win from Vivet Bhandari in the Mercuries Masters tournament at the Taiwan Golf and Country Club.

Mitchell Platts

Out of Necessity

For everyone involved in professional golf on both sides of the Atlantic, the sport is a wonderful and all-consuming passion. However, there are times when it is shown to be an irrelevance. That situation came sharply into focus on Tuesday September 11, 2001.

The 34th Ryder Cup Matches at The De Vere Belfry, scheduled for September 28-30, 2001, had, quite rightly, been the focus of the golfing world's attention for most of the year. But, after the enormity of the tragedy in America on that fateful day, postponement of the contest until September 27-29, 2002, was widely acknowledged as the reasoned, sensible and correct course of action.

Indeed, The PGA of America informed The European Ryder Cup Board that the scope of the tragedy was so overwhelming that it would have been impossible for The United States Ryder Cup Team and Officials to attend in 2001. The European Ryder Cup Board stated: "We have been placed in a position beyond our control and therefore the Matches, out of necessity, have been postponed."

Inevitably, the consequence of such a momentous decision was for the immediate Matches to be moved to even-numbered years, the superb support of The De Vere Belfry, the first host venue affected by the change, particularly appreciated.

After the PGA of America informed The European Ryder Cup Board of their decision, there were calls in some quarters for the 2001 Matches to be cancelled altogether. That would have resulted in a resumption of the contest in Detroit and a subsequent gap of eight years between 'home' Matches, a situation no-one relished. As Ken Schofield, the Executive Director of The European Tour, said: "The world changed on September 11, 2001, and that included The Ryder Cup."

European Captain Sam Torrance was another who added his weight behind the decision to postpone the Matches, revealing his Team felt the same way too. "They (The European Team) were delighted the Matches were going to be played but were also delighted they had been postponed as well," he said. "I did not think postponement was giving in to terrorism. I think it underlined the enormity of the horrors we had seen."

American Captain Curtis Strange said: "The tragedy caused us all to reflect and evaluate our lives and relationships with family and friends. The PGA of America's decision to postpone the Matches was appropriate in light of the situation."

Aside from the date change, everything will remain the same come September 2002, with both Torrance and Strange retaining their status as Captains and each leading the same 12 players - ten of whom qualified for each Team and two of whom were selected by the Captains.

Sam Torrance MBE

EUROPEAN TEAM CAPTAIN

Sam Torrance's appointment as European Ryder Cup Captain for The 34th Matches at The De Vere Belfry was a perfect example of combining nostalgia with common sense. It was at the superb Midlands complex in 1985 that Torrance, already a household name in Britain through his successful exploits on The European Tour, found global fame as the man who sank the historic putt which saw The Ryder Cup return to European shores for the first time since 1957.

So when a new leader was required to succeed Mark James for the next edition of golf's greatest team event, it was impossible to overlook the claims of a highly popular, universally respected and vastly experienced Ryder Cup campaigner with eight 'tours of duty' under his belt.

Torrance delivered the winning point against Andy North on the final green - and that defining moment for Europe in the glittering history of the competition ensured that Torrance's name would always be written in large neon letters whenever discussions arise surrounding Ryder Cups at The De Vere Belfry.

It remains his most cherished moment in a remarkable 31 year career as a playing professional on The European Tour which has seen the popular Scotsman accumulate no fewer than 21 titles on his home Tour and ten others world wide.

"I have many fond memories, but that particular moment in 1985 will stay with me forever. Nothing else comes close, not even my Tour wins," says Torrance.

His golfing passion began in earnest at the age of nine, four years after his father, Bob, the highly respected coach and club professional, introduced him to the game at Rossendale GC, Lancashire, England, before the family moved back to Scotland where Torrance Snr took up the post at Largs Routenburn GC in Ayrshire, on the west coast, not far from two of the world's greatest links courses, Royal Troon and Turnberry.

Young Sam proved to be a good pupil and a quick learner. He recalled: "The first time I broke 40 at Rossendale I rushed in to tell my dad and he didn't believe me. We then went back to the course together and I did it again!" As a youngster, he became hopelessly addicted to golf, playing three rounds a day - "sometimes four," he added - during the long, light summer nights in Scotland.

He left school at 13 and was employed in a variety of odd-jobs, including erecting television aerials and working in a supermarket, until turning professional in 1970 just short of his 17th birthday.

In 1971 he was sponsored by wealthy Sunningdale members, Angus Mackenzie and his sons, Norman and Gerald, to play on The European Tour. He managed to play only one tournament that year, the Agfa Gevaert at Stoke Poges, where he finished 39th and won the princely sum of £35 to be ranked 232nd on the Order of Merit.

The following season he finished 37th on the money list with £1,732 and collected the Sir Henry Cotton Rookie of the Year award on The European Tour. It was the first of 30 consecutive seasons Torrance has played on the Tour, during which time he has accumulated more than £3½ million in official money and approaching £5 million in total.

Torrance had to wait until 1976 to record his first victory in the Piccadilly Medal at Finham Park. Many others followed and he is especially proud of his victories in the 1981 Carrolls Irish Open at Portmarnock and the same title 14 years later in a play-off at Mount Juliet.

Of becoming the latest in a long line of well-respected European Captains, he said: "It's a fabulous honour to be The European Ryder Cup Captain. I've never made a secret of how much I enjoy being part of The Ryder Cup, and to be the Captain makes me feel very proud. It has been a privilege to be involved with four wonderful and very different Ryder Cup Captains in John Jacobs, Tony Jacklin, Bernard Gallacher and Mark James, and each of them is very special in their own way. Hopefully, I can take a little of what I have learned from all of them to live up to the very high standards set by my peers."

Europe

Thomas Björn

Darren Clarke

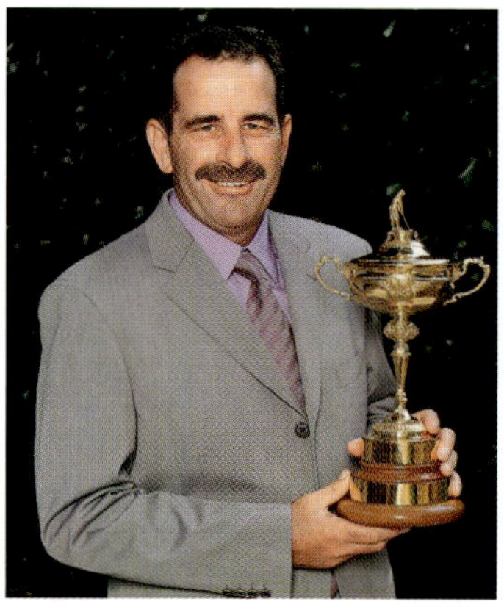
Sam Torrance
(Captain)

Niclas Fasth

Pierre Fulke

Sergio Garcia

Padraig Harrington

Bernhard Langer

Paul McGinley

Colin Montgomerie

Jesper Parnevik

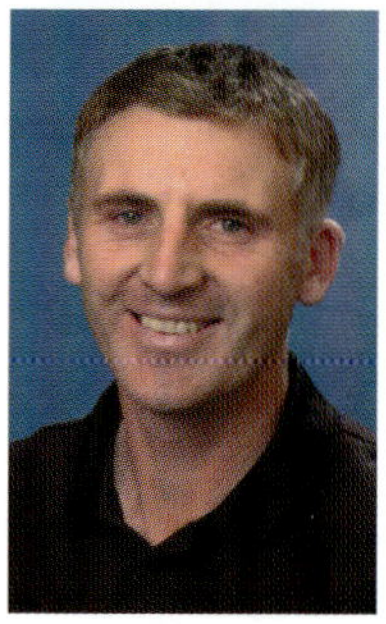
Phillip Price

Lee Westwood

RYDER CUP INDIVIDUAL RECORDS - EUROPE

Name	Years	Matches Played	Won	Lost	Halved
Sam Torrance (Captain)	1981-83-85-87 89-91-93-95	28	7	15	6
Thomas Björn	1997	2	1	0	1
Darren Clarke	1997-99	7	3	4	0
Niclas Fasth	Debut	--	--	--	--
Pierre Fulke	Debut	--	--	--	--
Sergio Garcia	1999	5	3	1	1
Padraig Harrington	1999	3	1	1	1
Bernhard Langer	1981-83-85-87 89-91-93-95-97	38	18	15	5
Paul McGinley	Debut	--	--	--	--
Colin Montgomerie	1991-93-95-97-99	23	12	7	4
Jesper Parnevik	1997-99	9	4	2	3
Phillip Price	Debut	--	--	--	--
Lee Westwood	1997-99	10	4	6	0

Curtis Strange

UNITED STATES TEAM CAPTAIN

It was Sam Torrance, at the time of being appointed The European Ryder Cup Captain, who summed up the character of Curtis Strange best of all when he said: "You know where you are with Curtis. It's laid down in front of you. No messing."

Further amplification was barely necessary. Torrance's implication was that, in Strange, the United States had a captain of substance - a man who can cut through a morass of red tape to get exactly what he wants and won't be deflected from his objectives.

The parallels are glaringly obvious. Like Torrance, Strange grew up in a golfing environment, the son of a club professional, Tom, who sadly passed away when young Curtis was a teenager. Like Torrance, he became a prolific winner on Tour and, just like Sam, he enjoyed a long and successful Ryder Cup career.

Torrance said: "He's a dear friend, Curtis. I've known him for almost 30 years. If you'd asked me to pick a Ryder Cup Captain in the last 20 years who I would like to be against when it eventually came to me, it would have been Curtis Strange because I love what he stands for in the game."

Strange won the Virginia State Junior Championship at the age of 15 and, in a poignant reminder of his late father, he won the Eastern Amateur in 1975, 18 years after his dad became the inaugural winner of the event.

He progressed quickly and became College Player of the Year in 1974 as a student at Arnold Palmer's alma mater of Wake Forest University and represented the United States in the Walker Cup the following year.

He turned professional in 1976 and earned his card at the US Tour Qualifying School in 1977. Strange's big break came relatively quickly when he captured the 1979 Pensacola Open.

Strange enjoyed several Ryder Cup highs and lows - and he crossed swords with Mr Torrance on a couple of occasions, with honours being shared. In 1987 at Muirfield Village, Tom Kite and Strange enjoyed a 4 and 2 win over Howard Clark and Torrance in the opening foursomes.

Then two year later, when The Ryder Cup was tied at The De Vere Belfry, Gordon Brand Jnr and Torrance took a measure of revenge by beating Paul Azinger and Strange by one hole.

However, Strange's most glorious moments came in 1988-89 when he emulated Ben Hogan's feat of capturing the US Open (1950-51) in successive years. The first victory at The Country Club, Brookline, came after an 18 hole play-off with Nick Faldo.

Twelve months later he defended successfully at Oak Hill, shooting a second round 64 on his way to a one stroke victory over Chip Beck, Mark McCumber and Ian Woosnam, who, coincidentally is Torrance's Vice Captain.

It was a superb achievement to follow in the footsteps of Hogan, but his most recent return to Oak Hill was less successful. The Virginian was selected as a wild card by United States Captain Lanny Wadkins for the 1995 Ryder Cup Matches and lost his three games, including a singles defeat by Faldo who exacted a measure of revenge for his 1988 US Open play-off loss.

Strange came close to collecting a third US Open title in 1994 but he fell one stroke short of the play-off which involved the eventual winner Ernie Els, Colin Montgomerie and Loren Roberts.

That first US Open win saw Strange become the first player on the US PGA Tour to pass the $1 million mark for a season, while one of his career highlights came at the Home of Golf, St Andrews, in 1987 when he reduced the Old Course to 62 blows, ten under par, which set a course record at that time.

Married to Sarah, with two sons, Strange has an identical twin brother, Allen, who also played on the US PGA Tour for a time. That 1989 US Open win was to be Curtis's last, and in 1997 he began a full-time assignment as an analyst for ABC Sports - a role which grew rapidly and resulted in his promotion to main analyst for the major US network.

United States

Paul Azinger

Mark Calcavecchia

Curtis Strange
(Captain)

Stewart Cink

David Duval

Jim Furyk

Scott Hoch

Davis Love III

Phil Mickelson

Hal Sutton

David Toms

Scott Verplank

Tiger Woods

RYDER CUP INDIVIDUAL RECORDS - UNITED STATES

Name	Years	Matches Played	Won	Lost	Halved
Curtis Strange (Captain)	1983-85-87-89-95	20	6	12	2
Paul Azinger	1989-91-93	13	5	6	2
Mark Calcavecchia	1987-89-91	11	5	5	1
Stewart Cink	Debut	--	--	--	--
David Duval	1999	4	1	2	1
Jim Furyk	1997-99	6	2	4	0
Scott Hoch	1997	3	2	0	1
Davis Love III	1993-95-97-99	17	6	8	3
Phil Mickelson	1995-97-99	11	6	3	2
Hal Sutton	1985-87-99	14	6	4	4
David Toms	Debut	--	--	--	--
Scott Verplank	Debut	--	--	--	--
Tiger Woods	1997-99	10	3	6	1

A Cause for Celebration

THE DE VERE BELFRY, SUTTON COLDFIELD, ENGLAND

10th hole from behind the green

When Peter Alliss and Dave Thomas first surveyed the site on which Ryder Cup history would in time be created, they were not filled with the same euphoria which so entranced Bobby Jones when he originally viewed the setting for Augusta National.

Jones instinctively knew on seeing Fruitlands, a 365-acre nursery where the progeny of a number of trees and plants imported from around the world had been nurtured, that the plunging terrain provided the ideal location for his golf course. "It seemed that the land had been lying there for years just waiting for someone to lay a golf course on it," Jones said.

What Alliss and Thomas said to each other as they cast their eyes over 15 potato fields at Sutton Coldfield, near Birmingham, is most probably unprintable. Yet it was there that they, having by then jettisoned their bag and clubs for pencil and drawing board, created at The Belfry, The Brabazon course on which for the fourth time The Ryder Cup will be played on September 27-29, 2002.

Initially, it would be criticised and maligned, causing some professionals to be so outspoken that they were fined. Now it sits proudly by the Lichfield Road as one of the most famous courses in Europe and part of a magnificent complex where the Professional Golfers' Association also has its home.

The birth of The Belfry can be traced to 1970 when Alan Hunter, the estates director of the Greenall Whitley company, asked Thomas to look at the site (a modest 49 acres that then went with the hotel)

RYDER CUP
1927 2004
OAKLAND HILLS C.C.
FOOTBALL EXPO
SINGAPORE '98
ASIANCUP
LEBANON 2000
RYDER CUP
1927 1999
THE COUNTRY CLUB
EMIRATES

and the adjoining land in other ownerships. Hunter said: "We asked them to tell us the preferred areas required to form an 18 hole championship course plus an 18 hole supporting course. Following this I acquired the necessary land options to purchase and following town-planning approval acquired the land on behalf of The Belfry Company."

In fact, it was in 1959 that Jimmy Burns, an entrepreneur, had purchased Moxhull Park, a private house at the time, for £18,500 and turned it into The Belfry. His expansion programme increased the number of bedrooms to 59 and made The Belfry a well known centre for wedding receptions and a place where in the 1960s such groups as Led Zeppelin, the Moody Blues, Slade and Status Quo performed live. In 1969 Burns sold The Belfry to a group called Allied Vintners Investments which in turn was bought by Greenall Whitley. At this time the PGA had their headquarters at the Kennington Oval and it was there, over a pie and a pint, that Colin Snape, then the new Executive Director of the PGA, lunched with Alliss. Snape felt that is was an imposition to be continually apologising for the surroundings as he ushered guests into the confined offices at the rear main stand of the cricket ground.

His dream of the PGA was a new headquarters which were geographically acceptable with two golf courses and modern offices. He had looked at both Royal Birkdale in Lancashire and Foxhills in Surrey, but the then 28-strong PGA Committee felt that his plan was no more than a pipe-dream since at that time in February, 1973, the PGA's assets were a paltry £40,000.

Alliss came to the rescue over lunch. He told Snape of an old hotel on the outskirts of Birmingham known as The Belfry which was being renovated and converted to a sports complex. Thomas and Alliss had originally been asked to design and build a pitch and putt course there.

Snape convinced the committee that expansion was a necessity and he must truly have felt he had the Midas touch. Ellerman Lines, the shipping company, was keen to diversify into leisure whereas Greenall Whitley, owners of The Belfry, lacked funds at that time as they were investing in a new brewery.

Thus Ellerman Lines formed a company called The Belfry (Sutton Coldfield) Ltd, taking 86.7 per cent of the equity with Greenall Whitley retaining 13.3 per cent for providing the hotel and land, and purchased a further 265.5 acres. In 1975 work began on two courses - The Brabazon and The Derby - by Thomas and Alliss. Brian Cash, a jocular but hard-nosed businessman, was brought in to oversee the operation, which included the refurbishment of the hotel. Cash, too, visualised the enormous potential of this triangular area of land near where the Tamworth and Lichfield roads merge at Wishaw. The access was splendid with close proximity to the M1, M5 and M6.

The PGA lacked the funds to become involved but The Belfry

Sam Torrance celebrates the putt with which Europe secured victory in 1985 – in 2002 he returns to The De Vere Belfry as European Team Captain

Company built the new PGA offices, funding the cost of approximately £100,000 as part of the overall deal with the PGA for two Ryder Cups. Meanwhile Accles and Pollock, the sports equipment company, funded the furnishings of the PGA's Headquarters at The Belfry in addition to investing a significant sum over ten years in the PGA's training school.

In 1977 the PGA waved farewell to The Oval to begin a new innings at The Belfry with a peppercorn rent for a 99-year lease. That year, with the existing hotel completely rebuilt, The Brabazon course was officially opened with a challenge match, Severiano Ballesteros and Johnny Miller against Brian Barnes and Tony Jacklin.

The first official tournament to be held on The Brabazon course was the Hennessy Cup, a Match between Great Britain and the Continent of Europe. This was played in September, 1978, and if any one player put the course on the map then it was Ballesteros who performed a feat that the designers had deemed impossible.

Winter forecast: warm and dry.
Enjoy perfect playing conditions all year round with our new golf suit.
Its specially woven fabric makes it windproof, waterproof and breathable,
so that you can play at your best, even if the weather is at its worst.
MARKS & SPENCER
EXCLUSIVELY FOR EVERYONE

The Spaniard watched as Nick Faldo, his opponent, hit an iron into the perfect position at the tenth from which to pitch over the water onto the green. Ballesteros reached for his driver and launched the ball into orbit. It was an imperious blow, for the ball soared then carried the trees strategically placed to stop such a shot before finishing eight feet from the hole.

The hole then measured 310 yards, and a plaque marks Ballesteros's achievement and remains as evidence of the moment when The Belfry was truly born.

Nevertheless, The Belfry, or more precisely The Brabazon course, had its critics as well as its supporters. The problem was the money supply. It had taken £2.3 million to refurbish the hotel and to build the two courses. Cash said: "We could not fool ourselves. We were aware that we did not have the perfect piece of land and that it would take time to get the course absolutely right."

Thomas quite rightly received praise for his fashioning of The Brabazon course, which was American in style, but there was little he could do now that it was in the hands of owners with, so it seemed, no funds to rectify matters.

In October 1981 Greenall Whitley purchased all Ellerman Lines shares in The Belfry Company, and immediately launched the resurrection of The Brabazon course. This was important because part of the agreement the PGA had with The Belfry Company was for The Ryder Cup to be played on the course twice in eight years and, following criticism during the English Classic in 1979, the match was switched to Walton Heath in 1981.

The course required the kiss of life and it started with the soil of the fairways being broken to a depth of nine inches so the stones which were causing so many complaints could be removed. Then the fairways were top-dressed with a mixture of fern peat and topsoil. In addition, 100 mature, 20-foot trees, costing £500 each, were planted to increase definition while at the same time strengthening the overall layout. It was coupled with an extensive drainage programme. Much of the work was carried out by floodlight so as not to disturb play during the day.

Off the fairways, Greenall Whitley spent a further £1.3 million on a new accommodation block - Jacklin House - of 48 bedrooms, a covered driving range and also opened a leisure centre. The chalet pub next to the famous tenth green became the Bel Air nightclub.

By now The Belfry had become part of The De Vere Group of hotels. With a further 56-bedroom extension - Trevino House - it was ready to stage The Ryder Cup which would be the ultimate test for The Brabazon course - and it unquestionably passed the examination. There were no complaints in 1985, when for the first time since 1957, the United States were beaten. The Matches drew

A round with the tournament favourite

The 1st **[Optimism]** The 4th **[Pessimism]** The 5th **[Anger]** The 10th **[Hope]**

The 15th **[Frustration]** The 17th **[Longing]** The 18th **[Anticipation]** The 19th **[Celebration]**

See you at the 19th . . .

Imported MICHELOB BEER

RYDER CUP 1927 2001 THE BELFRY OFFICIAL SPONSOR

OFFICIAL 19th HOLE TO THE 34TH RYDER CUP MATCHES

unprecedented crowds of more than 90,000 in comparison to 16,000 at Walton Heath in 1981. That the course itself was presented in superb condition was naturally important, especially as by now investment stood at £8.1 million.

The persuasive tongue of the enterprising Cash led to The De Vere board investing a further £8 million for the 1989 Matches which ended in a tie with Europe retaining the Cup following their historic 15-13 win at Muirfield Village in 1987 - the first time that the Americans had been beaten on home soil.

For 1989 two new lakes were constructed to control water flow and improve the aesthetics. An electrical irrigation system was installed. More importantly, as far as the spectators were concerned, special mounds were created to improve viewing and accessibility.

By now the management was convinced that from those small potato fields had grown a golf course of which everyone could be proud. Indeed The Ryder Cup returned to The De Vere Belfry in 1993, when the United States retained Samuel Ryder's elegant golden chalice following their win at Kiawah Island in South Carolina in 1991.

For 1993, when The De Vere Belfry made history by hosting The Ryder Cup for a third time, the De Vere Group spent a further £2.5 million remodelling The Brabazon course to enhance spectator viewing and to provide an even tougher test and improving the hotel facilities. No fewer than ten of the holes underwent improvement changes. Thomas said: "It was exciting to go back and do some of the things you would have liked to have done originally."

Seve Ballesteros and José Maria Olazábal: For many the finest partnership in Ryder Cup history

Christy O'Connor Jnr.

Stuart Reed, then the Chairman and Chief Executive of De Vere Hotels, pointed out that the "huge success and popularity of The Belfry, De Vere Hotel's flagship golf resort, has played a vital part in shaping the development of the group. The leisure and business guest who wants to play golf is becoming more and more discerning and quite rightly - more demanding. The programme of work at The De Vere Belfry focused on creating the best venue for The Ryder Cup because we wanted to make sure players from both teams, officials and sponsors were as comfortable as possible. But the benefit of that investment will be seen in the coming years by all those who visit The De Vere Belfry, play the course and enjoy the facilities."

Now, following another nine years of continued refurbishment and building of the hotel and in particular in the remodelling of The Brabazon course, The De Vere Belfry is ready to host The Ryder Cup for a fourth time. There have been many changes since 1993 with an overall investment in excess of £40 million on the complex including 120 significant changes and £3.5 million spent on alterations and improvements to The Brabazon course.

Mike Maloney, the Executive Director of The De Vere Belfry, has seen the complex grow since he first arrived at the hotel in May 1991, but the tremendous progress made in the last nine years have

HOW EXACTLY DO YOU TELL YOUR DOCTOR YOU'RE HAVING ERECTION PROBLEMS?

"Hello Doctor, I'm having erection problems."

Or: "Hello Doctor, I'm having difficulty maintaining an erection."

Yes, it is difficult to say but your doctor will understand.

Erection problems are common, affecting at least one in every ten men. But not talking only makes matters worse.

Remember that erection problems don't just affect the man - there's a relationship with a wife or partner which is affected too. And the longer this goes on, the more likely they are to drift apart.

Talking to your doctor gives you the best chance of sorting things out. Erection problems have a variety of causes and are often due to other medical conditions such as hypertension or diabetes.

So it is a health problem which should be checked out. Remember, you're not alone. You're one of many people with a problem that can usually be solved. So talk to your partner. And talk to your doctor. There are solutions to your problem that can make you both feel better.

Please send me more information on men's health. 13307

Title ☐☐☐☐☐ First name ☐☐☐☐☐☐☐☐☐☐☐

Last name ☐☐☐☐☐☐☐☐☐☐☐☐☐☐☐☐☐☐

Address ☐☐☐☐☐☐☐☐☐☐☐☐☐☐☐☐☐☐☐

☐☐☐☐☐☐☐☐☐☐☐☐☐☐☐☐☐☐☐☐☐

☐☐☐☐☐☐☐☐☐☐ Postcode ☐☐☐☐☐☐☐

E-mail ☐☐☐☐☐☐☐☐☐☐☐☐☐☐☐☐☐☐☐

For information post coupon to: informED, Freepost (PY917). PO Box 36, Plymouth PL1 1BR Or call 0870 129 0100

Email: info@informED.org.uk www.informED.org.uk

The Impotence Association

The MEN'S HEALTH FORUM

SUPPORTED WITH AN EDUCATIONAL GRANT FROM PFIZER LIMITED.

provided him and all his staff with a challenge that they have brought to fruition with enormous skill and diligence.

Even so Maloney acknowledged: "Our selection for this prestigious event could not have been achieved without the tremendous help received from the local community. I would particularly like to thank all the people at The De Vere Belfry together with North Warwickshire Borough Council, the Birmingham Marketing Partnership, the NEC Group and Birmingham City Council. We have enjoyed working with them all in the build up to what will be a magnificent week for golf."

The De Vere Belfry, part of the De Vere chain of hotels owned by The De Vere Group plc, also played host to the Benson and Hedges International Open in 2000 and 2001 and this famous tournament returns to the venue in 2002. De Vere Group Chief Executive Paul Dermody, said: "The European Ryder Cup Board's choice of The De Vere Belfry is a tribute to the management and staff who have done such an excellent job over the previous three Ryder Cup Matches. I am absolutely confident that the hotel, the staff and the course will live up to the high expectation entrusted in us by the Board.

"We have been totally committed to the standards of excellence worthy of this great event and Dave Thomas has spent six years enhancing The Brabazon course in a way that it has never been seen before."

Thomas also designed the PGA National Championship course, which opened in 1997. This further enhances the golf facilities at The De Vere Belfry and provides golfers with three demanding championship courses.

Sandy Jones, Chief Executive of the Professional Golfers' Association, said: "No one can deny that The De Vere Belfry has already staged three very successful Ryder Cup Matches. Taking this into consideration together with the superb development and refurbishment of The Brabazon course, and coupled with the fact that in 2001 The PGA, the oldest PGA in the world, celebrated its centenary, makes us believe that The De Vere Belfry is the ideal venue for the staging of The 34th Ryder Cup Matches. De Vere, owners of The De Vere Belfry, are loyal and long-standing supporters of the Association and of golf in general."

So in September, 2002, the eyes of the sporting world will focus on The De Vere Belfry and, once again, there will be ample evidence that from those small potato fields has grown a course of which all can be proud.

The Brabazon Course

HOLE 1

The tees have been lowered in a stepped formation to form an amphitheatre. The hole is essentially a straight away par four but alterations to the fairway bunkers and the addition of a further bunker on the right combined with changes in the mowing pattern creates a different effect. The green has remained the same although the greenside bunkers have been enlarged and reshaped.

HOLE 2

The tee formation has been altered and a new back tee has been built to make it play a little longer. The fairway bunker on the right has been removed and two new bunkers have been built in a more aggressive position on the left of the fairway which means the tee shot needs to be played more to the right. The green has been enlarged as have the formation and shape of the greenside bunkers. This makes it a much better hole from the tee where the golfer can appreciate the dramatic mounding which changes the playing characteristics and improves the aesthetic appeal.

HOLE 3

One of the major changes. The long par four has been replaced by a dramatic dog-leg right to left par five. The tees have been raised to give a better view of the existing fairway bunkers which have also been remodelled. A good drive will provide the opportunity to reach the green in two shots but the golfer will have to carry his second shot across a substantial new lake. A new green has been designed with deep bunkers in front and to the right with extensive mounding around it. It is anticipated that this will become a favourite spectator viewing point and should provide dramatic TV shots.

HOLE 4

The second major change. The hole now plays as a long par four with several new features. The drive must negotiate two new bunkers placed to encourage a left to right drive or a straight carry across the newly enlarged pond. The second shot must clear the widened stream to a new sloped green guarded by two greenside bunkers. Viewed from the tee the hole has been enhanced with new earthworks to provide greater interest and visual appeal.

HOLE 5

New tees have been created. The stream which previously crossed the fairway has been culverted but now flows into an enlarged pond on the left hand side. A substantial spectator viewing mound has been constructed which, in combination with the change of a bunker from the left side to the right side of the fairway, encourages a right to left tee shot. The green has not been altered but the three greenside bunkers have been enlarged and reshaped.

HOLE 6

Anyone who has played The Brabazon in the past will appreciate the dramatic change to this hole. The tees remain the same but the lake on the left has been reshaped and the fairway has been lowered by 1½ metres to give a greater visual role. The bunker on the right of the fairway has been enlarged and repositioned. The green remains unaltered although two new greenside bunkers have been added on the left and the existing right hand bunker has been remodelled.

HOLE 7

New tees have been constructed and a substantial bunker feature covering much of the approach to the green has been added to act as the main design feature of the hole. Interlocking mounds and fingers of grass have enhanced the impression that existed before of an island green surrounded by sand.

HOLE 8

New tees have shortened the hole but the tees have been raised to provide a better view of the hole and the lake on the left. New bunkers have been positioned on the right of the fairway as well as additional mounding to make it a more attractive tee shot. The green is unaltered but the greenside bunkers have been enlarged and deepened.

HOLE 9

New tees have been created and raised to provide a better view of the hole. The left hand bunker has been enlarged. The dramatic green beside the lake in front of the hotel is unaltered.

HOLE 10

Little has been done to this world famous hole. The fairway bunkers have been remodelled along with some minor fairway changes. Most interestingly, the green has been extended a few yards further towards the lake providing more flag positions tantalisingly close to the water's edge.

HOLE 11

New back tees have been created and raised to provide a better view of the hole. The left hand bunker has been remodelled to provide a wider opening for the drive. The fairway mowing pattern has been changed to make the hole look more attractive.

HOLE 12

This is another dramatic change to the original Brabazon design. The par three hole has been shortened by 26 yards and the tees raised substantially to provide a good view of a newly formed lake which has replaced the existing stream which used to run across in front of the green. The green has been altered to provide space to the right to encourage tricky flag positions just behind the newly constructed re-circulating stream and stone feature.

HOLE 13

The tees have been reshaped and extended. The existing fairway bunkers have been enlarged and the fairway mowing changed to encourage a more left to right positional drive. The green has been extended and slopes added for greater interest. A pot bunker added to the rear of the green and the two existing greenside bunkers have been remodelled.

HOLE 14

A new raised back tee provides a view of the newly created tee to green bunker which dominates the left hand side of this par three. The green has not been altered although the greenside bunker has been remodelled and substantial mounding added to the rear of the green and the right side of the fairway to create another amphitheatre for spectators.

HOLE 15

New tees have been constructed and the back tee substantially raised to provide a view down the entire length of the hole. Fairway bunkers have been enlarged and reshaped as has the bunker 100 yards short of the green.

HOLE 16

The fairway and greenside bunkers have been remodelled, but essentially this hole will remain the same except for substantial mounding to the left which gives it a slightly different look.

HOLE 17

New tees have been constructed and realigned to encourage more shots across the fairway bunker at the corner of the dog-leg. The fairway bunkers across the stream have been remodelled.

HOLE 18

Few playing changes have been made to this dramatic world famous finishing hole though substantial mounding has been added to provide better spectator viewing opportunities. All the tees have been raised to give the player a better view across the corner of the lake. The first fairway bunker which rarely troubled the top players has been removed, but the second one further up the fairway has been enlarged and reshaped.

CARD OF THE COURSE

Hole	Yards	Metres	Par
1	411	376	4
2	379	346	4
3	538	492	5
4	442	404	4
5	408	373	4
6	395	361	4
7	177	162	3
8	428	391	4
9	433	396	4
Out:	**3611**	**3301**	**36**
10	311	284	4
11	419	383	4
12	208	190	3
13	384	351	4
14	190	174	3
15	545	498	5
16	413	378	4
17	564	516	5
18	473	432	4
In:	**3507**	**3206**	**36**
Total:	**7118**	**6507**	**72**

Excitement...Elation...Exhilaration

Exasperation…Enjoyment…Ecstasy!

Opening the Gateway

The European Ryder Cup Board confirmed at a Media Conference held at Wentworth Club that the host countries for The Ryder Cup Matches in 2010 and 2014 would be Wales and Scotland respectively, and that The Matches would rotate through Continental Europe from 2018.

The 38th Ryder Cup Matches will be played at The Celtic Manor Resort, Newport, Wales, in September, 2010, and The 40th Ryder Cup Matches will be played at The Gleneagles Hotel, Perthshire, Scotland, in September, 2014. The 2018, 2022, 2026 and 2030 Matches will all be played in Continental Europe. Wales will be hosting The Ryder Cup Matches for the first time. Scotland was host nation at The Honourable Company of Edinburgh Golfers, Muirfield, Gullane, in 1973 when Great Britain and Ireland only used to contest The Ryder Cup Matches with the United States.

Sandy Jones, Chief Executive of The Professional Golfers' Association, said: "We congratulate Wales and Scotland and, specifically, all involved at The Celtic Manor Resort and The Gleneagles Hotel. Both bids were considered of equal quality, and with the timings of The Matches we will complete the cycle of England (2002), Ireland (2006), Wales (2010) and Scotland (2014) then open the gateway to a long and sustained run on the Continent. We also expressed our sincere appreciation to all involved in the bidding process and, specifically, acknowledged the professional and honourable way in which De Vere Slaley Hall through One NorthEast in England and Carnoustie, Loch Lomond and Turnberry Hotel in Scotland conducted their bids."

Ken Schofield, Executive Director of The European Tour, said: "We are delighted to welcome Wales and Scotland as new host nations to the European Ryder Cup Matches, and The Celtic Manor Resort and The Gleneagles Hotel as new host venues. The European Ryder Cup Board was unanimous in reaching these decisions. Furthermore we have ensured the opportunity for Continental countries to host each of the next four Matches. France, Germany, and Sweden have like Spain - the host nation in 1997 - long been at the forefront in advancing professional golf with their invaluable contributions to The European Tour International Schedule. We also recognise that Italy and other nations, many of whom are host countries on the Tour's schedule, will similarly see the opportunity to host future Ryder Cup Matches."

Since players from Continental Europe became eligible The Ryder Cup has become golf's greatest shop window. The European Ryder Cup Board recognised in awarding the host venue to Spain in 1997 the significant roles played by the Spanish players and by Spain in hosting no less than 117 tournaments since the birth of The European Tour 30 years ago. Now that recognition has been extended by putting in place a rotation system on the Continent which will further stimulate the game throughout Europe.

The Ryder Cup enjoys a privileged place in the sporting calendar alongside the Olympic Games and World Cup football. Like these events The European Ryder Cup Board must work through a four year cycle in that only once in every four years is there a "home" Ryder Cup Match. Therefore the Continental countries have ample time to prepare then prosper as the Home of The Ryder Cup in the 21st century. Candidate nations will be invited to take up the opportunity to start their European Ryder Cup campaigns ten years ahead of hosting The Matches. This is the blueprint for the future.

Wales hosted the Dunlop Masters in 1971 - the year which marked the birth of The European Tour - and other tournaments to have been played in the country include the Coral Classic, the Epson Grand Prix of Europe, the Murphy's Cup and, most recently, The Celtic Manor Resort Wales Open where in 2000 The PGA Cup Matches were held. The late Dai Rees captained a record five Ryder Cup Teams and Dave Thomas, also from Wales and captain of The Professional Golfers' Association in their Centenary year, played four times in 1959, 1963, 1965 and 1967. Also part of the "Team Wales" bid was an immensely proud Brian Huggett, who played in six Ryder Cups and, in 1977, Captained the last Team before The Matches embraced Continental Europe.

The Wales Ryder Cup Bid Committee led by the National Assembly for Wales, chaired by Tony Lewis, the former Chairman of the Wales Tourist Board, was a true partnership that included the Welsh Development Agency, the Wales Tourist Board, Sports Council for Wales, the Welsh Golfing Union, the Welsh Ladies' Golf Union, Newport County Borough Council and The Celtic Manor Resort.

Tony Lewis said: "The whole of Wales was behind the bid and I believe we gave The Ryder Cup Board the opportunity to place a new vibrant piece in the jigsaw of European golf. We are sticking to our campaign slogan that a Ryder Cup staged in Wales will be 'Good for Wales: Great for Golf.' Hosting The Ryder Cup will assist the National Assembly and its agencies in their work, to enhance perceptions of Wales, make it an even more suitable destination for inward investment, for tourism and for the game of golf itself.

"We continue to pay tribute to a remarkable patriot and

entrepreneur in Sir Terence Matthews, who was bold enough to think his Celtic Manor might one day host a Ryder Cup. Moreover we could not have developed our bid without the cross-party support of our politicians in the National Assembly led by our First Minister, Rhodri Morgan and backed by the Minister for Sport Jenny Randerson. We believe that bringing The Ryder Cup to Wales will have a positive impact on the game of golf."

Rhodri Morgan, First Minister for Wales, said: "Over the next nine years or so and beyond, key members of Team Wales, such as the Assembly, the Welsh Development Agency, the Wales Tourist Board and the Sports Council for Wales, can build on this to secure a step change in Wales's international profile. This will not only put us on the sporting map but will also help secure more top quality inward investment, besides increased numbers of visitors to Wales. We will ensure that the whole of Wales will benefit from this."

Sir Terry Matthews, owner of The Celtic Manor Resort, said: "This is a great time for Wales and The Celtic Manor Resort - and a huge opportunity for golf. It has brought a new dimension to the sport by adding another nation into the golfing premier league. Our win will mean that exciting proposals for golf development, new tournaments and the further expansion of the world class facilities at Celtic Manor can be fully implemented. The plans have been set, our sleeves are rolled up, the work has begun."

Ian Woosnam, who has played in no fewer than eight Ryder Cup Matches, said: "Naturally I'm delighted that the 2010 Ryder Cup will be going to Wales for the first time. Not only will this help build the profile of golf in Wales and help introduce youngsters to the game at the grass roots level, but I am sure it will also help golf tourism in Wales and the economy in general. It is a fantastic reward for the efforts of all involved. Whilst it is eight years away, I can't wait for 2010 to come round so that we can put Wales on the golfing map."

Colin Montgomerie, who has played in five Ryder Cup Matches, said: "I'm sure Wales will stage a wonderful tournament and this opportunity will provide a great boost for Welsh golf and the Welsh economy. My warmest congratulations to them. I have always strongly supported the campaign to take The Ryder Cup to Scotland, so I am thrilled that the committee awarded The 40th Ryder Cup Matches to be played there in 2014. My support for Scotland has always been a personal choice and the announcement of Wales in 2010, Scotland in 2014 and then the Continent would seem to be to the benefit of the game in Wales, Scotland and ultimately golf in Europe as a whole."

Scotland has hosted no fewer than 80 events on The European Tour International Schedule including in 2001 and 2002 The Scottish Open at Loch Lomond, The Gleneagles Scottish PGA Championship and the Dunhill Links Championship at St Andrews, Carnoustie and Kingsbarns. The PGA Cup Matches were also played at The Gleneagles Hotel in 1996.

Peter Lederer, OBE, Managing Director of The Gleneagles Hotel, said: "Gleneagles is very honoured to have been selected as the host venue for The 40th Ryder Cup Matches in 2014. It will be a particularly significant year for the resort, which will celebrate its 90th anniversary in the same year. It provides Gleneagles with a fabulous opportunity to strengthen the existing platform the resort already holds within the golf world, and it has given good cause for great celebration at Gleneagles and throughout the Scottish golfing community in general. We very much look forward to welcoming The Ryder Cup back to Scotland, the home of golf, in 2014."

The European Ryder Cup Board announced that agreement was reached by The European Tour and The Professional Golfers' Association to embrace The PGA of Europe within a new structure with The European Tour becoming Managing Partner. The shareholding will be revised following the postponed 2001 Matches - to be played at The De Vere Belfry on September 27-29, 2002 - with the new European Ryder Cup Board comprising Members from The European Tour, The Professional Golfers' Association and The PGA of Europe.

Sandy Jones said: "The Professional Golfers' Association, in tandem with The European Tour, reached agreement to fully embrace The PGA of Europe within a new structure with The European Tour becoming the Managing Partner. The Professional Golfers' Association agreed to reduce its shareholding to recognise the game across Europe . The Ryder Cup will commit funds in the form of a licence fee to acknowledge that The Professional Golfers' Association were made the custodians of The Ryder Cup by Sam Ryder - indeed we remain the Founder Partner - and also through a device such as a Trust Fund to support initiatives through and across Europe."

Ken Schofield added: "The strength of any partnership has much to do with planning and vision. We, like The Professional Golfers' Association, have a responsibility not only to our Membership, but also in broadening the interest in our sport which means growing the game at the grass roots. We are confident that by taking The Ryder Cup Matches to Continental Europe, and with good planning and for a sustained period, we will encourage many, many thousands, and indeed we hope millions, to play golf and support our sport. The European Tour respects that as the Managing Partner we will be entrusted to progress the Cup in a way which is good for golf. We must also make it abundantly clear that it is the Herculean efforts of the players over several decades which have ultimately galvanised the stature and universal popularity of The Ryder Cup."

THE K CLUB

The K Club - 2006

Given that The Ryder Cup is a collaboration between Europe and the United States, it is highly appropriate that the first Matches to be played in Ireland in 2006 will be staged at The K Club.

For the parkland gem at Straffan in County Kildare was originally designed by American legend Arnold Palmer before being altered and extended by the Palmer Design Team in recent years.

The combination produced a golf course which has received high praise from professional golfers and enthusiastic spectators alike and one which, through the staging of the Smurfit European Open since 1995, has shown that it has all the facilities required to host the most prestigious international match in golf.

Dr Michael Smurfit, Chairman and Chief Executive of The Jefferson Smurfit Group, said: "It has been the club's ambition since 1990 to bring The Ryder Cup to Ireland and build a complex worthy of hosting the most prestigious golfing competition in the world.

"The importance of this event for Irish sports, Irish tourism and for the country as a whole cannot be overstated. It will attract large numbers of visitors and will put Ireland at the forefront of the world's sporting stage for many months before the actual event."

The feeling of excitement and anticipation is shared by everyone at The K Club and exemplified by Chief Executive Ray Carroll.

"Talk of The Ryder Cup creates great excitment," he said. "It will be tremendous and we will be ready for it. I'll be nervous in the sense that you can never not be nervous until you've delivered. But that only means that we've got to plan and prepare properly and be ready and organised - that's the fun in the challenge and I relish that.

"It will be the highlight of my career and for all of us here at The K Club. I'm not a great golfer but on the staff we have some very good and keen golfers and for the likes of Gerry Byrne, our course superintendent who is doing a tremendous job, The Ryder Cup will be a mighty challenge and a great opportunity."

As with every Ryder Cup, being able to watch the action unfold will be paramount and The K Club have already taken steps to ensure as many people as possible will be able to do that in person.

The vast programme of remounding which has taken place in recent years will be further augmented along the sides of the eighth and ninth fairways until a point is reached where thousands will be able to watch the play from both holes.

"We are looking out for a situation where, say, Tiger Woods is playing Sergio Garcia and 30,000 people would want to see that," said Ray Carroll. "We're anticipating the difficulties and the bottlenecks and will plan and be ready accordingly."

You can bet your last punt that the whole of Ireland will be ready too.

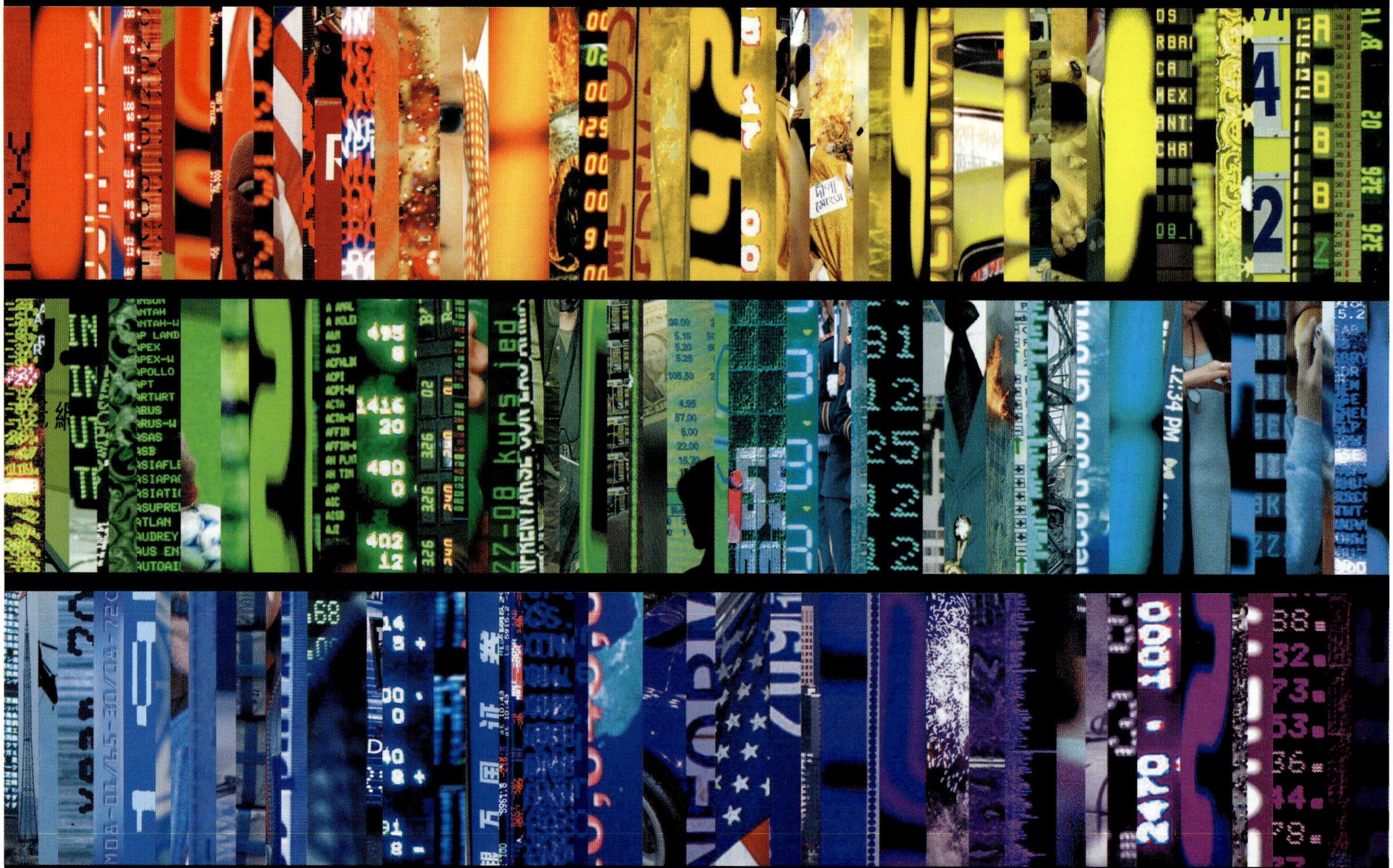

The Celtic Manor Resort - 2010

The magnificent splendour of The Celtic Manor Resort today is a far cry from the view that greeted owner Sir Terence Matthews as he drove along the M4 in the late 1970s.

The 19th century Manor House, which began life as the home of a steel magnate and subsequently became a maternity hospital, was boarded up - a casualty of Health Service reorganisation. However the entrepreneur in Matthews recognised the site's potential as a hotel and golfing location, and The Celtic Manor Resort story had begun. It would also be a case for Matthews of 'coming home.' For he was born in 1943 on the site - in that very maternity hospital. "I want Celtic Manor to be the best it can be at everything it does," he said. "I want to offer the local people a place they can be proud of and I want to help bring a bit of prosperity to my birthplace."

The facts support the promise. From an initial 17 bedroom hotel built in 1982, the resort now boasts a 400-room five star hotel set in 1400 acres of rolling parkland with 40 function rooms, a 1500 delegate convention centre, four restaurants, three championship golf courses and two health and spa clubs. Since 1999 it has won a string of accolades but the greatest prize came its way in September 2001, when it was awarded The 2010 Ryder Cup Matches.

Of the three Trent Jones-designed golf courses at the resort, the superb Wentwood Hills is the jewel in the crown and is where The 38th Ryder Cup Matches will unfold in eight years time. Already home to The Celtic Manor Resort Wales Open on The European Tour International Schedule, Wentwood Hills will have undergone a significant facelift by the time the most prestigious international match in golf gets underway. The remodelled golf course, under the supervision of European Golf Design, will feature seven completely new holes on new land and two redesigned holes on the lower level of the Usk Valley, all of which will provide a layout perfect for Ryder Cup requirements. It will also produce a course with a much smaller overall change in elevation. The new layout should be ready for the 2004 Celtic Manor Resort Wales Open.

The £12 million investment, which was given planning permission by Newport County Borough Council last summer, also includes the creation of a new clubhouse. Designed with The Ryder Cup in mind, each team will have separate, purpose built accommodation for their players, caddies and officials. In addition, security, physiotherapy, Tournament Officials and Ryder Cup administration has also been planned for.

Spectators have not been overlooked in the grand scheme either, and when the 2010 Matches are played, around 50,000 will be able to view the action while sitting on the natural amphitheatre banks that will run along the closing holes. In addition, the new layout will have only one hole that requires a crossing point.

The new course will start and finish at the new clubhouse overlooking the Usk Valley. There are spectacular views of the Brecon Beacons and the Severn Estuary. To the east, the Resort borders 23,000 acres of unspoilt woodland stretching to the beautiful Wye Valley.

Ireland

12

The Gleneagles Hotel - 2014

There can surely be no more fitting venue for the 2014 Ryder Cup in Scotland than The Gleneagles Hotel. For not only will the occasion represent the 40th playing of The Matches themselves, it will also see them return to the site of the first unofficial playing of the contest over 80 years ago. On June 6, 1921, a team of ten professionals from Great Britain & Ireland challenged their counterparts from the United States to a morning foursomes and afternoon singles contest at the Perthshire course and ran out 10 ½ - 4 ½ winners.

Scotland has, of course, hosted The Ryder Cup before, in 1973 at The Honourable Company of Edinburgh Golfers, Muirfield where the United States defeated Great Britain & Ireland 19-13 in The 20th Matches, but the 2014 contest will represent the first time a European Team has lined up north of the border.

A member of the victorious American Team in 1973 was the legendary Jack Nicklaus and it is highly appropriate that The Ryder Cup's return to Scotland will see it contested on The Golden Bear's first course design in that country. The PGA Centenary Course, formerly known as The Monarch's Course before being renamed in February 2001 to celebrate the Centenary year of the Professional Golfers' Association, was opened in May 1993 at a cost of £6 million.

Already the home to the Gleneagles Scottish PGA Championship on The European Tour International Schedule, the course - described by Nicklaus himself as "the finest natural parcel of land in the world I have ever been given to work with" - is also host to the WPGA International Match Play Championship. Even for a champion and acclaimed golf architect like Nicklaus, the PGA Centenary Course was a challenge. It had to be a great course and, set as it is in the heart of Scotland, the country which gave the world golf, it had to fit into the landscape in a way that did no violence to the Scottish tradition. It had to be unique in its challenge, a course in the modern design ethos that at its fullest stretch tested the greatest players, while, in the immortal phrase of Bobby Jones, "offered problems a man may attempt according to his ability... never hopeless for the lesser player nor failing to concern and interest the expert."

A consistent feature of The PGA Centenary Course layout is the feast of views of the spectacular countryside in which Gleneagles is set. Putting on the two-tier second green, you are distracted by the lush panorama of the rich Perthshire straths. As you move westwards over the next few holes, the rugged Grampians come into view on the right, then distantly ahead, Ben Vorlich and the mountains above the Trossachs.

As well as marvelling at Mother Nature, the Spectators at The 2014 Matches are also guaranteed excellent views of the action thanks to the natural amphitheatres around each hole which generate a true sense of grandeur and spectacle. "Gleneagles is very honoured to have been selected as the host venue for The 40th Ryder Cup Matches in 2014," said Peter Lederer, OBE, Managing Director of The Gleneagles Hotel. "It will be particularly significant for the resort which will celebrate its 90th anniversary in the same year."

match winning drive
The Royal Bank of Scotland is pleased to be the Official Bank to The European Tour.
Just like the game of golf (which originated in Scotland) our Corporate Banking & Financial Markets services reach around the world.
It means we can offer you the international strength and expertise you need. It means you can work with a corporate specialist or utilise modern banking services - from near or far - knowing we ll go the distance with you.
Give us a shot!
Make it happen.
EUROPEAN TOUR
OFFICIAL BANK
RYDER CUP 1927 2001
THE BELFRY
OFFICIAL BANK
Official Bank to The European Tour
www.rbs.co.uk
The Royal Bank of Scotland
The Royal Bank of Scotland plc. Registered in Scotland Number 90312.
Registered Office: 36 St Andrew Square, Edinburgh EH2 2YB. A member of the London Stock Exchange and regulated by IMRO, SFA and Personal Investment Authority.

PROUDLY SUPPORTING TH
We're already on
THE DE VERE BELFRY WEST MIDLANDS

The Good Life

Ian Stanley Senior British Open Champion

Ian Stanley is the first to admit that he did not fulfil his full potential while competing on The European and Australasian Tours during the 1970s and 1980s. The charismatic Australian will tell you that he believes he would have won a good deal more than once on The European Tour and 24 times "Down Under" had he been as dedicated as some of his rivals, and he will also insist that it was something he was determined to put right when he turned 50 on November 14, 1998, and decided to join the European Seniors Tour.

At first sight, Stanley would appear to be one of nature's more laid back characters. Certainly, he loves to enjoy himself but that penchant for the good life has not stopped him setting himself a series of goals since he embarked on his lucrative second career on the European Seniors Tour.

Stanley's goal during his first season on the European Seniors Tour was to consolidate a place in the top 25 on the Order of Merit and he accomplished that with some ease when he finished the 1999

Noel Ratcliffe

season in 21st place. The next season, he decided he wanted to progress to winning a first European Seniors Tour title and once again he succeeded in that aim when he emerged victorious at the Coca-Cola Kaiser Karl European Trophy at Haus Kambach, Germany.

By the end of the 2000 season, Stanley had moved up to fifth place on the European Seniors Tour Order of Merit behind his compatriot, Noel Ratcliffe, but he was determined not to rest on his laurels, going home instead, first to fulfil his contract as a golf commentator for Fox TV, and then to set his next goals for the 2001 season.

Last winter, while at home in Melbourne, Stanley decided that he wanted to progress to winning what he describes as one of the European Seniors Tour's two Major Championships. He set his sights on winning either the De Vere PGA Seniors' Championship at De Vere Carden Park, England, or the Senior British Open, presented by MasterCard, at Royal County Down Golf Club, Northern Ireland, but never in his wildest dreams did he anticipate collecting both.

In times to come, the 2001 European Seniors Tour season will be

Denis O'Sullivan

David Good

seen as the season Stanley finally fulfilled the potential that his heroes, Kel Nagle and Peter Thomson, had seen in him when he turned professional back in 1970. It was a process that started when he held off a determined challenge from England's Maurice Bembridge to win the De Vere PGA Seniors' Championship over the new Jack Nicklaus course at the De Vere Carden Park. "It is a great honour for me to win this title," said Stanley, after collecting the 55,191 euro (£33,320) first prize. "I've always believed it to be one of the senior Majors and it is particularly special to win it because two of my greatest idols, Kel Nagle and Peter Thomson, have won it before."

Stanley moved briefly to the top of the European Seniors Tour Order of Merit after winning that title and it was a position he was to consolidate two months later when he emulated a feat achieved by Neil Coles in 1987 by winning the Senior British Open, presented by MasterCard, and the PGA Seniors' Championship in the same season.

On that occasion, Stanley played some of the finest golf of his career, producing rounds of 70, 69, 70 and 69 to finish tied with Bob Charles and then defeating the veteran left hander on the first hole of the subsequent play-off. What's more, it was a performance that was all the more impressive because it was produced against the

Gary Player, Jack Nicklaus and Arnold Palmer

Darren Clarke

Ian Stanley receives from Andy Stubbs, Managing Director, European Seniors Tour, The John Jacobs Trophy which is awarded annually to the Number One player in the European Seniors Tour Order of Merit

strongest field ever assembled for this Championship. For the first time ever, the 'Big Three', Jack Nicklaus, Arnold Palmer and Gary Player, all played, helping to raise the Championship to a new level. Al Balding, aged 76, of Canada, also entered, creating headlines of his own when he beat his age with a second round 71. It was a marvellous moment and one that was emulated several months later when 68 year old Englishman, David Snell, shaved one stroke off his age with a second round of 67 in the Tunisian Seniors Open at Port El Kantaoui.

Given Stanley's outstanding victories at the De Vere PGA Seniors' Championship and the Senior British Open, presented by MasterCard, it was only fitting that, come the end of the season, he was confirmed as the winner of The John Jacobs Trophy, awarded to the leader of the European Seniors Tour Order of Merit following the European Seniors Tour Championship at PGA Golf de Catalunya in Girona, Spain. There, at the last event of the season, he finished tied sixth to take his winnings for the season to a record 287,025 euro (£178,460) which enabled him to finish ahead of Denis Durnian (276,623 euro; £171,993) and Ratcliffe (218,685 euro; £135,969). As Stanley savoured this delicious moment so he also learned that he had been nominated Australian Golfer of the Year by the Golf Digest magazine in his native Australia.

Bob Shearer

Denis Durnian

Nick Job

Seiji Ebihara

David Huish

During 2001, total prize money on the European Seniors Tour increased by a staggering 54 percent over the previous season and Stanley was not the only golfer to benefit. Elsewhere Durnian claimed the biggest first prize in European Seniors Tour history when he collected the 139,555 euro (£83,300) on offer at the inaugural Wales Seniors Open over the venerable Royal St David's Golf Club at Harlech and a total of 24 golfers ended the season with earnings in excess of 100,000 euro.

Stanley was the undoubted star of the 2001 season but he was not the only multiple winner because Japan's Seiji Ebihara (AIB Irish Seniors Open and Microlease Jersey Seniors Masters), Ireland's Denis O'Sullivan (Palmerston Trophy Berlin and STC Scandinavian International), Ratcliffe (Beko Classic and De Vere Hotels Seniors Classic) and America's David Oakley (Energis Senior Masters and Scottish Seniors Open) also all won more than once.

Other previous winners such as Brazil's Priscillo Diniz (The Royal Westmoreland Barbados Open), England's Nick Job (Lawrence Batley Seniors), David Huish (Bad Ragaz PGA Seniors Open) and Australia's Bob Shearer (STC Bovis Lend Lease European Invitational) added to their tally of European Seniors Tour titles but there was to be frustration for campaigners such as Neil Coles, Tommy Horton, Brian Huggett and John Morgan, none of whom won during the 2001 campaign. For Horton it was particularly significant because, by not winning what would have been a 24th European Seniors Tour title, it meant that for the first time since

Jerry Bruner

Russell Weir

Jack Nicklaus

Maurice Bembridge

Jay Horton

1992 he went through a whole season without a tournament victory. With Horton reaching the age of 60, and qualifying for the weekly Hardys Wines Super Seniors prizes alongside the likes of Bob Charles, John Fourie, Bill Hardwick, Joe McDermott, Bobby Verwey, Coles and Huggett, there was room for the newcomers to make a mark and it was significant that during 2001 no less than seven first-time winners emerged into the spotlight.

Ebihara, in his second season on the European Seniors Tour, was the first new winner to enter the 2001 winner's circle, finishing with a birdie on the final hole to defeat New Zealand rookie Simon Owen at the AIB Irish Seniors Open at Powerscourt Golf Club, Dublin, Ireland. Durnian reached the winner's circle next, producing rounds of 74-65 and 69 to claim the Wales Seniors Open and he was followed by the rejuvenated Australian, David Good, who confirmed his claim to be the European Seniors Tour's most improved player of the season when he defeated America's Jerry Bruner with a birdie on the first hole of a sudden-death play-off at the Legends in Golf tournament at Crayestein Golf Club at Dordrecht in The Netherlands. Incidentally, that was Bruner's eighth second place finish since joining the European Senior Tour in 1999 and he was to be the bridesmaid once more before the season was out, also finishing second at the Dan Technology Senior Tournament of Champions at Mere Golf & Country Club, Manchester, England, before his own moment of glory arrived.

The triumphs of Durnian, Ebihara and Good emphasised that the European Seniors Tour was witnessing a changing of the guard and that process was confirmed in the autumn when first time winners were crowned in five successive tournaments.

Michael Rayment from Hardy's Wines presents Tommy Horton with the winners cheque.

HARDYS SUPER SENIORS ORDER OF MERIT
Final after European Seniors Tour Championship

Pos	Name	Points
1	Bill Hardwick (Can)	4,250
2	Bob Charles (NZ)	3,500
3	Tommy Horton (Eng)	2,650
4	Bobby Verwey (SA)	2,250
5	Neil Coles (Eng)	2,000
6	John Fourie (SA)	1,300
7	Jay Dolan III (USA)	1,200
8	Joe McDermott (Ire)	1,150

Delroy Cambridge

Simon Owen

Tommy Horton

Scotland's Russell Weir was the first to be installed when, in just his sixth start after turning 50 in time for the Seniors British Open, presented by MasterCard, he won the TEMES Seniors Open at Glyfada Golf Club in Greece and he was swiftly followed by Jamaica's Delroy Cambridge (Dan Technology Senior Tournament of Champions), New Zealand's Simon Owen (Tunisian Seniors Open), England's Jim Rhodes (SSL International/Sodexho Match Play Championship, presented by The Daily Telegraph) and Bruner (European Seniors Tour Championship).

Cambridge, Owen and Weir, alongside the likes of England's Keith MacDonald and Ian Mosey, New Zealand's Barry Vivian, and Scotland's John Chillas and Mike Miller, were all members of one of the most promising group of rookies that the European Seniors Tour has ever attracted but the same cannot be said of Rhodes, a veteran of six seasons of competing on the European Seniors Tour. Rhodes, a former club professional from Cannock, came into the 2001 season in 15th place on the European Seniors Tour Career Money List with earnings of 271,372 euro, but even he was beginning to wonder if he would ever taste victory until he overcame Peter Cowen, O'Sullivan, Stanley and Oakley before defeating Welshman Craig Defoy in a stirring final to the SSL International/Sodexho Match Play Championship, presented by The Daily Telegraph, at Le Meridien Penina Golf & Resort on the Algarve of Portugal.

David Oakley

Neil Coles

The Englishman was in an emotional state when he collected his winner's cheque from the sponsors but not too overcome to put his victory into perspective. "This means an awful lot to me," he said. "I wouldn't say that I was beginning to wonder if I was ever going to win but to do it certainly takes a great weight off the mind. This season there has been a huge improvement in the standard of play on the European Seniors Tour and that means it is becoming increasingly difficult to win out here.

"Once, you could afford the odd bad shot, the odd bad round, and still do well, but not anymore. Suddenly, it's much more competitive and it's also a lot more lucrative as Ian, Denis and the other guys at the top of the money list have found."

The last word on 2001, however, must go to Stanley. He said: "It's huge to be Number One. Over the last five weeks of the season there were five consecutive first time winners which fully underlined the strength in depth of the European Seniors Tour. It is tough to do well out here so everyone knows what it means to win let alone finish Number One."

Colin Callander

Priscillo Diniz

John Morgan

Bernard Gallacher

Jim Rhodes

Ian Stanley, Arnold Palmer and Seiji Ebihara

EUROPEAN SENIORS TOUR FINAL ORDER OF MERIT

Pos	Name			€	£
1	Ian STANLEY	(Aus)	(20)	287,025.14	177,478.38
2	Denis DURNIAN	(Eng)	(22)	276,623.40	171,046.59
3	Noel RATCLIFFE	(Aus)	(20)	218,685.44	135,221.39
4	David GOOD	(Aus)	(22)	214,500.19	132,633.49
5	Jerry BRUNER	(USA)	(22)	214,457.29	132,606.97
6	Simon OWEN	(NZ)	(18)	199,341.67	123,260.41
7	David OAKLEY	(USA)	(21)	188,061.40	116,285.40
8	Seiji EBIHARA	(Jpn)	(13)	187,077.15	115,676.80
9	Delroy CAMBRIDGE	(Jam)	(21)	177,871.80	109,984.79
10	John MORGAN	(Eng)	(21)	171,750.33	106,199.65
11	Bernard GALLACHER	(Scot)	(19)	166,623.74	103,029.70
12	Denis O'SULLIVAN	(Ire)	(22)	165,919.98	102,594.53
13	Maurice BEMBRIDGE	(Eng)	(22)	143,651.84	88,825.31
14	Jay HORTON	(USA)	(20)	134,576.93	83,213.95
15	Priscillo DINIZ	(Bra)	(19)	126,670.77	78,325.27
16	Bob SHEARER	(Aus)	(16)	121,619.54	75,201.91
17	Barry VIVIAN	(NZ)	(16)	117,312.61	72,538.77
18	Keith MACDONALD	(Eng)	(19)	114,243.28	70,640.89
19	Nick JOB	(Eng)	(20)	111,083.86	68,687.31
20	Malcolm GREGSON	(Eng)	(19)	107,364.10	66,387.24
21	Peter DAWSON	(Eng)	(22)	107,174.87	66,270.23
22	Bob LENDZION	(USA)	(16)	105,483.34	65,224.29
23	Jim RHODES	(Eng)	(22)	104,274.06	64,476.55
24	David CREAMER	(Eng)	(22)	101,523.02	62,775.48
25	Craig DEFOY	(Wal)	(20)	97,787.52	60,465.68
26	Terry GALE	(Aus)	(13)	94,912.15	58,687.74
27	John GRACE	(USA)	(15)	93,615.54	57,885.99
28	Mike MILLER	(Scot)	(19)	89,715.49	55,474.45
29	Tommy HORTON	(Eng)	(19)	85,342.68	52,770.57
30	David HUISH	(Scot)	(19)	84,052.83	51,973.01
31	Eddie POLLAND	(N.Ire)	(21)	83,266.49	51,486.78
32	Bill HARDWICK	(Can)	(22)	82,922.68	51,274.19
33	Jeff VAN WAGENEN	(USA)	(22)	78,943.22	48,813.55
34	Bobby VERWEY	(SA)	(16)	75,749.83	46,838.95
35	John MCTEAR	(Scot)	(19)	75,002.57	46,376.90
36	Alan TAPIE	(USA)	(17)	70,491.63	43,587.61
37	Russell WEIR	(Scot)	(10)	69,548.49	43,004.43
38	Paul LEONARD	(N.Ire)	(16)	64,440.07	39,845.71
39	Alberto CROCE	(It)	(17)	56,530.46	34,954.90
40	Neil COLES	(Eng)	(11)	55,371.41	34,238.21
41	John IRWIN	(Can)	(15)	51,835.07	32,051.56
42	Hank WOODROME	(USA)	(16)	50,536.27	31,248.47
43	Peter TOWNSEND	(Eng)	(21)	47,274.57	29,231.63
44	Ray CARRASCO	(USA)	(13)	42,281.87	26,144.46
45	Brian HUGGETT	(Wal)	(8)	40,278.45	24,905.67
46	Steve WILD	(Eng)	(13)	38,185.52	23,611.54
47	Tommy PRICE	(USA)	(17)	36,748.52	22,722.98
48	Silvano LOCATELLI	(It)	(15)	35,520.20	21,963.47
49	Jay DOLAN III	(USA)	(20)	34,697.54	21,454.78
50	David VAUGHAN	(Wal)	(9)	34,441.23	21,296.30

Pos	Name			€	£
51	Trevor DOWNING	(Aus)	(18)	33,886.28	20,953.15
52	Roberto BERNARDINI	(It)	(13)	32,063.81	19,826.25
53	Renato CAMPAGNOLI	(It)	(14)	29,268.42	18,097.76
54	John CHILLAS	(Scot)	(5)	26,602.09	16,449.07
55	Antonio GARRIDO	(Sp)	(18)	24,627.91	15,228.36
56	Ross METHERELL	(Aus)	(16)	24,587.46	15,203.35
57	John FOURIE	(SA)	(19)	24,099.81	14,901.81
58	Liam HIGGINS	(Ire)	(16)	24,064.29	14,879.85
59	Lawrence FARMER	(Wal)	(15)	23,681.71	14,643.29
60	Randall VINES	(Aus)	(20)	22,931.80	14,179.59
61	Rodger DAVIS	(Aus)	(4)	21,535.67	13,316.31
62	Kenny STEVENSON	(N.Ire)	(16)	21,357.61	13,206.21
63	Brian WAITES	(Eng)	(14)	20,346.67	12,581.11
64	David OJALA	(USA)	(8)	20,250.14	12,521.42
65	Graham BURROUGHS	(Eng)	(9)	19,863.60	12,282.41
66	Manuel SANCHEZ	(Sp)	(15)	18,665.53	11,541.60
67	Geoff PARSLOW	(Aus)	(19)	18,500.33	11,439.45
68	Joe MCDERMOTT	(Ire)	(9)	18,174.90	11,238.22
69	Gordon MACDONALD	(Scot)	(14)	17,736.11	10,966.90
70	Ian MOSEY	(Eng)	(6)	16,199.84	10,016.97
71	Manuel BALLESTEROS	(Sp)	(13)	13,698.33	8,470.19
72	Jan BJÖRNSSON	(Swe)	(16)	13,289.28	8,217.26
73	Antero BABURIN	(Swe)	(18)	12,900.06	7,976.59
74	Leonard OWENS	(Ire)	(13)	12,155.45	7,516.17
75	Peter WARD	(Eng)	(14)	11,743.31	7,261.33
76	J.R. DELICH	(USA)	(9)	11,112.77	6,871.44
77	Glenn MACDONALD	(Can)	(16)	11,094.38	6,860.07
78	Raymond KANE	(Ire)	(17)	10,189.33	6,300.44
79	Pat KAYLOR	(USA)	(9)	9,762.55	6,036.55
80	John TOLHURST	(Aus)	(8)	8,869.55	5,484.37
81	Barry SANDRY	(Eng)	(9)	7,886.50	4,876.52
82	Norman WOOD	(Scot)	(10)	7,834.93	4,844.63
83	Tienie BRITZ	(SA)	(5)	7,282.69	4,503.16
84	Paul VAN BILJON	(SA)	(14)	6,987.59	4,320.69
85	Arnold O'CONNOR	(Ire)	(11)	6,573.14	4,064.42
86	Rick UHLIR	(USA)	(15)	6,301.95	3,896.73
87	Michael STEADMAN	(Eng)	(8)	5,729.88	3,543.00
88	William MILNE	(Scot)	(4)	5,168.31	3,195.76
89	Robert WEBSTER	(Scot)	(13)	4,998.66	3,090.86
90	John BENDA	(USA)	(4)	4,790.68	2,962.26
91	Paul HERBERT	(Eng)	(5)	4,622.91	2,858.52
92	Tomas PERSSON	(Swe)	(6)	4,426.09	2,736.82
93	Brad FRANKS	(USA)	(15)	4,369.60	2,701.89
94	Hugh DOLAN	(Aus)	(5)	4,309.49	2,664.72
95	Ian RICHARDSON	(Eng)	(10)	4,213.72	2,605.50
96	John GARNER	(Eng)	(5)	4,025.90	2,489.36
97	David SNELL	(Eng)	(6)	3,965.90	2,452.27
98	Bill LOCKIE	(Scot)	(4)	3,734.34	2,309.08
99	Richard BEER	(Aus)	(13)	3,703.72	2,290.15
100	TR JONES	(USA)	(6)	3,225.35	1,994.35

In Good Hands

Mark Foster

It may seem a curious golfing fact but you will always find someone, somewhere, bemoaning the lack of talent around. "Where is the next crop of European stars?" they cry. "How can we hope to compete with the skilful youngsters coming out of Argentina, Australia, South Africa and the United States," they add.

The Doubting Thomases will always drone on, but they seldom look further than their noses. If they did, they would see that European golf is in a very healthy state with the game in the good hands of a host of young, exciting and talented individuals.

If anyone wondered where the next generation of gifted players such as Severiano Ballesteros, Nick Faldo, Bernhard Langer, Sandy Lyle and Ian Woosnam were coming from they need only look at The European Tour. Since the "Famous Five" gave birth to a special era others such as Paul Lawrie and José Maria Olazábal have emerged to win Major Championships not to mention the record breaking achievement of Colin Montgomerie collecting seven successive Volvo Order of Merit Number One honours.

Jamie Donaldson

Sebastien Delagrange

Now we have good reason to enthuse about the future because the European Challenge Tour's claim to fame that it produces the "Stars of the Future" was fully endorsed in 2001 with graduates Tobias Dier and Henrik Stenson increasing the wins to 37 by different Challenge Tour players on The European Tour since 1991. The total number of wins reached 70 with Thomas Björn, Michael Campbell, Andrew Coltart, Thomas Levet and Ian Poulter all successful in 2001.

And there would appear to be much, much more to come for as the likes of Luke Donald, Nick Dougherty and Steven O'Hara were progressing from the winning Great Britain and Ireland Walker Cup team, Gregory Havret was advancing from three times French Amateur champion to his maiden European Tour triumph and Paul Casey was breaking through in only his 11th European Tour event, so the season-long battle for European Challenge Tour honours, and one of the prized 15 cards for The 2002 European Tour International Schedule, was producing another class of starry-eyed challengers led by Mark Foster of England and Jamie Donaldson of Wales.

Foster, like Donaldson, enjoyed a highly successful amateur career. Aged 26, he is a great friend of Lee Westwood. In fact they both hail from Worksop in Nottinghamshire and occasionally can be seen taking the odd pound off each other on the fairways. Foster's amateur campaign included being crowned English champion in successive years, and he played in the 1995 Walker Cup team at Royal Porthcawl that defeated the United States - Tiger Woods and all!

Klas Eriksson

Andrew Marshall

Foster made a frustrating start to his professional career but he was fast out of the blocks in 2001. He finished fourth in the Tusker Kenya Open at Muthaiga Golf Club in Nairobi then, the following week in Lusaka, took his maiden title by a shot with a victory in the Stanbic Zambia Open at Lusaka Golf Club.

That first win had been a long time coming and, two weeks later, when the Tour returned to Europe and the Spanish mainland, Foster filled third place behind Scotland's Euan Little in the Segura Viudas Challenge de España at Club de Golf Villamartin, Alicante, in Spain.

With that start, Foster took over at the top of the Rankings and there he remained for much of the campaign apart from a short spell when he was dislodged by France's Sebastien Delagrange, one of four multiple winners during the year. The two had a healthy rivalry, never more so that in the Charles Church European Challenge Tour Championship at the delightful Bowood Golf and Country Club in Wiltshire, England, in July when Foster secured his second title by two strokes from the Frenchman and Golding.

"I took the decision in 2001 to stay with the Challenge Tour for the entire season," said Foster. "I had new clubs, a new ball, I worked hard under Peter Cowen and I would have been disappointed if I had not done well. It was a fantastic season for me."

Foster earned 97,736 euro (£60,768) to finish Number One ahead of Donaldson (92,740 euro; £57,662), England's Philip Golding

Gary Clark

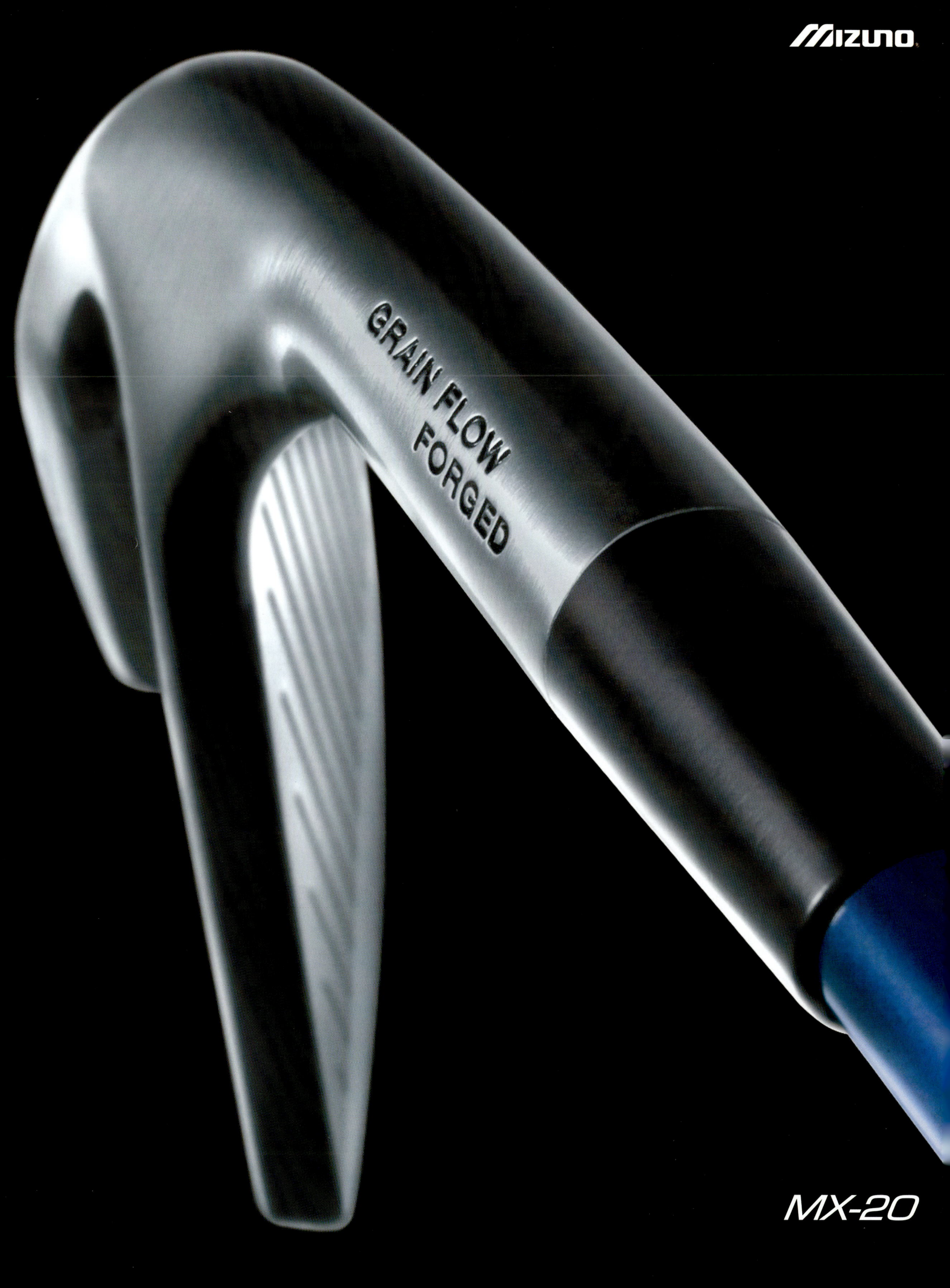
MIZUNO
GRAIN FLOW
FORGED
MX-20

Peter Hanson

(79,731 euro; £49,573), Andrew Marshall (75,840 euro; £47,154) and Gary Clark (72,949 euro; £45,347) with Delagrange (71,236 euro; £44,292) eventually finishing sixth. It was Donaldson, however, who chased Foster through to the season-ending Challenge Tour Grand Final at Golf du Médoc in Bordeaux, France.

Donaldson, who finished runner-up in the Brabazon and St Andrews Links Trophies, gained selection for the 2000 Great Britain & Ireland Eisenhower Trophy team that finished second to the United States in Berlin. His greatest disappointment was failing to make the 1999 Walker Cup team. But that is history and, having turned professional in November, 2000, the 26 year old had to rely on invitations to kick start his new career. "I had six on the Challenge Tour but managed to make the most of them," he said. "I'm always pushing for a win in every Tour event I play because it will open more doors."

After a promising start, he finished tied fourth in the Austrian Open, then was runner-up in the 5th Aa Saint Omer Open. But it was his victory in the BMW Russian Open at the Moscow Golf and Country Club in August which identified him as one of the emerging generation of young European talent.

To further underline his huge potential, Donaldson also came out on top in the Telia Grand Prix at Bro Bälsta, Stockholm, in Sweden in September. He said after the victory: "A win is always hard to achieve but this was similar to Russia in that I led for most of the way. I suppose Sweden was a little harder because it was an easier course where someone could have shot a really low round."

Donaldson further enhanced his growing reputation when on The European Tour he followed finishing tied fourth in The Celtic Manor Resort Wales Open and tied 13th in the Omega European Masters in Switzerland by closing with a 68 at St Andrews for a share of ninth place in the Dunhill Links Championship which launched him into the top 100 in the 2001 Volvo Order of Merit with winnings of 195,502 euro (£121,555). This was a remarkable achievement which earned Donaldson Category 7 Membership through the 2001 Volvo Order of Merit whereby those players in positions one to 16 in the 2001 European Challenge Tour Rankings earned Category 10 Membership for The 2002 European Tour International Schedule.

The man born in Pontypridd but based in Macclesfield has set himself some tough goals but he is pleased with his rapid progress. "As long as you put yourself in a position to play to the best of your ability anything can happen," he adds. "I set my standards high on the course and I practise a lot. I practise all day, every day. If you want to catch Tiger Woods you can't afford to lie in bed."

Golding secured third place in the European Challenge Tour Rankings with an excellent performance in the Challenge Tour Grand Final – closing with rounds of 65 and 66 to finish runner up as England's Richard Bland produced the round of his life with a 63

Robert-Jan Derksen

to take the title with an 18 under par total of 266. Golding's consistencey stems from experience – he turned professional 20 years ago after deciding to curtail a flourishing cricket career – and he will be looking forward to The 2002 European Tour International Schedule.

Marshall and Clark, like Golding, showed superb consistency throughout the season while Delagrange was one of four multiple winners. The 27 year old Frenchman held all at bay to win the 5th Aa Saint Omer Open at Aa Saint Omer Golf Club in France then two weeks later won the Nykredit Danish Open at Aalborg Golf Club in Denmark. "To win twice in a row and to be leading for all eight days was very special," he said.

Londoner Chris Gane, the 27 year old left-hander, was the other player to enjoy two victories by lifting the Austrian Open at Golf Club Murhof, Graz, in May and the Terme Euganee International Open Padova in October at Golf Club Padova, Valsansibio, Italy.

To say that 2001 was a celebration of British golf would be something of an understatement. There is little doubt that British players dominated, winning 16 of the 29 titles on offer. That was reflected by those gaining their cards with nine coming from Britain, one each from Denmark, France and Holland and four from Sweden.

Chris Gane

Philip Golding

Mads Vibe-Hastrup

The Dane is Mads Vibe-Hastrup, a name that is likely to initially prove a tongue-twister for commentators as the fans grow accustomed to this likeable 22 year old. His triumph late in the season in the San Paolo Vita & Asset Management Open at Margara Golf Club in Italy was a victory waiting to happen. On arriving in Italy, he had played in 12 events, recording six top-ten finishes and just three missed cuts. On top of that, the lad from Helsingor had topped the Nordic League, winning three titles in nine tournaments.

But the victory still came as a shock. "I never expected to win on the Challenge Tour this year," he said. "But I have a strong game and when I finished second in the Volvo Finnish Open in July I thought that if my game was working well I could finish high. This is far above my expectations."

Not only did Vibe-Hastrup win but he did it in style, picking up five strokes over the closing six holes to take the title by a shot on 21 under par. A talented amateur, Vibe-Hastrup won the Doug Sanders World Junior Championship in 1996 in Aberdeen, following the likes of Daniel Chopra, Fredrik Jacobson, Shaun Webster, Michael Welch and preceding Australian Adam Scott. That same year he played for Denmark in the Eisenhower Trophy in Manila. He might have taken the familiar route and gone to college in the United States, but chose instead to turn professional at the end of 1999.

He played just six times on the 2000 European Challenge Tour without commanding attention although he did share the first round lead, also in Italy, after firing a 65 in the Tessali Open del Sud. Joint 44th was his final placing but the promise was there. "Then I was inexperienced," he said. "I never managed to stay relaxed or focused. I didn't have the mental strength, but I have worked hard on this."

Considering he didn't have a category in 2001, Vibe-Hastrup has performed wonders. In 2002 he will boost the Danish contingent and join forces with compatriot Thomas Björn. The big league awaits Vibe-Hastrup, who certainly has the talent and the ability to become another great Dane.

He will certainly be a welcomed addition to The 2002 European Tour International Schedule as will all the European Challenge Tour graduates - a mix of young and experienced campaigners - as they join forces with other new faces for the global challenge that offers fame and fortune.

David Hamilton

Richard Bland

Mårten Olander

Peter Hedblom

Grant Hamerton

Stuart Little

Richard Bland and Mark Foster

EUROPEAN CHALLENGE TOUR FINAL RANKINGS

Pos	Name			€	£
1	Mark FOSTER	(Eng)	(23)	97,736.71	60,768.69
2	Jamie DONALDSON	(Wal)	(18)	92,740.20	57,662.06
3	Philip GOLDING	(Eng)	(21)	79,731.35	49,573.69
4	Andrew MARSHALL	(Eng)	(19)	75,840.90	47,154.77
5	Gary CLARK	(Eng)	(24)	72,949.77	45,357.18
6	Sebastien DELAGRANGE	(Fr)	(12)	71,236.94	44,292.21
7	Klas ERIKSSON	(Swe)	(22)	66,933.36	41,616.42
8	Robert Jan DERKSEN	(Hol)	(20)	61,595.11	38,297.32
9	Chris GANE	(Eng)	(25)	60,778.07	37,789.32
10	Richard BLAND	(Eng)	(21)	60,693.27	37,736.59
11	Mads VIBE-HASTRUP	(Den)	(16)	60,677.01	37,726.48
12	Peter HANSON	(Swe)	(6)	60,432.40	37,574.40
13	Grant HAMERTON	(Eng)	(24)	59,580.64	37,044.81
14	Stuart LITTLE	(Eng)	(25)	58,649.94	36,466.13
15	Mårten OLANDER	(Swe)	(20)	58,306.44	36,252.56
16	Peter HEDBLOM	(Swe)	(16)	57,680.47	35,863.35
17	Greig HUTCHEON	(Scot)	(18)	56,387.55	35,059.47
18	Scott DRUMMOND	(Scot)	(21)	54,058.29	33,611.23
19	Andrew SHERBORNE	(Eng)	(25)	53,173.13	33,060.88
20	André BOSSERT	(Swi)	(24)	51,080.59	31,759.82
21	Michael ARCHER	(Eng)	(21)	50,401.93	31,337.86
22	Benn BARHAM	(Eng)	(22)	49,664.27	30,879.21
23	Iain PYMAN	(Eng)	(23)	47,749.82	29,688.88
24	Mattias ELIASSON	(Swe)	(24)	47,025.45	29,238.50
25	Alberto BINAGHI	(It)	(21)	46,104.04	28,665.61
26	Ashley ROESTOFF	(SA)	(22)	44,466.12	27,647.21
27	Dominique NOUAILHAC	(Fr)	(22)	43,639.79	27,133.43
28	Mattias NILSSON	(Swe)	(21)	39,392.73	24,492.79
29	Didier DE VOOGHT	(Bel)	(25)	38,192.88	23,746.77
30	Euan LITTLE	(Scot)	(25)	36,965.02	22,983.34
31	Jesus Maria ARRUTI	(Sp)	(19)	36,047.64	22,412.95
32	Simon WAKEFIELD	(Eng)	(25)	33,882.37	21,066.67
33	Sam WALKER	(Eng)	(22)	33,031.27	20,537.49
34	Kenneth FERRIE	(Eng)	(15)	32,915.77	20,465.68
35	Joakim RASK	(Swe)	(19)	32,231.06	20,039.95
36	Magnus PERSSON	(Swe)	(19)	31,735.98	19,732.13
37	Kariem BARAKA	(Ger)	(21)	31,636.34	19,670.18
38	Ian HUTCHINGS	(SA)	(16)	31,443.68	19,550.39
39	Hennie WALTERS	(SA)	(21)	31,122.69	19,350.82
40	Marc PENDARIES	(Fr)	(18)	30,867.54	19,192.17
41	Christophe POTTIER	(Fr)	(19)	30,219.33	18,789.14
42	Miles TUNNICLIFF	(Eng)	(18)	30,214.34	18,786.04
43	Federico BISAZZA	(It)	(24)	29,871.06	18,572.60
44	Wolfgang HUGET	(Ger)	(14)	29,090.46	18,087.26
45	Johan SKOLD	(Swe)	(19)	28,847.98	17,936.49
46	Pehr MAGNEBRANT	(Swe)	(19)	26,536.21	16,499.13
47	Simon D. HURLEY	(Eng)	(15)	26,214.27	16,298.96
48	Mikael PILTZ	(Fin)	(20)	25,856.97	16,076.80
49	Lee S JAMES	(Eng)	(25)	25,364.57	15,770.65
50	Alvaro SALTO	(Sp)	(21)	24,766.88	15,399.03
51	James HEPWORTH	(Eng)	(23)	24,578.83	15,282.11
52	Damien MCGRANE	(Ire)	(11)	22,732.91	14,134.39
53	Jean-François LUCQUIN	(Fr)	(22)	22,405.83	13,931.03
54	Paul DWYER	(Eng)	(22)	21,828.50	13,572.07
55	Fredrik WIDMARK	(Swe)	(22)	21,807.41	13,558.95
56	Simon KHAN	(Eng)	(20)	21,062.83	13,096.01
57	Daniel CHOPRA	(Swe)	(11)	20,708.10	12,875.45
58	Peter LAWRIE	(Ire)	(25)	20,469.86	12,727.32
59	Gary MURPHY	(Ire)	(13)	19,709.26	12,254.41
60	Andreas LJUNGGREN	(Swe)	(21)	19,326.02	12,016.13
61	Sam LITTLE	(Eng)	(17)	19,264.43	11,977.83
62	Thomas HAVEMANN	(Den)	(20)	18,945.13	11,779.30
63	Dennis EDLUND	(Swe)	(13)	18,828.03	11,706.50
64	Gianluca BARUFFALDI	(It)	(20)	18,425.32	11,456.11
65	Tony EDLUND	(Swe)	(18)	18,264.87	11,356.35
66	Niels KRAAIJ	(Hol)	(11)	18,129.38	11,272.11
67	Peter MALMGREN	(Swe)	(17)	17,999.80	11,191.54
68	Kalle VAINOLA	(Fin)	(18)	17,777.72	11,053.46
69	Pasi PURHONEN	(Fin)	(15)	17,705.04	11,008.27
70	Simon HURD	(Eng)	(19)	17,265.10	10,734.73
71	Per LARSSON	(Swe)	(18)	17,100.12	10,632.16
72	Massimo FLORIOLI	(It)	(13)	16,804.70	10,448.47
73	Andrew BUTTERFIELD	(Eng)	(21)	16,334.85	10,156.34
74	Bjorn PETTERSSON	(Swe)	(18)	15,697.67	9,760.17
75	Tino SCHUSTER	(Ger)	(15)	15,122.63	9,402.63
76	Adam MEDNICK	(Swe)	(23)	14,961.71	9,302.58
77	Knud STORGAARD	(Den)	(19)	14,941.04	9,289.73
78	Ulrik GUSTAFSSON	(Swe)	(21)	14,780.80	9,190.10
79	Marcel SIEM	(Ger)	(14)	14,286.91	8,883.02
80	Francesco GUERMANI	(It)	(18)	13,524.29	8,408.85
81	Marcello SANTI	(It)	(7)	13,522.12	8,407.50
82	Patrik GOTTFRIDSON	(Swe)	(18)	13,153.91	8,178.57
83	Hampus VON POST	(Swe)	(14)	13,043.27	8,109.77
84	Robert MCGUIRK	(Eng)	(21)	12,194.99	7,582.35
85	David DRYSDALE	(Scot)	(21)	12,139.14	7,547.62
86	Martin ERLANDSSON	(Swe)	(23)	12,073.89	7,507.05
87	Ben MASON	(Eng)	(15)	11,885.30	7,389.80
88	Carlos LARRAIN	(Ven)	(14)	11,680.92	7,262.72
89	Raimo SJÖBERG	(Swe)	(18)	11,656.85	7,247.75
90	Franck AUMONIER	(Fr)	(18)	11,639.84	7,237.18
91	Kalle BRINK	(Swe)	(20)	11,500.56	7,150.58
92	Lee THOMPSON	(Eng)	(16)	11,433.25	7,108.73
93	Paul NILBRINK	(Swe)	(21)	11,412.44	7,095.79
94	Frédéric CUPILLARD	(Fr)	(7)	11,319.86	7,038.23
95	Thomas BESANCENEZ	(Fr)	(15)	11,242.41	6,990.07
96	Benoit TEILLERIA	(Fr)	(14)	10,822.49	6,728.98
97	Thomas NORRET	(Den)	(24)	10,639.82	6,615.40
98	Olivier DAVID	(Fr)	(20)	10,569.95	6,571.96
99	Richard DINSDALE	(Wal)	(13)	10,312.35	6,411.80
100	Jamie LITTLE	(Eng)	(10)	9,740.77	6,056.41

NB: Jamie Donaldson has earned Cat 7 ranking through the 2001 Volvo Order of Merit and therefore those players in positions one to 16 in the 2001 European Challenge Tour Rankings have earned Cat 10 ranking for The 2002 European Tour International Schedule.

Wages of Sin

It must rank as the shortest distance a golf ball has travelled to win The European Tour Shot of the Year, but Paul Lawrie's 40 foot putt from the infamous Valley of Sin at the Old Course at St Andrews was a colossal effort by any standard.

The 32 year old Scot had watched his approach to the 18th green spin off the putting surface and gather in that small pocket which has been the graveyard of many a golfer, professional and amateur, down the years.

However, the hallowed turf of the Old Lady provided Lawrie with similar inspiration to that which he had displayed two years earlier just a few miles across St Andrews Bay at Carnoustie where he captured the Open Championship after a thrilling play-off.

He had not won since that historic day at Carnoustie, but Lawrie arrived at the 72nd hole of the Dunhill Links Championship knowing that another huge victory was again within his grasp.

Lawrie, who had established a new course record of 63, nine under par, for the revised Old Course layout in his third round, was tied with Ernie Els playing the final hole after he had three putted the 17th and the South African had rolled in a birdie effort at the last.

As Els sat in the warmth of the Recorder's Office adjacent to the 18th, Lawrie could only watch in disbelief as his soft sand iron approach sucked back off the front of the green. Now the Scot faced the daunting task of attempting to get down in two to match Els's 17 under par total of 271.

To those watching enthralled, memories flooded back of Costantino Rocca's remarkable putt to tie John Daly in the 1995 Open Championship from a near identical spot, and Miguel Angel Martin's equally improbable putt from the 'Valley' in the 2000 Alfred Dunhill Cup which was the catalyst for Spain's victory.

Undaunted, the quietly-spoken Aberdonian went about his business, lined up his 40 foot putt with the Dunhill Links Championship title and 881,251 euro (£551,040) resting on the stroke and took dead aim. The ball trundled up and over the ridge and, with perfect line and pace, dropped into the cup.

Lawrie, normally the most reserved of characters, broke into a spontaneous victory jig as Els, wreathed in smiles, emerged from his sanctuary to embrace the victor in a massive bear hug.

With his 18 under par aggregate, Lawrie was the champion and drove the 70 miles home to Aberdeen with the plunder in his back pocket and a massive, glittering silver trophy to admire.

The Scot reflected on that dramatic climax to this celebration of links golf, played over three marvellous courses, St Andrews, Carnoustie and Kingsbarns, by admitting: "I wasn't thinking of what Rocca had done until I came off the course and someone mentioned it.

"When I am playing and in contention I am focused on nothing but the job in front of me. In this case my priority was to get down in two to force a play-off and not three putt. But, having said that, I always felt I had a chance of holing it. Of course I knew that would be a bonus, but I had putted well that week and felt good about my stroke.

"I have an excellent caddie but I read all the putts myself - so that there is no-one else to blame if it goes wrong! I reckoned it was a double-breaker with a bit of left to right movement at the start and from right to left near the hole. It worked out perfectly and as soon as I hit it, I knew it wasn't going to be far away.

"That has to be the most important putt of my life. When I won the Open Championship at Carnoustie I had three putts from about three feet to win the title, but this was real pressure, knowing what was riding on that one stroke. It was a great tournament to play in and it doesn't get much better than to win at the Home of Golf."

Lawrie's outstanding putt is another worthy winner of The European Tour Shot of the Year following some wonderfully executed strokes such as Nick Faldo's wedge in the 1995 Ryder Cup; Colin Montgomerie's driver off the fairway in the 1996 Dubai Desert Classic and his 18th hole tee shot in the 1997 Ryder Cup; Miguel Angel Jiménez's chip in at the 1998 Trophée Lancôme; Sergio Garcia's six iron at the US PGA Championship in 1999 and Pierre Fulke's five wood in the 2000 Volvo Masters.

Gordon Simpson

Paul Lawrie
Callaway
GOLF
ABERDEEN
ASSET MANAGEMENT

Asprey & Garrard Golfer of the Month Awards 2001

Justin Rose, Asprey & Garrard Golfer of the Month in January, receives a silver salver from Edward Asprey, Corporate Director of Asprey & Garrard

The Asprey & Garrard Golfer of the Month Awards are presented throughout the year followed by an Annual Award. Previous winners have been:

2000 Lee Westwood
1999 Colin Montgomerie
1998 Lee Westwood
1997 Colin Montgomerie
1996 Colin Montgomerie
1995 Colin Montgomerie
1994 Ernie Els
1993 Bernhard Langer
1992 Nick Faldo
1991 Severiano Ballesteros
1990 Nick Faldo
1989 Nick Faldo
1988 Severiano Ballesteros
1987 Ian Woosnam
1986 Severiano Ballesteros

Aaron Baddeley – **FEBRUARY**

Thomas Björn – **MARCH**

José Coceres – **APRIL**

Andrew Oldcorn – **MAY**

Retief Goosen – **JUNE**

Darren Clarke – **JULY**

Paul Casey – **AUGUST**

Sergio Garcia – **SEPTEMBER**

Ian Woosnam – **OCTOBER**

REUTERS

FOR THE 2001 EUROPEAN TOUR SEASON

STROKE AVERAGE

1	Padraig HARRINGTON (Ire)	(77)	69.23
2	Retief GOOSEN (SA)	(77)	69.32
3	Sergio GARCIA (Sp)	(36)	69.53
4	Colin MONTGOMERIE (Scot)	(77)	69.75
5	Paul MCGINLEY (Ire)	(87)	69.82
	Bernhard LANGER (Ger)	(49)	69.82
7	Ernie ELS (SA)	(40)	69.90
8	Angel CABRERA (Arg)	(66)	69.95
9	Ricardo GONZALEZ (Arg)	(80)	70.00
10	Darren CLARKE (N.Ire)	(83)	70.02
11	Adam SCOTT (Aus)	(74)	70.12
12	Thomas BJÖRN (Den)	(81)	70.19
13	Niclas FASTH (Swe)	(79)	70.27
14	Peter O'MALLEY (Aus)	(81)	70.35
	Anthony WALL (Eng)	(93)	70.35
16	Warren BENNETT (Eng)	(101)	70.37
17	Robert KARLSSON (Swe)	(77)	70.39
18	Phillip PRICE (Wal)	(81)	70.42
19	Ian WOOSNAM (Wal)	(73)	70.45
20	Anders HANSEN (Den)	(98)	70.47
21	Richard GREEN (Aus)	(84)	70.50
22	Steve WEBSTER (Eng)	(100)	70.52
23	Paul LAWRIE (Scot)	(81)	70.54
24	Eduardo ROMERO (Arg)	(60)	70.60
25	Dean ROBERTSON (Scot)	(94)	70.62
	José Maria OLAZABAL (Sp)	(58)	70.62
27	Raphaël JACQUELIN (Fr)	(102)	70.66
28	Paul CASEY (Eng)	(57)	70.67
	Miguel Angel JIMÉNEZ (Sp)	(61)	70.67
30	Greg OWEN (Eng)	(107)	70.69
31	Thomas LEVET (Fr)	(93)	70.71
32	Mathias GRÖNBERG (Swe)	(77)	70.79
33	Ignacio GARRIDO (Sp)	(83)	70.82
34	Justin ROSE (Eng)	(99)	70.83
35	Michael CAMPBELL (NZ)	(64)	70.84
36	David LYNN (Eng)	(105)	70.88
37	John BICKERTON (Eng)	(101)	70.89
38	Ian GARBUTT (Eng)	(101)	70.91
39	Emanuele CANONICA (It)	(42)	70.93
40	Alex CEJKA (Ger)	(77)	70.94
	Jean VAN DE VELDE (Fr)	(31)	70.94
42	Fredrik JACOBSON (Swe)	(79)	70.97
43	David HOWELL (Eng)	(109)	70.98
44	Peter LONARD (Aus)	(77)	70.99
45	Nick O'HERN (Aus)	(48)	71.02
46	Andrew OLDCORN (Scot)	(69)	71.03
47	John SENDEN (Aus)	(76)	71.04
	Henrik BJORNSTAD (Nor)	(71)	71.04
49	Scott GARDINER (Aus)	(42)	71.05
50	Andrew COLTART (Scot)	(92)	71.07
	Greg TURNER (NZ)	(74)	71.07
52	Brian DAVIS (Eng)	(82)	71.09
53	Anders FORSBRAND (Swe)	(66)	71.11
	Soren HANSEN (Den)	(94)	71.11
55	Nick DOUGHERTY (Eng)	(40)	71.13
	Jeev Milkha SINGH (Ind)	(53)	71.13
57	Mark MCNULTY (Zim)	(62)	71.16
	Markus BRIER (Aut)	(92)	71.16
59	Christopher HANELL (Swe)	(78)	71.17
	Gary ORR (Scot)	(76)	71.17
61	Carl PETTERSSON (Swe)	(80)	71.18
	Diego BORREGO (Sp)	(73)	71.18
	Stephen LEANEY (Aus)	(61)	71.18
64	Jonathan LOMAS (Eng)	(100)	71.19
65	Jeremy ROBINSON (Eng)	(63)	71.21
	Soren KJELDSEN (Den)	(99)	71.21
67	Joakim HAEGGMAN (Swe)	(74)	71.23
	Olle KARLSSON (Swe)	(81)	71.23
69	Brett RUMFORD (Aus)	(72)	71.25
70	Mikko ILONEN (Fin)	(33)	71.27
71	Jorge BERENDT (Arg)	(85)	71.28
72	Raymond RUSSELL (Scot)	(93)	71.30
73	Desvonde BOTES (SA)	(59)	71.31
	Gary EVANS (Eng)	(98)	71.31
	Jarrod MOSELEY (Aus)	(78)	71.31
	Roger WESSELS (SA)	(81)	71.31
	Fredrik ANDERSSON (Swe)	(74)	71.31
78	Costantino ROCCA (It)	(66)	71.33
	Sven STRÜVER (Ger)	(84)	71.33
80	Mark MOULAND (Wal)	(88)	71.34
	Trevor IMMELMAN (SA)	(88)	71.34
82	Jean HUGO (SA)	(87)	71.36
	Nick FALDO (Eng)	(36)	71.36
84	Bradley DREDGE (Wal)	(85)	71.38
85	Johan RYSTRÖM (Swe)	(90)	71.39
86	Stephen DODD (Wal)	(86)	71.40
	Robert COLES (Eng)	(82)	71.40
88	Ian POULTER (Eng)	(94)	71.44
	Steen TINNING (Den)	(63)	71.44
90	Peter HANSON (Swe)	(76)	71.46
	Daren LEE (Eng)	(97)	71.46
	Stephen GALLACHER (Scot)	(84)	71.46
93	Mikael LUNDBERG (Swe)	(88)	71.47
94	Jose Manuel LARA (Sp)	(44)	71.48
95	Matthew BLACKEY (Eng)	(55)	71.51
	Gregory HAVRET (Fr)	(94)	71.51
97	Santiago LUNA (Sp)	(82)	71.54
	David CARTER (Eng)	(90)	71.54
99	Barry LANE (Eng)	(85)	71.56
100	Des SMYTH (Ire)	(69)	71.61

( ) = rounds played

DRIVING ACCURACY (%)

1	Peter O'MALLEY (Aus)	(81)	83.7
2	Richard GREEN (Aus)	(84)	81.9
3	John BICKERTON (Eng)	(101)	77.1
4	Gary ORR (Scot)	(76)	76.0
5	Mark PILKINGTON (Wal)	(80)	75.1
6	Michele REALE (It)	(74)	75.0
7	Anders HANSEN (Den)	(98)	73.7
8	Matthew BLACKEY (Eng)	(55)	73.4
9	Paul EALES (Eng)	(88)	72.7
10	Sergio GARCIA (Sp)	(36)	72.6
11	Ian GARBUTT (Eng)	(101)	72.1
12	Nick FALDO (Eng)	(36)	71.4
	David CARTER (Eng)	(90)	71.4
14	Simon D. HURLEY (Eng)	(26)	71.0
15	Miguel Angel JIMÉNEZ (Sp)	(61)	70.9
	Nick O'HERN (Aus)	(48)	70.9
17	Pierre FULKE (Swe)	(53)	70.3
18	Darren CLARKE (N.Ire)	(83)	70.1
	Eamonn DARCY (Ire)	(56)	70.1
	Dean ROBERTSON (Scot)	(94)	70.1

DRIVING DISTANCE (YDS)

1	Angel CABRERA (Arg)	(66)	303.5
2	Ricardo GONZALEZ (Arg)	(80)	303.3
3	Emanuele CANONICA (It)	(42)	298.8
4	Jean HUGO (SA)	(87)	297.6
5	Adam SCOTT (Aus)	(74)	297.4
6	Mark PILKINGTON (Wal)	(80)	295.7
7	Robert KARLSSON (Swe)	(77)	295.3
	Elliot BOULT (NZ)	(79)	295.3
9	Carl SUNESON (Sp)	(83)	294.5
10	Scott GARDINER (Aus)	(42)	293.4
11	Gary EMERSON (Eng)	(86)	293.1
	Sandy LYLE (Scot)	(47)	293.1
13	Greg OWEN (Eng)	(107)	292.4
	Steve WEBSTER (Eng)	(100)	292.4
15	Darren CLARKE (N.Ire)	(83)	291.8
16	Sergio GARCIA (Sp)	(36)	291.4
17	Roger CHAPMAN (Eng)	(77)	291.3
18	Paul CASEY (Eng)	(57)	291.1
19	Retief GOOSEN (SA)	(77)	291.0
20	Jose Manuel LARA (Sp)	(44)	290.7

SAND SAVES (%)

1	Jean VAN DE VELDE (Fr)	(31)	85.2
2	Tony JOHNSTONE (Zim)	(60)	81.6
3	Bernhard LANGER (Ger)	(49)	78.9
4	Miguel Angel JIMÉNEZ (Sp)	(61)	78.7
5	Brett RUMFORD (Aus)	(72)	78.3
6	Simon HURD (Eng)	(24)	76.9
7	John SENDEN (Aus)	(76)	76.0
8	Seve BALLESTEROS (Sp)	(42)	72.5
9	José Maria OLAZABAL (Sp)	(58)	72.2
10	Padraig HARRINGTON (Ire)	(77)	71.1
11	Fredrik JACOBSON (Swe)	(79)	69.0
12	Michele REALE (It)	(74)	68.4
13	Christophe POTTIER (Fr)	(27)	67.9
14	Scott GARDINER (Aus)	(42)	67.4
15	Dean ROBERTSON (Scot)	(94)	66.9
16	Jamie SPENCE (Eng)	(66)	66.3
17	Gustavo ROJAS (Arg)	(73)	66.1
18	Miguel Angel MARTIN (Sp)	(28)	65.5
19	Jarmo SANDELIN (Swe)	(61)	64.7
20	Mathias GRÖNBERG (Swe)	(77)	64.6

Padraig Harrington

Peter O'Malley

AVERAGE PUTTS PER ROUND

1	Seve BALLESTEROS (Sp)	(42)	27.9
2	Pierre FULKE (Swe)	(53)	28.1
3	Thomas BJÖRN (Den)	(81)	28.2
	Joakim HAEGGMAN (Swe)	(74)	28.2
5	Jeev Milkha SINGH (Ind)	(53)	28.3
6	Nick FALDO (Eng)	(36)	28.4
	Mathias GRÖNBERG (Swe)	(77)	28.4
8	Gerry NORQUIST (USA)	(26)	28.5
	Olle KARLSSON (Swe)	(81)	28.5
10	Gary EMERSON (Eng)	(86)	28.6
	Robert KARLSSON (Swe)	(77)	28.6
	Andrew MARSHALL (Eng)	(30)	28.6
	Fredrik JACOBSON (Swe)	(79)	28.6
	Henrik BJORNSTAD (Nor)	(71)	28.6
	Bradley DREDGE (Wal)	(85)	28.6
	Phillip PRICE (Wal)	(81)	28.6
17	Russell CLAYDON (Eng)	(73)	28.7
	Scott GARDINER (Aus)	(42)	28.7
	Dennis EDLUND (Swe)	(38)	28.7
20	Paul BROADHURST (Eng)	(69)	28.8

Greg Owen

Angel Cabrera

Seve Ballesteros

GREENS IN REGULATION (%)

1	Greg OWEN (Eng)	(107)	77.1
	Sergio GARCIA (Sp)	(36)	77.1
	Padraig HARRINGTON (Ire)	(77)	77.1
4	Peter O'MALLEY (Aus)	(81)	76.5
	Retief GOOSEN (SA)	(77)	76.5
6	Paul MCGINLEY (Ire)	(87)	75.6
7	Steve WEBSTER (Eng)	(100)	75.5
8	Richard GREEN (Aus)	(84)	75.4
9	Colin MONTGOMERIE (Scot)	(77)	75.1
10	Adam SCOTT (Aus)	(74)	74.6
	Bernhard LANGER (Ger)	(49)	74.6
12	Thomas LEVET (Fr)	(93)	74.3
13	John BICKERTON (Eng)	(101)	73.4
14	Gary ORR (Scot)	(76)	73.2
15	Eduardo ROMERO (Arg)	(60)	73.0
16	Raphaël JACQUELIN (Fr)	(102)	72.7
17	Ian GARBUTT (Eng)	(101)	72.6
18	Ian WOOSNAM (Wal)	(73)	72.3
19	Michele REALE (It)	(74)	72.1
20	David CARTER (Eng)	(90)	71.9

Sergio Garcia

Jean Van de Velde

PUTTS PER GREEN IN REGULATION

1	Padraig HARRINGTON (Ire)	(77)	1.723
2	Michael CAMPBELL (NZ)	(64)	1.731
	Thomas BJÖRN (Den)	(81)	1.731
4	Colin MONTGOMERIE (Scot)	(77)	1.738
	Retief GOOSEN (SA)	(77)	1.738
6	Pierre FULKE (Swe)	(53)	1.739
7	Darren CLARKE (N.Ire)	(83)	1.742
8	José Maria OLAZABAL (Sp)	(58)	1.744
9	Niclas FASTH (Swe)	(79)	1.745
10	Phillip PRICE (Wal)	(81)	1.746
	Brian DAVIS (Eng)	(82)	1.746
12	Seve BALLESTEROS (Sp)	(42)	1.747
13	Joakim HAEGGMAN (Swe)	(74)	1.748
	Mikael LUNDBERG (Swe)	(88)	1.748
	Russell CLAYDON (Eng)	(73)	1.748
16	Anthony WALL (Eng)	(93)	1.749
17	Dennis EDLUND (Swe)	(38)	1.750
18	Nick FALDO (Eng)	(36)	1.751
	Fredrik JACOBSON (Swe)	(79)	1.751
20	Robert KARLSSON (Swe)	(77)	1.754

Volvo Order of Merit 2001

Pos	Name & Country		Total Prize Money €	£
1	Retief GOOSEN (SA)	(23)	2,862,806.13	1,779,975.71
2	Padraig HARRINGTON (Ire)	(22)	2,090,165.54	1,299,579.40
3	Darren CLARKE (N.Ire)	(23)	1,988,055.29	1,236,091.43
4	Ernie ELS (SA)	(12)	1,716,287.45	1,067,117.31
5	Colin MONTGOMERIE (Scot)	(23)	1,578,676.04	981,556.16
6	Bernhard LANGER (Ger)	(16)	1,577,129.63	980,594.67
7	Thomas BJÖRN (Den)	(22)	1,474,802.31	916,971.73
8	Paul MCGINLEY (Ire)	(25)	1,464,433.67	910,524.93
9	Paul LAWRIE (Scot)	(25)	1,428,830.50	888,388.34
10	Niclas FASTH (Swe)	(23)	1,224,587.60	761,398.46
11	Angel CABRERA (Arg)	(19)	1,183,349.62	735,758.37
12	Michael CAMPBELL (NZ)	(21)	1,065,464.79	662,462.41
13	Adam SCOTT (Aus)	(22)	898,625.71	558,728.70
14	David HOWELL (Eng)	(31)	886,146.38	550,969.56
15	Robert KARLSSON (Swe)	(23)	877,179.66	545,394.42
16	Mathias GRÖNBERG (Swe)	(24)	854,296.03	531,166.31
17	Peter O'MALLEY (Aus)	(22)	847,547.18	526,970.16
18	Ian WOOSNAM (Wal)	(22)	837,808.53	520,915.06
19	Thomas LEVET (Fr)	(29)	801,747.31	498,493.67
20	Miguel Angel JIMÉNEZ (Sp)	(19)	788,201.82	490,071.64
21	Phillip PRICE (Wal)	(27)	763,862.75	474,938.60
22	Paul CASEY (Eng)	(17)	760,692.09	472,967.21
23	Pierre FULKE (Swe)	(19)	751,174.26	467,049.42
24	Ian POULTER (Eng)	(31)	736,460.08	457,900.74
25	Ricardo GONZALEZ (Arg)	(22)	721,853.25	448,818.81
26	Andrew OLDCORN (Scot)	(22)	717,344.30	446,015.33
27	Sergio GARCIA (Sp)	(11)	715,287.63	444,736.58
28	Raphaël JACQUELIN (Fr)	(29)	656,556.00	408,219.66
29	Warren BENNETT (Eng)	(28)	653,472.36	406,302.37
30	Steve WEBSTER (Eng)	(30)	648,067.88	402,942.09
31	Andrew COLTART (Scot)	(27)	647,006.40	402,282.10
32	Greg OWEN (Eng)	(29)	626,201.07	389,346.20
# 33	Justin ROSE (Eng)	(28)	620,992.88	386,107.96
~ 34	Jean HUGO (SA)	(28)	594,025.80	369,340.93
35	José Maria OLAZÁBAL (Sp)	(17)	578,594.78	359,746.56
36	Dean ROBERTSON (Scot)	(27)	572,927.33	356,222.77
37	Soren HANSEN (Den)	(28)	540,207.30	335,878.79
38	Fredrik JACOBSON (Swe)	(24)	532,168.37	330,880.52
39	Anders HANSEN (Den)	(27)	500,544.31	311,217.97
40	David LYNN (Eng)	(29)	488,289.32	303,598.32
41	Barry LANE (Eng)	(28)	477,088.41	296,634.05
42	Nick O'HERN (Aus)	(16)	473,828.53	294,607.19
43	Gary ORR (Scot)	(24)	453,666.61	282,071.33
~ 44	Henrik STENSON (Swe)	(26)	442,150.83	274,911.29
45	Daren LEE (Eng)	(31)	428,404.00	266,364.08
46	John BICKERTON (Eng)	(30)	427,058.98	265,527.80
47	Mark MCNULTY (Zim)	(20)	414,923.97	257,982.75
48	Anthony WALL (Eng)	(28)	409,381.31	254,536.55
49	Richard GREEN (Aus)	(24)	406,911.15	253,000.70
50	Soren KJELDSEN (Den)	(31)	400,696.05	249,136.41

Retief Goosen

Padraig Harrington

Darren Clarke

Ernie Els

Colin Montgomerie

Bernhard Langer

Thomas Björn

Paul McGinley

Pos	Name & Country		Total Prize Money €	£
51	Alex CEJKA (Ger)	(25)	399,347.90	248,298.18
52	Lee WESTWOOD (Eng)	(20)	390,612.92	242,867.13
53	Brian DAVIS (Eng)	(24)	386,811.69	240,503.68
54	Peter LONARD (Aus)	(22)	367,437.68	228,457.71
55	Greg TURNER (NZ)	(22)	361,414.48	224,712.74
56	Ian GARBUTT (Eng)	(28)	361,364.23	224,681.49
# 57	Brett RUMFORD (Aus)	(23)	355,183.53	220,838.59
58	Roger WESSELS (SA)	(28)	354,955.72	220,696.94
59	Gary EVANS (Eng)	(30)	352,718.60	219,305.99
# 60	Gregory HAVRET (Fr)	(29)	343,180.01	213,375.29
# 61	Carl PETTERSSON (Swe)	(27)	342,812.96	213,147.07
# 62	Mark MOULAND (Wal)	(29)	338,102.31	210,218.18
~ 63	Mikael LUNDBERG (Swe)	(29)	325,407.75	202,325.22
64	Raymond RUSSELL (Scot)	(30)	325,404.51	202,323.21
65	Stephen GALLACHER (Scot)	(27)	321,417.69	199,844.37
66	Nick FALDO (Eng)	(11)	315,858.17	196,387.69
67	Sven STRÜVER (Ger)	(26)	314,285.20	195,409.68
# 68	Olle KARLSSON (Swe)	(27)	303,036.21	188,415.51
69	Tony JOHNSTONE (Zim)	(22)	291,933.74	181,512.45
70	Markus BRIER (Aut)	(27)	283,439.66	176,231.18
71	Jarrod MOSELEY (Aus)	(24)	280,167.64	174,196.78
72	Bradley DREDGE (Wal)	(27)	276,979.96	172,214.80
73	Eduardo ROMERO (Arg)	(17)	274,678.95	170,784.13
74	Costantino ROCCA (It)	(22)	259,565.84	161,387.42
75	Roger CHAPMAN (Eng)	(25)	257,790.54	160,283.61
# 76	Jorge BERENDT (Arg)	(28)	254,159.43	158,025.93
77	Jonathan LOMAS (Eng)	(32)	252,135.62	156,767.61
78	Gary EMERSON (Eng)	(30)	251,294.44	156,244.60
79	Des SMYTH (Ire)	(22)	249,550.63	155,160.37
80	Joakim HAEGGMAN (Swe)	(23)	248,508.35	154,512.33
81	John SENDEN (Aus)	(21)	248,267.52	154,362.58
82	Peter BAKER (Eng)	(29)	245,083.82	152,383.09
# 83	Henrik BJORNSTAD (Nor)	(22)	238,136.12	148,063.30
84	Diego BORREGO (Sp)	(25)	233,501.39	145,181.61
85	David CARTER (Eng)	(29)	232,156.66	144,345.51
86	Jean-Francois REMESY (Fr)	(24)	230,338.51	143,215.06
# 87	Simon DYSON (Eng)	(29)	230,293.97	143,187.37
~ 88	Trevor IMMELMAN (SA)	(29)	222,242.74	138,181.44
89	Ignacio GARRIDO (Sp)	(25)	220,420.96	137,048.74
90	Stephen LEANEY (Aus)	(19)	213,336.69	132,644.02
91	Christopher HANELL (Swe)	(29)	210,742.63	131,031.14
92	Anders FORSBRAND (Swe)	(23)	209,018.38	129,959.07
93	Patrik SJÖLAND (Swe)	(27)	202,291.66	125,776.67
# 94	Mark PILKINGTON (Wal)	(28)	201,974.40	125,579.42
95	Paul EALES (Eng)	(29)	201,806.16	125,474.81
$ 96	Jamie DONALDSON (Wal)	(7)	195,502.12	121,555.22
# 97	Stephen DODD (Wal)	(27)	192,554.38	119,722.43
98	Marc FARRY (Fr)	(29)	189,935.43	118,094.08
~ 99	Johan RYSTRÖM (Swe)	(27)	188,870.17	117,431.74
100	Jarmo SANDELIN (Swe)	(21)	188,865.68	117,428.95

Pos	Name & Country		Total Prize Money €	£
# 101	Stephen SCAHILL (NZ)	(27)	188,516.68	117,211.96
$ 102	Darren FICHARDT (SA)	(20)	187,904.79	116,831.51
103	Maarten LAFEBER (Hol)	(32)	183,434.74	114,052.21
104	Henrik NYSTROM (Swe)	(29)	183,198.55	113,905.36
# 105	Desvonde BOTES (SA)	(20)	181,737.33	112,996.83
~ 106	Carlos RODILES (Sp)	(27)	177,237.99	110,199.33
107	Jean VAN DE VELDE (Fr)	(11)	175,746.55	109,272.01
108	Jeev Milkha SINGH (Ind)	(17)	174,011.42	108,193.18
109	Steen TINNING (Den)	(19)	173,152.10	107,658.89
# 110	Malcolm MACKENZIE (Eng)	(25)	171,163.52	106,422.47
111	Mark ROE (Eng)	(28)	168,250.02	104,610.98
112	Richard S JOHNSON (Swe)	(28)	166,483.82	103,512.83
113	Rolf MUNTZ (Hol)	(25)	165,793.13	103,083.39
114	Lucas PARSONS (Aus)	(26)	163,252.97	101,504.02
~ 115	Christian CÉVAËR (Fr)	(30)	161,617.30	100,487.02
116	Alastair FORSYTH (Scot)	(31)	157,723.28	98,065.88
# 117	Elliot BOULT (NZ)	(27)	156,210.77	97,125.46
* 118	Scott GARDINER (Aus)	(13)	155,630.27	96,764.53
* 119	Mikko ILONEN (Fin)	(11)	151,628.33	94,276.29
# 120	Peter HANSON (Swe)	(26)	150,954.26	93,857.18
# 121	Graeme STORM (Eng)	(30)	148,883.14	92,569.44
# 122	Fredrik ANDERSSON (Swe)	(25)	143,254.44	89,069.75
123	Peter MITCHELL (Eng)	(29)	142,399.94	88,538.45
~ 124	David HIGGINS (Ire)	(33)	136,398.35	84,806.91
125	Massimo SCARPA (It)	(31)	135,330.94	84,143.24
$ 126	Peter FOWLER (Aus)	(25)	133,740.02	83,154.07
# 127	Robert COLES (Eng)	(29)	133,000.44	82,694.23
~ 128	Tobias DIER (Ger)	(28)	129,996.43	80,826.46
129	Santiago LUNA (Sp)	(28)	125,366.46	77,947.73
$ 130	Russell CLAYDON (Eng)	(24)	124,230.82	77,241.64
131	Van PHILLIPS (Eng)	(33)	123,802.80	76,975.52
132	Emanuele CANONICA (It)	(11)	123,568.34	76,829.74
133	Gordon BRAND JNR. (Scot)	(25)	121,200.75	75,357.67
134	Carl SUNESON (Sp)	(28)	119,239.84	74,138.45
135	David PARK (Wal)	(30)	115,354.95	71,722.99
136	Des TERBLANCHE (SA)	(25)	114,164.41	70,982.76
# 137	Shaun P WEBSTER (Eng)	(25)	111,867.33	69,554.53
~ 138	Erol SIMSEK (Ger)	(30)	111,758.27	69,486.72
# 139	Gustavo ROJAS (Arg)	(28)	109,880.23	68,319.03
140	Olivier EDMOND (Fr)	(28)	108,964.68	67,749.78
141	Jamie SPENCE (Eng)	(23)	107,476.75	66,824.64
142	Roger WINCHESTER (Eng)	(30)	106,600.13	66,279.60
143	Nicolas VANHOOTEGEM (Bel)	(28)	106,263.68	66,070.41
144	David GILFORD (Eng)	(21)	105,573.68	65,641.40
# 145	Nic HENNING (SA)	(27)	105,272.38	65,454.06
$ 146	Jeremy ROBINSON (Eng)	(20)	104,134.20	64,746.39
# 147	Hennie OTTO (SA)	(18)	91,297.80	56,765.23
$ 148	Dennis EDLUND (Swe)	(12)	88,696.85	55,148.07
$ 149	Eamonn DARCY (Ire)	(20)	87,255.39	54,251.83
150	Thomas GÖGELE (Ger)	(30)	82,043.70	51,011.41

$ = *2001 Challenge Tour Members* * = *Affiliated Members* # = *2000 Qualifying School Graduates* ~ = *2000 Challenge Tour Graduates*

• *Figures in parentheses indicate number of events played*

The European Tour

(A COMPANY LIMITED BY GUARANTEE)

BOARD OF DIRECTORS

N C Coles, MBE *Chairman*

A Gallardo, *Vice Chairman*
R Claydon
D Cooper
B Gallacher, OBE

T A Horton, MBE
M H James (alternate K J Brown)
D Jones

M Lanner
J E O'Leary
D J Russell
O Sellberg

Sir Michael F Bonallack OBE *(Non Executive)*
P A T Davidson *(Non Executive)*
B Nordberg *(Non Executive)*
K S Owen *(Non Executive)*

TOURNAMENT COMMITTEE

M H James (Eng), *Chairman*
M Lanner (Swe), *Vice Chairman*
A Binaghi (It)
R Chapman (Eng)
D Clarke (N Ire)
P Eales (Eng)
A Forsbrand (Swe)
T Gögele (Ger)
B Langer (Ger)
R Lee (Eng)
C Montgomerie MBE (Scot)
O Sellberg (Swe)
J Spence (Eng)
S Torrance, MBE (Scot)
J Van de Velde (Fr)

EXECUTIVE MANAGEMENT

Executive Director	K D Schofield CBE
Deputy Executive Director	G C O'Grady
General Counsel	M D Friend
Assistant to Executive Director and Ryder Cup Director	R G Hills
Director of International Policy	K Waters
Marketing Director	S F Kelly
Director of Corporate Affairs and Public Relations	M S Platts
Director of Tour Operations	D W Garland
Assistant Director of Tour Operations	D A Probyn
Chief Referee	J N Paramor
Senior Referee	A N McFee
Managing Director, European Seniors Tour	K A Stubbs
Championship Director, World Golf Championships	P Adams
European Challenge Tour Director	A de Soultrait
Company Secretary	M Bray
Senior Tournament Director and Qualifying School Director	M R Stewart
Director of Tournament Services	E Kitson
Director of Tournament Development	J Birkmyre
Chief Financial Officer	J Orr
Director/Player Liaison	M MacDiarmid
Director of IT and New Media	M Lichtenhein
Director of Communications	G Simpson
Sales Director	T Shaw

The Contributors

Mike Aitken *(The Scotsman)*
The Scottish Open at Loch Lomond

Colin Callander
European Seniors Tour

Phil Casey *(PA Sport)*
Sao Paulo Brazil Open

Jeremy Chapman
Victor Chandler British Masters

Bruce Critchley *(Sky Sports)*
US Open Championship

Scott Crockett *(The European Tour)*
WGC - Accenture Match Play
Qatar Masters
Cannes Open

Norman Dabell
Moroccan Open
North West of Ireland Open

Bill Elliott *(The Observer/Today's Golfer)*
Volvo Order of Merit
Volvo PGA Championship
130th Open Golf Championship

David Facey *(The Sun)*
The Compass Group English Open

Andy Farrell *(Independent)*
Dunhill Links Championship

Alan Fraser *(Daily Mail)*
Trophée Lancôme

Mark Garrod *(PA Sport)*
Volvo Masters Andalucia

David Hamilton
European Challenge Tour

Martin Hardy
Dubai Desert Classic

Alan Hedley *(The Journal)*
The Great North Open

John Hopkins *(The Times)*
US PGA Championship

John Huggan *(Golf World US)*
Gleneagles Scottish PGA Championship

Renton Laidlaw *(The Golf Channel)*
Alfred Dunhill Championship
Mercedes-Benz South African Open

Derek Lawrenson *(Daily Mail)*
Masters Tournament

Jock MacVicar *(Scottish Daily Express)*
Algarve Open de Portugal

Lewine Mair *(Daily Telegraph)*
Benson and Hedges International Open

Michael McDonnell
The Year in Retrospect

Bernie McGuire
Carlsberg Malaysian Open

James Mossop *(Sunday Telegraph)*
Deutsche Bank - SAP Open TPC of Europe
Omega European Masters

Graham Otway
BMW International Open

Mitchell Platts *(The European Tour)*
Johnnie Walker Classic
Heineken Classic
Greg Norman Holden International
Wins Around the World
The 34th Ryder Cup Matches

Philip Reid *(Irish Times)*
Murphy's Irish Open

Gordon Richardson
Novotel Perrier Open de France
The TNT Open
Linde German Masters

Tony Rushmer *(Golf Weekly)*
The Celtic Manor Resort Wales Open

Gordon Simpson *(The European Tour)*
WGC - NEC Invitational
WGC - American Express Championship
WGC - EMC^2 World Cup
The European Tour Shot of the Year

Colm Smith *(Irish Independent)*
Smurfit European Open

Mel Webb *(The Times)*
Madeira Island Open
Via Digital Open de España
Volvo Scandinavian Masters
Telefonica Open de Madrid

John Whitbread *(Surrey Herald)*
Cisco World Match Play Championship

Roddy Williams *(The European Tour)*
Caltex Singapore Masters
Open de Argentina
Atlanet Italian Open

The Photographers

Charlers Rex Arbogast/AP Photo
255 bottom, 256 top

Hamish Blair/Allsport
25 right, 27 top, 28

Simon Bruty/Allsport
330, 336 top left

David Cannon/Allsport
2, 12, 14, 18-20, 21 top, 22 top, 23, 66, 67 top, 68-69, 97 top, 98-99, 138, 140 top, 143 top, 145, 147 bottom, 156-160, 199 bottom, 222 bottom, 223, 280, 282, 284, 286 bottom, 322, 324, 326, 333-335, 336 bottom right, 346, 386-387

Robert Cianflone/Allsport
26, 27 bottom

Phil Cole/Allsport
180-181, 182 bottom, 183-184, 346

Jonathan Ferrey/Allsport
312

Stuart Franklin/Allsport
6-7, 9 bottom, 16 top, 84-88, 90, 95, 132-136, 202-204, 206, 208-213, 242-243, 245-246, 258-263, 264-268, 270-275, 288-292, 370, 374, 376, 386

Scott Halleran/Allsport
15 bottom, 231 bottom, 232, 234, 316 top, 317 left

Julian Herbert/Allsport
216 bottom, 217

Harry How/Allsport
21 bottom, 22 bottom, 97 bottom, 193 top, 198 bottom, 200, 221, 222 top, 230, 231 top, 233, 235, 312, 313 bottom

Phil Inglis Photography
354 top, 355 top, 356 bottom, 357 bottom, 358, 361 bottom, 362 bottom

Rusty Jarrett/Allsport
224

Craig Jones/Allsport
165 bottom, 220-221, 314-315, 336 bottom middle, 337 top right, 337 middle middle, bottom left

Ross Kinnaird/Allsport
78-83, 108-112, 120-124, 127 bottom, 168-171, 172 top, 173, 187, 189 bottom, 199 top, 244 bottom, 277 top, 278 bottom, 318

Warren Little/Allsport
129 bottom, 285 top, 351 top, 352 top, 354 bottom, 355 bottom left, 356, 360, 361 top, 362 top, 363

Andy Lyons/Allsport
317 right

Bob Martin/Allsport
332

Richard Martin-Roberts/Allsport
187 top, 364, 368 top, 371 bottom, 374 top

Darren McNamara/Allsport
24, 25 left, 49 bottom

Donald Miralle/Allsport
165 top, 167

Stephen Munday/Allsport
Front Cover, 8 top, 9 top, 11, 15 top, 16 bottom, 17, 38, 42-47, 96, 100, 130, 139, 141 top, 141 bottom, 142, 143 bottom, 146 bottom, 147 top, 175 bottom, 177-178, 183 top, 193 bottom, 195, 244 top, 248-253, 255 top, 294-298, 300-304, 305 top, 308-309, 310 bottom, 311, 313 top, 328, 336 middle left, 337 top left, bottom right, 365-366, 368 bottom, 372, 374 bottom, 376

Andrew Redington/Allsport
1, 10, 13, 67 bottom, 70, 72-77, 102-107, 114-118, 126, 127 bottom, 128, 129 top, 140 bottom, 141top, 142, 146 top, 147 top, 148, 150-154, 172 bottom, 174, 175 top, 176, 179, 182 top, 186, 188, 189 top, 190, 192, 194, 196, 198 top, 205, 226-229, 236-240, 247, 256 bottom, 276, 277 bottom, 278 top, 279, 283, 285 bottom, 286 top, 287, 305 bottom, 306, 310 top, 320, 336 top right, middle right, bottom left, 337 middle left, middle right, 350, 351 bottom, 352, 355 bottom right, 357 top, 359, 362 top, 363, 371 top, 379

Joe Raedle/Getty Images
254, 257

Paul Severn/Allsport
30-34, 36-37, 39-41, 342

Tom Shaw/Allsport
214-215, 216 top, 218

Jamie Squire/Allsport
8 bottom, 164, 316 bottom, 225

Matthew Stockman/Allsport
162-163, 166

Matt Turner/Allsport
48, 49 top, 50 bottom, 51 bottom, 52, 54-58, 60-65

Nick Wilson/Allsport
50 top, 51 top, 53